WORKING MOTHERS AND THE CHILD CARE DILEMMA

WORKING MOTHERS AND THE CHILD CARE DILEMMA
A History of British Columbia's Social Policy

Lisa Pasolli

UBCPress · Vancouver · Toronto

© UBC Press 2015

All rights reserved. No part of this publication may be reproduced, stored in a retrieval system, or transmitted, in any form or by any means, without prior written permission of the publisher, or, in Canada, in the case of photocopying or other reprographic copying, a licence from Access Copyright, www.accesscopyright.ca.

23 22 21 20 19 18 17 16 15   5 4 3 2 1

Printed in Canada on FSC-certified ancient-forest-free paper (100% post-consumer recycled) that is processed chlorine- and acid-free.

Library and Archives Canada Cataloguing in Publication

Pasolli, Lisa, author
Working mothers and the child care dilemma : a history of British Columbia's social policy / Lisa Pasolli.

Includes bibliographical references and index.
Issued in print and electronic formats.
ISBN 978-0-7748-2923-6 (bound). – ISBN 978-0-7748-2924-3 (pbk).
ISBN 978-0-7748-2925-0 (pdf). – ISBN 978-0-7748-2925-7 (epub)

1. Child care – Government policy – British Columbia – History – 20th century.
2. Working mothers – British Columbia – Social conditions – 20th century.
3. Motherhood – British Columbia – History – 20th century.   4. British Columbia – Social policy – History – 20th century.   I. Title.

HQ778.7.C32B7 2015   362.70971109'04   C2015-901020-9
                                                                                                                     C2015-901021-7

UBC Press gratefully acknowledges the financial support for our publishing program of the Government of Canada (through the Canada Book Fund), the Canada Council for the Arts, and the British Columbia Arts Council.

This book has been published with the help of a grant from the Canadian Federation for the Humanities and Social Sciences, through the Awards to Scholarly Publications Program, using funds provided by the Social Sciences and Humanities Research Council of Canada.

Printed and bound in Canada by Friesens
Set in Stone by Artegraphica Design Co. Ltd.
Copy editor: Stacy Belden
Proofreader Lana Okerlund
Indexer: Christine Jacobs

UBC Press
The University of British Columbia
2029 West Mall
Vancouver, BC V6T 1Z2
www.ubcpress.ca

For Grandma Helen

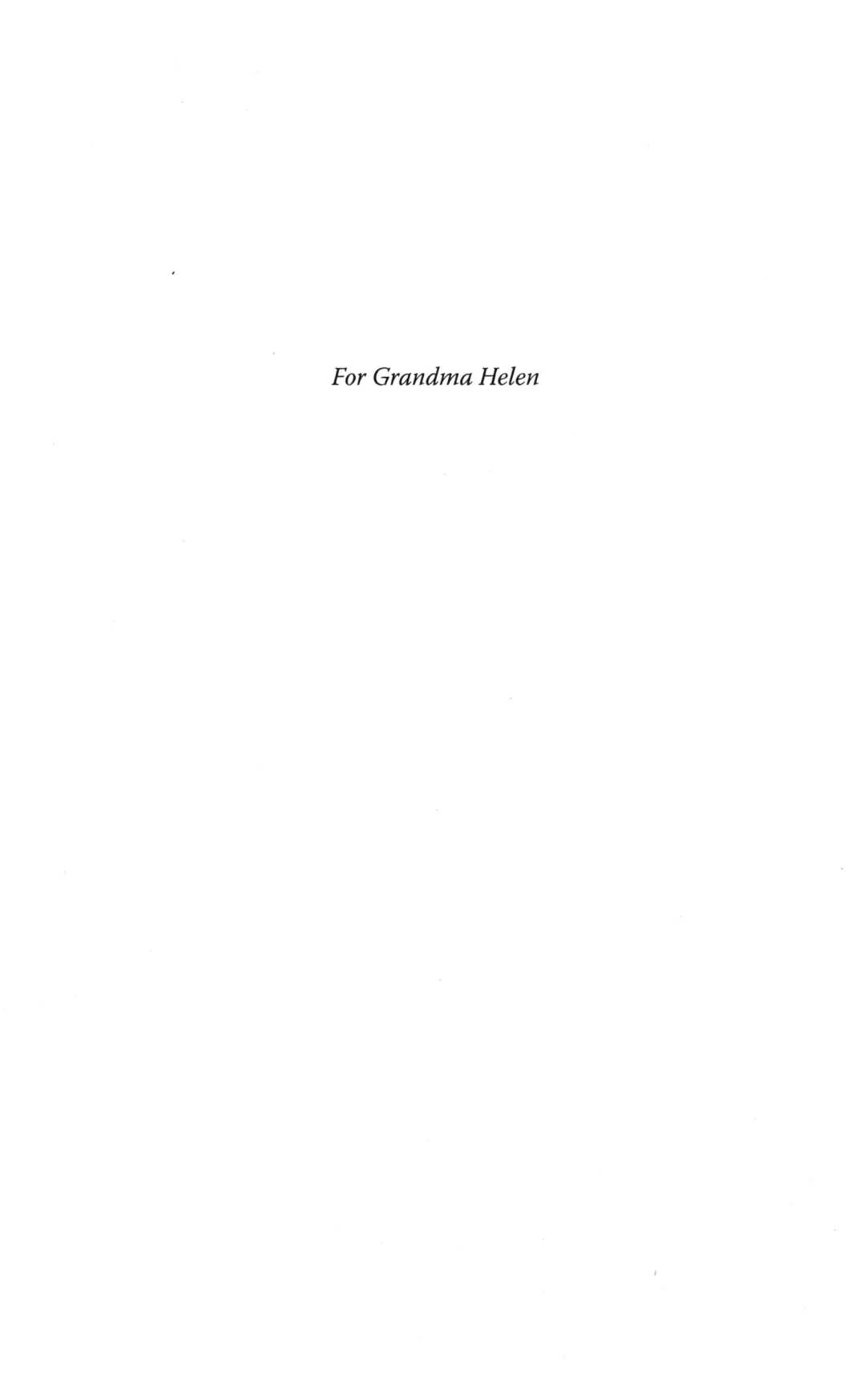

Contents

List of Illustrations / ix

Acknowledgments / xi

Introduction / 3

1 "A proper independent spirit": The Vancouver City Crèche, 1909–20 / 25

2 "Self help is to be encouraged to the fullest extent": Working Mothers and the State in the Interwar Years / 48

3 "It takes real mothers and real homes to make real children": Child Care Debates during and after the Second World War / 74

4 "The working mother is here to stay": The Making of Provincial Child Care Policy in the 1960s / 101

5 "Talkin' Day Care Blues": Feminist Child Care Battles in the 1960s and 1970s / 126

6 "The feeling lingers that day care just isn't nice": Provincial and National Child Care Politics since the Mid-1970s / 152

Conclusion / 178

Notes / 187

Bibliography / 243

Index / 261

Illustrations

1 Group portrait of children at Vancouver City Crèche, c. 1917 / 43

2 Mrs. Mary Ellen Smith, c. 1920s / 53

3 Mrs. Anne Walsey working at the Burrard Shipyard, 1943 / 77

4 Mrs. Fraudena Eaton, 1933 / 79

5 Women protesting government inaction on day care, 1973 / 146

Acknowledgments

It is a pleasure to be able to thank those who provided support along the way to the completion of this book. First on the list is my PhD supervisor, Penny Bryden, whose guidance and advice kept (and keeps) me on the right track. I would also like to offer my gratitude to Lynne Marks, Eric Sager, Helga Hallgrimsdottir, Jim Struthers, and Joan Sangster, who have all provided thoughtful and important critiques of my work.

Several others have read parts of this book and related projects over the years and have offered valuable insights. Thank you to Shirley Tillotson, Scott Sheffield, and Veronica Strong-Boag. Thanks also to my supportive colleagues at the University of the Fraser Valley, who took an interest in my work and made me feel very welcome during the year I spent teaching there. I would like to acknowledge *BC Studies* for allowing me to reproduce a version of "'A Proper Independent Spirit': Working Mothers and the Vancouver City Crèche, 1909–1920" as the first chapter in this book and offer particular thanks to editor Richard Mackie and the anonymous reviewers who helped to make that article better. I am grateful to those who offered tips and feedback when I have presented portions of this work at conferences. Their many small comments often made a big difference in the direction my work has taken. My thanks also to Jason Ellis for generously sharing his research with me.

Financial support from the Social Sciences and Humanities Research Council of Canada has made this book possible. I would also like to acknowledge the contributions of the University of Victoria History Department, the University of Victoria Centre for Co-operative and Community-Based Economy, and the Frost Centre for Canadian Studies and Indigenous Studies at Trent University. Staff at various archives were accommodating and helpful with access requests: the British Columbia Archives, the City of Vancouver Archives, Simon Fraser University Archives, the University of British Columbia Rare Books and Special Collections, the BC Legislative Library, the University of Victoria Archives, and Library and Archives Canada. Thanks to Sandra Boutilier and Jeannie Hounslow for facilitating permission to reproduce photographs.

It has been a pleasure to work with the team at UBC Press and especially Darcy Cullen, Megan Brand, and Stacy Belden. I offer my thanks to them, and to the rest of the production team, for their patience, efficiency, and expertise. Thank you also to the anonymous reviewers whose incisive comments made this a better book.

The writing of this book has been sustained by advisors, colleagues, and friends around the country. I would like to acknowledge Heidi MacDonald and Marg Conrad, who continue to be supportive of my academic career though I am no longer their responsibility. My thanks also to everyone in the history department at the University of Victoria. The west coast felt like home for many years because of Lianne Charlie, Kaitlyn Charlie, Megan Harvey, Christa Hunfeld-Murray, Margaret Robbins, Derek Murray, and Michael Thessel, whose friendships will always serve as the best reminder that graduate school was a good decision. In Ontario, Kristy MacDonald, Mike Wilcox, Julia Smith, Sean Carleton, Kristi Allain, Diane Therrien, Phil Abbott, Dave Tough, Steve Grainger, and Grant Burns have been generous research trip hosts, project collaborators, and friends. Trent University has been a wonderful place to see this book through to completion, and I would especially like to extend my thanks to the entire Frost Centre crew for their support.

Finally, I offer my gratitude to my family – my mom and dad, my sisters, Grandpa Sev, and Grandma Helen – and to James MacGregor, for the many dimensions of emotional and moral (and financial) support they have always offered and that they continue to provide. Thank you.

WORKING MOTHERS AND THE CHILD CARE DILEMMA

Introduction

"The place for the mother of her family is at home," declared an editorial in the 10 April 1920 issue of the *Victoria Daily Times*.[1] For the most part, it seemed, British Columbians agreed. The previous day, in front of full galleries and "graced with feminine loveliness," the provincial secretary had introduced the *Mothers' Pensions Act*, a piece of legislation widely celebrated for its potential to allow mothers to devote their energies to the "maintenance of [their] home[s], and the proper care and education of [their] children."[2] With a pension cheque arriving monthly, an indigent mother, in theory at least, would be free from the pressure of earning a wage and would no longer have to send out her children to be cared for by others. Her children, the *Victoria Daily Times* editor insisted, should not be "given to the State to populate its charitable institutions."[3]

Almost twenty-five years later, in the midst of the Second World War, another editorial waded into the debate about mothers' responsibilities to their homes and their children. The wartime need for women workers was seemingly at odds with the sanctity of the family home – that bastion of democratic freedom over which the mother presided. "The country's future depends far more on the quality of children turned out from the country's home," this author insisted, "than it does on the quality of factory output."[4] However, many mothers found satisfaction in the personal and financial rewards of wage earning, and by the late 1960s it was clear that mothers had taken their place as a permanent part of the labour force. Newspaper commentary in these years warned of women who were "trying to bring their incomes up to $8,000 a year" so that they could buy "two cars and a big stereo set."[5] Another forty-five years later, during the May 2013 provincial election, working mothers were again in the spotlight when BC advocates proposed a universal, $10-a-day child care system. A massive demographic shift suggested the need for such a program – approximately three-quarters of mothers with young children worked outside the home – yet public commentators were still given to framing working motherhood as somehow unnatural, and they criticized mothers who "farm[ed] out [their] children to be raised by virtual strangers."[6]

Yet what about those mothers who "*need[ed]* to work" to support their families?[7] Despite the powerful prescriptions against "abandoning" their children, British Columbian mothers always worked, and not all of them were subject to the same brand of condemnation. When the residents of Victoria debated the possibility of establishing a day nursery in 1922, one sympathetic woman pleaded for the need to provide child care to poor mothers who "work hard and are too proud to let their poverty be known."[8] When provincial day care subsidies were introduced in the 1960s, commentators were willing to concede that some working mothers were deserving of help, particularly those "in the poorer districts," mothers "who may temporarily or permanently be unable to help themselves."[9] Amidst a spate of welfare reforms at the turn of the new millennium, observers insisted that the province's limited public resources should be reserved for deserving mothers who "eschew the poverty cycle, hold their heads high, work hard and raise their children with a bred-in-the-bone work ethic."[10]

These moments represent only a small sampling of controversy about BC women who combined motherhood with paid work. By the same token, public commentary in newspapers offers only a limited glimpse into more widespread views. But these authors, with the span of almost a century between them, gave voice to enduring public perceptions of working mothers. With remarkable consistency throughout the twentieth century, women who were both mothers and labour force participants were characterized in one of two ways: either selfish or pitiable. Selfish mothers were those who worked outside the home despite having the financial security of a male breadwinner. They were thought to be putting their own interests ahead of their children's and putting material desires ahead of their children's wellbeing. Alternatively, the wage earning of impoverished, indigent, and otherwise pitiable mothers was considered necessary for a number of reasons. Though being away from her children for long stretches of time was not ideal, the thinking went, at the very least a poor mother could work to keep her family free from charity, to provide a model of work ethic to her children, and to fill the demand for "women's work" such as housekeeping. No matter the decade or historical context, BC mothers were always subject to scrutiny around whether they worked too much or not enough. These perceptions were informed by gendered, classed, and racialized norms about the family and the workplace. A woman's "sacred" role was to stay home to care for her children unless she was working class, working poor, non-white, or an immigrant, in which case her wage earning was proof that she was imbued with a work ethic and personal responsibility, a guard against the shiftlessness to which the lower classes were considered prone.[11]

A mother's relationship to paid work was never more closely examined than when someone asked: who was caring for her kids? This question was especially controversial when it was framed in terms of government responsibility. Was it up to the state to subsidize the care of her children? Did working mothers deserve public support and protection? These questions were debated fiercely throughout twentieth-century British Columbia. The nature of these debates, the parents, policy-makers, politicians, advocates, welfare officials, and child care providers who took part in them, and the child care programs that were offered – or not offered – to working mothers are the subjects of this book. *Working Mothers and the Child Care Dilemma* begins with the controversial founding of the Vancouver City Crèche in the 1910s, an institution that still bore the name of the infant-focused centres of nineteenth-century France but, like other day nurseries around North America, had evolved significantly to include the care of older, preschool-aged children and to provide employment services for their mothers.[12] It moves through the prominent debates about the care of working mothers' children – variously called day nurseries, day care, and, most broadly, child care – that took place in the context of municipal, provincial, and national politics in the twentieth century. It closes with the stalled attempts at universal child care programs in the opening years of the twenty-first century.

This study reveals how child care policy and politics in British Columbia have been shaped by a deeply rooted societal uneasiness about working motherhood. With a remarkable degree of consistency over one hundred years, an ambivalence about working mothers was embedded into the rocky landscape of BC child care and reflected in the letters, editorials, and commentary mentioned earlier. The contours of these policies and programs, and, just as importantly, the absence of them, hinged on prevailing expectations about whether mothers should work, what kinds of work they should do, and what role the state should play in shaping and regulating their relationships to their families and the labour force.

Susan Prentice, one of Canada's leading child care scholars, points out that the "meaning of childcare services has long been contested."[13] This study untangles the intertwined threads of "meaning" that waxed and waned throughout twentieth-century BC child care politics. In the chapters that follow, the focus is on how the state has interpreted the meaning of child care: what programs were offered and on what basis. Just as importantly, this study considers the gendered, classed, and racialized cultural assumptions about the family, labour market, and welfare that were reflected in and reinforced by policy and programs. In one sense, a simple story emerges. Federal, provincial, and municipal governments, not to mention a significant proportion of the BC and Canadian public, primarily understood the care of young children to be a private responsibility, and, more specifically, a mother's responsibility, whether it meant within the family or the market. The state thus consistently distanced itself from the provision of universal child care.

However, British Columbia's child care history is not just the story of a policy vacuum. There is another important story about child care – another thread of meaning – that emerges by looking more closely at the making of these policies and programs, including municipal initiatives, provincial subsidy programs, and various kinds of government support for community-based child care. These programs were informed by the same cultural expectations that explain the absence of universal care – above all, that working mothers were not considered "normal." A working mother was the signal of family breakdown, including poverty, single motherhood, an incapacitated male breadwinner, or the like, circumstances to which working-class, low-income, non-white, and immigrant families were considered more vulnerable. Child care services were targeted at these "needy" families, which did not conform to middle-class ideals because they were considered to be in need of rehabilitation through paid work. As services such as the Vancouver City Crèche and provincial day care subsidies revealed, state-sponsored child care was considered a compromise. It was a response to family crises that also fulfilled important welfare goals, which included promoting self-sufficiency among families that had otherwise "failed"; protecting the work ethic and guarding against chronic dependency in poor and working-class families; and helping to meet the demand for low-paid workers in traditionally feminine jobs.

Throughout the twentieth century, this residual welfare orientation dominated day care debates and configured child care policy and practice.

But British Columbians concerned about the well-being and social inclusion of mothers, children, and families, as well as about the general prosperity of society and the economy, offered a range of other rationales for government-sponsored child care, articulating alternate threads of meaning in this complex twentieth-century web. Child psychologists and early childhood educators argued that preschool programs offered the foundation of moral education necessary for democratic citizenship, a view that gained traction in the 1940s and 1950s. In a similar vein, advocates worked to position child care for working mothers as part of early learning and education programs that fostered healthy development for all children, an angle that has been especially resonant within advocacy efforts since the 1980s. More recently, as Prentice points out, a "business case" has been made, one that links child care to women's full employment and the long-term investment in an educated workforce.[14] These threads have had varying degrees of prominence throughout the century, but hints of all of these intertwined meanings have been present to some extent in virtually all historical moments.

Of particular importance to this study is the equality- and rights-based meaning assigned to universal child care. Especially during the feminist-inspired campaigns of the 1960s and 1970s, but present since at least the 1910s and continuing into the new millennium, advocates have argued that child care should be more than a residual service for poor mothers. Every woman, they have insisted, regardless of her social location or economic status, should have the choice and the right to be a wage earner as well as a caregiver, and an affordable, accessible, high-quality, comprehensive, and even universal child care program is necessary to secure this right. They have argued, in other words, that publicly funded child care is a crucial component of women's social rights as citizens and that it belongs on the spectrum of social services that secured economic independence, well-being, and equality for women.

In this respect, then, *Working Mothers and the Child Care Dilemma* is not just a story about the competing meanings woven through child care politics, but also a study of the contested nature of social citizenship in British Columbia. Child care debates have been part and parcel of the bigger questions about the construction of social citizenship's boundaries: who was entitled to the support and protection of the state? What kinds of services should the state offer and on what basis? The answers to these questions were never entirely fixed. The rights, responsibilities, privileges, and obligations that operated at the boundaries of social citizenship could and did shift, especially during moments of societal upheaval. It is no surprise that the provision of social services, child care included, came under intense scrutiny during the two world wars, the Great Depression, and major social movements such as second-wave feminism.

A long history of negotiations about the rights and responsibilities of citizenship, Judith Shklar argues, has resulted in a social and political system in which we are considered "citizens only if we 'earn.'"[15] A vast body of scholarship has shown, furthermore, that the citizenship rights associated with earning have been largely reserved for male breadwinners.[16] However, this history of British Columbia's child care politics reveals a complex tangle of expectations about the gendered, classed, and, to some extent, racialized dimensions of wage earning that have operated at the boundaries of social citizenship. It also reveals enduring debates about the relative value of wage earning and caregiving as the "passports" to social rights.[17] The universal child care advocates that have come to be a key part of the policy landscape have long insisted that women have a right to the social benefits that facilitated their equitable wage earning. Others, such as the maternal feminist supporters of the 1920 *Mothers' Pensions Act* and the "Wages for Housework" campaigners of the 1970s, sought to divorce citizenship from its association to earning a wage and, instead, insisted that social rights should derive from caregiving and motherhood.[18] These debates were part of the "contested meanings" of child care: whether motherhood was at the root of women's oppression or the source of their status as citizens and whether the state should facilitate full-time caregiving or equality in the paid workplace. Like the fight for meaningful child care policies, these debates have a long historical trajectory and they continue today.

Ultimately, though, these multi-dimensional challenges were no match for the entrenched social citizenship paradigm that privileged the wage earning of male breadwinners and thus fed into the enduring image of a working mother as a "problem." In this long history of BC child care politics, we see a story about the uneasy relationship between working mothers and the state. As the safeguards against their families' permanent dependency and impoverishment, mothers who were marginalized by their class and race were offered child care so they could enter the low-paid labour force. But the work that these "problem" mothers did was not a positive source of social rights. They were always second-class workers, forestalling any possibility of universal child care as a social citizenship right. Working mothers were caught between the pressure, and their desires, to be stay-at-home mothers, to prove their worthiness for public support, to provide for their families, and to work for reasons of personal fulfillment. None of these options offered the possibility for child care as a component of fully realized social citizenship.

Caring, Earning, and Social Citizenship

Writing about the history of child care is a daunting prospect. In her remarkable history of American child care policy, *Children's Interests / Mothers' Rights*, Sonya Michel "partakes of several historiographies: those of women, families, children, labor, early childhood education, social welfare, and the welfare state."[19] This study draws on a similarly wide range of historical work. The moments of child care controversy examined in the chapters that follow – the operation of the Vancouver City Crèche; the implementation of the *Mothers' Pensions Act* in the interwar years; Second World War day nurseries; the introduction of provincial day care subsidies; the battles over day care during the second-wave women's movement; and the ins and outs of BC child care amidst welfare reforms and national initiatives since the 1970s – draw understanding from studies of the family, the construction of childhood, and women in the labour force, and even from historical investigations into fatherhood that have emphasized the importance of the "male breadwinner image" as a key element of "masculine self-definition and of public ideals about family and fatherhood."[20]

An understanding of these moments is enhanced, furthermore, by a consideration of the historical evolution of nursery school and preschool education, kindergartens, and early childhood education. The nature of these services had important class-based implications for working mothers' access to child care, a subject that is discussed in more detail later in this chapter. At the centre of this analysis, though, is a study of child care policy and politics within the parameters of ideas about work, motherhood, and the state. (Of course, motherhood, caregiving, and homemaking are also work, but, throughout this study, "work" is used as a shorthand for paid work or labour force participation.) It is a study of societal assumptions about women's roles within their families and the labour market, how these assumptions have been embedded in and reinforced by social policies, and the challenges that have been launched and the alternatives that have been voiced. These particular historical episodes have been chosen because they mark the introduction of new legislation or policy directions or, in the case of Chapter 5, the emergence of a new social force in the form of "second-wave" feminism. As such, these were noteworthy moments for the degree of attention paid to the tensions embedded in the making of child care policy and, more broadly, for how societal ideas about work and motherhood shaped the contours of social citizenship.

British political theorist T.H. Marshall first articulated the notion of social citizenship in the 1940s. He defined it as "the right to a modicum of economic welfare and security," along with "the right to share to the full in the social heritage and to live the life of a civilized being according to the standards prevailing in the society."[21] In other words, Marshall suggested that if a citizen's earning capacity was interrupted or prevented, the state had a responsibility to step in to restore well-being and independence. Marshall certainly did not envision child care as part of social citizenship – nor did the social planners who were building the welfare state that Marshall was describing in the 1940s and 1950s.[22] As scholars of gender and welfare have pointed out, Marshall's analysis cast this "civilized being" as an independent, white, male family head. He did not consider the "sorts of resources a *female* worker might need to achieve equality."[23] However, feminist (and, in the United States, anti-racist) critiques of Marshall have not completely undermined the usefulness of the concept of social citizenship. Instead, the shortcomings of Marshall's analysis have inspired scholars and activists to imagine a framework of social rights and benefits that takes into account the unequal relations of gender. A full and inclusive version of social citizenship, they argue, must include social programs to ensure that women's roles as mothers and caregivers do not hinder their equality in the labour force. Universal child care is one such social program, along with reforms to the tax system, to welfare regulations, to legal practices, and to discriminatory structures in employment, politics, and education. Indeed, as Alexandra Dobrowolsky and Jane Jenson argue, universal child care is the "cornerstone for women's full social citizenship, economic autonomy, and well-being."[24]

What this literature also makes clear is that citizenship is not an all-or-nothing proposition nor is it confined to the strict rights and obligations of citizens and national state institutions. Instead, social citizenship is more usefully considered a fluid and conditional "marker of boundaries," to borrow a phrase from Lara Campbell, that helps us to understand the uneven development of welfare policy as well as the multiple contexts of individuals' sense of belonging.[25] Inclusion within the boundaries entitled a citizen to the protection and supports of the state, but neither inclusion nor exclusion were static categories. Social citizenship's boundaries were flexible and permeable; they were often opened only temporarily; and they were subject to expansion and contraction based on particular economic, political, and social contexts. One's inclusion within social citizenship's boundaries was contingent on class, race, gender, and other factors of difference. The rights of social citizenship were often granted on only a limited or partial basis, which may have included the assumption that social benefits were granted as a privilege rather than as a right. The meaning of inclusion could also vary according to different scales of citizenship – for some, citizenship could be more relevant at the level of a local "little state" or community rather than the nation-state.[26]

Scholars of Canadian social welfare history have produced rich explorations of the dynamic and provisional nature of social citizenship in the twentieth century. This book relies on their historical insights as well as those of American and international scholars of social welfare and policy. Of particular importance is the significant (and growing) body of literature that reveals how state welfare programs have served to "constitute and reinforce" unequal relations of gender in different historical contexts.[27] It is now well understood, thanks to these gender-conscious analyses of the welfare state, that policies and programs have worked to prop up the independent, male-breadwinner family in which women were dependent wives and mothers. Based on the dominance of this white, middle-class model, women's social entitlements were subordinated to men's both in the home and in the workplace.

Such findings are at the centre of major works such as Nancy Christie's *Engendering the State* and Alvin Finkel's *Social Policy and Practice in Canada: A History*, which reveal how programs such as workmen's compensation, unemployment insurance, pay legislation, and family allowances privileged the entitlements of male wage earners while reproducing women's dependence in the home and family.[28] Their studies join a host of others in challenging previous gender-blind analyses of such social programs.[29] Unequal gender relations explain the broad acceptance of mothers' allowances in the first half of the twentieth century because they were premised (at least in theory) on the preservation and protection of women's roles as mothers.[30] Other studies point to the ways that the state "regulated" gender roles, including the ideals around femininity, domesticity, and dependency as well as those around masculinity and wage earning.[31] Still others highlight women's difficulty in claiming health benefits, pensions, and other social benefits that depended on "regular" (that is, male) labour force participation.[32]

The history of child care is not well represented in this body of literature. In part, this is because child care policies and programs themselves were limited. The most notable aspect of Canadian child care history, perhaps, is the absence of a universal program comparable to those established in Sweden, France, and elsewhere, and it is admittedly difficult to study a policy void. For the most part, child care in British Columbia and Canada was left to private and charitable social agencies, and when public services did exist, they operated at the margins of welfare policy, where they did not attract as much attention from historians interested in major welfare state programs such as medicare, old age pensions, unemployment insurance, mothers' allowances, and family allowances.[33] Furthermore, the history of working mothers' child care arrangements has often been "subsumed" in the literature of child welfare and child saving, as Michel suggests, especially in the pre–Second World War decades.[34] To a significant extent, this observation is true of the Canadian scholarship. Historians have examined crèches, day nurseries, and orphanages, including the Vancouver City Crèche, with respect to their implications for children but rarely for mothers.[35] Child welfare histories, moreover, are often silent on day care services.[36]

Studies of the patchwork of child care policies constructed in the post–Second World War period are more common, reflecting the higher profile of working mothers and their child care arrangements on the public and political agenda during those years. Alvin Finkel has provided a brief but useful overview of pan-Canadian child care politics since the Second World War, and Rianne Mahon has traced the influence (or lack of it) of "state feminists" in the federal bureaucracy in the making of child care policy through the provisions of the *Canada Assistance Plan* (*CAP*).[37] Mahon, Prentice, Suzanne Morton, and Tom Langford have offered more focused provincial and local studies in Ontario, Nova Scotia, and Alberta, and Prentice's edited collection *Changing Child Care* reveals "select pieces of a large puzzle" of day care advocacy and policy in the post-war years.[38]

Québec, of course, was and is home to a child care story remarkably distinct from the rest of Canada, culminating in the 1997 introduction of the $5-a-day, later $7-a-day, universal day care program as part of a three-pronged family policy that included a targeted family allowance and generous parental leave. Scholars have explored the political motivations and social and economic objectives behind Québec's policy, including analyses of the Parti Québécois' concern with "fostering social solidarity," promoting full employment, fighting poverty, and improving children's "school-readiness."[39]

Much of the most current child care scholarship has been the domain of political scientists, political economists, sociologists, and legal scholars. Indeed, Prentice, Mahon, and Langford's work emerges from these disciplines, and one of the most detailed analyses of national approaches to child care to date is political economist Annis May Timpson's *Driven Apart: Women's Employment Equality and Child Care in Canadian Public Policy*.[40] These studies help paint a more complete picture of child care policy, politics, and the shifting fortunes of advocacy movements in postwar Canada. They also enhance our understanding of the contemporary challenges of building gender equity into the state. Moreover, these social science-oriented studies have helped to insert child care policies into the debates about welfare regimes, a compelling comparative framework that begins with Gøsta Esping-Andersen's three typologies of welfare states: conservative-corporative; social democratic; and liberal. Canada, along with the United States, Australia, and Great Britain, clearly falls into the liberal regime, meaning that social benefits have been (and continue to be) residually offered as "means-tested assistance, modest universal transfers, or modest social-insurance plans."[41]

Social scientists have been interested in whether and how child care policies are characteristic of this liberal regime, especially amidst the modern decline of the male breadwinner family and the resulting "crisis of care." In the contemporary Canadian context, Mahon has shown that child care has largely been left to the market, and the limited public support that is offered takes the form of tax deductions or credits and a "safety net" approach for low-income families. In other words, the Canadian liberal regime has responded to the caregiving crisis in largely "path-dependent" ways – ways, furthermore, that are rooted in and reproduce gender and class inequalities.[42] However, welfare regimes are not static. The liberal path, and the child care policies embedded within it, have developed out of particular historical forces and "universe[s] of political discourse."[43]

As the first history of child care policies and politics in British Columbia, *Working Mothers and the Child Care Dilemma* provides the kind of nuanced historical analysis required to take account of the factors that have shaped and reshaped the liberal path, particularly with respect to "the influence of the male breadwinner ideologies as a cornerstone of the liberal welfare state."[44] It also reveals the "twists and turns" along this path, as the politics of maternalism, feminism, early childhood investment, the New Right, and other social and political forces have offered policy choices that swerve towards social or "inclusive liberalism."[45] This study, then, sheds light on the historical dimensions of the Canadian welfare regime, and it provides the kind of focused analysis required for provincial comparisons.[46] British Columbia, as the "west beyond the west," was distinct among the Canadian provinces in many respects, particularly in its strongly polarized political culture.[47] The need for more provincial comparisons within the Canadian federal system, as Mahon points out, is suggested by Québec's deviation from the liberal path.

Besides offering historical fodder for the debates about welfare regime frameworks, this study also contributes to historiographical discussions about working mothers and welfare. The question of "who is a citizen in a welfare state," as Ruth Lister explains, is fundamentally linked to "which activities should attract social citizenship rights": wage work, domestic caregiving, or some combination of both.[48] Social scientists who analyze the social organization of care and the "woman-friendliness" of welfare regimes are taking up this debate in a contemporary context. With a common starting point – that women's inequality has its roots in the unrecognized value of feminized care work – scholars and activists nevertheless disagree about the appropriate role for the state in promoting gender equality. For some, true equality requires compensation for caregiving and mothering. Lister, though, warns that the "problem is how to provide this recognition without locking women further into a caring role which serves to exclude them from . . . power and influence."[49] For others, then, the solution is women's full and equal participation in the labour market, facilitated by programs such as maternity leave, flex-time, and universal child care. Others advance policy solutions that break down the barrier between the gendered public and private divide to ensure the "universalization of care."[50] Paul Kershaw advocates, for instance, for a policy approach based on "integrat[ing] care as a constitutive responsibility and right of social citizenship that binds men as much as women."[51]

Taking stock of these contemporary debates helps to identify patterns in the historical development of social citizenship. Historians' interpretations of mothers' pensions and allowances are particularly revealing when it comes to the value assigned to earning and caregiving. In her study of American mothers' pensions, for example, Barbara Nelson identifies two "channels" of welfare: one for motherhood and one for wage work. For Nelson, maternally based programs were not invested with the same level of entitlement as those for male breadwinners – mothers' pensions were discretionary and considered a privilege rather than a right – but they at least represented public validation of caregiving work.[52] This interpretation is closely linked to Nancy Fraser and Linda Gordon's "genealogy of dependency." Rooted in gendered family norms and expectations about the family wage system, Fraser and Gordon argue, there still existed the possibility in the early twentieth century that women's (and children's) ties to the household were considered "good dependency."[53] Programs such as mothers' pensions, therefore, were not shrouded in the stigma that would come to characterize welfare dependency later in the century. Canadian historians have also identified a strong current of care-based welfare entitlement around mothers' pensions and mothers' allowances in the interwar years. British Columbia was a particularly interesting case, as Margaret Little has argued, because mothers' pensions in this province were understood as rights-based and embedded in a cultural acceptance of the value of mothers' "service to the state."[54]

So what does this mean for the history of child care? For one thing, the value placed on maternally based social rights certainly helps to explain the absence of virtually any public discussion about child care for a prolonged period between the First and Second World Wars. In those years, as Chapters 1 and 2 show, mothers' pensions were the preferred method of social welfare delivery to mothers, and the tentative public forays into public child care such as the Vancouver City Crèche lost favour. In other words, instead of programs that assisted mothers in balancing work and motherhood, governments prioritized stay-at-home caregiving. The reinforcement of domesticity for women was also enshrined in welfare policies in the decades immediately following the Second World War, another period of significant public opposition to public child care. In those years, Alvin Finkel observes, policy-makers "favoured social security measures that would make it possible for most households to function without mothers having to seek paid employment."[55] Even during the Second World War, when women's paid labour was extolled as their patriotic duty, welfare officials in British Columbia were reluctant to expand the gender-typed boundaries of social citizenship in ways that included child care for working mothers. These wartime attitudes, and their implications for working mothers and their child care options, are explored in Chapter 3.

Yet as Tammy Findlay notes, "it is not only the lack of construction of child care that has gender consequences. The pattern and type of construction matter as well."[56] In this sense, the history of child care in British Columbia forces us to reconsider the ways in which the tenuous boundaries of social citizenship were regulated, shifted, and policed, especially when working mothers came up against the state. There is no doubt that, historically, the social rights of male worker-citizens – and the accompanying expectations about their work ethic – were at the core of social welfare policy.[57] Many of the workers who came into contact with the state, however, were also mothers. When we take a closer look at the child care services offered to these women, it becomes clear that notions of work were central to their social inclusion as well. In other words, mothers were not necessarily slotted into the channel of welfare designed around maternalism and domesticity. Rather, welfare officials were actually more interested in their labour force participation, their economic behaviour, and their work ethic. This interest was apparent, as Chapter 1 shows, in the administration of the Vancouver City Crèche, while Chapter 4 explores how these work-based expectations were also inherent in the provincial day care subsidies in the 1960s. Working mothers were enmeshed in the expectations of worker citizenship and the "fundamental" goals of welfare policy that, in a sense, overrode their gender: preserving the work ethic in their needy families, striving for economic independence that did not require long-term welfare dependency, and filling the gaps in the labour market.[58]

In this sense, this study follows on the work of social welfare scholars such as Eileen Boris, who cautions that we should not overlook the importance of the "working" in "working motherhood."[59] Dependency within the maternal and domestic sphere was not necessarily considered "good" for all mothers, especially mothers marginalized by class and race. In both the United States and Canada, policy-makers expected that "poor women, often the racial or ethnic 'other'" should participate in wage labour for reasons of "uplift," to sustain some measure of family independence, and to maintain the work ethic. This expectation was especially apparent during the 1960s, when racialized and poor mothers were targeted for workforce "activation" as part of their receipt of social assistance.[60]

In Chapter 6, we see how class and race hierarchies played into BC debates about reforms to social assistance for working mothers in the 1970s and 1980s. However, these expectations were present throughout the century in Canada, in a variety of ways in which women encountered the state. Little points out that Asian and indigenous women were excluded from mothers' pensions legislation in British Columbia and that, in Ontario, economic behaviour was crucial to poor mothers' receipt of mothers' pensions and social assistance.[61] Joan Sangster has shown how state policies channelled Aboriginal women into domestic service placements.[62] Even for Anglo-Saxon widows, James Struthers has revealed, deservedness was a vulnerable category. Ontario's superintendent of labour advocated excluding widows with one child from pensions legislation in that province because they could earn a living as housekeepers.[63] *Working Mothers and the Child Care Dilemma* shows how child care policies were folded consistently into this type of welfare delivery throughout the twentieth century.

To borrow a phrase from Joy Parr, though, the "gender of breadwinners" remained crucially important.[64] Some women were obligated to work in order to receive social benefits – but the unequal relations of gender, class, and race followed breadwinning mothers into the work force and served also to reinforce inequality between women based on class, race, ethnicity, and marital status.[65] No matter the reason or the rationale behind their labour force participation, mothers could not escape their subordinate status as second-class workers. Work-based social citizenship rights were never offered to women on the same terms as men. Poor, working-class, and racialized mothers were considered a labour reserve that could help alleviate the demand for domestics, as was the case in Vancouver during the 1910s.[66] Obligated to work to prove their deservedness for mothers' pensions in the interwar years and welfare-linked day care subsidies from the 1960s on, mothers were nonetheless denied equal pay, protection, or any of the rights that were assumed inherent to the work of male breadwinners. One of those rights that was always beyond their reach was universal child care. The limited and contingent public child care support offered to those mothers was ideally just a temporary measure – one preferable to direct income supplements, which just encouraged welfare dependency – on the road to the restoration of "normal" family life.

A complete understanding of the construction of social citizenship, Lara Campbell argues, has to take into account the ways in which people expressed their "needs, as well as duties and responsibilities."[67] Throughout this book, then, also runs a story of how parents, advocates, concerned citizens, and, at times, sympathetic politicians and government officials pushed back against the restrictive notions of social citizenship and against a welfare system that characterized women either as dependent mothers or as second-class workers.[68] Their efforts ran throughout the century, albeit with widely varying degrees of visibility and influence. Advocates from within the second-wave women's movement of the 1960s and 1970s were especially instrumental in shaping public discourses about child care. Their strategies and messages are explored in Chapter 5. A central plank of their child care campaigns hinged on women's right to equality in the workplace, an argument that was also articulated, however faintly, long before second-wave feminism emerged and one that has since continued to be an important part of child care politics.

However, as this BC story reveals, there was not always an entirely united front on child care from within the women's movement, especially when feminist activism intersected with welfare rights lobbyists, as it did in the 1970s and 1980s. Some of the advocates featured in Chapters 5 and 6, for example, argued that mothers' "employability" with respect to welfare reforms was too narrowly defined and that full-time caregivers had just as much right to social benefits as paid workers. In exploring the battles at the intersection of women's liberation, the New Left, and welfare rights activism, Chapters 5 and 6 provide important historical analysis of an understudied part of child care history. These historical battles help to explain why "feminists," as Prentice says, "are still struggling with the vexing meaning and politics of motherhood."[69] The conflicts that unfolded in the 1960s, 1970s, and 1980s represent a prelude to contemporary theoretical discussions about a universal child care policy's potential to ameliorate women's subordination in the workplace as well as in the family.[70]

Advocates have played an important role in creating an imagined ideal about a child care system that is part of a full and inclusive social citizenship for women. But their successes were limited throughout the twentieth century in British Columbia. The boundaries of social citizenship, both in the sense of rights and obligations, remained conditioned by gendered and classed assumptions about work and welfare. Mothers' partial and conditional inclusion within the boundaries of social citizenship was and is keyed to their wage work, yet their wage work was – and often still is – understood as a problem. This tension helps to explain the absence of universal child care as well as the fact that the provision of child care is treated as a marginal welfare issue. *Working Mothers and the Child Care Dilemma* reveals that those attitudes have a long history in British Columbia.

Caring for and Educating Young Children: A Brief History

This study is the first to tell the history of child care in British Columbia as a story about the politics of working motherhood. The story could not be told, though, without drawing on the insights from the rich body of literature that examines child care as part of the range of services that includes kindergartens, nursery schools, and preschools. As this historiography shows, the provision of early childhood services in British Columbia and Canada was infused with tension between ideas about "care" and "education" and class-based assumptions about the kinds of services to which mothers, families, and children were entitled.

The often divergent courses of childhood care and education were set in the mid-nineteenth century. In this Victorian era of social reform, some reformers began to suggest that the "educational enrichment" of young children was necessary as long as it only supplemented and did not replace maternal care – and only for the children of middle- and upper-class families, who required a foundation of training and socialization for long-term success. Friedrich Froebel's notions of a play-based, part-time kindergarten education were "perfectly suited to meet this need," according to Larry Prochner.[71] The first Canadian kindergartens were established in east coast cities at the tail end of the nineteenth century. Within a few years, several had been established in British Columbia. Most of them, like St. Margaret's Kindergarten School in Victoria, catered to the children of privileged families who wanted their children to spend a bit of time each week being prepared for academic success. Many of these operated out of the homes of well-to-do families or in church basements.[72] Nursery schools and, later in the twentieth century, playschools and preschools were similar to kindergartens in that they largely had a middle-class orientation.

A very different kind of social provision was established for the children of labouring classes who were denied their mother's care during the work day. These "childcare centres for the needy" also began to appear in the late nineteenth century, variously called crèches, day nurseries, and day cares. In a similar vein, this era saw the establishment of "foster day care," wherein children were placed in the homes of caregiving mothers (similar to services that would today be called day homes).[73] In establishing these custodial centres, charity-minded reform women, church groups, and philanthropic organizations targeted worrisome gaps in social welfare for children. Many mothers, especially those without family support networks, were forced to rely on orphanages, Children's Aid Society homes, and other long-term boarding institutions when they could not arrange reliable and affordable care for their children while they worked.[74] Crèches and day nurseries offered a more attractive option than these long-term solutions, and they also provided care for children younger than four or five years of age who were often excluded from boarding homes.

By the later nineteenth century, some reformers had adopted the kindergarten model as a "vehicle of mission work and social reform" and established centres in ethnic and working-class neighbourhoods (such as the international kindergarten in New Westminster, which was specifically for Japanese and Chinese children).[75] For many immigrant and working mothers, these free kindergartens served important child care functions. However, if a mother had infant- or toddler-aged children or if she worked long or irregular hours, kindergartens did not suffice. A crèche or a day nursery was more suited to her needs. By 1910, most of Canada's big cities were home to at least one such institution: Montreal, Toronto (the Victoria Crèche, East

End Day Nursery, and West End Day Nursery), Hamilton (operated by the Women's Christian Temperance Union), the Jost Mission in Halifax, the Edmonton Crèche, and, of course, the Vancouver City Crèche.

Many, if not most, of these crèches and day nurseries included an employment bureau for mothers alongside their child care services. Poor mothers, together with their morally vulnerable children, were the targets of social reform efforts meant to turn them into hard-working, morally upright, self-sustaining citizens. The mission statement of the Victoria Crèche in Toronto reveals the interconnected goals of day nurseries:

> To provide a home during the day for children whose mothers have to go out to work; to assist in securing day work for the mothers needing it; to encourage habits of thrift among the parents and children, and to enable Christian and charitably disposed women to come in touch with the home life of the mothers and children and take such action as may from time to time seem best to brighten their homes.[76]

These earliest crèches and day nurseries established a pattern that persisted throughout the twentieth century – that working mothers and their children were viewed as the objects of charity and that through the provision of child care working mothers' relationships to the labour market could be regulated and policed.

After this spate of day nursery development in the first decade of the twentieth century, however, changing trends in child welfare initiated something of a "stagnant" period in child care. As legislation dealing with mothers' pensions was introduced across the country, the importance of mother care held sway, and institutional care was increasingly viewed with distaste.[77] In the meantime, however, the (admittedly still limited) world of education services for young children underwent something of a transformation between the two world wars. Most historians point to 1925 as a turning point. In that year, the St. George's Institute for Child Study – later the University of Toronto's Institute of Child Study – was established under the direction of Dr. William Blatz, a psychologist who would have a "profound influence" on early childhood education in Canada.[78] Blatz created the model of a preschool centre that combined child study with parent education, one that was emulated across the country. Most centres were accessible only to parents who had the resources and time to be involved alongside their children. In other words, Blatz did not advocate for centres that met the needs of working parents. Furthermore, many of his ideas began to permeate the operation of mid-century day nurseries in ways that made them less convenient for working parents. Their hours were shortened, for example, so as to lessen the strain on children, and some institutions raised their minimum age to two or three years.[79]

Although care and education developed largely along separate tracks for several decades, the Second World War marked something of a convergence. The *Dominion-Provincial Wartime Day Nursery Agreement* (*WDNA*), though adopted unevenly across the country, had a significant influence on public attitudes towards child care.[80] "For the first time," Prochner argues, "group child care was promoted as a normal support for families."[81] Mothers were encouraged to "share the care" of their children with professionally trained day nursery staff, overseen in Ontario by Dorothy Millichamp, a graduate of the Institute of Child Study.[82] In provinces that did not sign on to the *WDNA*, including British Columbia, private child care enterprises faced less resistance during the war. In Vancouver, for example, three "playschools" were founded to care for the children of mothers who were not necessarily working in war industries, but who were filling the jobs left vacant by enlisted men.[83] The wartime context helped to move these child care centres away from their welfare orientation.

The wartime "normalizing" of day nurseries took root most firmly in Ontario, where mothers fought to maintain day care services even after the *WDNA* was cancelled.[84] However, British Columbia's experience was more typical. In the 1950s, the practices of care and education returned to pre-war patterns as "normal" gender norms were reinforced, including the emphasis on maternal caregiving. Day care services for working mothers were even further relegated to residual status during the immediate post-war years – a fifteen-year period that Loren Lind and Prentice have called the "doldrum years" in terms of public attention to child care for working mothers.[85] In the same period, though, the moral training of future democratic citizens became important, and middle-class-oriented playschools, kindergartens, and nursery schools proliferated. Blatz and the Institute of Child Study continued to have an important influence and continually sought to distance themselves from the charity-type needs of working mothers. Indeed, the Institute of Child Study "made continuous efforts to assure the public that it was not relieving mothers of their duty, but was providing training so they could better carry out their roles."[86]

Support for Blatz-inspired preschools was part of broader impulses towards educational reform in the 1950s and 1960s – what historians have called the "watershed years" in terms of education policy.[87] In British

Columbia, much of this reform impulse emerged around the University of British Columbia's Child Study Centre, which, like its counterparts around the country, was part of a growing post-war concern with the science of child development and best practices in preschool education. The benefits of educating four and five year olds gained favourable attention in 1960 when the BC Royal Commission on Education called for the province-wide establishment of public kindergartens – something that had been an issue since the war when Vancouver and Victoria school boards had turned to kindergartens rather than throw their support behind the *WDNA*.[88] Eventually, in 1973, provision was made for kindergartens in all BC public schools (although they were not required to establish them).[89]

With the post-war focus on early childhood education came a "new scrutiny" of older, charitable child care institutions.[90] The spotlight was put on these institutions for another reason as well. In the 1960s, several provinces, British Columbia included, made a commitment to subsidize low-income mothers' child care costs. The funds available through the *CAP* made this possible, but it also meant that day care subsidies were cast as being part of the "war on poverty."[91] Reminiscent of what occurred with the Vancouver City Crèche, subsidies were linked to mothers' labour force participation and they were not made available for children under three years of age, thanks in large part to a view espoused by child psychologists that infants suffered developmental damage if they were away from their mothers. However, thanks to subsidy programs, as well as the capital and operating grants made available by provincial governments, the number of day care centres grew significantly in the 1960s and 1970s. What remained firmly imprinted in all of these new policies, though, was a stigma about the welfarist nature of child care for working mothers.

This stigma remained powerful throughout the 1980s and 1990s, and it endures today. Thanks to this long legacy, child care is still often characterized as something that only poor mothers need (or that selfish mothers want). It is viewed within the framework of anti-poverty programs rather than in terms of social entitlements. Early childhood education, on the other hand, has been viewed in a much more positive light. Recognizing this distinction, child care advocates have sought to fuse ideas about education with practices of care. The terminology reflects their efforts. In the 1980s, "child care" replaced "day care" as the preferred label, as advocates, parents, and staff rejected the older stigma associated with custodial "day care." More recently, attempts to integrate the two goals are reflected in phrases such as early childhood education; early childhood learning; early childhood education and care; and early learning and care.[92] Linda White points out that contemporary academic research into child development, behaviour, and long-term success has partly fuelled the shifting currents of care and education. As a result, programs that focus "attention on the importance of a child's experiences in the early years on subsequent development" in ways that emphasize the "explicit" connection between learning and care – such as the federal government's 2003 *Multilateral Framework on Early Childhood Learning and Care* – are relatively politically palatable.[93] BC advocates have taken a similar path in recent years. Since 2010, the Coalition of Child Care Advocates of British Columbia and the Early Childhood Educators of British Columbia have been championing a proposal for a $10-a-day public child care program that not only represents an important coalition between preschool educators and day care advocates but is based on a "public system of integrated early care and learning."[94]

In policy terms, though, Martha Friendly and Prentice maintain that the "long historical split between early childhood education and childcare continues to shape the national political debate about how to meet the needs and rights of Canadian families and children today."[95] Not all child care workers and advocates think that the infusion of education principles into child care is a good thing. Warnings have surfaced about the "schoolification" of child care, which some feel recreates the class-based, two-tiered precedent established earlier in the century.[96] Some argue, furthermore, that focusing on education-based principles results in gaps in the provision of child care. Full-day kindergarten was made available to all BC children in 2010, for example, but working mothers remained without infant and toddler care, before- and after-school care, and care during the summer months. As Tammy Findlay notes, education-based programs are the "main event[s]" that attract public funding, while child care remains an "afterthought."[97]

For many advocates, a feminist framework has also become an afterthought in child care campaigns. Contemporary lobbying focuses heavily on early childhood investment and development. Rarely does gender equity and working mothers' social citizenship take centre stage.[98] Is this because the rhetoric of feminism is not politically palatable? Studies of advocacy movements in Alberta suggest that may be the case – that focusing on the interests of children leads to better policy gains than does focusing on women's rights, especially in the context of rightward government turns at both provincial and federal levels in recent years.[99] The ineffectiveness of feminist advocacy, of making child care a "women's rights" issue, speaks to the enduring uneasiness about working mothers and ambivalence about the ways in which the state was expected to foster their social and economic inclusion.

Tammy Findlay's observation – that child care is an "afterthought" – would come as no surprise to BC working mothers. Throughout the twentieth century, as they struggled to find affordable and quality child care, they would have been well aware that politicians, social planners, and a significant portion of the public pushed their child care needs to the backburner. In the meantime, those mothers and their families sought out alternatives in the range of private, family, and community-based options that emerged out of necessity. We get glimpses of mothers' varied strategies throughout this study: children were cared for by grandparents or other family members; mothers relied on neighbours and friends; and groups of women formed child care co-operatives.[100] Left to the private sphere, however, mothers' child care arrangements, like so much of women's private lives, are largely invisible in the historical record and thus left relatively unexamined.

However, working mothers' options were always shaped by the debates, policies, and programs that are at the core of this study. As they moved between their worlds of caregiving and wage earning, they navigated a tangled set of social, cultural, and political threads of meaning about child care and about their roles as mothers and workers. Some of these threads suggested the importance of early childhood educational opportunities. Others represented a feminist, rights-based understanding of a public child care system. These threads, though, ran up against more powerful meanings that worked to forestall the development of universal child care and explained the limited nature of child care provision that was crafted throughout the century: the dominance of discourses about the male breadwinner family and women's accompanying dependency; the belief that women's predestined role was to care for young children and that child care outside of the home was unnatural; that the overriding goal of state welfare policy was to regulate the work ethic in underprivileged families; and that child care could be used as an anti-poverty measure to prevent chronic welfare dependency in mother-headed families. All of these meanings fed into the enduring image of a working mother as a "failure" who should either be encouraged to leave the labour force or who should have her low-paid labour policed as a condition of her receipt of social assistance. Either way, negotiating expectations about work, both paid and unpaid, at the boundaries of social citizenship was complex and often contradictory for mothers. This negotiation is as apparent today as it was in the 1910s in Canada's first publicly funded child care centre, the Vancouver City Crèche.

1
"A proper independent spirit": The Vancouver City Crèche, 1909–20

The Vancouver City Crèche opened its doors to much fanfare on 4 April 1912. Amidst an enthusiastic crowd, volunteers and invited dignitaries made many congratulatory remarks about the unselfish work of charitable women who spearheaded the crèche's establishment, and guests were given tours of the "pretty and restful" new quarters in a wing of the Women's Building on Thurlow Street. Visitors were encouraged to take note of the child-sized chairs and tables, the numbers of cots available for napping, and the variety of educational toys, games, and books with which the playroom was equipped. They were paraded through the dining room, where the children would receive a "good plain meal properly cooked" at noon and another meal at 5 pm. Upstairs were two "tastefully furnished" rooms for the matron, Miss Ada McLean, and her assistant, Miss Needle, both of whom were trained nurses with overseas experience. The Vancouver public was assured that McLean and Needle, along with a volunteer roster of "generous-hearted women" who would provide arts and crafts and kindergarten classes, were doing good work in "making proper citizens" of otherwise-neglected children.[1]

These glowing reviews may have been exaggerated for the benefit of donors, but, nevertheless, the crèche's value to Vancouver's working families was clear. Over the next few months, the numbers of mothers and children who arrived at the crèche each morning grew steadily. By the fall of 1912, daily attendance averaged just over twenty children, and by 1913 it was not unusual for the matrons to have thirty-five or forty children in their charge on a given day. The mothers who appeared with their children each morning reported a range of troubles: their husbands were out of work, they had been deserted, or they were left to care for their children alone while their husbands left town to look for a job.[2] The crèche gave these mothers an opportunity to find work and provided them with peace of mind while they earned a wage to support their families.

Accounts of neglected children kept safe by nurturing matrons played well in the press, but it was the working mothers who were the real object of concern for those who administered the crèche. The middle- and upper-class reform women who founded the crèche as a private institution in 1909 envisioned it as a way to get white mothers working as domestic labourers in respectable homes in order to replace undesirable Chinese men. The interest in mothers' labour was continued by city welfare officials when they took over the crèche in 1912, making it Canada's first publicly funded child care centre, one that also functioned as an employment bureau for mothers. This municipal investment was justified because it was considered to be cheaper and more morally sound to put poor mothers to work rather than to provide them with direct relief. Through all of its administrative shifts in the 1910s, the crèche remained entwined much more tightly with the politics of mothers' employment and relief than with the currents of child welfare. In a city wracked with poverty and a crisis of unemployment, the crèche functioned essentially as a work-for-relief project for poor mothers, who were distinct from men only in their need for child care.

The Vancouver City Crèche adds another dimension to our understanding of the complex array of gendered, classed, and racialized regulatory objectives behind British Columbia's early social welfare programs. Much of what we know about this period comes from historical analyses of a bourgeoning provincial welfare regime, including acts for the protection of children (1901), workmen's compensation (1916), a female minimum wage (1918), and mothers' pensions (1920).[3] In Vancouver, local officials were also centralizing welfare services in the 1910s because the "voluntary, piecemeal" approach to relief was no longer adequate to deal with the scope of poverty and unemployment in a rapidly growing city.[4] Although T.H. Marshall would not coin the term for another thirty or so years, the development of these programs represented the expanding boundaries of social citizenship.

The parameters of this expansion were conditioned by the cultural expectations of the day. For women, it meant that their social entitlements were afforded less importance than the protection of male worker-citizens and when they were offered social benefits, it was on the basis of their "service to the state" as mothers.[5] But for many marginalized women, maternal service to the state was not enough. The crèche mothers' claims to public support were based on wage earning and their roles as family breadwinners. Their encounters with the boundaries of social citizenship, in other words, were policed according to their economic behaviour. The crèche administrators' approach to supporting working families showed that gender roles could be suspended for working poor and working-class women in the name of holding up the more fundamental goal of welfare provision – to promote the work ethic and prevent the chronic dependency of poor and working-class families.[6] However, the crèche always represented an uneasy compromise in response to the pressing issues of labour shortages, relief provision, and family poverty. It was rarely considered more than a stopgap measure to "rehabilitate" mothers and restore a male breadwinner at the head of the family. It is perhaps no surprise, then, that mothers' pensions replaced the crèche as the preferred approach to mothers' welfare by the end of the decade.

The Origins of the Crèche

In the first decade of the twentieth century, Vancouver was home to a small, but influential, group of female social reformers and suffragists. From this energetic group came the "founding mothers" of the crèche: Helen Gregory MacGill, Mary Ellen Smith, Mrs. T.E. Aikins, and Mrs. J.O. Perry. MacGill, a member of the University Women's Club, the Women's Christian Temperance Union (WCTU), and the Local Council of Women, was an influential advocate for women's and children's legal rights and the province's first female juvenile court judge.[7] Smith, a former schoolteacher, was a prominent suffragist and a member of assorted women's organizations including the WCTU and the Imperial Order Daughters of the Empire (IODE). When her husband Ralph died in 1917, Smith was elected to his seat in the BC legislature, and she became the province's first female member of the legislative assembly (MLA).[8] Perry did not occupy such a prominent political position, though she was certainly part of the middle- and upper-class social strata from which female reformers were drawn. Her husband John was a businessman who manufactured and sold bank and office supplies.[9] Less is known about Aikins, though it is likely that her position was similar to Perry's.[10]

The establishment of the Vancouver crèche in 1909 was very much a product of these women's spheres of charitable activities.[11] MacGill and her colleagues were involved in a range of activities aimed at improving the lot of indigent women and children, including orphanages, hospitals, and Children's Aid Society homes. The crèche operated with a similar rationale. It was a place where working-class children could be fed and clothed and where mothers could have access to both material and moral help with child rearing.[12] The crèche's "founding mothers," who were part of a broader network of "clubwomen" that spanned the continent, would no doubt have been aware of other crèches and day nurseries that dotted the United States and Canada by the early twentieth century, and they would have considered that their city needed a similar service to relieve the suffering of poor families. The Methodist Jost Mission in Halifax, for example, established a day nursery as part of its larger community service functions that included motherhood education and relief work for the "poorer sisters."[13] In Toronto, the West End Crèche began with a young Anglican woman named Penelope Harvey who, in 1908, was motivated by a desire to engage in community charity work.[14] In Ottawa, Winnipeg, Montreal, and elsewhere, crèches were located in the city's poorest districts, their purpose being to provide charity to families struggling to ensure basic survival and to provide care to otherwise "neglected" children.[15] Elsewhere in British Columbia, a group of women from the Victoria chapter of the IODE spearheaded the creation of a day nursery in 1913, highlighting the importance of helping poor children.[16] Vancouver's clubwomen, though less motivated by religious impulses in their relatively "irreligious" city, were nonetheless similarly inspired to help relieve the plight of poor families.[17]

MacGill and the other founding mothers' work was framed by the ideology of maternal feminism, which highlighted the importance of women's natural roles and responsibilities as mothers that should extend to the public sphere. Yet their idealized version of motherhood did not extend across class boundaries, and, like their contemporaries across the country, MacGill and her cohort were "firmly rooted in the middle-class experience and expectations."[18] Their campaigns rarely included calls for class equality. Rather, their political work was based on a preservation of the status quo for middle- and upper-class families. As Gillian Weiss observes, Vancouver's clubwomen assumed that working-class women would work their entire lives, and their charitable projects were designed to help working women carry out their duties, not to challenge entrenched class norms.[19] Their role in establishing the crèche was part of this logic. The crèche helped to preserve the class-based status quo in one particularly important way: it ensured that white working-class mothers could be employed as domestic servants.

In the years immediately preceding the crèche's establishment in 1909, Vancouver's white middle- and upper-class families were reporting difficulties in finding suitable domestic help, a situation that had long plagued British immigrants looking to establish respectable households in British Columbia. The uneven demographics of the province and the city largely explained the dearth of female domestic servants. The resource-based economy of British Columbia attracted far more men than women, and by 1911 women represented only 36 percent of British Columbia's population. The proportion was only slightly higher in urban centres, at 39 percent.[20] The scope of the "servant problem" was such that various assisted immigration schemes were attempted throughout the late nineteenth century as a way to ensure a steady supply of young white women to do household work, but they were largely unsuccessful.[21] By the first decade of the twentieth century, changing labour force opportunities also meant that young working women were taking up positions as clerks, stenographers, and other service occupations, causing even more consternation among British Columbia's elite women who could not secure the kind of household help they desired.[22]

As the economy expanded, so too did employment opportunities for women in stores, offices, restaurants, and hotels. Data from 1911 show, for example, that two-thirds of Vancouver's female workers (who comprised 12.7 percent of the total labour force) were stenographers, teachers, and nurses or worked in retail and service industries.[23] Furthermore, given British Columbia's gender imbalance, many "well-trained women" were quickly "snapped up as wives" and thereby removed from the labour market, compounding high turnover rates in middle- and upper-class homes.[24] By 1907, the Provincial Council of Women declared that the domestic servant problem had reached "crisis proportions."[25] At the National Council of Women's annual meeting during the same year, Vancouver's clubwomen called for the creation of a committee to investigate "the impossibility of procuring women to help in housekeeping," which they characterized as "a situation that threatens to annihilate our homes."[26]

Vancouver's domestic help crisis in the early 1900s was also complicated by the racism that permeated every aspect of city life. Without a readily available supply of female domestics, many families throughout the late nineteenth and early twentieth centuries had hired Asian men as household workers. According to Eric Sager's study of domestic servants, almost two-thirds of live-in household help in British Columbia at the turn of the century was male, "and a majority was born in either China or Japan."[27] Chinese men had begun arriving in British Columbia in the mid-nineteenth century to work in the gold fields or to build the Canadian Pacific Railway. When the railway construction was complete, many remained and found work as domestic servants. For the most part, members of BC society considered it acceptable for Chinese men to work in domestic service because it kept them out of competition with white men and because stereotypes about their "submissive" and feminized nature reconciled white families to employing them in their homes.[28] Indeed, by the turn of the century, many of Vancouver's middle-class women, horrified at the "exorbitant" wages that in-demand white domestic servants charged, expressed a preference for Chinese "houseboys" because they could be employed at a much cheaper rate and because they were reliable and hard-working. Helen MacGill herself relied on a "Chinese cook" to run her household and help care for her children, as did many other elite families.[29]

Chinese men were such an important source of domestic servants by the early twentieth century that middle-class women began to agitate for the relaxation of immigration laws. The federal government, under pressure from British Columbia, had introduced a Chinese head tax of $50 in 1885 and raised it to $100 in 1901 and $500 in 1903. In 1907, women circulated a petition calling for a reduction in the head tax, which they believed would help "increase the supply of household servants."[30] MLA Ralph Smith, speaking of his wife Mary Ellen, privately deplored that "his gallant wife should have to roast her comely face over the kitchen fire every day because the Chinese Head Tax makes it impossible for him to get a Chinese cook."[31]

The desperate position of households such as the Smith's, however, could not entirely override deeply held anti-Asian views, and there remained an ongoing concern in Vancouver and across the province that "good white help was rare."[32] As Patricia Roy explains, "in the minds of many electors, it was better to go without help than to hire Asians."[33] High-status residents, after all, were invested in efforts to protect British Columbia as a "white man's province." This anti-Asian prejudice stemmed, Roy notes, from the "threat they allegedly posed as 'cheap labour' and the fear that 'hordes' of Asians could overwhelm a white British Columbia."[34] At the height of the clubwomen's domestic crisis, the city was in the midst of violent anti-Asian agitation, including a riot through Chinatown and Little Tokyo in September 1907, which was fuelled by the newly formed Asiatic Exclusion League. In this milieu, it was not surprising that the popular press deplored the employment of "Oriental" men in respectable white, middle- and upper-class homes.[35] Fear mongers suggested that Chinese domestics were "sexual deviants" who would coerce children into lives of immorality and danger.[36]

The establishment of the crèche offered a solution to these intertwined labour problems – the racist opposition to hiring Chinese men even though their labour was desperately needed. In 1909, Vancouver's clubwomen began to offer the combined services of child care and employment placement, likely in a home in the west end nearby employers' homes (though the exact location of this first iteration of the crèche is not known). In doing so, they tapped into the reserve of white middle-class domestic labour that they considered was not being used to its full potential. In this respect, the crèche actually had more in common with the dozens of employment bureaus dotting the city in the early years of the century, most of them designed to place workers in specialized sections of a labour market segregated by race and sex. Bureaus that facilitated women's domestic placements were particularly prolific due to the "almost insatiable demand for household servants" that remained steady even through periods of economic fluctuation.[37]

The crèche essentially functioned as a specialized employment service designed specifically to meet the needs of its middle-class clients. Women, most of them from the prosperous west end, would place a request for a domestic worker, who would be supplied from the ranks of the crèche's working mothers. Working mothers, for their part, were much more likely to take on waged work if they could be assured of reliable child care. After all, as future matron Lilian Nelson later reflected, mothers were often all too "glad to return as a day worker to bring grist to the mill, if their little ones could be well cared for in their absence."[38]

The Vancouver City Crèche as Public Welfare

Between 1909 and 1911, the crèche remained a privately run operation, its day-to-day activities largely unobserved by history's record keepers. In late 1911, however, the crèche appeared on the city's agenda when a motion was raised during a November council meeting to "erect, establish, and equip" a "Day Nursery."[39] This motion also included plans for a city-run "old people's home" and a free dispensary – a set of welfare measures that were indicative of a larger push towards consolidating social services in the city. In the decade or so leading up to 1911, Vancouver had undergone dramatic population growth, from 27,196 residents to 123,902 – its economy fuelled by lumber, mining, and the business opportunities that arose from its position as the west coast terminus of the Canadian Pacific Railway.[40] A new scope of social problems resulted from this rapid growth and industrialization, and it became clear to welfare officials that the city's patchwork approach to relief could no longer keep up with the demand. Council's proposal to establish a crèche took place in the context of the "rationaliz[ation]" and centralization of Vancouver's municipal welfare administration, which included a range of other services designed to protect and support neglected children, unemployed men, deserted wives, unwed mothers, and services for the "elderly infirm" and the "sick and convalescent."[41]

One important component in the spate of reforms to city welfare was the increasing consolidation of voluntary organizations with the municipal bureaucracy. The Associated Charities was the most important of these organizations. The roots of the Associated Charities lay in the Friendly Aid Society, which was established in 1895 to provide volunteer investigators to act in concert with city health officials. Through the first decade of the twentieth century, it was increasingly absorbed into official municipal channels. In 1906, the Friendly Aid Society became the Friendly Help Society, and its welfare investigators handled all of the city relief cases. In 1909, the Friendly Help Society evolved into the Associated Charities, a "more widely based operation of concerned citizens and societies."[42] Funded primarily through city grants (with the difference made up through public subscriptions), the Associated Charities had an even closer relationship with the city's Health Department, which included a joint board of management.[43] Through the Associated Charities, city relief was meted out in the form of food and meals, rent assistance, clothing, and coal.[44]

Even as the Associated Charities was being integrated into the city administration, though, the relief work it provided was still very much the domain of middle-class women. City council's measures with respect to the "day nursery" proposal represented the extent to which private and public welfare provision continued to overlap in Vancouver. Soon after the November 1911 council meeting, officials decided that rather than establishing a new crèche the city would take over the existing one being operated by the clubwomen. In January 1912, council passed a bylaw earmarking $7,500 to be put towards renovating and equipping a space for the crèche.[45] However, while the city assumed financial responsibility, the day-to-day operations of the crèche remained largely in the purview of charitable women. Management and oversight were assigned to the Associated Charities and, more specifically, to two of its female members, Lillian Forbes MacDonald and Desiré Unsworth.[46] Both women were well established in reform circles. Unsworth was the wife of a United Church minister and would eventually become the president of the Local Council of Women and co-founder of the Women's Employment League.[47] MacDonald, the wife of a local doctor, was deeply involved in women's employment issues in Vancouver, including wages and working conditions in stores and factories.[48] Both women were founding members of the Richard McBride chapter of the IODE and in fact drew on their IODE chapter to populate the twelve-member Associated Charities subcommittee given responsibility for fleshing out the details of the crèche's new place within municipal welfare services.[49]

Under MacDonald's guidance, the committee decided that the best location for the crèche was in the Vancouver Women's Building at 752 Thurlow Street. Also known as the "Tait House," the Vancouver Women's Building was the brainchild of Helen MacGill, who felt that the city's clubwomen deserved a dedicated space for their activities.[50] In early 1912, the crèche committee leased an annex of the Tait House, an arrangement that everyone considered suitable because the crèche would have access to the resources and support of the clubwomen who gathered there. Furthermore, the location was convenient for the client mothers of the crèche since the Tait House was nearby to the west end houses where they would be working during the day.[51]

MacDonald and her committee used the $7,500 allocated by the city to undertake a series of renovations to the Tait House wing, and the grand opening was held on 4 April 1912. After the much-publicized opening speeches and tours, the real work of the crèche began the next day. The matron and her assistant performed the bulk of the daily work at the crèche. They greeted the mothers and children when they arrived at 7 am, at which point the children were changed into the "blue striped rompers" designed to maintain a sanitary environment. The children's mothers, in the meantime, checked in with the crèche secretary, who oversaw the employment services. Most mornings, mothers could be sure of being placed in domestic day work, although record books show that some mothers were put to work in the crèche, helping with cleaning, cooking, or laundry (the crèche also employed a housekeeper), while other mothers had jobs independent of the employment bureau. Those who did crèche-assigned domestic work could expect to earn $2 for an eight-hour day, which included a noon meal. When mothers returned to the crèche at the end of the day – initially at 6 pm, but later at 7 pm to accommodate those who travelled long distances – they paid the fee of 10 cents per child and returned home with their children.[52]

For all of the congratulations and fanfare that surrounded the opening of the crèche, however, its establishment as a city institution was marked with a significant degree of controversy.[53] Other Vancouver children's institutions were also under the microscope at the time for alleged abuse of children, which no doubt contributed to concern about the crèche. However, by all accounts, the children in the crèche were "healthy and happy."[54] Rather, it was their mothers who loomed large in these debates. Did poor and working mothers "deserve" the kind of public assistance that the crèche offered? On what basis was their deservedness measured? What were their obligations to the city in return?

Two outspoken city aldermen, Malcolm McBeath (who would be elected mayor in December 1915) and Frank E. Woodside, expressed deep misgivings about the crèche, which no doubt reflected widely held views. In their minds, the crèche represented an irresponsible squandering of public funds. At the crux of their criticism was suspicion of any welfare scheme that was at variance with women's ties to their homes and children. Was it appropriate, they asked, to devote public money to a service that encouraged mothers to leave their homes and take up employment? In the first few months after the crèche's opening, McBeath and Woodside used the press to warn that its services would be used by "selfish" west end mothers who needed someone to look after their children "when they went to bridge parties." When pushed, Woodside was willing to concede that the crèche served a useful function for poor mothers, but he urged careful administration so that its services would not be misused by middle-class mothers. Perhaps, he suggested, the crèche was better off located "somewhere nearer Main Street," in closer proximity to the working-class mothers who needed to work.[55]

Views such as McBeath's and Woodside's, though, also inspired passionate and wide-ranging defences of the crèche. Many defenders trotted out familiar justifications that included its ability to ensure a steady supply of white domestic help as well as the charitable assistance it offered to "bereaved" widows and their pitiable families.[56] However, for many observers, the crèche's importance to the city was not simply about poor children or even the domestic servant problems of elite families. These factors were certainly still important, but so too were the labour and character of its working clientele. As Lillian MacDonald declared, the crèche was designed to make families "self-supporting" and to ensure that "no woman need go without work who is willing and able."[57] Besides MacDonald, a chorus of voices that included city councillors, sympathetic members of the press, welfare officials, and, of course, Unsworth and the crèche committee members insisted that these "self-respecting," working-class, breadwinning mothers were suitable candidates for public support.[58] As the crèche was further folded into the city's modern relief administration over the next several years, the terms of welfare provision to these working mothers were at the crux of the crèche's status among the expanding roster of city social services.

From "Founding Mothers" to "City Fathers"

Debates about the crèche took on new urgency by the end of 1912, only a few months after its move into the Vancouver Women's Building. The crèche was outgrowing its quarters; daily attendance had grown from an average of three children per day in April 1912 to thirty per day by the end of the year.[59] Furthermore, the lease on the building was due to expire in the spring. The crèche committee recognized the opportunity – and the need – for expansion. Lillian MacDonald was still heading up the crèche's operations, and she began to champion for increased public responsibility for the crèche. Her committee recommended that the city purchase a lot on Haro Street, not far from the Vancouver Women's Building in the downtown core, and erect a completely new crèche building designed specifically for the purposes of an employment bureau and day nursery. MacDonald also recommended that the crèche become a completely public institution, entirely under the financial and administrative control of the city instead of the arms-length control of the Associated Charities. Her proposal was bold and required a substantial commitment from the city as the plans were estimated to cost $70,000.

Alderman McBeath took up his refrain of suspicion about the crèche's purpose and became an outspoken critic of MacDonald's plan. Questioning why the city should be responsible for such a project, he also accused MacDonald's committee of engaging in "extravagant" spending and of mismanaging the Vancouver Women's Building crèche. (He also accused them of pocketing donated money, a claim that both the Associated Charities and the press dismissed as a "cock-and-bull story."[60]) His protests, however, were largely in vain. Not only did the steadily growing attendance rates prove the crèche's usefulness, but it also enjoyed a high degree of public support. Both the *Vancouver Sun* and *The Province*, Vancouver's two major dailies, published editorials praising the Haro Street plan and the "invaluable" service that the crèche provided to the city's working mothers.[61] Positive public opinion no doubt helped to sway the rest of council. In December 1912, they passed a bylaw that allocated $70,000 for the purchase of the Haro Street lot and construction costs, and a subcommittee of council, called the Associated Charities and Relief committee, was given responsibility for overseeing the crèche's construction. The committee consisted of five aldermen, the mayor, the relief officer, and three representatives of the Associated Charities, whose role was maintained despite MacDonald's suggestion otherwise.[62]

A seemingly endless stream of contract disputes and construction problems delayed the crèche's completion throughout 1913 and well into the spring of 1914. It finally opened in July 1914 to wide public accolade – as a wholly public institution "entirely under the control of the city fathers" and, more specifically, as the administrative responsibility of the city's Health Department.[63] The facilities were modern and functional, having been designed with input from the staff. The lower level housed a separate office for the employment bureau, which could be accessed with a "sloping cement way for buggies," if needed. As with the old crèche, the employment service was designed specifically to place mothers in domestic service positions, and the daily 10 cent fee remained the same. Across the hall from the employment office was the "culinary department," which was complete with electric dumbwaiter and a laundry room. The two main floors contained numerous "spacious and sunny rooms" in which the children would play, nap, and dine and where the older children would attend kindergarten classes. A room was also reserved for doctor's visits. The top level of the new building housed a small apartment for Miss Ada Paul, who replaced McLean sometime in 1913. Paul was a British-trained nurse with experience in "maternity and massage" work. She moved into the crèche position after having served as the matron of the Senior House University School in Victoria.[64]

Paul's time at the crèche was brief. She was soon replaced by Lilian M. Nelson, a native of England who had moved to Vancouver in 1901 and who had worked as the matron of the city's hospital before taking up the crèche position. Nelson's experience in various welfare institutions would lead to her appointment in 1916 as the city's first female welfare officer, but until that point she was a central figure in the evolution of the Vancouver City Crèche.[65] As matron, she ushered it through several significant years when its purpose was largely defined by its importance as a relief institution.

Key to understanding Nelson's tenure as matron, as well as the crèche's new administrative home in the Health Department, was the economic context of the decade's middle years. The crèche opened in July 1914 in the midst of very different economic circumstances than had shaped its earlier years. Vancouver was no longer flush with the financial health that had allowed the city to designate $70,000 towards the crèche in 1912. The first decade of the century was a prosperous period of economic and demographic expansion for British Columbians, but dwindling outside investments and a declining real estate market, as Jean Barman observes, "highlighted the extent to which the city had grown faster than the economy warranted."[66] The boom years under Premier Richard McBride came to an end, and the province entered a recession.[67] The province's economic collapse was exacerbated by the country's entry into war, together putting an unprecedented strain on both public and private welfare services in Vancouver.

The scope of the crisis became apparent in 1913 and into 1914, as skyrocketing rates of male unemployment caused widespread panic among social agencies. The Vancouver Trades and Labour Council (VTLC) painted a picture of "thousands" of out-of-work men "walking the streets lacking food and shelter, and thousands more silently starving."[68] Helena Gutteridge, the only female executive of the VTLC, sought to keep the plight of unemployed women at the forefront of public consciousness as well. A recent immigrant from England and a "single working woman until well into middle age," Gutteridge was a high-profile reformer whose activist efforts on behalf of women were much different than MacGill and her cohort of clubwomen. Gutteridge's focus was on the struggles of women in the labour force, and in her monthly reports to the *Labour Gazette*, she drew attention to the astronomical unemployment rates facing women in the summer of 1914 – as high as 75 percent for women working as tailors, dressmakers, and milliners.[69]

The situation was similarly dire among stenographers and clerical workers laid off by downsizing business firms.[70] Gutteridge was especially worried about the numbers of married women and mothers seeking support. With their husbands out of work, more women were "seeking employment to help keep the family."[71] Gutteridge's male colleagues on the VTLC's executive believed that the solution to female unemployment was "to see that men were provided with employment," their assumption being that women would no longer have to search for work if they were provided for by a breadwinner.[72] But Gutteridge was more practical in seeking a solution, and together with Desiré Unsworth, one of the original members of the crèche committee, she spearheaded the creation of the Women's Employment League as a job placement and make-work project for unemployed women. However, even this effort made only a small dent in the problem. Of the 1,189 women who registered with the league between October 1914 and February 1915, only 483 found work.[73] The employment crisis, furthermore, was particularly troubling for mothers with children to support. About one-third of the women who registered with the Women's Employment League in October 1914 were in just such a position.[74]

The unemployment crisis turned into a relief crisis. Not even the outbreak of the war improved employment prospects. British Columbia's wartime economy would not reverse the recession until 1916, and as husbands signed up to serve overseas or travelled to Britain to take jobs in munitions factories, rising numbers of working-class families were left without breadwinners. The Canadian Patriotic Fund, a pension for soldiers' wives established in 1914, provided only a limited scope of assistance.[75] The bulk of family relief work was left to private agencies and the city. The VTLC, for example, reported in February 1915 that it had so far spent "$14,000 on the destitute," and half of those were families.[76] J.H. McVety, the VTLC president, reported that "some soldiers' families were so desperately poor that fourteen wives had applied for relief funds before their husband's signature was dry on the enlistment roll."[77] The Women's Employment League, unable to find work for all who needed it, resorted to giving out meal tickets to mothers.[78] Other relief agencies stretched their resources as thin as possible to ensure that at the very least children were fed and warm.[79] City relief rolls showed that by mid-1915 families represented one-third of the relief recipients.[80] In that year, the city responded to the urgent situation by establishing a permanent city relief department, which could co-ordinate the provision of assistance more effectively.[81]

Amidst these pressures, the crèche represented an opportunity for the city; it could serve as relief project for working-class mothers and their families. By 1914, the logic of the crèche had moved firmly into the realm of relief provision because it offered the possibility of turning mothers into breadwinners. For the city, this was a much preferable alternative to families' permanent place on the city's relief rolls. Similar reasoning was at play across the strait in Victoria, which was facing the same pressures on its relief services. In this city, a committee made up of city representatives as well as members of the IODE, the Social Service Commission, the Children's Aid Society, the Friendly Help Society, and the Local Council of Women established a day nursery in 1913 and declared it an essential service for working-class and poor families. Without such a service, the committee said, "a great deal of charity will of necessity have to be dispensed by the city during the coming Winter."[82]

In both Victoria and Vancouver, this crèche-based approach to relief provision was made easier by the relatively stable demand for domestic service throughout the recession. Indeed, many of Vancouver's commercial female employment agencies had given up placing stenographers, office workers, cooks, waitresses, clerks, and hospital workers and confined their business solely to domestic placements. As Robin John Anderson explains, the unemployment crisis meant that "domestic service was the only work available for women after the summer of 1913."[83] By 1915, half of the Women's Employment League's successful job placements were in housework.[84] Working women's advocates within the VTLC also recognized that domestic service represented the only real employment opportunity for women, largely because of the persistent anti-Asian sentiment that continued to colour the province. "There [are] still a great many [women] out of employment," reported the *British Columbia Federationist*, whose concern about women workers was tinged with the familiar racism that surrounded Chinese domestics. These women "could do much of the work now being done about hotels by Orientals; as chambermaids, cooks, workers in the kitchens and as housekeepers. A good many people talked about a 'white British Columbia' and a good place to make a start was in domestic service. The duty of a community [is] towards its own subjects first."[85]

The weighing of financial considerations featured largely in deliberations about the crèche. Critics wondered whether the crèche was "serving its purpose ... considering the investment it represented" and whether it was, in other words, a financially prudent relief strategy.[86] After all, the wages that a mother earned as a housekeeper were not, for the most part, sufficient to support a family. Before the recession, women could expect to earn 40–50 percent less than (white) men, and with the economic crunch women workers reported that their wages were being cut another 25–50 percent.[87] But, at the very least, crèche supporters argued, a mother's employment income could help offset the amount that the city (or another private agency) would otherwise have to pay in direct relief. During the worst of the recession, at least, the crèche offered the chance to lessen the load on the city's relief department.

Along with these financial considerations, though, were moral ones. A mother's reliance on relief and/or charity not only was expensive but also made her prone to laziness and an unsuitable role model for her children. The crèche, then, filled a less tangible, but still vital, role in the city's relief provision: the promotion of a work ethic and the prevention of dependency. Matron Lilian Nelson called this role the "moral effect of the crèche system," and she felt that it "fully justified its existence."[88] The crèche was part of the broader need to stimulate work and the work ethic in the welfare provision of the turbulent mid-1910s. Relief measures were undertaken cautiously so as not to encourage long-term reliance on the city coffers. In 1914, for example, the city established a work camp for 2,000 unemployed men, which the relief officer called "a work test ... to prevent the creation of a 'chronic crowd of dependents.'"[89] Crèche mothers were subject to the same standards. They were essentially treated as the objects of a work-for-relief project distinct only in the recognition that care for their children determined their capacity to work.[90]

Over and over, city welfare officials and concerned observers claimed the prevention of a "class of dependents" as the crèche's most important function. Indeed, it was usually the crèche's role in preserving women's (and their families') work ethic that allowed its opponents to reconcile themselves to its existence and to the city's increased responsibility for working mothers. Alderman McBeath insisted that if the city was going to invest in the crèche, the client mothers had to "establish their bona fides by going out to work by the day."[91] Others lauded the crèche mothers who, "by their own hard work," were "supporting two or three little children and doing it without a murmur" and felt that they thus deserved some measure of public support.[92] Even the crèche's most ardent supporters did not think mothers should receive something for nothing. Working mothers had to earn their access to public welfare by proving that they were humble, were hard working, and did not desire to become dependent on the charity of others. It was these independent and self-reliant mothers – who would "indignantly refuse" direct charity because of its "pauperizing" and "stigmatizing" effects – who made the crèche a worthwhile investment for the city.[93] "There was no doubt," Nelson declared, "that being enabled to go to honest work kept a proper independent spirit among the women."[94]

For Nelson and others, the crèche's importance as a morally sound relief measure was borne out by the kind of mothers and children who used it on a daily basis. Annual reports from the city's Department of Health showed that the crèche operated at or above capacity, with numbers increasing after the opening of the new crèche on Haro Street. The number of days of care provided in 1916 was 25 percent higher than in 1913.[95] The majority of client mothers were from the working-class, industrial neighbourhoods of the city. Crèche register books list clusters of addresses around Hastings and Main Streets as well as to the east of the downtown core – the areas of the city where industry was concentrated and where wives often took over breadwinning responsibilities.[96] Moreover, the women using the crèche were much more likely to be married than single (although there were three single fathers among the crèche clientele). While the press was eager to play up the plight of bereaved and noble single mothers, records show that the typical crèche mother was married and that her husband was unemployed or unable to work due to illness, injury, or otherwise. This was especially true in the years of economic depression – although single mothers averaged only about 20 percent of the crèche clientele through the mid-1910s, entries for married women were even more common after 1912.[97] Mrs. Cheadle's husband, for example, was an out-of-work painter, and she left her son and infant daughter in the crèche while she was at her job. Mrs. Ross's husband was "unable to find work," and Mrs. Charles's husband was "not working" for unspecified reasons. Several mothers reported their husbands "idle," and others explained that their husbands were "looking for work," were "out of work," or, as in the case of the Frost family, had left town in search of employment.[98]

While in most cases, then, crèche mothers were serving as their families' sole breadwinner, in rarer instances both parents were employed yet the family was considered sufficiently "needy" enough to warrant the use of the crèche. The McGrath family, for example, who had recently immigrated from the United Kingdom, used the crèche so that both parents could work to save money for a new home. In the Bernetti family, the six children stayed at the crèche during the day so that Mrs. Bernetti could "help" her husband at the store they owned.[99] As the Bernettis' situation suggests, not all mothers relied on the crèche's employment bureau to help them find work. Among the entries was a woman who worked as a cashier in the Vancouver Hotel, another who worked as a cleaner in the Empress Theatre, one who was a piano player in cafes, and others who were employed as store clerks, chambermaids, stenographers, waitresses, and, of course, domestic workers in jobs they acquired independently of the crèche's employment bureau.[100] Many of these women were no doubt new immigrants without networks of family and friends on which to rely for child care. For them, the crèche was invaluable not only because it allowed them to work but also because it prevented them from resorting to other, less desirable child care options such as placing their children in homes or orphanages. Diane Purvey has shown, for example, that the majority of children at the Alexandra Orphanage came from working-class families headed by a deserted parent, most often the mother. Of those mothers who declared an occupation, 53 percent had chosen or been forced to use the orphanage as a place for child care.[101]

Despite the variety of occupations and backgrounds among the clientele, what they all had in common was a strong conviction that their use of the crèche did not render them "charity cases." Just as city welfare officials wanted the crèche to promote independent families, so too did the mothers who used its services want to be perceived as hard-working and self-reliant. As Helena Gutteridge explained, these "self-respect[ing]" women "shrink from charity" – they "did not want charity, but employment."[102] The payment of the daily 10 cent fee was one important way in which mothers laid claim to their independence from charity. Although the immediate circumstances of "destitution" sometimes prevented that day's payment, mothers often returned days later to repay debts.[103] During the worst of the economic slump in 1915, the city actually suspended the fee thinking that mothers deserved a break, but mothers' insistence on payment prompted the city, only a month later, to authorize the matron to "collect fees from persons using the Crèche, who are desirous to pay for services rendered."[104] Though the fee was admittedly "nominal," it was still "sufficient to remove the stigma of charity from the minds of the mothers."[105] The freedom from welfare dependency was a key part of the mothers' own conceptions of their status as deserving and contributing citizens.

"A mother cannot support her children and look after them properly at the same time"

After several wearying years, the BC wartime economy kicked in in 1916, and employment prospects for both men and women improved.[106] The re-established labour market brought with it new questions about women and work. In industrial occupations (including munitions work), campaigns for equal pay for women gained steam, although advocates were more concerned, as Gillian Creese argues, to protect male wages and ensure jobs for returning soldiers.[107] Cordoned off in predominantly female sectors of the labour market, crèche mothers were largely immune, at least in theory, from these debates about women's wages and working conditions. Yet the fate of the crèche was tied up in the larger discussions about women, work, and family that preoccupied city planners as the end of the war approached and as the rebounding economy alleviated the urgency around relief provision.

In late 1916 and early 1917, several city councillors and relief officials used the opportunity of a recovering economy to renew their suggestions that the crèche was not a cost-effective or appropriate use of public resources. A report commissioned by city council suggested that it would actually be cheaper for the city to board children year-round, orphanage-style, than it would be to provide daytime child care and employment services through the crèche.[108] In fact, this is what had happened to the Victoria Day Nursery. Soon after its establishment in 1913, it began to board girls for whom there was not enough room at the Children's Aid Society home. By 1917, full-time boarding was essentially its main function, and the children were permanently moved into the Children's Aid Society home. The day nursery was no longer necessary, "owing to the fact," city officials claimed, "that there are few, if any ... mothers who go out to work by the day."[109] Although no one seriously proposed a city-run orphanage in Vancouver, one alderman suggested that rather than "keep up the crèche" it would be "more economical for the city to maintain the mothers at home" by providing them with direct relief.[110] Several councillors, including frequent critic Alderman Woodside, wanted to see the city give up its responsibility to the crèche entirely. Based on reports he received from a delegation of seven concerned (but unnamed) women, Woodside insisted that several of the crèche mothers were "under no obligation to go out [to work] at all" and were taking advantage of the crèche's child care services for selfish reasons.[111]

The city's medical health officer, Dr. Frederick T. Underhill, also took an interest in the crèche in the fall of 1916. He insisted that the almost-new building on Haro Street should be repurposed to allow "a wider scope for more important work."[112] What he had in mind was an infant's hospital, an institution he (and others) considered necessary for a modern city that should place children at the centre of post-war rebuilding efforts. Some councillors continued to insist that the crèche was doing "necessary" work, but Underhill redoubled his efforts in the spring of 1917. His campaigning was rewarded when council decided to turn the crèche building over to an infants' hospital and allocated funding to undertake the necessary renovations.[113] The services of the crèche would continue but in the "Old Hospital Building" at the corner of Pender and Cambie Streets. This physical transfer coincided with an administrative shuffle that made the scaled-down crèche the responsibility of the city's Relief Department. The crèche, in every sense, had been demoted in the ranks of the city's welfare services.

Figure 1 Group portrait of children and supervisors at the City Crèche, located at the corner of Pender and Cambie Streets, Vancouver. This photo was likely taken sometime in 1917 after the crèche had moved into the "Old Hospital Building" at Pender and Cambie.
Credit: Courtesy of City of Vancouver Archives, Major Matthews Collection, AM54-S-:Bu P48, Photographer W.J. Moore.

Shifting trends in child welfare circles help to explain the declining support for the crèche. Supporters sought to frame the crèche as an essential support to allow the children of delinquent working-class families to become productive and healthy citizens, but, in the aftermath of the war, even this argument lost ground.[114] "Institutional" care for children was falling out of favour across a range of welfare organizations in the city. Charles South, the president of the Vancouver Children's Aid Society, advocated for the replacement of boarding house–style care with a foster care system, so that children could be rehabilitated in "real homes."[115] These changing local attitudes were influenced by a wider context. The founder of the Toronto Children's Aid Society, J.J. Kelso, insisted that children in institutional care were harder to "save" because they were in constant contact with other morally suspect children. His views carried great weight with child savers across the country.[116]

Intertwined with this concern about institutional care was a rising tide of enthusiasm for maternalist social reform. The emphasis on care in "real homes" implied that the best thing for children was to be looked after by their mothers and, if necessary, these mothers should be compensated in order to provide full-time care. Vancouver city councillors began to suggest that this was a much preferable system to the crèche, not only because it was "cheaper" but also because it was "better ... for mothers and children."[117] In the initial stages of these kinds of proposals, supporters of the crèche pointed out that such an extensive provision of direct relief – right into the hands of mothers – was "morally objectionable." But it was increasingly becoming even more objectionable to encourage mothers to give up their natural roles as mothers in the home.[118]

Among the most outspoken critics of the crèche by 1917 were, somewhat ironically, middle-class women. For Helen Gregory MacGill, Mary Ellen Smith, and their peers, the crisis-level shortage of domestic servants was a thing of the past, and, in their view, the crèche's continued existence only served to undermine the sanctity of home life. A delegation of women from the New Era League, one of Vancouver's leading women's groups, suggested to city council that,

> if the money that was spent in the maintenance of the crèche were given direct to the mothers under the administration of a board from the various women's organizations, the crèche could be done away with and the mothers, through being able to look after their children personally, it would be better for them [sic].[119]

As this delegation pointed out, mothers' earnings were less than the city spent in providing child care, and thus it made more sense to "give that amount to the mothers in the way of a pension or a grant."[120]

This plan, of course, described mothers' pensions almost exactly. By this time, a powerful female-led campaign for provincial mothers' pensions was taking shape across the province, inspired by the international popularity of maternalist politics.[121] In social policy terms, mothers' pensions represented the epitome of maternalist ideology, and British Columbia's social reformers were eager to see the province keep up with progressive welfare reform in the United States and Europe. The overwhelming support for mothers' pensions, as Margaret Little shows, was rooted in the belief that mothers did not belong in the labour force but, rather, in the home and that their maternal "service to the state" should be compensated. Since the pensions were cast as a mother's "right," they were not associated with the stigma of charity and, thus, even those reluctant to endorse public handouts could support the idea.[122]

Mothers' pensions, furthermore, were closely aligned with the broader currents of social reform taking shape in the same period, similarly designed around the protection of women's "natural" connection to home and motherhood. Pensions campaigns coincided, for example, with the introduction (by Mary Ellen Smith) of female minimum wage legislation in 1918, which had less to do with women's rights to be paid fairly and much more to do with concern over their "health and morals." Advocates wanted to ensure a high enough wage that women would not be tempted into prostitution and, at the same time, to prevent lower-paid women from providing unfair competition to men. The level was set at subsistence for one individual, not taking into account children or other dependents. The minimum wage, in other words, both reinforced women's "natural" connection to domesticity and motherhood and was based on the assumption that women were single, childless, and, ultimately, temporary members of the labour force.[123] Labour activists such as Helena Gutteridge, taken up with union organizing and wage disputes, based their work on the same assumptions. Women workers' need for child care services was very rarely part of the reform landscape.[124]

The crèche did not fit comfortably alongside these reform efforts and, not surprisingly, was a frequent target of mothers' pensions advocates. In the public hearings on pensions that crossed the province through 1919 and 1920, several respondents invoked the crèche as an example of how not to provide public support to mothers and their children. A member of the Nelson WCTU described her visit to the Vancouver crèche as an appalling experience, one that inspired pity for the children who were stuffed together like a "lot of little chickens" for hours everyday. "It would be a splendid thing," she urged the hearing's commissioners, "to have these mothers care for their children instead of having to send them to some institution."[125] Another respondent in Nelson declared simply that "a woman cannot support her children and look after them properly at the same time."[126]

Evidence also suggests that many of Vancouver's working mothers were in favour of mothers' pensions as an alternative to the crèche. The long hours and low pay of domestic work took its toll, and many mothers, as matron Lilian Nelson observed, were eager for the chance to give up the double day and devote more time to their children. "It is no small matter," she told the commissioners, "for these women to come out as they do every day at 8 o'clock in the morning with three or four children, [and] it is bad for the children having to get them up and take them out so early."[127] A mothers' pensions cheque was an attractive option, especially if their receipt of state assistance was considered an entitlement rather than charity. As Nancy Christie has shown of working-class mothers elsewhere in Canada at this time, often "women preferred government aid to outside work that compelled them to leave their children unattended" and that allowed them to avoid "the double-burden of paid and unpaid work."[128]

The lead up to, and passage of, mothers' pensions legislation in 1920 did not mean the end of the crèche, but it did mark a significant shift in its purpose and status. In 1919, crèche administrators stopped offering employment placement services since the city did not want to be seen to be encouraging mothers' employment.[129] Despite maternalist reformers' hopes, however, mothers' pensions did not eliminate working motherhood, especially since only widowed and deserted mothers were eligible for a pension cheque. The crèche continued to be used heavily through the 1920s. At the end of the decade, daily attendance sat at forty to fifty children.[130] However, the working wives and "failed" families that made up the crèche clientele stood in marked contrast to the more "respectable" pension recipients. As a last resort service for mothers and their otherwise neglected children, the crèche was relegated to the margins of municipal social welfare – its status helping to further stigmatize mothers who needed public support in their child care arrangements. The crèche remained in operation until 1932, at which point it was replaced by the privately run Vancouver Day Nursery Association, a home-based child care placement program for working mothers.[131]

The first decade of the Vancouver City Crèche's existence was marked by tumultuous economic conditions, unemployment and relief crises, and the consolidation and centralization of local and provincial welfare services. The decade was also marked by changing public opinion towards the crèche. Established by middle-class clubwomen, then cautiously embraced as a work-for-relief project for mothers, it was denounced within ten years as an inferior form of public welfare by many of those same women. However, whether concerned officials and citizens were expressing support of the crèche or in opposition to its existence, their statements always reflected the conflicting public attitudes towards the labour and moral character of the crèche's working-class client mothers. The Vancouver City Crèche's evolution as a public institution was very clearly a story about the politics of mothers' employment and about public responsibility to working mothers. The crèche enjoyed support when working-class mothers were needed for domestic labour or when the imperative to promote the work ethic and working-class family independence was foremost. Its value as a public institution declined when planners and politicians did not want to be seen encouraging mothers' employment amidst the post-war preoccupation with women's domestic and maternal "service to the state."

Despite the far-reaching consensus about mothers' pensions, however, the issue of motherhood, work, and welfare was far from settled in British Columbia. Throughout the 1920s and the 1930s, as women across British Columbia interacted with the provincial welfare state through the administration of mothers' pensions, new questions arose about working mothers' citizenship. Mothers' pensions seemed to offer a radical departure from the crèche: access to social rights on the basis of motherhood, entirely removing the criteria around mothers' labour force participation. The nature of BC women's relationship with the state in the interwar years, however, suggests that the history of women, work, and welfare was one of continuity as well as change.

2
"Self help is to be encouraged to the fullest extent": Working Mothers and the State in the Interwar Years

In late 1921, a group of social reformers in Victoria launched a campaign for the re-establishment of a day nursery, a service that the city had lacked since 1916. An impressive array of local social agencies weighed in on the proposal, including the Children's Aid Society (CAS), the Young Men's Christian Association, the Victorian Order of Nurses, and the Victoria Trades and Labour Council.[1] The representatives of these groups were not the only ones who recognized a gap in services for working mothers: editorials and letters to the editor also hinted at the extent of popular support for a day nursery. Mothers wrote in to tell of the "crying need" for a place where "working women could leave their babies while they are at work."[2] Another declared that a day nursery would be "a boon and a blessing to us mothers who have the whole burden of providing for a young family."[3] Ultimately, however, the campaign went nowhere. The development of a day nursery was impeded in part by a shortage of financial support from the city as well as by the lack of a common vision from its supporters. While, for some, the needs of working-class mothers were at the core of the day nursery's mission, others imagined it as a place for "relaxation" for middle-class mothers, while they "d[id] their shopping or t[ook] their recreations."[4] Most importantly, though, the day nursery was rejected for the threat it represented to home and motherhood. The "aim sought in the establishment of a Day Nursery," according to the CAS, "should be attained through the operation, and if need be the extension of the principle of the Mother's Pensions [sic]."[5]

By 1921, the *Mothers' Pensions Act* had been in force for a year, and hundreds of mothers had seen their incomes increase and stabilize through their receipt of a monthly cheque.[6] For the Victoria reformers, pensions were the "solution" to the "problem" of working motherhood and a much more desirable way to assist mothers than to provide them with child care services. A remarkable number of British Columbians, from ordinary citizens to political leaders, agreed. The passage of mothers' pensions legislation in 1920 was precipitated by a powerful and widespread maternalist campaign, at the core of which was the belief that motherhood was women's sacred duty. Pension advocates urged the provincial government to provide compensation to indigent mothers so that they would not have to spend their days apart from their children, toiling in low-wage work. Not surprisingly, then, alongside the rising tide of enthusiasm for mothers' pensions was diminishing support for services such as the Vancouver City Crèche, the (proposed) Victoria Day Nursery, and any sort of publicly funded child care initiative. Municipal and provincial welfare officials distanced themselves from the provision of these services in the interwar years and positioned motherhood and domesticity, at least rhetorically, at the centre of an expanding roster of social programs.

However, the relationship between mothers' pensions and mothers' work outside the home – the expectation that the former would put an end to the latter – was not so straightforward. As the experiences of hundreds of mothers throughout the 1920s and 1930s demonstrates, the receipt of a pension did not necessarily remove the need for wage work. In fact, in many cases, the opposite was true. The pension, after all, was still marked with the stigma of state "charity," and participation in paid work was considered an important guard against mothers' chronic dependency. Certainly, as Margaret Little has suggested, there is a case to be made that the passage of pension legislation in 1920 represented a new type of welfare entitlement, one based around the "good" dependency of mothers within the family.[7] Compared to the rest of Canada, BC pensions were generous, at least when it came to white women. Unwed, divorced, and deserted mothers could receive a cheque, and there is evidence to suggest that recipients and their advocates understood the pension as their right.[8] Underneath this rhetoric of maternalism and mother-citizenship, though, was a pension administration driven by the moral and economic imperatives of mothers' wage work. Officials were reluctant, for example, to grant pensions to mothers they deemed capable of doing "productive" work, especially mothers with "only" one child. Administrators were also satisfied with a low monthly amount that acted only as a supplement to earned income. This limitation, they argued, ensured the preservation of the work ethic and some semblance of self-sufficiency in families that relied on public support.

In the public discourse of British Columbia's interwar years, mothers' pensions were situated as the antithesis of publicly funded child care initiatives. Yet mothers' pensions and services such as crèches and day nurseries were, essentially, just different solutions to the same problem: how to provide public support to working poor and working-class mothers. Should they be encouraged to stay at home or to earn a wage to support their families? Both solutions were problematic. Poor mothers who stayed at home were at risk of becoming permanent drains on the public purse and reproducing patterns of dependency within their families. Wage-earning mothers were neglecting their children and their sacred duty to the home and to the nation. BC welfare officials were not the only ones facing this dilemma in the early twentieth century, as different jurisdictions around North America experimented with crèches, day nurseries, and mothers' pensions and allowances. For officials in Philadelphia, Elizabeth Rose notes, the working mother represented a "puzzling figure." "Reformers seemed uncertain," Rose observes, "about whether to treat her more like a breadwinner, who should be encouraged to achieve 'independence,' or more like a mother, who should be properly supported."[9]

Just as the Vancouver crèche reformers had in the 1910s, provincial pension administrators in British Columbia confronted this dilemma throughout the 1920s and 1930s. The public debates and bureaucratic decision making about pensions eligibility represented the same battleground on which crèche politics had played out: which mothers were deserving of public support and what did they "owe" the state in return? The provincial welfare state continued to grow, but how were working mothers going to be brought inside the expanding boundaries of social citizenship?[10] Despite paying lip service to motherhood's importance to the state, though, provincial welfare officials remained first and foremost concerned with preventing "bad" dependency, which was associated with pauperism and charity, among poor and working-class mothers. Expectations around paid work as a measure of deservedness figured strongly in the pensions administration. The bureaucrats and social workers working in the provincial government made this feeling clear virtually from the moment that the legislation passed in 1920. When Charlotte Whitton reported on BC pensions in 1931, she powerfully reaffirmed wage work as the gatekeeper to social benefits.[11]

As women in the work force, though, those mothers ran up against gendered inequalities that precluded any possibility that they would receive rights as worker-citizens. Pensioned mothers, in other words, were encouraged and even obligated to enter the labour market to achieve independence, but they were not given "the resources to do so."[12] They were confined to female occupation ghettos with low wages, limited opportunities, and few workplace supports – least among them, child care. As the province slid further into the Great Depression, women, and especially married women and mothers, faced increasing hostility amidst accusations they were taking jobs that rightfully belonged to male breadwinners. The Depression-era panic about women's threat to male employment may not have been based in reality, but it nonetheless had significant consequences. The "man as breadwinner," Lara Campbell explains, "was ultimately encoded into the social policies" of the welfare state.[13] This perception had a double effect on women – not only was maternally based social entitlement sidelined to the point of invisibility, but so too were mothers' tenuous claims on the state as workers.

The Mothers' Pensions Lobby and Hearings

During and after the First World War, women's organizations, labour groups, politicians, and welfare reformers were searching for ways to restore "normalcy" to society. Years of social upheaval due to wartime separations and dismal economic conditions, as well as the 1918 influenza epidemic, had taken its toll on communities and families. At the core of reconstruction efforts, many reformers argued, were mothers. The caregiving and domestic work that mothers did in their homes was "essential to the future of the nation" and thus needed to be encouraged and sustained through public support.[14] These kinds of arguments were not unique to the BC context. Campaigns for mothers' pensions and allowances also emerged elsewhere across North America as well as in Europe and Australia. Spearheaded by powerful coalitions of women's organizations, politicians, clergy, and social welfare groups (to name a few), these maternalist campaigns "exalted women's capacity to mother and applied to society as a whole the value they attached to that role," including "caring, nurturance, and morality."[15] The common goal of these transnational movements, as Seth Koven and Sonya Michel explain, was to transform motherhood from "*private* responsibility into *public* policy."[16] In Canada, mothers' pensions and mothers' allowances acts began to appear on provincial agendas beginning in the 1910s. By 1920, British Columbia along with Alberta, Saskatchewan, Manitoba, and Ontario had legislation on the books.

The introduction of such programs represented a significant new way of thinking about social entitlement within developing provincial welfare states. Social protections were no longer just for male workers – certain mothers could also be entitled to benefits based on the maternal services that they performed for the greater good and because they were doing essential work as "mothers of the nation." The nature and degree of this entitlement varied in different jurisdictions. In the United States, Barbara Nelson suggests, mothers' allowances represented a secondary "tier" of welfare entitlement. Unlike the rights-based, rationally organized workmen's compensation for male breadwinners, mothers' aid was characterized more like charitable benefits that were privileges rather than rights.[17] Historians have viewed Canadian mothers' pensions and allowances in a somewhat different light. In Ontario, for example, James Struthers argues that mothers' allowances represented "a new basis for thinking about welfare as entitlement rather than as charity," with this entitlement rooted in women's reproductive work.[18] Little's research suggests that BC mothers were uniquely positioned to make claims upon the state, especially since the parameters of pension eligibility were so broadly conceived (for white women) in British Columbia relative to the rest of Canada.[19]

Social, economic, and political circumstances help to explain British Columbia's unique approach to mothers' pensions. Besides wartime losses and family turmoil, British Columbia's socio-economic equilibrium had been upset by dangerous working conditions (for men and women) and visible poverty created by rapid urbanization and industrialization and by large-scale immigration that fuelled anxiety about "race suicide" of the white Anglo-Celtic population. The insistence on protecting white mothers stemmed from a "great fear that the family unit was being destroyed," according to Little. Providing widowed, deserted, and even unwed and divorced white mothers with a monthly pension, reformers argued, was one way to restore families to something approximating "normal." Pensions were part of the blueprint for re-establishing a prosperous society built upon the white middle-class status quo.[20]

British Columbia's powerful coterie of maternalist reformers were among the most vocal proponents of mothers' pensions. Among them were former supporters of the crèche, including Helen Gregory MacGill and Mary Ellen Smith. By 1917, Smith was sitting as the province's first female member of the legislative assembly (MLA), and she acted as the government point person for the coalition of mothers' pensions lobby groups, helping them to navigate access to senior politicians and ensuring that pensions remained on the government's agenda.[21] A number of other high-profile women overlapped with MacGill and Smith in suffrage campaigns, public health initiatives, and other social welfare projects, including the crèche. Susie Lane Clark, for example, who co-ordinated and led delegations to the provincial government, was the president of the New Era League, one of the province's most prominent women's rights associations. These Vancouver women were joined by representatives from Victoria's reform community, including Cecilia Spofford and Maria Grant. Spofford was on the executive of both the CAS and the Women's Christian Temperance Union (WCTU), and Grant was the WCTU president.[22]

Maternal feminists were not the only ones making the case for mothers' pensions. Lobbying efforts also came out of religious, medical, and child welfare organizations as well as labour representatives. In fact, the Vancouver Trades and Labour Council (VTLC) was one of the earliest supporters of mothers' pensions, thanks in large part to their lone female executive member, Helena Gutteridge. During the worst of the province's economic troubles in 1914 and 1915, Gutteridge convinced the VTLC to pass a resolution calling for state aid for the many desperate single mothers and those with unemployed husbands.[23] However, their motives were not entirely driven by a deep desire for maternalist social reform. The protection of male jobs was at the centre of the VTLC's agenda. Accompanying their pension resolution were other efforts to prevent women from working in, and undercutting the wages of, jobs that rightfully belonged to family men. A resolution from August 1913, for example, called for co-operation from "trade unionists" to "prevent the employment of women in the foundries," a plan they insisted

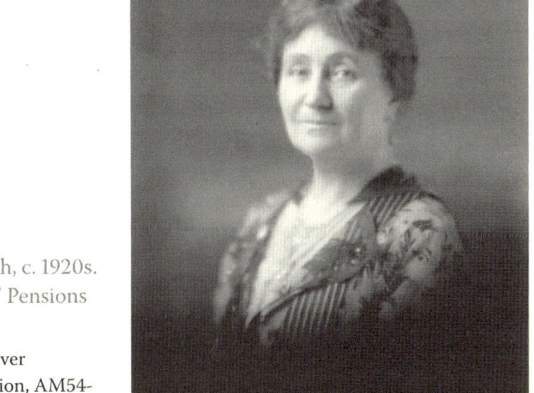

Figure 2 Mrs. Mary Ellen Smith, c. 1920s. Smith introduced the Mothers' Pensions Act.
Credit: Courtesy of City of Vancouver Archives, Major Matthews Collection, AM54-S4-:Port N32, Photographer Walter H. Calder.

emerged from their concern for women's and "the race's" physical and moral health.[24] No matter how they framed it, however, labour organizations had the same agenda as women's groups: a pension "adequate to support the mother and child without her having to go out to work."[25]

The extent of support for mothers' pensions was made apparent when the campaign became official in 1918 and 1919. A delegation of over fifty women's, labour, religious, medical, and welfare organizations, led by Susie Lane Clark, made presentations before the government in Victoria on two separate occasions in those years. Liberal Premier John Oliver called this group "the most businesslike and representative delegation that had ever appeared before the Government."[26] He was particularly impressed by the second of the delegations, in January 1919, which saw thirty-five speeches by thirty-five women in just one hour. Oliver agreed with Clark and her colleagues that the pensions were a "necessity," although he may have been thinking more in terms of his political fortunes than of the needs of widowed mothers. The female voting bloc represented by the pensions lobby ensured that mothers' pensions featured prominently in the 1920 election, and it was in Oliver's best interests to capture their support.[27] Citing the huge financial commitment that pensions entailed, however, he requested further study of the matter by the Royal Commission on Health Insurance and Maternity Benefits. He appointed E.S. Winn, the chairman of the Workmen's Compensation Board (WCB) and thus the chief administrator of the largest welfare program in the province, to head the commission. Victoria's Cecilia Spofford was also made a commissioner, as were Dr. T.C. Green from New Westminster and D. McCallum, also from Victoria.

The commissioners were tasked with investigating the broader possibility of province-wide health insurance, but it soon became clear that mothers' pensions were foremost on everyone's minds.[28] Through late 1919 and early 1920, the commission travelled to eighteen municipalities throughout the province and heard arguments from local women's organizations, medical and social work professionals, welfare experts, charities, clergymen, and labour representatives. A clear consensus emerged from all of these hearings. For the proper training of future citizens, mothers without a breadwinner must be compensated by the state in order to preserve home life. A pension would allow a mother to "remain in her home and maintain it for the welfare of her children."[29]

At the very core of this wholesale support for mothers' pensions was the insistence that mothers, especially white mothers, did not belong in the labour force. Mothers' work outside the home, commissioners heard again and again, was damaging to the entire family. Many respondents, such as Reverend Robert Herbison of Princeton, warned that the children of working mothers "run the streets for the greater part of the day," contributing to juvenile delinquency.[30] The Revelstoke Women's Canadian Club issued similar warnings, advocating the pension as a way to let mothers "take care of their children in the home instead of going and scrubbing and letting the children run the streets."[31] The alternative to giving children free rein – putting them into institutions – was equally unappealing. Lilian Nelson, the Vancouver City Crèche matron, spoke in favour of mothers' pensions, as did Maria Grant, who ran the Victoria WCTU home for children (many of whose parents did not have access to child care). "I think it is high time," Grant argued, "when a mother should be able to live with her children and not have to leave her home or take them to some place and leave them."[32] Paying a mother a monthly sum, Provincial Secretary J.D. MacLean explained, would enable her to "keep her family at home under her watchful care," which would prevent juvenile delinquency, institutional placements, and mothers resorting to "doubtful modes of living." These outcomes would "insure a better and higher type of citizenship" and would serve the interests of children, mothers, and the state.[33]

Other respondents focused not just on the neglected children of working mothers but, rather, on the burdens borne by the mothers themselves. In this respect, concern came mostly from the (limited) evidence presented by working-class representatives, who knew first-hand the challenges of wage earning and mothering. In Nanaimo, the commission heard from coal miner Joseph Dickson, who related the story of a widowed mother with six children who made her living "out scrubbing" for $1.50 per day:

> "She had to turn in after seven or eight o'clock and do her own housework. That woman cannot go out and work and do her own housework and keep her children clean and in proper health, she cannot do it and I think there should be something done for people like her."[34]

Dickson was one among many respondents who insisted that the support to which these mothers were due did not stem from pity. This view pervaded the proceedings in every corner of the province and was echoed in 1920 by none other than Charlotte Whitton, the country's recognized expert on social work. A mother's receipt of a pension, Whitton declared, should be considered "state recognition, not charity."[35] This sentiment featured strongly in the commissioners' final report, which they released in the spring of 1920. Not only did the report strongly endorse mothers' pensions legislation, but the commissioners were also careful to place aid to mothers in the same category as soldiers' pensions – a state entitlement that was based on an important contribution to society.[36]

The remarkable consensus around the need to support mothers in the home was the real story of the pension hearings, but there were outliers. Several respondents, chiefly labour representatives, took a different stance on the question of mothers' "rights" and questioned whether a mother's receipt of state support could ever really be divorced from the stigma of charity. Mrs. Edith Booth, the Prince Rupert representative of the Ladies Auxiliary of the One Big Union, warned that pensions would create "handicaps" for women and "saddle" them with the judgment of a paternalistic state. Booth used England as an example to illustrate her point: "There is always some person prying around to see that they do this or get something else – it is too much like charity – a woman is doing her best to bring up her family." "If the state interferes as to the way the mother should spend the money," Booth argued, "the mother might as well earn the money."[37] Jack Kavanagh, the president of the VTLC, agreed. Moreover, he argued, some mothers "prefer taking part in industry," and "such women might desire that the child be taken care of by the state in order to allow her to take her place" in the work force.[38] Kavanagh's statements highlighted the "limits of maternalism" and raised the troubling question of state-funded child care, and the commissioners were obviously wary.[39] For the most part, responses such as Booth's and Kavanagh's were dismissed as the views of radical labour organizers and socialists – a characterization that, in fact, accurately described both respondents – and although they reveal intriguing hints of a discourse that would emerge later in the century, their positions remained on the margins of public debate in 1920.

Legislation Enacted

Considering the degree of public support that had emerged from the cross-province hearings, introducing mothers' pensions legislation was a no-brainer for Oliver's government. Provincial Secretary J.B. McLean introduced the *Act to Provide Pensions for Mothers* in April 1920.[40] It passed easily, and by 1 July of the same year the government began accepting applications. The base rate of the pension was set at $42.50 per month, which applied to mothers with one child. $7.50 per month was available for each additional child. The fact that one-child mothers could apply for a pension set British Columbia apart from other provincial jurisdictions; so too did the provisions that made pensions available to deserted wives, those whose husbands were imprisoned or incapacitated, and even, through a discretionary clause, those who were unmarried or divorced.

Despite these relatively inclusive terms, some highly placed officials thought that the legislation did not go far enough. Mary Ellen Smith regretted that many unwed mothers would have to rely on the generous interpretation of the discretionary clause to gain access to a pension. "May God forgive us," she lamented, for "brand[ing] a mother who has not gone through a marriage ceremony [as] different [than] ourselves."[41] Smith's concerns were not without merit. Despite the broad parameters of the legislation, widowed mothers remained the state's priority. Through the 1920s and 1930s, widows represented roughly two-thirds of all of the mothers on the pension rolls.[42] Neither Smith nor any other public official, though, put forward criticism of the other ways in which the legislation was narrowly conceived. The act required that recipients of mothers' pensions had to be British subjects, which was clearly meant to exclude women from many immigrant communities and particularly, as Margaret Little shows, those of Asian background. Eligibility was further restricted to mothers who were residents of British Columbia for at least eighteen months and whose children were under the age of sixteen.[43]

The government assigned responsibility for administering mothers' pensions to George Pyke, the superintendent of neglected children (despite Winn's recommendations that the Department of Education should be responsible). Pyke set about creating thirteen local advisory boards throughout the province in 1920 and four more in 1921. Appointments to these boards, while not paid positions, were nonetheless highly coveted. Most of the boards were filled with prominent and well-placed women. In Vancouver, Pyke appointed Susie Lane Clark, Mrs. McNair (whose first name is not given, and who was affiliated with the CAS, the King's Daughters, the Local Council of Women, the Women's Canadian Club, and the Presbyterian Rescue Home for Girls), and Mrs. Sheasgreen (who was also listed only by her last name and who had a long history of work with the Juvenile Court, the Catholic Orphanage, and St. Paul's Hospital). Cecilia Spofford was appointed to the Victoria board.[44] While the advisory boards did not have the authority to officially approve or deny a pension, "to a very large extent" their reports "were taken as the recommendation upon which the applicant will be brought under the operation of the law."[45] Information on applications was also provided by local welfare investigators, who undertook home visits "to see that proper home life is being maintained, the health of the children safeguarded and that those of school age are making satisfactory progress."[46]

Over 1,000 pension applications arrived in George Pyke's office in the fall of 1920, more than double the government's expectations.[47] The overwhelming response put a larger than expected strain on provincial finances, which did not bode well for the long-term sustainability of mothers' pensions, let alone for the short-term bureaucratic hurdles. Officials decided that reforms were needed sooner rather than later. In March 1921, the first set of amendments was introduced to the *Mothers' Pensions Act*, less than a year after the legislation was first introduced. The eligibility restrictions were tightened to include only those mothers whose husbands' incapacitation had occurred while they were residing in British Columbia, whose disability was medically certified, and who did not own assets in excess of $2,000, which was later raised to $2,500.[48] There was also talk of reducing the monthly base amount from $42.50 to $35 as a cost-saving measure. Cecilia Spofford, who advocated the reduction, assured mothers that since the cost of living was falling, this change would "permit a reduction in pensions without discomfort." (An astute reader of the *Victoria Daily Colonist*, which printed Spofford's comments, pointed out that elsewhere in the paper an increase in the salaries of members of parliament was justified by the increased cost of living).[49]

Vigorous protestations, mostly from women's groups, helped to ensure that the monthly amount remained $42.50. But Spofford and her colleagues made convenient scapegoats for the shaky start to pensions administration. Indeed, they were under fire from all sides: the government blamed the female board members for ineffective oversight and unwarranted generosity that overextended the government's financial resources.[50] The advisory boards were also the target of criticism from mothers' advocates, who accused them of "spying" and "catechizing."[51] Labor MLA Thomas Uphill, who would become a passionate spokesman for pensioned mothers throughout the 1920s, told the House of Commons of his many constituents who "declared that they would rather scrub for a crust of bread than go through the ordeal of being investigated by the committee."[52] Citing all of these complaints, the government abolished the local advisory boards as part of the March 1921 amendments.

The revised 1921 act contained one final amendment, one that was important for its symbolic significance if not its procedural reforms. Responsibility for oversight and administration of pensions was transferred away from the superintendent of neglected children to E.S. Winn, the pensions commissioner who had since returned to his position as chairman of the WCB. Winn's "reputation for fairness" was expected to provide a renewed "vision" for mothers' pensions that included a rational and streamlined administration.[53] Winn was put in charge of a new mothers' pensions board, which oversaw an operation that did not actually differ much from pre-1921 practices, despite the amendments. The board still relied on recommendations from "visiting committees," especially in far-flung areas of the province. Many women from the former advisory boards were retained in this capacity, although Winn also relied on local police, clergy, and even businessmen to report on mothers' eligibility and character.[54]

The pension's new home alongside the WCB, however, represented an alignment with the social welfare principles of workmen's compensation, at least in theory. Provincial officials took the opportunity to remind everyone that, in their view, mothers' pensions were essentially workmen's compensation by another name and with another clientele – mothers were simply "indigent" for reasons other than industrial accidents. Winn described a mothers' pension recipient as a "non-industrial widow" who "should not be treated by the Government less generously than the industrial widow was treated by the employers of the Province." Like WCB payments, mothers' pensions "were intended as a substitute in part for the pay-cheque" of a husband.[55] Granting pensions to mothers was a matter of "equity and fairness," according to Provincial Secretary MacLean, one that went "beyond the pale of charity."[56]

"Satan finds some mischief still for idle hands to do"

Much of the discourse around pensions throughout the 1920s echoed Winn and MacLean's public sentiments. In press debates and in their letters and appeals to the government, concerned commentators insisted that the state should value mothers' work in the home and that a pension was a (certain) mother's right. Community members, for example, often intervened in the cases of mothers who they felt were unfairly denied a pension. A group of concerned citizens wrote MacLean in 1921 on behalf of Mrs. E, a widow whose "heroic efforts in rearing such a family" of four children "by her own labour, thrift, and sense of duty" surely entitled her to a government cheque.[57] The press held the same line. "Most important," a *Victoria Daily Colonist* editorial proclaimed, was "the establishment of a principle which will assure the beneficiaries that they are not the recipients of State charity, but that the enjoyment of a pension is a right."[58] Perhaps most revealingly, the extent of the rights-based understanding of pensions was evident in provincial officials' frustrations that "too many" mothers expected a pension. "Our greatest difficulty in administering this Act," Winn informed the premier in 1925, "is to get the affected parties to realize that it is not a general pension scheme, but only a matter for allowance in cases where the parties are . . . indigents."[59]

Public expectations did not match the reality of pension administration, however. As pension operations unfolded throughout the decade, it became clear that mothers' claims on the state were more complicated, and less secure, than many British Columbians expected they should be. At the level of actual decision making about mothers' cases, officials did not simply consider pensions to be their right, nor were pensions awarded based on the straightforward recognition of maternal service to the state. In fact, maternal labour did not figure nearly as strongly as paid labour in officials' assessments of mothers' eligibility. A mother's relationship to wage work was just as important, if not more important, in determining whether or not she deserved to be supported by the state. Underneath the public declarations of the rights-based nature of pensions, those tasked with managing mothers' cases were much more concerned about work ethic, "earning power," income levels, and employment status.[60]

For many mothers, work-based judgments could mean an outright denial of pension eligibility. Winn and his colleagues were more than willing to turn down a pension application if they deemed a mother capable of supporting herself. Mothers with one child were especially vulnerable to suspicion. Although technically within the scope of the act, mothers with one child who demonstrated a lack of wage earning were often a cause of concern for officials. Mrs. W, for example, a widowed mother of one living in Duncan, had her pension terminated suddenly in the spring of 1922 based on a technicality that many prominent local citizens considered ridiculous (her husband had died while the family was "sojourning" in Washington, rendering her ineligible). The technicalities of the act, however, did not interest Winn as much as Mrs. W's employment status. "The Board also takes the attitude," he explained to Premier Oliver, "that where the mother is in sufficiently good health to work and where her age is not against her, she should be able to earn sufficient to maintain herself and one child."[61] Senior officials staked out a similar position throughout the decade. George Pyke, the assistant superintendent of neglected children, insisted in 1923 that a mother "should be able to support herself and child without assistance from the Government."[62] Perceptions of a mother's work ethic figured heavily into these decisions. Mrs. T was a "young and healthy woman" who was "quite capable of earning sufficient to maintain herself and child if she wishes to," explained Pyke in one letter: "The unfortunate part seems to be lack of desire. Self help is to be encouraged to the fullest extent."[63]

Winn and Pyke's rationale, and their focus on one-child mothers, was partly about financial restraint. The government admitted that it had underestimated mothers' need and overestimated its ability to provide pensions to all who needed them and that limiting the numbers of mothers on support was one way to cut costs.[64] But the moral imperatives of paid work also factored strongly into their justifications. From the board's point of view, it was better to deny a pension and ensure wage earning than it was to grant a pension and foster a mother's chronic reliance on state assistance. Public pronouncements that pensions were not a "charity dole" belied very real concerns at the administrative level that they had the potential to destroy "self reliance" and "creat[e] a class that would tend to relax personal effort and lean on public benevolence."[65] And while statements such as these highlighted the importance of work in the assessment of mothers' entitlements, they also revealed the accepted level of wage discrimination for mothers – who were obviously expected to make enough to support only one child.

For the same work-based reasons, Winn and his colleagues considered it perfectly appropriate that pensions were designed to replace a husband's paycheque only "in part." In this respect, pensions represented a version of the "principle of less eligibility" – to keep benefits low so as to preserve a work ethic.[66] "Generally speaking," one annual report noted, "the mothers realize that this assistance is not intended to be sufficient for all their wants or requirements."[67] Indeed, the mothers' pension base rate of $42.50 was lower than the lowest female minimum wage rate in 1920. An adult woman working in the mercantile industry was considered entitled to at least $51.00 per month, a rate derived from the assumption that she had no dependents.[68] Based on the government's own standards, $42.50 for a mother and one child was remarkably low. To make ends meet, mothers' wage earning was required and expected. Officials heartily agreed, explaining that this was the best way to protect against the "grave danger to society" that chronic welfare dependency represented.

"Self help," "initiative," "resourcefulness," and "enterprise" – those were the watchwords of administrative oversight throughout the decade and the standards against which deserving mothers were measured. "We do believe in that old quotation," Winn explained, "that 'Satan finds some mischief still for idle hands to do.'"[69] Moreover, these fears of pauperization extended to the entire family since a lack of work ethic could infect other family members.

The board was often reluctant to grant a pension unless every possible option for family self-support had been explored. Such options included the earnings of older children and other relatives. It would establish a "bad precedent," Pyke explained in 1921, to grant a pension to a Fernie mother whose son was out of work: "I do not think it was ever intended that the Mothers' Pensions should be used as an unemployment fund."[70] In another case, he denied a pension to a mother whose two oldest children "are employed and earning $110.00 per month each."[71] "If the same effort were made towards getting the family to contribute to her support as are made in trying to get the Government to do so, perhaps something might be accomplished," another highly placed official explained in rejecting another mother's application.[72] Charlotte Whitton would express sentiments very similar to this when she arrived to investigate mothers' pensions in 1930.

Charlotte Whitton Comes to British Columbia

Largely because of a growing population, the numbers of BC mothers on the pension rolls increased steadily through the 1920s.[73] Rising pension costs were an issue of some worry for Conservative Premier Simon Fraser Tolmie, who was elected in 1928 with the support of the province's business community. His concerns were magnified when the Great Depression hit British Columbia. Tolmie was initially slow to act on the unemployment crisis. "Conservative thought," Jean Barman observes, "still held that poverty and unemployment resulted from personal failings."[74] By 1931, however, British Columbia's 28 percent unemployment rate was the highest in the country, and, as politicians elsewhere were doing, Tolmie had to confront some very hard questions about social welfare spending priorities.

Work-for-relief camps for unemployed men were among Tolmie's first forays into the Depression-era provision of aid, but relief efforts of all kinds were inhibited by sharply declining government revenues. Desperate for ways to cut back on government spending, the premier commissioned a series of reports in the early 1930s to determine how it could be done. One of the most high-profile commissions was chaired by George Kidd, a former president of the BC Electric Company. The 1932 Kidd report called for drastic cuts to spending on a wide swatch of social services including education and transportation.[75] Spending on mothers' pensions was also one of Tolmie's targets. For advice on how to streamline and roll back pension operations, he called on Charlotte Whitton, who had been in British Columbia not long before investigating child welfare in the province.[76]

Whitton, the director of the Canadian Council on Child Welfare and the country's recognized expert on social work, was in high demand by governments in the early 1930s. Besides her professional credentials, she had also developed a reputation as a harsh critic of the "expanding boundaries" of government social programs.[77] Whitton's best-known advisory role in this period was to Prime Minister R.B. Bennett, who hired her in 1932 to report on unemployment relief in the western provinces.[78] Mothers' pensions and allowances were a particular area of expertise for Whitton. In addition to British Columbia, she conducted studies on mothers' allowances for Manitoba and Nova Scotia, and she advised on reforms in Ontario and Québec. Her reports followed the same themes in all of these jurisdictions. She called for the withdrawal of government from family life and for cautious intervention, managed by trained social workers, only for families who conformed to her standards of "fit and proper" behaviour.[79] Whitton's social welfare ideology aligned closely with Premier Tolmie's, and in June 1931 he welcomed her to British Columbia, anticipating a series of recommendations for radical cutbacks.

Over the spring and summer of June 1931, Whitton and her team of investigators travelled throughout the province interviewing pension recipients and field workers. She returned in December 1931 with a decidedly critical report. Whitton characterized British Columbia's mothers' pensions administration as one of "exploitation, abuse and heavy expenditure," the blame for which she placed largely on the overworked and undertrained field staff.[80] British Columbia's spending on mothers' pensions, Whitton argued, was disproportionate in comparison to other provinces as well as to other provincial expenditures. While the national average of per capita pension spending was 72 cents, British Columbia's rate was the highest at $1.21. Within the province, the pension budget was eating up 3.5 percent of the entire annual provincial budget, an excessive amount considering that it only served 1,550 families.[81] The problem was not that pension amounts were too high in British Columbia but, rather, that they were haphazardly awarded to too many undeserving mothers, often with the collusion of investigators who encouraged mothers to "evade" regulations.[82] In Whitton's view, the best way to cut costs was to strictly limit eligibility and thus cut down on the number of pension cheques issued.

Whitton's recommendations essentially amounted to a stricter policing of social citizenship's boundaries, with mothers' economic behaviour being the central reference point. In their present state, she insisted, pensions were actually doing more harm than good. Negligent administration, despite Winn and Pyke's efforts to constrain the number of pensions handed out, had multiplied the cases of "chronic dependency," and the situation threatened to get worse.[83] Like Winn before her, Whitton identified many cases in which pensions were, in her view, entirely unwarranted. Mothers with one child were once again particular targets, especially since they represented one-third of the total caseload at the end of the 1920s (up from one-quarter in 1921).[84] Many of those cases were similar to Mrs. AB's. A widow with a school-aged daughter, Mrs. AB decided to leave her rural home and rent an apartment in Vancouver so her daughter could attend a better school. In Whitton's view, though, Mrs. AB was simply living off the state while she indulged in her desire to live in the city and enroll her daughter in private lessons. This was not a case of "serious need," Whitton concluded, but one of a woman "not very fond of work."[85] Her analysis of the 1930–31 caseload led Whitton to conclude that, although one-third of applications were denied because they had "resources deemed sufficient to maintain them without public aid," many more should have fallen into the same category and that one-child cases should be the first to be cut.[86] Except in "very exceptional" cases of poor health or incapacitation of a family member, the state should insist upon "the maintenance of the child by its mother."[87] Furthermore, the inability to find work was not an excuse. As Whitton argued, it was much simpler for a mother with only one child to find work as a live-in domestic.[88]

Whitton also called for a closer surveillance of pension rates. By 1931, it was common practice for administrators to reduce a mother's pension amount because of income from other sources, namely wage work. Whitton approved of this policy, citing "wholesome and profitable" employment as the best way to ensure that mothers – all mothers, not just those with one child – developed "habits of industry and thrift and ambition for independence."[89] Children's earnings, support from relatives, or the absence of rent payments also factored into this sliding scale of pension rates.[90] Whitton's concern was the lackadaisical attitude towards enforcing this policy. In many cases, pensions were awarded above "the family's minimum requirements," thus encouraging dependence on the state. Such was the case with Mrs. P, a widow with seven children who otherwise was a model pension recipient: "The reports of this family showed good conditions throughout, as to health, school attendance and environment." Nevertheless, Whitton suggested that Mrs. P's pension should have been reduced as her children were old enough to work and as her father-in-law (in whose house they lived) became old enough to qualify for an old age pension.[91]

As Mrs. P's case makes clear, Whitton's fears about dependency had implications for the entire family. Without regulation, a mother's lack of ambition risked being passed down to create a second generation of "shifting, unattached social dependants."[92] If family independence could be achieved through participation in the paid labour or income of any family member, then it was the responsibility of investigators to insist on it.[93] In Mrs. AC's family, for example, Whitton advocated for cancelling her pension and "throwing" her, her husband, and their two older, earning children "on their own resources." The combined income of the four of them, Whitton argued, would give them the resources to remain independent of public assistance and, at the same time, provide "some assurance that the problem of the reproduction of similar stock ... would not continue."[94] All of the family members were implicated in Whitton's vision for state intervention in the family, which was based on "the development of initiative, independence, self respect, and self-reliance at the earliest possible date, and to such a degree and strength as to avoid future dependency."[95]

Whitton's pronouncements on mothers' moral fitness was indistinguishable from her expectations about their economic pursuits.[96] In her view, a good mother was one who taught her children to be good workers, and, to do so, it required that she be a good worker herself. A clean house and well-behaved children were signs not just of moral integrity but also of a vigorous work ethic and healthy attitude towards work and of a commitment to passing those traits on to her children. "Children reared in good, humble and poor homes," Whitton wrote, "thrive much better ... their general health is likely to be better; they have more individuality, adapt themselves better to ordinary life, are more resourceful, and more likely to develop lives of self-reliance and independence."[97] A tidy home, "wholesome" children, and well cared for vegetable garden, in Mrs. B's case, symbolized her "good management" skills and her ability to budget resources carefully.[98] Conversely, mothers whose homes were "slovenly" and who had been found to be consorting with numerous male friends in the evenings should ideally have the "expenditure of [their] monthly allowance" approved by social workers so that their limited financial resources were spent in a manner considered appropriate by the state.[99] In Whitton's view, morality and economic behaviour were intertwined in "the sense of responsibility which is the very amalgam of our social structure."[100]

The one issue on which Whitton had little to say was the child care arrangements of all of the mothers she expected to be in the work force. In focusing on family self-sufficiency, though, Whitton's attitude towards child care was implicit: it was a mother's responsibility to make arrangements in the private sphere, either through relatives or paid caretakers. One brief pronouncement on one-child mothers provides some insight into Whitton's thinking. She was more willing to be sympathetic to a mother with a young (preschool aged) child (or children) if the mother was "so situated in relation to the lack of any home or relatives that it is otherwise impossible for her to support her child."[101] Although Whitton was clear that this pronouncement did not extend to unmarried mothers, whose lack of moral fitness should automatically disqualify them, this was virtually her only admission that access to child care could determine a woman's ability to work and thus her claim to state support. In giving this discussion such a marginal place, however, Whitton signalled that working mothers' child care arrangements were not a matter for state concern.

Mothers' Pensions in the 1930s and Beyond

Premier Tolmie was largely receptive to Whitton's proposals. Depression conditions required fiscal restraint and, from a cultural perspective, demanded welfare policy that was designed to prevent dependency. Though Tolmie could not afford to hire the roster of professional social workers that Whitton recommended for this oversight, he did hire Miss Elizabeth King of the Canadian Council of Child and Family Welfare to serve as acting supervisor of mothers' pensions. King, in turn, hired five new welfare visitors to more closely monitor pensioned mothers throughout the province.[102] A series of reforms followed, including one that deemed one-child families officially ineligible for a mothers' pension unless "special circumstances" warranted one.[103]

Tolmie introduced his most controversial reform in 1932, when he amended the *Mothers' Pensions Act* to transfer half of the financial responsibility for pensions to municipalities. Not surprisingly, the BC Union of Municipalities reacted with outrage at this offloading of welfare responsibility, especially during a time when they were struggling under mounting relief pressures.[104] Opposition to this reform also came from mothers' advocates who objected to the equation of mothers' pensions with "city relief." Helen Gregory MacGill, Susie Lane Clark, Mary Ellen Smith, and their colleagues in the New Era League and the local councils of women held a protest in March 1932 to oppose Tolmie's reforms.[105] But government officials were unsympathetic, and Winn (echoing a common refrain of Whitton's report), in fact, urged the attorney-general to consider renaming the act the Mothers' Assistance Act "to get the term 'pension' out of the minds of our people."[106]

These early 1930s reforms were just the beginning of a tumultuous decade. The place of mothers' pensions in the 1933 election, for example, was a far cry from 1920, when both the Liberals and the Conservatives had been eager to take credit for the legislation. In 1933, Tolmie and Liberal leader Duff Pattullo traded accusations about the "racket" that was the pensions program.[107] The reasons for the newly maligned political position of pensions stemmed from their marginalization, as MacGill and her colleagues had feared, to a level just barely above general relief.[108] Not only were monthly base rates reduced to $35, but pensions had also been stripped of their "special status" as a welfare program with some higher, nobler goal of compensating motherhood.[109] By the early to mid-1930s, the pension program essentially functioned as unemployment relief for mothers.

The pension's function as "mothers' relief," to use the words of Harry Cassidy, the provincial director of welfare, was apparent in the ways that fluctuating expenditures paralleled female unemployment trends.[110] Pension spending dropped immediately following the Whitton reforms but started a steady rise in the middle to late 1930s as unemployment worsened. Officials readily attributed this increased generosity to the shortage of jobs for mothers and their older children.[111] Cutting pensions, after all, only "forc[ed] women on a labor market that was unable to absorb them."[112] Even mothers with one child were considered in a more sympathetic light due to the desperate unemployment they faced.[113] Conversely, at the first sign of economic recovery in the latter years of the decade, provincial administrators encouraged closer scrutiny of mothers who should be expected to serve as the family breadwinner.[114] On the advice of Cassidy, the newly created Mothers' Pensions Advisory Board undertook a study in 1937 to determine which mothers were "likely prospects for employment," and it recommended that welfare field workers encourage mothers to pursue domestic work (for which there was a high demand in Vancouver at the end of the decade), to enrol in dressmaking or secretarial evening training courses, or to consider taking advantage of the Dominion provincial youth training programs to prepare them for employment.[115] One board member even suggested that Vancouver should re-establish a crèche to facilitate such efforts. The board also urged Cassidy to find work opportunities for older children, especially boys, through co-operation with officials in other departments such as agriculture, mines, and forestry, so that they could contribute to their families' upkeep.[116]

In many respects, Whitton's report and the reforms initiated in its aftermath represented a markedly different path for pensions than they had been set on in the early 1920s. No longer were public officials making proclamations about maternal entitlement. Mothers' pensions were clearly "charity based" in the 1930s, as Nancy Christie contends.[117] Yet in another respect, there was a significant degree of continuity between the two decades. From the beginning, a mother's access to state benefits had been measured by her relationship to wage work and her susceptibility to welfare dependency. In the late 1930s, as in the early 1920s, officials worried that the pension program would undermine a mother's drive to become independent and "self-supporting."[118] The Great Depression meant that mothers' pensions were given a new rhetorical context that focused on relief and charity rather than on maternalism and entitlement, but the administrative principles established from the beginning remained remarkably similar. Mothers' paid work remained a consistent determinant of inclusion and exclusion with the boundaries of social support.

Mothers, Workers, and Citizens in British Columbia's Interwar Years

Given that Whitton was so determined that more mothers should be working, she also included in her report an analysis of the provincial labour force to prove that her stance was not unreasonable. She argued that "opportunities for the employment of women in British Columbia in the age groups, in which many of these mothers falls, compare very favourably with those of other provinces [sic]." She pointed in particular to the continued high employment rates, despite the Depression, in female-dominated industries: "laundries, cleaning, and dying industries," along with garment making, stenography, waitressing, food service, and, especially, char work and domestic service.[119]

Whitton's analysis was mostly accurate. It was true that many women's jobs were sheltered from the effects of the Depression. Eric Sager's investigations of British Columbia between 1929 and 1934 show that there was actually an increase in the proportion of women workers in the industrial labour force because "proportionately fewer women were being laid off" from their positions in the gender-segregated industries of "inelastic demand": food products, garment making, laundries, and street railways/utilities. These industries accounted for more than 80 percent of female wage earners in British Columbia. Sager also notes that this was part of a larger story of women's increasing labour force participation in the interwar years and beyond. In British Columbia, the growth rates of women's employment in industry outpaced female population growth between 1921 and the Second World War. These "official" labour force statistics, though, reflect only those jobs deemed worthy of recording by the provincial Department of Labour. Many more women were employed in domestic work and other non-industrial positions, which remained a relatively stable source of work for women through the interwar years.[120]

However, even if pensioned mothers managed to find and keep a job during the Depression, work did not necessarily provide them with the stability and independence that Whitton and other provincial officials expected it would. Women's jobs were unstable and low paid. Adult women's average wages in the Depression years ranged between 55 and 66 percent of men's. These gender inequalities were magnified by a woman's marital status and motherhood. Of the women working in industrial occupations in the 1930s, 75 to 80 percent of them were young, single, and presumably childless.[121] For women who had children, their labour force opportunities were constrained by their domestic and caregiving responsibilities. For many mothers, then, domestic work (among the lowest paid jobs for women) was the only option. Relying on these low wages, balancing work and home life was a constant struggle. Widowed mother Mrs. C was just one among many who worked in domestic service but who "[could not] earn enough to pay for the children being kept while at work."[122]

These tangible gendered inequalities in the labour force were accompanied in the Depression era by ideological panic about women's work. Jobs were scarce, commentators argued, and women were not entitled to a paycheque when so many male breadwinners were out of work. Their concerns, as Sager's historical analysis of the 1930s labour force has shown, were not based in reality. As a result of the gender-segregated labour force, it was unlikely that employers were replacing men with women.[123] Some officials at the time urged the public not to demonize women workers – especially married women, who critics insisted should be supported by a husband – and instead to consider the facts. "We hear a great deal about the married women workers," wrote Fraudena Eaton, of British Columbia's Board of Industrial Relations. But "over a period of years" that spanned the worst of the Depression, she pointed out, married women's labour force participation held steady at 20 percent of all female workers. Moreover, Eaton added, "in most cases necessity, and not choice, is the compelling factor of the married women's employment, and criticism of her holding a place in the business world is usually levelled at her by persons with a somewhat superficial knowledge of the circumstances surrounding her employment."[124] Despite these calls for reason, the perceived threat to masculinity and the male breadwinner norm was a powerful discursive force during the Depression.

So powerful, in fact, that it contributed to a reorientation of social welfare policy in the 1930s. The provision of social services on the whole was altered by the Depression. "Traditional perspectives on the causes of poverty," Alvin Finkel writes, were "radically shaken" by the sheer scope of the unemployment crisis.[125] Concern about how to support the unemployed laid bare the prevailing beliefs about family and work. Women, especially married women and mothers, had no inherent right to work; while men, as family breadwinners, did. When this right was undermined because of fluctuating economic conditions beyond a man's control, the state had a responsibility to step in. "This persistent concern with upholding the status of male breadwinners," Nancy Christie argues, led to a privileging of "paid labour as the sole foundation of welfare rights" and, more specifically, the privileging of male paid labour.[126] Although Finkel points out that the 1930s saw little in the way of concrete social policy reforms compared to the following decades, the Depression era's focus on male breadwinners laid the foundation for the changes to come. The one significant policy undertaking of the decade, federal unemployment insurance (UI), provided a "glimmer" of later approaches to the social welfare provision.[127] UI, which was proposed in 1935, deemed unconstitutional in 1937, and eventually agreed to as a constitutional amendment once the war started in 1940, embodied this gendered welfare paradigm. Male breadwinner independence and female mother/homemaker dependence, as Ruth Roach Pierson shows, were inscribed into the UI legislation, beginning with the simple fact that women workers were not eligible for coverage.[128]

As workers, then, BC mothers' welfare entitlements were virtually non-existent. As mothers, their access to benefits was being further undermined in the 1930s by more reforms to mothers' pensions. Effective on 1 January 1938, the *Mothers' Pensions Act* was repealed and replaced with the *Mothers' Allowances Act*, a move that Whitton had advocated in her 1931 report.[129] As Whitton explained, "pensions" were payments "in recognition of services already rendered," while allowances were payments to those who would otherwise be indigent. With this amendment, the "maternal rights" basis of mothers' aid was even further worn away, and allowances entered the realm of needs-based charity.[130] Women were not entitled to social rights as mothers nor as workers.

Working mothers and their advocates pushed back against the shrinking boundaries of social citizenship throughout the 1920s and 1930s, yet this opposition was not widespread or even particularly public. For the most part, married women's rights as workers were mostly left out of interwar BC labour politics, especially during the Depression, when even British Columbia's "militant mothers" focused their efforts on the plight of unemployed men.[131] Some Vancouver women on the left, including Co-operative Commonwealth Federation (CCF) MLA Dorothy Steeves, bucked the provincial trend somewhat by speaking to the concerns of working women, but they too were preoccupied with the immediate concerns around providing relief and did not engage in much political action around working mothers' rights.[132] If resistance was not visible in the political realm, though, it was discernable in mothers' individual interactions with state officials as well as in the rhetoric of sympathetic politicians and welfare visitors. Negotiations over mothers' pensions was one important site of this resistance. Mothers insisted that they had a right to public support, a right derived from a range of sources: their loyal party voting records, their status as "native daughters" of British Columbia and Canada, and their work in rearing the future citizens of the nation.[133]

Women also understood their social rights to be rooted in their interlocking identities as mothers, workers, and citizens. Pensioned mothers, as well as those who felt they had been unfairly denied a pension, highlighted the role that their work – both paid and unpaid – played in their dignity and value as mothering citizens. It was precisely because she was both worker and mother that a woman was entitled to the services and protection of the state. Mrs. A, for example, appealed to Premier Oliver in 1926 to reinstate her cancelled pension: "I was foolish enough to actually believe that this Mother's Pension business was intended to help working mothers to keep a home up for their children." Surely, she continued, the premier could see that she was entitled to a pension after all her "years of hard and patient labor."[134] Like Mrs. A, other mothers claimed a right to a pension not to give up their paid work but, rather, in order to maintain some dignity and security in the balance between work and motherhood.[135]

In the face of entrenched ideas about their second-class status in the workforce, though, mothers like Mrs. A had a hard time making their case for support as workers, mothers, and citizens. The province and municipalities felt no responsibility in the interwar years to assist mothers in their dual roles as caregivers and wage earners, and so private organizations, if they had any resources to spare, tried to pick up some of the slack. Yet they too took the view that a working mother was a sign that something had failed in the family, and they provided support that was laden with moral judgments and pity. Vancouver mothers' only organizational option for child care in the 1930s, the Vancouver Day Nursery Association (VDNA), was infused with such beliefs. The VDNA was created privately in 1932 in the aftermath of the city's decision to close the Vancouver City Crèche. The city cited financial restraint as the reason for the crèche's closure, although its status as a welfare institution (though not its attendance levels) had been dwindling throughout the 1920s.

The private interests behind the VDNA recognized the need for some kind of continued child care service for working mothers but opposed the "congregate care" that the crèche had provided. Care in "real homes" was considered much more desirable, and so the VDNA established an in-home service that they referred to as foster day care, wherein the children of working mothers were placed in the individual homes of caregiving mothers.[136] The VDNA's mission extended far beyond providing mothers with "a convenient place to leave their children," however. Working with the caregivers, the VDNA was intent on saving the children of the "underprivileged class" and on supplying their mothers with "sound instruction in child training, correct habits and diets."[137] VDNA volunteers considered themselves voluntary social workers whose services were inspired by charitable benevolence rather than by any sort of belief that working mothers were entitled to child care.

In the absence of public support throughout most of the interwar years, working mothers were left to cobble together child care arrangements of their own. Their strategies of "maternal invention," as Sonya Michel calls it, do not often appear in historical records, at least not to any great extent.[138] Mothers left their children in the care of older siblings, grandparents, other relatives, neighbours, or, in cases of last resort, alone to fend for themselves – arrangements in the private sphere, in other words, where governments were confident that they belonged. When these kinds of private provisions could not be made, mothers may have had to rely on charitable provisions such as orphanages or the foster homes of the VDNA. Since it was often the poorest and most marginalized families who used such services, institutional child care was marked with the stigma of poverty, charity, and desperation. Child care services for working mothers were considered vastly inferior to the part-day nursery schools and child study centres that were increasing in popularity in the 1920s. Nursery schools were geared towards middle-class families who wanted to provide their children with educational and social benefits, goals that were not equated with the working-class mother's need for child care.[139] Working mothers' need for child care was considered a matter for charities and welfare officials, who were equipped to deal with such "problem" families.

In 1920, British Columbians were optimistic that a "solution" to working motherhood was to be found in the form of mothers' pensions. A new notion of maternally based entitlement offered the possibility that mothers could be compensated for the important work they did for their homes and for the nation and that the need for wage earning and outside-the-home child care would recede. The experiences of pensioned mothers throughout the 1920s and 1930s, however, revealed just how big the gap was between expectations and reality. Pensions did not eliminate the need for a mother's paid work. Instead, a mother's wage earning was still necessary to supplement the inadequate monthly cheque. It was also a condition of receipt of the pension within a welfare system geared towards preserving the work ethic, preventing chronic dependency, and maintaining the self-sufficiency of poor and working-class families.

However, amidst powerful Depression-era public discourses that maligned women in the workforce, mothers remained second-class workers. Their lesser status in the labour force took on many dimensions, including low wages, tenuous positions, and unsafe conditions. Inattention to working mothers' child care needs was another aspect of this formula. The 1930s marked a beginning of the expanded claims of worker-citizens within the Canadian welfare state, but the boundaries of those social rights were almost entirely shaped by the entitlements ascribed to male breadwinners, the rightful earners of a family wage. There was no consideration from provincial or municipal governments in the interwar years that publicly funded child care could be offered as a way to secure equal opportunities and fair treatment for mothers in the labour force.

All of these assumptions – the stigma of child care, the inferior status of women workers, the importance of male breadwinners' social rights – were carved deeply into the framework of social citizenship by the end of the 1930s. But all of these assumptions would be unsettled by the changing social, economic, and cultural conditions of waging war on the homefront and by the high-profile public debates about child care for wartime working mothers.

3

"It takes real mothers and real homes to make real children": Child Care Debates during and after the Second World War

Prior to the Second World War, it was relatively easy for governments and the general public to push the child care needs of working-class and poor mothers to the margins of welfare policy, where "failed" families were dealt with. That all changed with the mobilization of female workers into the wartime labour force. In a very short period of time, an unprecedented number of women, including mothers and members of the middle class, became members of the paid workforce and a crucial piece of the country's war effort. Who, concerned Canadians asked, was going to look after these women's children?

For the first time in the country's history, the federal government decided to assume some responsibility for working mothers' child care arrangements, albeit only in cases of women working in "essential" war industries. This support took the form of the *Dominion-Provincial Wartime Day Nurseries Agreement (WDNA)*, an initiative that was cost shared with the provincial governments.[1] Not all provinces were eager to sign on. Ontario and Québec, the sites of the largest clusters of wartime factories, were ultimately the only two governments that established day nurseries under the *WDNA*. Over the course of the war, twenty-eight centres were opened in Ontario and six in Québec. British Columbia, claiming not enough of a concentration of war industries to justify public investment in child care, declined to adopt the *WDNA*. Senior welfare officials in British Columbia insisted that private interests could meet any increased demand for wartime child care.

Evidence from around the province suggested otherwise. The official – and simplistic – rationale behind British Columbia's decision belied the existence of heated debates about wartime child care needs as well as ardent on-the-ground campaigns for government-supported day nurseries. These debates contained the customary uneasiness with working motherhood, though this uneasiness was magnified by the scope and nature of mothers' employment. While British Columbians may have accepted the employment of poor and working-class mothers because their families' survival and work ethic depended on it, the mobilization of the so-called "reserve army" of middle-class mothers threatened, commentators warned, to increase juvenile delinquency, undermine family life, and compromise a moral citizenry. Alternatively, the wartime years also offered a public platform for a discourse about mothers' social citizenship that had been trivialized to this point. Politicians on the left, women's groups, social agencies, and community-based child care providers cautiously advanced the argument that the experience of war marked a new and even permanent relationship between women and paid work that warranted government involvement in child care as a matter of women's social rights.

While Québec and especially Ontario saw significant transformation in their day care services thanks to the *WDNA*, in British Columbia the provision of child care for working mothers changed more incrementally during the wartime years. In Vancouver, at least three day nurseries were established with very limited public financial support. Despite the efforts of women's rights advocates to reframe these kinds of child care centres as an essential public service for women, though, these new services were run according to familiar logic: the need to assist pitiable mothers so that they could remain free of public assistance, to keep families together, and to counteract the immorality represented by working-class neighbourhoods. However, in another sense, these day nurseries were pioneering, and in the final stages of the war their operation was injected with a new type of discourse emerging in child psychology and early education circles around the training of young children.

This popular (and politically safe) rationale translated into the establishment of playschools and kindergartens around the province in the immediate post-war years, which no doubt made life easier for some working families. But these play- and education-based centres were considered entirely distinct, in policy terms, from the programs designed to serve working mothers. In the post-war ubiquity of nuclear family ideology, any mother who worked outside the home was once again assumed to be acting out of economic desperation, and child care services such as the Vancouver Day Nursery Association (VDNA) continued to treat working mothers like charity cases. The wartime years, then, revealed that the ground had shifted somewhat – but pre-war ideologies about women, work, and welfare still largely determined the contours of child care provision and of working mothers' social citizenship well into the second half of the twentieth century.

Working Mothers and the WDNA

Canada entered the Second World War on 10 September 1939. Waging an effective war overseas meant ensuring that the Canadian labour force was operating at full capacity on the homefront, and, as such, the federal government closely regulated and controlled domestic employment through the National Selective Service, headed by Arthur MacNamara. Central to MacNamara's plans was employing unemployed men, a task that was not difficult given the unemployment crisis of the Great Depression. However, as men enlisted for service overseas, the male reserve of labour soon dried up. MacNamara looked to the next obvious pool of workers: women. He gave Fraudena Eaton, a former member of the BC Labour Relations Board, the responsibility of heading up the National Selective Service Women's Division (NSSWD), which began in 1942 to measure the national supply of female workers. Eaton's first targets were single and childless women between the ages of twenty and twenty-four. With relatively few family obligations, these young women were more easily able to devote themselves to training and retraining for industrial jobs and to take up factory work in places where shortages were most acutely felt, which often meant moving across the country to industrial centres in Ontario and Québec. Eaton soon realized, however, that the pool of young single women was not deep enough. The war effort required the mobilization of married women and even mothers. They could help fill factory shortages, but, just as importantly, they could take up work in domestic and service positions, thereby freeing younger women for full-time factory work.[2]

The NSSWD recruitment of married women and mothers raised the question of child care. If the government was explicitly mobilizing mothers for wartime work, was it the government's responsibility to provide care for their children? And what about child care for the vast numbers of married women who had already entered the revitalized wartime labour force, most of them driven by economic need? Did there exist some collective responsibility, in the wartime context, to set up child care services for those mothers? In British Columbia, the Department of Labour had begun to report in 1941 that women were taking the place of men in the reinvigorated lumber, shipbuilding, and manufacturing industries, performing such "unfamiliar" occupations as:

> welding, machine-tending in sash and door plants and other wood-working establishments, assembly and checking in electrical, gun, and aeroplane factories, or sanding and glueing in furniture plants. Others are doing lathe-work, spot welding, operating stamp-presses, working on winding and small cable machines in establishments making metal tanks, drums, or wire ropes.[3]

Women were employed in lumber factories and saw factories; they operated "machines of all sizes" and performed "mechanical operations of all kinds," which, according to the labour department, "no longer hold mysteries for these nimble-fingered workers." By 1942, reports noted, "practically every line of industrial work sees women and girls engaged in occupations that a few years ago were considered to be men's work."[4] Although the idea of women working in industry was not an entirely new phenomenon in British

Figure 3 Mrs. Anne Walsey was one of many British Columbian women who took up paid work during the war. Here, she operates the precision grinder at the Burrard Shipyard in Vancouver in 1943.

Credit: Courtesy of City of Vancouver Archives, Williams Bros. Photographers Collection, AM1545-S3-:CVA 586–1136, Photographer Don Coltman, Steffens Colmer.

Columbia – their proportions had been increasing since the mid-1920s – the scale and proportions of married women and mothers in the wartime context were remarkable.[5] By 1944, married women made up 34 percent of all female workers, up from 22 percent in 1939.[6] The well-being of their children – not only in British Columbia but also around the country – was a matter of serious concern to all levels of government. As Eaton noted, the demand for child care in heavily industrialized centres had become "a burden too heavy for private agencies" to carry alone.[7]

Facing a prospective campaign for the recruitment of even more mothers in war work, government planners began to float the idea that providing them with day care services was the responsibility of the state. Throughout the spring of 1942, federal and provincial officials held consultations to explore the possibility of government-supported child care centres. The recognized national experts in child welfare were brought into the discussion, including George Davidson, the executive director of the Canadian Welfare Council, and Dr. William Blatz, the director of the Institute of Child Study at the University of Toronto.[8] By the end of May, the consultations resulted in a major announcement – the creation of the *WDNA*, a shared-cost program available to any province that wished to establish public day care services for the children of mothers working in "essential" war industries.[9] Full-day child care offered through the *WDNA* nurseries would be available to any child from two to six years of age, along with out-of-school care for children aged six to sixteen. Funds from the *WDNA* could also be used to provide home-based care for infants. Parents were responsible for a fee of 35 cents per day per child for nursery care and slightly less for after-school care.[10] The day nurseries' capital and operating expenses were to be shared equally between the federal and provincial governments, and, similar to private services, the *WDNA* nurseries would continue to rely on the voluntary assistance from women's groups for their day-to-day operation.

Ontario and Québec, as the provinces containing the most wartime industrial activity, were the first to adopt the agreement (Ontario on 29 July 1942 and Québec on 3 August 1942).[11] Alberta originally signed the agreement but later backed out, claiming, in a controversial decision, that demand for wartime day nurseries was scarce.[12] Over the course of the war, Québec operated six *WDNA* nurseries, all of them located in Montreal. Ontario established twenty-eight, many of them located in close proximity to factories that employed mothers. Others operated in community halls and church basements. Blatz and the Institute of Child Study played a "lead role" in establishing the programs of the day nurseries, incorporating the latest standards and techniques in the field of child development and "mental hygiene." The institute also provided the training for women who volunteered in the nursery, and graduates of Blatz's program comprised much of the paid staff that worked in the centres.[13]

The governments of other provinces, British Columbia included, argued that they were not "sufficiently industrialised [sic]" to merit public investment in child care.[14] In British Columbia, decisions about the *WDNA* fell largely to Isobel Harvey, the superintendent of neglected children. Harvey and Fraudena Eaton were familiar with each other from Eaton's days at the BC Department of Labour, and when word of government day nurseries reached the west coast in the spring of 1942, Harvey immediately got in touch with her former colleague in Ottawa. Recognizing that the *WDNA* was no more than a "rumour" at that point, Harvey was nonetheless anxious about the details should such a policy materialize. Would the centres be self-supporting, she asked Eaton, or would they rely entirely on government funding? Would day nursery care be available only to mothers working in defence industries or to all working mothers?[15]

Eaton's response was vague. Although she provided Harvey with a draft of the federal government's agreement with Ontario, she gave no indication of support for a BC wartime day nursery plan. In fact, Eaton had likely already made up her mind about the unsuitability of the *WDNA* for British Columbia, and soon after this initial contact with Harvey she began to

Figure 4 Mrs. Fraudena Eaton, director of the National Selective Service Women's Division during the Second World War. Eaton is pictured here in 1933, when she was president of the Vancouver Council of Women.
Credit: Courtesy of City of Vancouver Archives, Major Matthews Collection, AM54-S4-:Port P1332, Photographer not listed.

actively discourage it.[16] Harvey, for her part, largely agreed with Eaton's assessment that private organizations and arrangements were sufficient to meet any increased demand for wartime child care. More specifically, the home-based foster day care services of the VDNA (the daytime care of children in the private homes of caregiving mothers) could, and should, be replicated in communities around the province. "Mrs. Eaton knows very well," Harvey explained, "our capabilities regarding foster-home care, and has told us we are not to branch into day nurseries until we have exhausted our foster-home possibility."[17]

Throughout the spring and summer of 1942, Harvey and other provincial welfare officials held this line. In response to a query about day nurseries from the Canadian Welfare Council (CWC) in March, both Harvey and Laura Holland, a senior welfare advisor and supervisor of the Welfare Field Service, reiterated that home-based foster day care programs were the province's preferred option to meet the demand. "We have worked so hard in some of the provinces to do away with institutionalizing of children," Harvey explained, "and I would hate to see them take a backward step. [It] seems to me that foster home care would be better for the children, both from a social and physical standpoint, and much less costly."[18] Holland took the further step of consulting with local social agencies in Vancouver and reported the same general consensus from several welfare organizations. "The representatives of the social agencies present did not consider as yet in British Columbia there had been a real increase in the demand from clients for placement of children due to employment in war industries," she told the CWC. "In other words our regular resources have so far been adequate to meet this demand on an individual basis."[19] Victoria's social welfare groups provided the CWC with a similar report, as did the Vancouver Council of Social Agencies.[20]

For Harvey, Holland, and Eaton, the issue was straightforward: were married women, those with family responsibilities, needed to keep wartime factories running in British Columbia? It seemed clear that they were not. Holland consulted with local businesses in Vancouver and reported to the CWC that there was more than enough of a reserve of young, single women in the province. Boeing Limited, for example, which began employing women in 1941, had 3,000 applications on file but employed only about 100 women. No direct wartime need for married women's labour, then, meant no real justification for spending public money on setting up day nurseries. Government responsibility to "safeguard" children "from the social hazards created by the breaking up of the child's home" came into play only in very specific circumstances, namely when "war conditions necessitate the letting down of those child welfare principles which public departments have built up, i.e. keeping the family together."[21] Officials advised keeping a "very close check" on the problem, but they maintained that the *WDNA* was not necessary for British Columbia.[22]

British Columbia's Wartime Child Care Needs: Perception and Reality

Senior provincial officials conceived of the wartime child care question very narrowly, as one that was in direct correlation with industrial labour needs. The issue was not quite that simple, however. Mothers' employment in the early 1940s was not just a matter of wartime industry – it was widespread and multi-faceted. So too were their child care needs, as reports from around the province indicated. The official rationale that Harvey, Eaton, and Holland provided to Ottawa and to the public, in other words, obscured a more complex story about working mothers during the wartime years and the dimensions of their need for child care.

British Columbia may not have been a heavily industrialized province, but the war nonetheless created myriad employment opportunities for mothers. In the initial years of the war, mothers easily found domestic work in the homes of middle-class and upper-class families, which provided them with a much-desired income after long years of struggle through the Depression.[23] As young women began moving into higher-paid factory work, mothers' job opportunities expanded into their vacated positions. By 1942, the VDNA was reporting that their client mothers were working at jobs as varied as "canning, factory work, making . . . war uniforms, cleaning of railway coaches" as well as "waitress work, clerking, hotel, laundry and cleaning plants, elevator operators, repairing steel drums."[24] Likewise, Marjorie Bradford of the Vancouver Council of Social Agencies reported that "a good many mothers known to the Day Nursery have recently taken day work in cafes, laundries, apartment houses, etc., to replace other women who had gone to work in war industries."[25]

As mothers' employment grew, so too did their child care troubles. By the fall of 1942, local officials in Vancouver were starting to report worrying pressures on the VDNA. The demand on their services had seen a "tremendous increase" since the war started, although the numbers had to that point been manageable (some neighbourhoods even reported vacant foster day homes in 1941).[26] However, in 1942 and 1943, there were indications that the VDNA was unable to keep pace with requests. Even Harvey admitted that the foster home system in Vancouver threatened to become overtaxed, a situation made worse by wartime housing shortages.[27] But since private foster day care was "much the cheapest and best procedure," Harvey and Holland's solution was to recruit more caregiving volunteers using campaigns that emphasized "that such care of children is a war service."[28]

Holland also admitted in December 1942 that provincial officials, despite their rejection of the *WDNA*, were prepared to get a clearer sense of the "extent of the need" for child care.[29] Reports from around the province had been arriving in Victoria, which no doubt led to Holland and Harvey's somewhat reluctant admission that child care shortages were more serious than they had initially thought. Particularly troubling were the reports from welfare field visitors stationed in resource towns around the province.[30] In Trail, for example, Madge York urged Harvey to pay heed to a developing child care crisis. "Ever since the Smelter starting employing women" in the fall of 1942, York informed Harvey, "I've seen the need developing." The regional welfare supervisor, as well as the smelter company president Mr. Blaylock, suggested along with York that government action on child care provision was needed.[31] So too did community members in Trail, one of whom told Harvey that "what women are going to do with there [sic] children is becoming [a] problem," and one offered to set up "a home" to care for the children of mothers working at the smelter.[32] The town of Kimberley faced similar issues. There, the field worker Berna Holt, along with the school board, the Parent-Teacher Association (PTA), and women involved in various voluntary agencies in the community, urged Harvey to consider assistance for mothers who worked at the town's concentrator. The PTA said, in fact, that they had found the province's rejection of the *WDNA* "rather staggering," given the demonstrated need in their town and others. The lack of child care resources in Kimberley, according to these agencies, was leading to the "inadequate supervision" – some claimed "neglect" – of children of all ages, but especially of school-aged children who were left alone outside of school hours and fell into delinquent behaviour and truancy.[33]

Harvey's response to both towns was virtually the same. To Madge York in Trail, she advised that "foster-home care such as is given by the Vancouver Day Nursery should suffice . . . [T]here should be no difficulty whatever in providing proper care for the children of Trail, if the smelter needs mothers for working."[34] To Berna Holt in Kimberley, she also urged stepping up efforts to secure private child care services. Holt was actually able to establish a foster home system similar to Vancouver's, which pleased Victoria officials because it "entailed no expense" for the provincial government. Though they would have preferred a day nursery, Kimberley's concerned citizens were somewhat appeased by the foster day care system since it ensured at the very least that "no woman would have the excuse that she did not know where to have her child cared for."[35] In these cases and others, Harvey was adamant that direct government intervention was an option of last resort.[36] Her correspondence with the welfare field visitors also revealed that she considered the matter of day nurseries to be somewhat trivial, especially for the newly hired male regional supervisor. "Tell Mr. Smith," she joked to York, "that I just love the idea of his starting day nurseries – I never would have thought he would start out this way."[37]

Port Alberni was another resource town particularly affected by the wartime employment of mothers. In the fall of 1942, the Alberta Pacific Lumber Company hired 200 women, 30 percent of whom were married with children. Field officer Zella Collins warned Harvey about the town's lack of child care resources and the issues with the neglected, delinquent, and truant children of working mothers. Since she was always reluctant to pledge government support, but recognizing that Port Alberni's problems were perhaps more serious than elsewhere, Harvey asked Collins to investigate more closely the social and economic conditions of the town's working families. Along with the public health nurse, the school principal, and an official from the Department of Labour, Collins visited as many homes as possible to record the ages and numbers of children, the parents' occupations, the children's attendance records, and reports from the community about the conditions of the mother and family. Her reports spoke to much more than the need for child care. Collins passed judgment on mothers' behaviour and on the condition of their households, linking mothers' perceived moral failings to their employment outside the home. Mrs. E, for example, who took up work at the lumber company after her husband deserted her, was criticized for being "very friendly with a man . . . who spends a good deal of time at the home." In the meantime, her children were left to "shift for themselves," while Mrs. E was at work.[38]

The solution to Port Alberni's problems, Collins suggested, was not the establishment of government day nurseries or even foster home care – it was convincing mothers to give up their jobs. "I think with a little reasoning," Collins suggested, the lumber mill "would not employ any more married women if it could secure single girls." This decision meant that the mill would have to provide housing, recreation, and other services suitable for young female employees, which Collins was eager to help acquire. There were indications that the lumber company was receptive to the idea. "The day we called," Collins noted approvingly, "Mr. Wright refused to employ a woman with four small children . . . on the basis that she could not work and give them proper care." Not only would the woman's mothering responsibilities impede her effectiveness as a worker, since "she would be likely to miss a good deal through illness of small children, such as colds and sore throats," but, as a worker, she would also be less of a mother.[39] Collins was not alone in suggesting such an approach. The executive director of the Vancouver Council of Social Agencies, for example, recommended that the city's child care challenges could be met by setting up a counselling service that would advise women "as to whether or not they should enter war industries" or to establish an employment agency that discouraged businesses from hiring mothers.[40]

Around the province, it was clear that circumstances on the ground suggested a pressing need for some kind of child care provision. Within bureaucratic channels, though, officials were unwilling to admit that the need was legitimate. Harvey and her colleagues saw no convincing evidence that there was "such a labour shortage in BC to warrant the employment of women with young children" and, thus, no obligation on the part of the government to provide child care.[41] Instead, the solution to the problems created by working motherhood were, in effect, to put an end to working motherhood.

Debating Mothers' Employment

Working mothers had long raised "anger and fear of some sections of the community."[42] During the war, however, the debates that perpetually encircled working motherhood reached a new order of magnitude, not only among welfare bureaucrats but also in wider public discourses. The wartime context meant that the debates were tied up in patriotic fervour as well as in questions about whether a woman best contributed to the country's war effort by remaining in the home or by taking up paid work. Just as importantly, wartime debates about working motherhood implicated all mothers and families. Participation in the labour force was no longer just an unfortunate, but inescapable, reality for poor mothers whose child care needs were very low on the list of social welfare priorities. During the war, employed mothers came from the ranks of the respectable working and middle classes. Child care became a mainstream issue. Although British Columbia declined to participate in the *WDNA*, the notion that publicly supported day care was even on the table forced British Columbians to face a question that, until that point, had been easy to ignore. Was BC society facing a new reality, one in which mothers were paid workers and the government had a responsibility to support them and their children?

To some extent, there had always been a section of BC society that supported a mother's right to choose wage earning and the provision of social supports to help her achieve that right. The war created an opportunity, however, for that argument to gain public and political prominence in ways that had previously not been possible. In large part, the political visibility of child care could be credited to women on the left, particularly those in the BC Co-operative Commonwealth Federation (CCF). The CCF had been an important part of the provincial political landscape since its founding alongside the national party in 1933, and several women members were particularly influential within it: Dorothy Steeves, a founding member of the party who won a seat during a 1934 by-election; Grace MacInnis, the daughter of founding CCF leader J.S. Woodsworth, who won one of the fourteen CCF seats during British Columbia's 1941 election; and Laura Jamieson, elected as a member of the legislative assembly (MLA) for Vancouver Centre in 1939. Despite what Susan Walsh calls the party's "half-hearted commitment to feminist causes" in its early years and the ongoing tension between feminist and socialist goals, these women helped to ensure that women's issues, such as equal pay, access to birth control, divorce reforms, and day nurseries, remained part of the CCF landscape through the 1930s and during the war.[43]

Laura Jamieson was a particularly vocal advocate for the wartime rights of working women – rights, she insisted, that should be maintained once the war was over. Her history as a social activist on behalf of women and children extended back to suffrage campaigns as well as her role as a juvenile court judge, a position she had held (as a working mother) since 1927. It was largely due to her lengthy experience with the problems of juvenile delinquency, child welfare, and family poverty, Walsh notes, that explained Jamieson's political commitment to the "fundamental restructuring of social welfare."[44] She outlined many of these views in *Women, Dry Those Tears*, a socialist feminist tract that circulated widely through wartime British Columbia.[45] At the heart of her political work was a desire to improve working women's wages, working conditions, and the social supports required to balance work and family, including government-sponsored day care. Mothers' employment, she insisted, was a permanent reality for many families, and after the wartime years it would be an even more deeply engrained part of BC society. "Women who have learned to enjoy economic independence," she argued, "are not going back to that barbarian state in which their husbands can ill afford to keep them."[46] Jamieson advocated public day nurseries as a way to alleviate mothers' stress, provide educational and social opportunities for children, and equip mothers with the information needed to build a "more satisfactory home life."[47]

Jamieson's CCF colleagues voiced similar views. Dorothy Steeves, like Jamieson, devoted much of her political life to improving the lives of working-class women. Among her many initiatives was the introduction of legislation for the inclusion of domestic servants in the minimum wage laws. Together with Grace MacInnis, Steeves and Jamieson "consistently championed such feminist causes as access to birth control, adequate child-care support and facilities, mother's allowances, compensation for deserved wives, equal pay for equal work and fair employment practices."[48] In MacInnis's case, the calls for day nurseries in wartime British Columbia were an early indication of her commitment to such issues when she served as the New Democratic Party (NDP) member of parliament (MP) for Vancouver-Kingsway from 1965 to 1974. The need for day care supports was particularly acute, she told the House of Commons in 1967, among working-class and poor women who "are faced with the choice of either going out to work and leaving the children neglected or staying at home and facing a very thin type of life for their families."[49]

However, while MacInnis, Steeves, and Jamieson emphasized the plight of poor working-class women – the traditional targets of child care politics – their demands for better social welfare measures also took place within a framework of freedom and choice for all women to "undertake any kind of work according to their ability."[50] In other words, they insisted that women be viewed as legitimate, permanent members of the labour force and afforded the social rights required to take their place within it. Such thoughts were echoed on the national stage by Dorise Nielsen, the MP for North Battleford, Saskatchewan, who won her seat as a Unity candidate in the 1940 election. Nielsen was also a member of the Communist party, an association she did not reveal publicly until 1943, and her left politics, along with her experience as a working mother (she was the first politician to hold office while her children were still young), guided her campaigns to improve the conditions of women's working lives, including access to day care. "The emancipation of women as wage earners has come to stay," she declared during the war. "I feel I am speaking the views of every Canadian woman when I say that the women of Canada do not want, after the war is over, any suggestion that the only place fit for them is in the home."[51]

Individual women also sought to defend the rights of mothers to be wage earners. For many women, their decision to speak out came from a reaction against accusations that they were neglecting their children in pursuit of extra income. Mrs. F, for one, was disgusted with those who would have her give up her job. "This is so ridiculous," she wrote, that "if it weren't such an important issue one would be inclined to laugh." She continued: "Let every woman realize, as so many of us do, that as women we are individuals, citizens of a democratic country, in which we should, and will, have the right to decide for ourselves that for which we are best suited."[52] Mothers like Mrs. F resented the implication that women were "using child-care centres to unload their responsibilities." When Grace McGaw, who was in charge of female personnel at the North Vancouver shipyards, got wind of these charges, she mounted a spirited defence of working mothers. "We have no reason to believe that any of the married women are working just to shirk the responsibilities of their homes," she argued. "These women are doing a real wartime job and only some crank wanting to shove women back into the homes would make such a statement."[53]

While the conditions of war on the homefront opened up a new space in which working mothers could make a case for public support, others considered the wartime disruption to family life to be a threat rather than an opportunity. A counterpart to her colleagues on the left, Tilly Rolston, the Conservative MLA for Point Grey (Vancouver), frequently voiced disdain for mothers who gave up their domestic responsibilities in favour of wage earning. Rolston's confrontations with Laura Jamieson and Grace MacInnis led, as the press gleefully reported, to "unseemly hair-pulling in the House."[54] While Jamieson promoted day nurseries, Rolston insisted that working mothers were undermining the war effort and, indeed, the very foundations of democratic society. "The absentee mother problem already has produced the most critical juvenile delinquency situation in our history," she warned, and the strain on families caused by working motherhood was making British Columbia a "centre for divorces." Instead of encouraging mothers to abandon their domestic duties, "women should be drafted for duty in the homes of the nation, to preserve those homes and stay the rising tide of juvenile delinquency."[55] Rolston urged British Columbians to consider the long-term consequences of working motherhood:

> Military victory will be a hollow mockery if we produce a generation of demoralized and delinquent Canadians while winning this war to preserve our way of life. Your daily newspaper and local police record will show you how serious this threat has become. We have thousands of underfed, neglected children who are key carriers, while mother wields a blow torch.[56]

The suggestion that the state should provide care for children was "an insult to British Columbia mothers," according to Rolston. What mothers wanted most of all was to "bring up their own children," not to leave child rearing to "some parched, dried-up, starched and cultured academician" in a day nursery.[57]

Rolston's declarations touched a nerve with many BC citizens. The press was eager to scare the public with images of children "hungry and running wild," who lacked mothers to prepare home-cooked meals and instead went to "a movie with a bag of peanuts."[58] One woman, identified only as "Plain Jane," warned of the threat that working mothers represented to society:

> Look at many of your young mothers of today, one shudders as to the habits their children will achieve from their bad example . . . From scarlet painted lips dangles a cigarette, their legs encased in ill-fitting pants, of which one leg is often rolled up to the knee to show a bare unbeautiful leg. Their feet are poked into shoes that have loose heels and go clickaty clak as they slop along. Looking up at these bedraggled females are the innocent eyes of young children, how can one expect but that a girl will grow up sloppy as her mother, or hope for a boy to turn out manly, when his mother isn't even womanly. Let us remember it takes real mothers and real homes to make real children.[59]

For Plain Jane and many others, the provision of child care was entirely outside the boundaries of acceptable public services. It was the government's duty to preserve home life, not to encourage its destruction.

These debates revealed just how far apart British Columbians remained on the question of working mothers and their access to public day care services. However, the very public profile of these debates did mark a shift in British Columbia's child care politics. Advocates such as Jamieson provided a platform for thinking about child care as a matter of women's rights, choices, and opportunities, not simply as an inconsequential welfare measure for poor families. The unprecedented numbers of wartime working mothers, in industrial jobs or otherwise, challenged the dominant assumption that there was something wrong with families in which mothers worked. These kinds of arguments presaged the dimensions of child care politics of the late 1960s and early 1970s. Ultimately, however, the idea of day nurseries as a women's right gained little traction in the wartime years. In the efforts to establish day nurseries in Vancouver, rights-based rhetoric meant very little to the child care providers working on the ground.

"Mother love hasn't a chance at Jackson and Powell"

Provincial officials may have been keen to minimize the government's responsibility for wartime day nurseries and public figures eager to engage in the ideological battles around women and work, but in the meantime something still needed to be done for the province's steadily growing numbers of working mothers. The province's rejection of the *WDNA* frustrated day care supporters, but they continued their efforts in the ways they had always done, by relying on committed community workers and private donors. The need for child care services was especially acute in Vancouver. Many local organizations in the city devoted resources towards the establishment and maintenance of day nursery services and lobbied, mostly unsuccessfully, for municipal, provincial, and even federal support. Despite the circulation of new ideas about working mothers' rights, the work of these community-based child care providers remained in familiar territory. Their campaigns for day nurseries centred on the prevention of juvenile delinquency, the promotion of moral standards, and the need for social supports to prevent the total breakdown of family life. To borrow a phrase from Susan Prentice, they "manipulated a conservative idea without challenging it," by suggesting that day care was at the very least a stop-gap measure to prevent all of the problems that Rolston and her supporters feared most.[60]

The Vancouver Council of Social Agencies was the focal point for wartime day nursery initiatives in the city. A subcommittee of the council's Children's Division kept a close eye on mothers' employment rates and through 1941 and 1942 engaged in negotiations with provincial officials, including Zella Collins, around the possibility of publicly funded child care services. Initially, the council's efforts were redirected away from day nurseries and towards a Counselling Service for Mothers Committee, which included provincial representation (likely Collins). As one 1940s social worker explained, the counselling service was considered an adequate interim measure because "it was believed that many mothers were wandering from agency to agency, looking for help and perhaps taking jobs, when, if given the opportunity to talk it over, they might decide to stay home with their children." There were reports that approximately seventy-five mothers were referred to the counselling service, "and their individual problems were discussed."[61]

Hundreds of other mothers, however, did not have the option of giving up their jobs. The Vancouver Council of Social Agencies and the Children's Aid Society (CAS) reported that those with preschool-aged children were resorting to troubling child care arrangements: inattentive landladies, older siblings, and even, according to one report, children "left in the school yard to play while the older brothers and sisters attended school." Problems were compounded by the shortage of foster day homes and of rental housing.[62] These troubling circumstances were of great concern to many social agencies in the city but particularly to the Vancouver Housewives' League, and by late 1942 the league had established its place among the most vocal advocates for day nursery services for the city's working mothers – the mothers for whom the province and the federal government had refused responsibility under the *WDNA* because they were not war workers but, rather, "waitresses, telephone operators, and workers in dry-cleaning plants."[63] The Vancouver Housewives' League had roots in the Depression-era Mothers' Council and was led by women who were also members of the Communist party and who, through the 1930s, were active in relief protests and offered support for striking workers. During the war, the league became more of a consumer advocacy group that worked to combat the rising price of household goods, but its efforts also extended to other issues that affected mothers' lives, including rent controls, low-cost housing, and child care.[64] The league established a Day Nurseries Committee and assigned Lillian Newitt, also a member of the Vancouver Council of Social Agencies, to the role of spokeswoman.

The care of preschool children was of particular concern for the Housewives' League, but they and other welfare groups were also worried about young school-aged children. Crowded wartime housing conditions forced many children onto the streets after school and on weekends, not just because their mother worked but also because "they had neither yard nor house room in which to play."[65] In the spring of 1943, the Housewives' League encouraged the Council of Social Agencies to consider what would happen to all of those children over the summer vacation. Representatives from a variety of local organizations – the Indian Day Camp Committee, the PTA, the school board, the Junior League, the Daily Vacation Bible Schools, the CAS, and public health nurses – were similarly concerned. One solution that emerged from all of the discussion, study, and consultation through the spring was the establishment of three day nurseries, overseen by the Council of Social Agencies, for children from ages three to six: Gordon House Play School in the West End, Alexandra House Play School in Kitsilano, and Strathcona Nursery School, which was located in a Japanese church at the corner of Jackson and Powell streets in the working-class downtown east side.[66] Although all three of these centres were described as playschools, they were explicitly designed for "supervised play for children of working mothers" and to serve "homes where the mother is away working all day." Much of the clientele also reported using the centres so that children could be kept away from their households during the day if parents needed to sleep after a night shift.[67]

Between these three day nurseries, eighty-eight mothers and 122 children were provided with child care services during the summer. At least twenty other families indicated that they would have liked to use the service, but the hours did not fit with their schedules.[68] A qualified nursery school teacher was in charge at each centre, assisted by volunteers from the Women's Voluntary Service. The day nurseries were so successful that the decision was made to keep them open in the fall. In order to do so, though, a more sustainable source of financial support had to be found. Through the summer, the Vancouver Council of Social Agencies had relied on the Welfare Federation and other private organizations to pay staffing and equipment costs and rents. The Housewives' League had been a particular "tower of strength" behind the Strathcona Nursery School, enlisting the financial support of several unions to keep the centre going.[69] In the long term, however, parent fees (50 cents weekly at Alexandra and Gordon Houses and $1.75 at Strathcona, where a hot lunch was served) and charitable contributions were not sufficient. As the end of summer approached, the Council of Social Agencies, the Housewives' League, and the Consumers' Council of Vancouver began to put pressure on all three levels of government to pledge support. The Strathcona Nursery School's officials, in particular, remained optimistic that the province would rethink its decision on the *WDNA*. E. Stanway Scanlon, the Consumers' Council representative who also sat on the Council of Social Agencies, appealed to city council to exert pressure on the province to reduce the numbers of war-working mothers in *WDNA*-eligible centres from 75 percent to 50 percent to better capture the needs of the day nursery clientele.[70] As he explained to the city and the provincial government, Strathcona presented the perfect opportunity "to set a pattern for government supported nurseries for children of mothers engaged in war industries," and doing so, the implication was, would benefit all working mothers in need.[71] After consulting with Zella Collins (the provincial field officer who worked closely with the Council of Social Agencies), the city declined for the customary reason that the day nurseries were not essential for the war effort: "To date the number of existing war industries in Vancouver has not necessitated the employment of women with children."[72] "The time," the city clerk argued, "was not 'ripe' for public day nurseries."[73]

In one sense, of course, city officials were right. Very few of the day nursery mothers were engaged in industrial war work – not nearly enough, even, to make up the 50 percent of clientele that Scanlon suggested could make the nursery eligible for amended *WDNA* funding. In fact, Collins reported that only one mother of the eighty-eight served over the summer was engaged in "an actual war industry." Many others, according to Collins's reports, were not in the formal paid labour force at all and, instead, sent their children to day care because of cramped housing conditions, because they had access to more nutritious food at the nursery, or to keep them away from bad neighbourhood influences.[74] However, to Scanlon, Newitt, and other members of the Vancouver Council of Social Agencies, the make-up of the day nursery clientele did not let the city and the province off the hook. Instead, it proved that the time was ripe for day nurseries and always had been. Waging war on the BC homefront may not have required mobilizing mothers into factory work, but it did exacerbate the social conditions that made day nurseries necessary.

As the Housewives' League and the Consumers' Council continued to push for government support in 1943 and 1944, their efforts revealed the extent to which they viewed day nurseries as the instruments of charity and child welfare. For Scanlon, Newitt, and others, the "working mother" and the "underprivileged child" were two sides of the same coin. They were not arguing for the inclusion of working mothers on the rights-based social policy landscape but, rather, for a welfare service to expose children to the social and educational environment that their own homes and neighbourhoods sorely lacked. According to Newitt, not even a mother's pension was enough to improve the conditions of Vancouver's most underprivileged children. In the depraved neighbourhoods such as those around Jackson and Powell streets, Newitt declared, "mother love hasn't a chance."[75] Collins agreed. "The conditions existing call for something more than a temporary war measure," she argued, "if these children are to become the type of citizens we both want and need, in Vancouver."[76]

The campaign for day nurseries in Victoria took on a similar tenor. There, a delegation of voluntary welfare agencies warned the minister of labour that "large numbers of Victoria women are working outside their homes, in the place of men who were in uniform" and that it was "obvious that in most cases their pre-school-aged children [were] not receiving proper care and attention."[77] Eventually, they decided to create the Greater Victoria Nursery School Association to "co-ordinate the activities of all individuals and groups furthering the nursery school movement" as well as to provide educational and research services.[78] According to the association, in one three-block radius alone in Victoria, over seventy-five preschool-aged children were left unsupervised while their mothers worked. They urged the province not only to sign on to the *WDNA* but also to press the federal government to enlarge the definition of "war-working mother" to include any women who were taking men's jobs (not just "essential" war jobs).[79] Not enough working mothers could be found to justify the day nursery, however, and so day nursery organizers redirected their efforts towards nursery schools to benefit "children from underprivileged homes" who were otherwise headed for lives of "delinquency and crime."[80]

In both Victoria and Vancouver, the push for public responsibility for day care arose from pity rather than entitlement – from a desire to "help families to help themselves" in the face of unfortunate circumstances. The war may have changed the rhetorical landscape of women and work, but, for the most part, British Columbia's working mothers continued to be lumped in with other families who needed day nursery services as an option of last resort and as a way to rehabilitate impoverished children and their families. The day nurseries established during the war continued to operate with private support, but with a mandate that had little to do with the entitlements of working mothers and much more to do with older, charity-style notions of child welfare.

"The day nursery is a training ground for democracy, not a dumping ground for babies"

As the end of the war approached, politicians and welfare officials in British Columbia, like their federal counterparts, began to consider how to manage a return to "normal." The "demobilization" of working women was of particular concern. In Ottawa, a subcommittee of the General Advisory Council on Reconstruction led a national discussion about the "post-war problems of women" and particularly on what should be done when men started returning home to the jobs that women had filled during the war. Two BC women, MacInnis and Evelyn Lett, were members of the subcommittee, and they reported that women and their employers in Vancouver-area war plants saw for the most part "women as an integral part of the future economic structure."[81] Observations like this led to the report's inclusion of declarations about a woman's "right as a citizen ... to work at whatever occupation she wished and subsequently to enjoy 'equality of remuneration, working conditions and opportunity for advancement' with men."[82] The report went so far as to recommend that "nursery schools" be available for working mothers, who were imagined as part of the post-war labour force, albeit only on a part-time basis.[83]

Yet post-war declarations about women's equality in the labour market, as Jennifer Stephen argues, were little more than "gestures." The report did not offer any substantial challenge to the belief that "preference in the post-war economy went to men" and that the preferred place for mothers was in the home.[84] Indeed, this ideology was inscribed into post-war policy-making across the country, which was uniformly focused on preserving the middle-class male-headed home as the bastion of a productive democratic society. The major policy undertaking in this respect was family allowances, which Nancy Christie interprets as a "means to foster postwar consumption, which in turn would ensure full employment, economic equilibrium, and social stability." Full employment meant, of course, full male breadwinner employment.[85] It was a given, therefore, that wartime day nurseries were not part of the post-war policy menu, a fact that Fraudena Eaton made very clear.[86] The *WDNA*, accordingly, was cancelled in June 1946.

The cancellation of the agreement was very controversial in Québec and especially in Ontario, where day nurseries had had such a beneficial impact on working mothers' lives. As Prentice has documented, a broad-based coalition of welfare reformers, women's organizations, and religious leaders in Toronto worked together to keep day nurseries open, rallying around the popular cause of preventing juvenile delinquency. Prentice credits this movement with helping to convince the Ontario government to pass the *Day Nurseries Act* in 1946, which provided for the cost sharing of day nurseries between the provincial and municipal governments.[87] Even after this legislative victory, though, Toronto child care activists continued to lobby for more spaces in the city. Members of the Communist party played a key role in the post-war day care fight, especially through the Day Nurseries and Day Care Parents Association, and Prentice shows that their membership in the coalition, which also included CCF women, was important for the collaborations it fostered with Communist and "sympathetic" city aldermen and Board of Education trustees. More broadly, Prentice suggests, the Communist-led day care campaigns in the late 1940s were part of an effort "to defend the rights of families with working mothers to government-funded services," including free milk for their children, although the red-baiting of the early 1950s and an overall suspicion of "undeserving" working mothers eventually undermined Toronto's nascent child care movement.[88]

Toronto's post-war day care fight was not replicated anywhere else in the country, most obviously because the *WDNA* had not resulted in such a dramatic reorientation of working mothers' child care expectations as it had in Ontario. Nevertheless, the cancellation of the *WDNA* did not necessarily put to rest the child care politics that had bubbled to the surface during the war. For many commentators in British Columbia, the agreement's cancellation came as a relief and even as a victory. Tilly Rolston, for one, was "glad" that "no large program for day nurseries" had been established during the war.[89] With the return of women to their homes, Rolston hoped, there would be "less need for day nurseries" and the commotion around centres such as Strathcona Nursery School would dissipate.[90] Even Rolston admitted, however, that the need for day nurseries would not disappear entirely. The efforts to restore female domesticity were implicitly understood to be a middle-class concern. Working-class women and non-white women still needed to work, a fact that policy-makers accepted.[91] What Rolston and others hoped and expected, therefore, was that working mothers and their day care demands would disappear from mainstream policy discussions, once again demoted to that realm of social services concerned with the welfare and rehabilitation of failed families. No longer would day nursery debates be caught up with the troublesome claims that working mothers were entitled to the public provision of child care, but instead they could return to their proper place, which was "a peacetime welfare activity to give assistance to those with large families and low incomes," preferably one handled by private social agencies.[92] Many of Vancouver's day nursery operators agreed that it was "foolish" to continue offering child care services to the extent that they had been offered during the war. This would only encourage mothers, as Gordon House's Kathleen Gorrie argued, to work for selfish reasons. The risk was that day cares would become a vehicle for "middle-class privilege rather than a need."[93]

This sentiment put the Strathcona Nursery School in a tricky position. Newitt and the Housewives' League, like their Communist colleagues in Toronto, wanted to garner as much public support as possible to sustain the nursery, but they had to do so without day nurseries being cast as a threat to family life. In Toronto, as Prentice shows, the rhetoric of juvenile delinquency mobilized day care activists from both sides of the political spectrum.[94] In British Columbia, day care debates contained strains of the post-war preoccupation with juvenile delinquency as well as of the familiar charitable framework, and in the mid-1940s a new emphasis on education and citizenship training also appeared. Day nurseries and nursery schools were touted as places where children could receive the lessons required to become upstanding democratic citizens, the foundation of a new peaceful society. The nursery school movement in Britain, which provided "working lessons in democracy," provided a model for Canadians such as Dr. William Blatz, who endorsed a vision of a network of nurseries that could be used to "train the child to fit the social pattern."[95] In Vancouver, Strathcona's officials harnessed this rhetoric wholeheartedly. "The day nursery," Newitt told the Women's School for Democracy in April 1944, "is a training ground for democracy, not a dumping ground for babies. Here, children learned self-discipline, order, co-operation – the art of living together."[96] Mothers benefited too because they were able to "learn a great deal about the physical and psychological needs of their children from contact with this kind of community life."[97] Newitt also insisted that day nurseries had a distinct advantage over home-based foster day care (which the VDNA continued to operate) because lessons in democracy were best learned in peer groups.[98] Children, Newitt argued, "learned to share toys, take turns, and play happily with other children, as well as improving in disposition [and] concentration."[99]

What this line of argument did, however, was further demote the particular child care needs of working mothers. Woven into education- and play-based rhetoric, nursery schools and kindergartens became almost entirely removed from the issue of working motherhood. "Whether or not mothers go out to work," one mother urged, "let us have more nursery schools, the children need them."[100] This view was shared by many welfare officials even during the war who, as Gillian Weiss has noted, did not object to the expansion of half-day preschools. Mothers who remained at home, ran errands, or even worked part-time while their children attended preschools remained "perfectly respectable," in sharp contrast to full-time working mothers.[101] Even as officials expressed increasing misgivings about day nurseries, for example, they were more than willing to support the establishment of five "play time" centres for the school- and preschool-aged children of servicemen and their wives. These centres, which opened in March 1944, were open from 1 to 6 pm on weekdays so that deserving mothers could have leisurely time to themselves to run errands or do volunteer work.[102]

As the popularity of early childhood services grew, the Vancouver School Board began to consider the role that it could play in the nursery school movement. In early 1944, representatives of the board approached the minister of education to request an amendment to the *School Act* that would allow children as young as three to enrol in kindergartens.[103] Based on their analysis of Vancouver neighbourhoods, the board identified several target schools, all of which were in the areas of low socio-economic status and which did not already have private kindergartens operating.[104] This proposal was supported by none other than Tilly Rolston, who endorsed educational programs for young children provided that "we ... have a knowledge that the mothers using the nursery schools are not doing it for their own particular benefit, but for the benefit of the children."[105] The province was also on board and gave the school boards permission to extend their services to four to six year olds. Spring Ridge kindergarten in Victoria and Henry Hudson and Dawson School kindergartens in Vancouver opened their doors in the fall of 1944.[106] The enthusiasm around kindergarten and preschool education continued to grow, represented in the post-war institutionalization of such services: the BC PTA endorsed preschools in 1946, the Co-operative Play School Association was formed in 1945, and the Institute for Child Study was established at the University of British Columbia in 1961.[107]

By getting directly into the kindergarten business, government officials were making an important statement about what kinds of child care were considered legitimate. Another bureaucratic mechanism also drove this point across. In 1938, the provincial government had passed the *Welfare Institutions Licensing Act*, which established a board to oversee licensing and regulations of various kinds of welfare institutions.[108] Beginning in 1943, all child care facilities – whether centre-based or home-based – were required to apply for licensing through the board and were held to health and safety standards determined by the province.[109] This was an important symbolic move in that it signalled that the province considered child care services to be in the same realm as other welfare functions. Moreover, the regulatory intervention of the Welfare Institutions Licensing Board (WILB) assumed a clear distinction between two tiers of child care services. In the upper tier were education-oriented kindergartens, playschools, and nursery schools. The WILB's annual reports through the late 1940s and into the 1950s offered much praise for these expanding services, which were almost always offered on a part-time basis – they were training grounds for democratic citizenship, they provided socialization opportunities for children, and they gave hard-working mothers a few well-deserved hours to themselves. Their utility for working mothers was rarely discussed. By 1950, the province was home to more than 100 licensed facilities in this category, including centres in Ocean Falls, Port Alberni, Sidney, Vancouver, and Victoria.[110]

The subordinate second tier that came under the WILB's purview was foster homes for day care. Under this category, the province kept track of the services of the in-home daytime services facilitated by the VDNA, which was known by the 1950s as the Foster Day Care Association, and a similar program established in Victoria in 1952. As in Vancouver, the Victoria foster home system was explicitly welfarist and economic in its rationale – without these homes, "the family would have been forced to ask for public assistance."[111] The framing of such services illustrated just how little had changed for working mothers, despite the disruption of the war years. In the pervasiveness of post-war nuclear family ideology, "women who both raised children and worked outside the home" were made "virtually . . . invisible."[112] These families, as they had been prior to the war, were treated as charity cases according to classist notions of dependency, assumed to be in need of rehabilitation. As the Foster Day Care Association explained, their service continued to play a "triple role":

(1) It preserves the self-respect and independence of Mothers.
(2) It benefits home life by keeping Mother and family together.
(3) It saves the City a large amount of money by giving these Mothers the opportunity to work.[113]

Most of all, though, the association nurtured the "fervent hope that employment conditions for fathers of young families will improve so that more Mothers will be able to stay home."[114] This focus on the nuclear family, on the one hand, and the threat of poor mothers' dependency, on the other, was a far cry from the "defence of democracy" taking place in kindergartens and playschools.[115]

While the gap between education-based child care and welfare-based services to poor families was inscribed in provincial policy, the distinction was often not so clear at the level of private local service provision. The changing nature of the Strathcona Nursery School in the 1950s showed this to be the case. Immediately after the war, Strathcona had been available as a "general service" to any child as a playschool, but by the 1950s administrators began to narrow their services "to the more specific problem faced by the working mother." In this new orientation, "both education and home supplementation [were] closely interwoven." There was recognition on Strathcona's part that working mothers were not necessarily charity cases and that their children deserved the play-based educational benefits that went beyond the custodial care in foster home programs. Indeed, Strathcona's client mothers worked for a number of reasons. Economic need was most commonly cited, but mothers also insisted that they worked for "enjoyment," because they "found it satisfying," and because they "were not content to stay at home to be 'just a housewife.'" Virtually all of the Strathcona mothers also insisted that there was a great need for similar facilities throughout the city since there was a lack of "desirable facilities for child care while [mothers] worked."[116]

The case of the Strathcona Nursery School illustrated an important reality in post-war British Columbia. Mothers had not retreated back into the home, but, rather, they continued to work for both economic and personal reasons, and there was a continued need for a more meaningful approach to child care policy and practice in provincial politics. While some provincial officials clung to the belief that "nurseries give mothers too much time for beer parlors," others were willing to acknowledge that the public provision of child care was an ever more important component of the provincial political agenda.[117] The social welfare department reported in 1953 that requests for day care "for children of mothers who do not *need* to work to supplement the family income but who *want* to work are increasing."[118] This reality raised an important question, asked quietly by the Social Welfare Branch in 1953:

> While everyone agrees it is important for mothers to stay at home and that their most important job is to care for their children, should disapproval be shown about a mother going to work if good care for her children can be provided and she prefers it that way?[119]

In the coming years, policy-makers would be forced to grapple with this question and to carefully consider the government's responsibility to these working mothers.

In an ideological sense, not much changed for British Columbia's working mothers during the Second World War. To be sure, the opening of new day nurseries and the expansion of foster day care services helped to lighten the load for many mothers, and there were more mothers than ever in the labour force, thanks to the opportunities created by the wartime economy. Despite an unprecedented level of attention to working motherhood, though, the gendered and class-based expectations around family, work, and welfare remained entrenched. The war years were essentially business as usual for the working-class and poor mothers whose child care needs were considered best left to charities. Elsewhere in Canada, particularly in Ontario and Québec, the mobilization of the "reserve army" of female labourers resulted in dramatic reforms to the public provision of child care services.[120] But in British Columbia, where the need for women in wartime industry was not so clear cut, working mothers were not assigned any sort of special status. Prescriptions against respectable mothers' work outside the home continued to carry a great deal of weight in British Columbia, even in the unusual circumstances of the war. Provincial and local welfare officials viewed working mothers in the same ambivalent light they always had. Their work was a necessary evil whose repercussions, including the provision of child care, was the responsibility not of the government but of private welfare organizations.

In another sense, though, the ground shifted during the war. Child care politics in British Columbia were infused with a new rhetoric about the rights and choices of working mothers, thanks largely to the efforts of women on the left. The public began to recognize and accept the benefits of preschool and nursery school education for children and of the government's role in providing such services. The community-based providers of child care services began to think of themselves not just as charity-oriented, last-ditch services but, rather, as places where the interests of children and of working mothers were not incompatible and where children were given educational care while their mothers earned wages either out of necessity or desire. From the level of the provincial government down to local welfare providers, there was a tentative and growing sense in British Columbia that child care could no longer be considered simply a residual service for deviant families but that it might be considered a legitimate public service in recognition of the social rights of working mothers.

4

"The working mother is here to stay": The Making of Provincial Child Care Policy in the 1960s

In the years immediately following the Second World War, mothers did not disappear from the labour force to the extent that many assumed (or hoped) they would. If the introduction of public child care services was to be determined by some minimum quantity of working mothers in society – as provincial officials insisted during the war – few could deny that by the 1960s a critical mass had been reached. By the middle of the decade, over half of British Columbia's working mothers had children under the age of fourteen who required either full-day or after-school day care or both.[1] Mothers' presence in the labour force was still accompanied by a great deal of anxiety, but it was becoming harder to deny the significant policy implications of their employment. Rather than "attempting to devise means of keeping the mothers home," Alvin Finkel explains, politicians and planners across the country had to start thinking about "insuring the best child care" for their children.[2] The BC Department of Social Welfare admitted as much as early as 1956: "If it is to become a permanent part of Canadian culture that married women with young children are needed as part of the labour force, then a good day-care programme must be worked out for the care of these children."[3]

The creation of a child care policy became part of the provincial political landscape for the first time in the 1960s. Social policy reform in British Columbia in the 1960s was overseen by Social Credit Premier W.A.C. Bennett, who had come to power in 1952 and immediately set about to transform the BC economy through natural resource and infrastructure development projects.[4] Despite his ambitious economic policies, Bennett was largely "unwilling to spend money on social programs" through his entire twenty-year administration (1952–72). In the middle of the 1960s, however, a "growing population and rising social service demands" left Bennett's government with few options but to invest in a modest day care program, as Cheryl Collier notes.[5] Tangible action became feasible in 1966 thanks to newly available money from the shared-cost *Canada Assistance Plan* (*CAP*), the federal government's effort to consolidate social service spending.[6] Under the *CAP*-sponsored day care program, BC mothers who were social assistance recipients were eligible for subsidies to help offset the costs of child care.[7] There were strict conditions attached to eligibility, however, and government support did not extend to capital or operating expenses for day care centres. The state's involvement in day care was about the specific need of certain mothers, not the broader societal concern for widely accessible day care.

Despite its limitations, though, this subsidy program represented the vanguard of provincial child care policy. But did this modest day care program represent a reshaping of social citizenship's boundaries in British Columbia? After all, not since the Vancouver City Crèche had any level of government within the province acknowledged that working mothers were entitled to public support for the care of their children. As working mothers inched their way towards the mainstream, these first limited forays into provincial day care programming offered the potential to open the boundaries of social citizenship in such a way as to legitimize the combination of earning and caring, rather than assuming that overlap to be a sign of failure in marginalized women and their families. This reading of day care policy in the 1960s should not be taken too far, however. The narrowly targeted subsidies, the program's relationship to the "war on poverty," and the ways that local welfare groups made their imprint on provincial policy reveal little alteration in long-standing approaches to working mothers' social citizenship. Day care subsidies occupied the same framework in which support for working mothers had long been entrenched: child care was a "service for the poor," one that facilitated mothers' "rehabilitation" through waged work or job-training programs and provided their children with the moral and educational training considered to be in short supply in their own homes.[8] Women may have been begrudgingly accepted as workers, but the idealization of the nuclear, male-breadwinner family in which mothers and children were dependents still "constituted the ideological backdrop to women's work outside the home."[9] The rationale for day care subsidies as a welfarist, anti-poverty strategy remained the preferred policy approach in the 1960s because it "left the nuclear family unchallenged."[10] Local welfare groups may have been cautiously optimistic about the new provincial program, but as the 1960s drew to a close it was clear to many, including those among the ranks of an emerging women's rights movement, that until social citizenship was premised upon women's right to work rather than their obligation to do so, provincial day care services would remain inadequate.

Growing Concern

In 1941, 4 percent of married women in Canada worked outside the home. By 1961, this proportion had grown to 22 percent and would increase to 41 percent in 1975.[11] In British Columbia, women made up nearly one-third of the 1960s labour force, and almost one-half (45 percent) of those women were mothers, which was slightly above the national average.[12] Put another way, 21 percent of BC mothers with children under the age of fourteen were labour force participants, which translated to 105,000 children who required care.[13] For many mothers, a "two-phase" cycle of wage work had developed, in which they worked until they had their first child and then again when their children were older.[14] However, it was also increasingly common for mothers to work even when their children were young. Their child care strategies, as a result, were increasingly a matter of public concern.

In the mid-1960s, the Women's Bureau within the federal Department of Labour recognized that the rates of working motherhood showed no sign of slowing down and wondered what kinds of arrangements mothers were making for their children. Officials gathered data from around the country and in 1967 released a report entitled *Working Mothers and Their Child-Care Arrangements*.[15] The report did not provide province-specific data about mothers' specific labour and child care patterns, but national figures hinted at BC trends. The Women's Bureau investigations revealed that 84 percent of children with working mothers required non-mother care, whether school or preschool aged. In two-thirds of these cases, mothers were able to arrange care in their own homes, provided by fathers, older relatives, or friends. Care by family and friends outside of the home was the strategy of 15 percent of working mothers, while the same proportion had no regular arrangement and were forced to seek out child care on an ad hoc basis. Only 1 percent of working mothers could rely on the services of a day nursery or nursery school, a figure that rose slightly to 3 percent when children aged three to five were considered as a group.[16]

Those BC mothers who needed some type of centre- or program-based support for child care had few options. Aside from the licensing and regulatory responsibilities of the Welfare Institutions Licensing Board (WILB), the provincial government was virtually absent in day care services before 1966. As they had been during the war and in the decades prior, local agencies and community groups were left to cobble together child care provisions on a small scale, occasionally with meager short-term grants from municipal governments. The growing numbers of kindergartens and playschools throughout the province – which were given a vote of support by the 1960 Royal Commission on Education – were likely a help to many working mothers. For those who worked shift work, those who could not afford to pay for private preschool services, and especially those with children younger than three years old, the home-based foster day care system was the primary type of child care available well into the 1960s.[17] Even private nursery schools that had developed around wartime working women's needs, such as the Strathcona Nursery School, had shifted their operations to focus on the management of foster day care, which by that point was becoming known as family day care.[18] But, while kindergartens and preschools proliferated, the same could not be said for family day cares. Through the late 1950s and early 1960s, there were never more than thirty-five licensed private homes in the province.[19] Furthermore, the family day care system remained deeply entrenched in child welfare for "broken families" and those with "social problems."[20] The department even suggested in 1962 that the family homes should be subject to the same oversight as boarding homes for troubled and disadvantaged children.[21] Providing convenient services for respectable working mothers was not among these administrative objectives.

However, the policy implications of the changing patterns in work and family life were impossible to ignore. As one BC social agency remarked, "the working mother is here to stay."[22] Around the province, working mothers and their child care arrangements began to preoccupy many social agencies, and reports and studies began to appear in the early 1960s calling attention to the inadequacy of child care in the province. Rising concern about access to day care was fuelled in part by growing dissatisfaction with the foster/family day home system. Local welfare officials in Vancouver, for example, made public their concern about the "shocking conditions" in many foster home settings.[23] Among these studies was a 1961 report commissioned by the provincial government that identified "substitute day care for the children of working mothers" as a key policy area requiring research.

The report's author, Michael Wheeler, observed that although more than 40 percent of working women were married (and thus likely had children), little was known about the quality and quantity of day care available in the province.[24]

The most thorough and pointed critique of British Columbia's day care situation came from the Vancouver Community Chest in its 1965 *Report on Day Care Needs*.[25] The committee behind the report represented an impressive array of local welfare officials, including representations from the Foster Day Care Association of Vancouver, Vancouver's Child Day Care Centre, Vancouver co-operative preschools, the city's Department of Social Services, Catholic preschool services, the University of British Columbia's Institute of Child Study, Vancouver Children's Aid Society (CAS), the city's health services, the provincial WILB, and the Community Chest and Council's Welfare and Recreation Committee.[26] The report not only focused on practical problems and solutions but also represented hints of an important rhetorical shift in the way that Vancouver's local agencies talked about day care. It was no longer appropriate, the committee said, to think about day care as a residual welfare service or as a "last resort" for poverty-stricken families. The new realities of the workplace and family life meant that day care should be available even to "normal families with normal children" – that is, not necessarily just those who had suffered some kind of social breakdown.[27] Day care had "unique values of its own," the report said, to offer to all children and their parents.[28]

The demands that issued from the Community Chest report were simple. More day care spaces were needed to match the growing numbers of working mothers in the city and the province. The report estimated that the rates of working motherhood in Vancouver were higher than provincial figures and that up to 55 or 60 percent of the city's female labour force were mothers compared to 45 percent throughout the entire province. The high rate of mothers' employment combined with inadequate child care services meant that 11,000 of the city's children were without adequate day care.[29] Of these children, 6,000 "acutely" required improved care. The report's authors suggested that this number likely underestimated the actual need for day care since many mothers were reluctant to admit to needing child care when working outside the home since it was still largely stigmatized. "There was a natural tendency," the committee observed, "for mothers to be protective in replying to questions about the care of their children." This was especially true of mothers with infants and very young children. For the committee, the results did not mean that there was less demand for care for children under three years of age; if anything, it meant that focusing on quality care for infants and toddlers was even more imperative.[30]

The Community Chest's high-profile report did much to publicly catapult day care onto the provincial political agenda for the first time since the war. A sense of deep dissatisfaction with the government's approach to child care permeated every section of the report. The list of the committee's grievances resonated widely, especially with day care providers throughout the city and the province who had been struggling for years to maintain their operations based only on the inconsistent support of private donors and whose appeals for help had been repeatedly dismissed by provincial welfare officials.[31] This report laid out a detailed vision of the government's role in day care – despite some suggestion from provincial officials that local organizations should take full responsibility for day care in exchange for a provincial homemaker-housekeeper program[32] – and, in doing so, laid the onus for action on the province. "All departments dealing with health, welfare and education" were implicated in the subject of day care, according to the Community Chest. The report's practical suggestions focused on increasing the number of child care spaces, hiring more staff on the WILB "to enable an aggressive program of licensing and inspection," and urging the city to ease its fire and health regulations to allow more homes to qualify for licensing.[33]

Yet for all of its insistence that day care was a service to which every "normal" family should have access, the report was still largely imbued with the enduring welfare rhetoric about working mothers and welfare. The report's authors earmarked the Department of Social Welfare for the bulk of day care responsibility, where child care programming could be developed along class-specific conditions. While middle- and upper-class families deserved increased access to services, they should also be expected to pay for day care. For the report's authors, this expectation was apparently self-explanatory. It was simple common sense that if a working mother was in a financially comfortable situation, she should pay for child care. Accordingly, the services designed for these families – commercial and for-profit day cares – received the least amount of attention in the *Report on Day Care Needs*. It was families in "economic need" who were of the most interest to the committee. These were the families that most required additional child care spaces because of day care's ability to ameliorate social problems. According to the committee, day care functioned as an important "preventive" public welfare measure because it could help alleviate issues of child neglect, mental illness of mothers, delinquency, social "maladjustments" of children, and all of the damaging effects that accompanied poverty, including "social isolation, lack of educational, social and work opportunities, lack of intellectual and emotional stimulation, [and] the destruction of initiative, motivation, and hope."[34] Whether in subsidized private centres or publicly run day cares, the children of working-class and poor families could thus receive the kind of preventive care that they lacked in their own homes.

The calls for more and better day care in the early and mid-1960s were based on the recognition that working mothers were "here to stay," but working mothers' status as "normal" was still clearly up for debate. For the most part, working motherhood remained synonymous with low-income families and potential welfare dependency. These views would be entwined into the provincial government's first real foray into child care provision.

The CAP and Day Care Subsidies

Growing concerns about day care in the 1960s were part and parcel of developing awareness around the causes of, and solutions to, poverty. Since the Great Depression, British Columbia's social welfare policy had undergone a wholesale renovation and expansion, alongside federal initiatives such as unemployment insurance (1940) and family allowances (1945). Provincially, John Hart's coalition government introduced the *Social Assistance Act* in 1945, which represented an effort to replace municipal and charitable relief with a provincial program that provided assistance "on establishment of need to residents of the Province irrespective of race, creed, citizenship or political affiliation."[35] In the mid-1950s, W.A.C. Bennett's Social Credit government entered into new cost-sharing arrangements with the federal government that allowed for the creation of provincial programs of assistance for the disabled and the permanently unemployed as well as for provincial health insurance.[36] The twenty or so years after the Depression saw efforts towards "amalgamation" of provincial social welfare services (administratively housed in the Social Welfare Branch of the Department of Health and Welfare and, after 1959, in separate Departments of Social Welfare and Health Services and Hospital Insurance), the expansion of a professional staff of social workers (including the formation of the BC Association of Social Workers in 1956), more emphasis on analysis and planning, and efforts to create consistent standards of support in rural and urban areas of the province.[37]

Social welfare initiatives continued at both the federal and provincial levels into the 1960s, when they were made more urgent by the declaration of a "war on poverty." As James Struthers explains, the issue of poverty "exploded into public consciousness" across Canada in the middle of the decade, inspired by American president Lyndon Johnson's anti-poverty rhetoric.[38] The centrepiece of the response by Lester Pearson's government was the *CAP*, a national program designed to "promote adequate levels of assistance so that Canadians will not, through poverty, be denied an adequate standard of food, clothing, shelter and other essentials for normal living and the preservation of family life."[39] The *CAP* consolidated a range of welfare programs, including unemployment assistance, mothers' allowances, medical care for the poor, and child welfare programs into one centrally administered, shared-cost program, in a way that governments hoped would curb out-of-control social spending. National Health and Welfare officials also hoped that the *CAP* would bring "rationalization and reason" to welfare programs, many of which were simply fostering long-term dependency. "Rehabilitation," therefore, became the watchword of the *CAP*, which incorporated job training and placement among its network of programs.[40]

The rediscovery of poverty in the 1960s was accompanied by a growing recognition that poverty was a particularly female problem. Women, especially elder women and single mothers, made up a disproportionate number of poor and low-income families on social assistance.[41] In the BC Department of Social Welfare, officials were beginning to identify the particular challenges faced by mothers on social assistance, especially since the *Mothers' Allowance Act* had been repealed in 1956 and all remaining cases were rolled into the social assistance caseload. By the 1960s, single mothers made up approximately one-quarter of this caseload.[42] The department's emphasis was on "vocational training" and "rehabilitation" projects for social assistance recipients, efforts that resulted in modest success for single men and male family heads. But for single mothers, department officials explained, employment-based rehabilitation "did not usually produce the desired result." Lack of access to affordable, accessible child care was largely to blame. The amount that mothers earned in the low-paid jobs they were able to secure was not enough to cover their "living costs" as well as their additional child care expenses.[43]

This emphasis on the feminization of poverty and the particular trials of poor mothers helped to (further) establish child care's association with other welfare initiatives. The social welfare department was not necessarily day care's inevitable home, however. BC officials kept a close eye on national policy developments, where "state feminists" within the federal bureaucracy were calling for better day care provision as an issue of women's employment equity. Marion Royce, the director of the Women's Bureau in the

Department of Labour, was insistent that day care was required to combat the particular needs of mothers as worker-citizens, a point she tried to reinforce through studies such as *Day Care Services for Children of Working Mothers*, released in 1964.[44] As Rianne Mahon has shown, however, Royce's position gained "little sympathy" from other federal bureaucrats or indeed from the wider public, who were willing to recognize working mothers in theory but were not willing to inscribe the matter of their distinct employment concerns into public policy. Instead, Royce and the Women's Bureau followed the lead of the Family and Child Welfare Division of the Canadian Welfare Council, which was advocating for the inclusion of day care on the federal policy agenda not as a labour issue but, rather, as a welfare one.[45]

By the early 1960s, the same principle was also firmly established in British Columbia. In large part, this movement was due to pressure from below. Alongside the Community Chest's high-profile *Report on Day Care Needs*, other social work and community welfare groups released a flurry of studies and reports in the mid-1960s that drew attention to the problems and solutions that the feminization of poverty demanded. The ramifications of increased poverty, after all, were being absorbed by those underfunded local agencies. Along with other "home helps" and job-training services, publicly funded day care was frequently included on the list of services that could help families "to help themselves" in gaining self-sufficiency and escaping poverty.[46]

There is little evidence that national officials imagined day care as one of the *CAP*'s priorities, although the *CAP* did mark the first time that federal contributions were used to support single mothers.[47] However, this pressure from local agencies had an impact on *CAP* negotiations with the BC welfare bureaucracy. The preventive benefits of day care outlined by the Community Chest and others fit nicely into the government's plan to use *CAP* funds to alleviate "social crisis" in low-income families. Besides providing mothers with peace of mind that allowed them to earn wages towards their family's financial independence, day care also allowed for early intervention into the social problems that resulted from poverty. "As day care is extended," a report from the Department of Social Welfare explained, "particularly to children whose homes provide limited opportunities, it is foreseen that fewer children will encounter major problems in adjustment to school and in their homes and communities."[48]

In the fall of 1966, the provincial government announced that *CAP* funding would be used to provide day care subsidies in British Columbia. Since they were funded by the *CAP*, like other means-tested income supports, the subsidy program had to be designed to meet the cost-sharing requirements of the federal government.[49] Subsidies, as a result, were available only to the "neediest" of mothers. *CAP* funding was not used to establish or support child care centres but only to subsidize the day care spaces occupied by the children of social assistance recipients and only for those children who attended licensed and approved non-profit "public" day care centres. Furthermore, *CAP* provisions left mothers with infants and toddlers with very few options, since the WILB regulations did not allow for the licensing of day care centres for children under three – an issue that would become the source of considerable grievances in the coming years. These narrow constraints were loosened somewhat in 1968 when the government extended subsidy coverage to include any low-income family who demonstrated need and to any licensed day care centre or home, public or private.

Subsidy levels were on a sliding scale set by the Department of Social Welfare and determined by an evaluation of the family's residual income. Social assistance recipients were entitled to $3 per day per child to attend a child care centre or $2.50 per day for an under-three child to attend a day home. Families who were deemed to have less than $10 per month to spend on child care also qualified for this "Plan C" funding. "Plan B" families, those with $11 to $25 of residual monthly income to put towards child care, were eligible for $2 per child per day for centre-based care and $1.50 for home-based care. In addition, as of 1 January 1969, a $1 per day per child universal subsidy was available to non-profit day care centres who met several conditions, among them that they reserved at least 10 percent of their enrolment for Plan C families, submitted their audited financial statements to the province, and charged a sliding scale fee to all parents except those on Plan C.[50]

One major problem with this new provincial program was that licensed, subsidy-eligible day care spaces were in short supply. Without financial support, social agencies and community groups had a hard time establishing and maintaining day care centres that could meet WILB licensing standards. In January 1967, only nine day care centres were licensed and approved for subsidy payments: four in Vancouver, two in North Vancouver, and one each in Richmond, Surrey, and Terrace, for a total of only 331 subsidy-eligible child care spaces in the province. Considering that the Community Chest had identified 6,000 children in Vancouver alone who were in desperate need of day care, the province's initial efforts hardly made a dent, even with the promise to fast-track the approval of centres in Prince Rupert, Victoria, and Alert Bay.[51] The onus to increase the number of licensed child care spaces, however, was still entirely on local agencies, community organizations, and parent groups. The province also relied heavily on local and municipal officials to administer the new provincial program. In both Vancouver and Victoria, local "administering agencies" oversaw subsidy authorizations and payments and supervised the billings for family day homes.

For their part, provincial officials were happy to pass much of the responsibility for the growth of day care on to organizations familiar with child care undertakings: the Vancouver CAS, the Community Chest (which became the United Community Services or UCS), the City of Vancouver's welfare department, and, in Victoria, the Family and Children's Service (FCS), which was a Community Chest agency.[52] These agencies, usually in conjunction with other charitable organizations, began to ramp up their efforts around day care initiatives in the aftermath of the *CAP* announcement. In Victoria, the city's first group day care explicitly designed for the needs of working mothers opened in January 1967 in the basement of the Centennial United Church, with the support of the FCS, the Lion's Club, and the Community Welfare Council as well as church members. Although the church had been the site of a playschool for some time, the day care centre was the community's attempt to provide "a home away from home for the children of mothers who have to work to make a living ... The children are fed hot meals at lunch time, take afternoon naps and are provided with the affection and attention they require."[53] Similar projects followed at St. Paul's Anglican Church in Victoria West and in Saanich.[54] (Churches were popular sites for day cares not only because their kitchen and bathroom facilities easily met WILB regulations but also because of the traditional association of churches with social welfare.[55])

In all of these locations, there was an explicit recognition that these day care centres differed in form and function from playschools and kindergartens. Their purpose was not "educational" but, instead, care oriented while mothers "earned their cheques."[56] Not surprisingly, these centres also generated familiar criticism and debate. Controversy about a day care in Saanich, for example, gave one municipal councillor a platform to argue that women were simply "working to boost family incomes into the $8,000-a-year class" so that they could afford "two cars and a big stereo set. The impact of the mass media is forcing them to work, requiring the children to be left somewhere."[57] In their defence of working mothers, FCS officials such as Victoria's Jane Gurr insisted that mothers who used day care were "forced" to work and that it was up to generous community organizations to "find a way to assist them to fulfill their duties both at home and in the labor [sic] field."[58]

In Vancouver, the UCS took the lead in the creation of new day care spaces, drawing on its long heritage of administering such services, which included the Strathcona Nursery School. Under the guidance of the UCS, the number of licensed day care centres began to increase in Vancouver, as they did around the province. Reports from 1967 identified twenty-one subsidy-eligible day care centres in the province. The number increased to twenty-seven in 1968. The government declared that centres (as well as licensed family homes) were developing "in gratifying numbers," and it pointed to the "steady and significant growth" in all types of day care in 1967 and 1968, the first years that they began collecting statistics on such institutions.[59] Though the number of child care spaces was still far short of the demand, the UCS suggested that day care activity throughout the province was "moderately encouraging," and they remained hopeful that numbers would continue to rise.[60] Their optimism was fuelled when E.R. Rickinson and J.A. Sadler, the deputy minister and assistant deputy minister of social welfare, respectively (and thus the civil service leads on day care), asked the UCS to establish an Advisory Committee on Day Care. Since the UCS had staked out its position as a day care authority with the release of the *Report on Day Care Needs*, and because it was also involved with preschool enrichment projects, Rickinson and Sadler trusted it to provide expertise and leadership for the fledgling provincial program.[61] The advisory committee was tasked with "stimulat[ing] interest in day care . . . coordinat[ing] the efforts of those involved in providing services . . . review[ing] and evaluat[ing] the overall program" and making recommendations regarding financing.[62] Representatives from day care centres, social agencies including the Catholic CAS, the Family Services Agency and neighbourhood houses, the city's Department of Social Welfare, the WILB, and child welfare organizations joined UCS officials on the twenty-four member committee.[63] Throughout the late 1960s, this group of representatives was the hub of child care policy and practice, and it had significant access to provincial officials in charge of day care administration.[64] The limits of their influence, however, would soon be revealed.

Unmet Expectations: The Case of Marpole Day Care Centre

One of the advisory committee's first undertakings was the development of a Plan for Public-Private Partnership for Day Care (PPP Plan), which was intended to increase the number of child care spaces in the province as well as ease the transition from entirely private day care to the involvement of provincial authorities.[65] The PPP Plan essentially set the agenda for the issues that needed to be addressed: subsidy levels, grants to non-profit groups, and the organization of family day homes. The plan also secured a central role for the advisory committee in the negotiations around these issues. Beginning in early 1967, the committee began meeting every two to three months to assess the state of day care in the province and to provide advice to a range of organizations on improving the quality and quantity of care.

Besides this ongoing consultative role, the advisory committee's most tangible contribution to day care policy and program development was the establishment of the Marpole Day Care Centre, a "demonstration project" to test the new provincial policy. The committee felt that it could oversee the operation of a centre that would act as a model for other groups and that such efforts could be used to work out the kinks in the subsidy schemes. In early 1967, they identified a fledgling day care centre in the Marpole area of Vancouver as an ideal test case because it was located in "an average low to middle class community with a large number of single parent families in need of Day Care."[66] The Marpole Area Council had already secured licensing for the St. Augustine's Church Hall, but resources were scarce and the centre was struggling to get off the ground.

An impressive array of day care practitioners and policy-makers converged on the Marpole project. The five-member Marpole Day Care Committee, led by Dorothy Behesti, took the lead, guided and supported closely by the advisory committee. Other UCS representatives also regularly attended the Marpole meetings, as did several from Vancouver's Family Services Agencies. The provincial welfare department also kept a careful eye on how things unfolded; Behesti was required to send regular updates to Dan Campbell, the minister of welfare. Together, these committees and agencies developed a projected budget for the Marpole centre's operation. The total capital costs needed to do the minor adjustments to the church required by the licensing regulations was $1,600, which had already been secured through private donations. To keep food costs as low as possible, families were required to provide lunches and snacks, although the centre would supplement the noon meal with hot soup. The largest portion of the budget was dedicated to staffing costs. A supervisor earned a monthly salary of $350, and with assistants, support staff, and janitors, personnel expenses totalled $850 per month. Taking into consideration all operating costs (less a small monthly donation from the St. Augustine's Church), the committee expected that the minimum monthly operating budget would total $1,100. Based on a twenty-two-day work month, with an average of

85 percent occupancy, the Marpole Day Care Centre would have to charge $3.85 per day per child in order to break even.[67]

With the majority of families eligible for the $1 daily provincial subsidy, the Marpole committee determined that parents' fees needed to be set at $2.85 in order for the centre to remain in the black. Many on the committee felt, however, that this amount was much too high for most parents in the Marpole neighbourhood. Furthermore, the committee was under pressure from the church to limit day care services to those families in "genuine need," and $2.85 was well out of the affordability range for the low-income families and social assistance recipients that the church wanted to serve. Ideally, the committee argued, they should be able to establish a fee structure based on each family's "ability to pay." Based on their analysis of the area's employment and income statistics from the BC Federation of Labour, the average daily fee that families could afford – an amount they decided was between 7.5 and 10 percent of a woman's net income – was $1.50 per child. Even with the subsidy, though, and assuming an occupancy rate of at least 85 percent, this rate would leave the centre with a monthly operating deficit of almost $400. This gap between costs and revenues in the Marpole figures hinted at the financial difficulties that would threaten the success of this test case.

Despite these early concerns, the Marpole Day Care Centre opened in June 1967. After only a few months, budgetary problems revealed themselves. The advisory committee reported to the provincial government that it was "evident that the income generated through the provincial subsidy and parent fees is inadequate."[68] The centre did not immediately run at full capacity, and since subsidies were paid based on daily attendance and not on monthly registration, the expected income from the province was not available. For the same reasons, neither was income from parent fees. Despite staying on (or even slightly under) budget for staffing and program expenses, Marpole had amassed a substantial deficit by the fall of 1967.[69]

Since these financial troubles were not particularly surprising, the committee moved quickly to make recommendations for making the centre more sustainable. Marpole's failure or success, after all, had implications for other day care centres and, indeed, for the entire provincial day care subsidy program. The committee was keenly aware that if Marpole, with its access to experienced welfare practitioners and government and community consultants, could not remain operational, other day care centres were surely doomed. Committee members also recognized that Marpole was under the microscope by those who remained ideologically opposed to the very idea of public involvement in day care. In making suggestions for reform, committee members emphasized that Marpole's shortfalls were not, as some suggested, due to "uninterested citizens" or "lack of demand" – it was simply that parent fees and subsidies did not generate enough income to keep the centre afloat. They put forward a simple solution: provincial funding that was more responsive to the actual requirements of operating a day care centre. Foremost among them were staffing costs. The committee called for 100 percent government funding to cover the salaries of teachers, teachers' assistants, and day care directors. Alternatively, they recommended public coverage of 90 percent of the teaching and administrative costs, combined with subsidies for "auxiliary services" such as food preparation and janitorial services. The committee acknowledged, however, that the likelihood the government would cover staffing to that extent was low, and so it urged, at the very least, for an increase in the per-child subsidy to meet the budgeted difference between total operating costs and revenue from fees.[70] Anything less would undermine the efforts of Marpole's staff as well as those of the growing number of day care providers throughout the city.

The experiences of other day care centres in Vancouver and around the province were indeed bearing out the committee's concerns in the late 1960s. At least fifteen to twenty Vancouver groups had inquired about setting up licensed centres, and although the spaces were solely needed the advisory committee urged caution. Without a significant revision to its funding schemes, any new centre would surely collapse under financial pressure. "With Marpole in mind," the committee declared, "we cannot, in all conscience, encourage them to open."[71] Gladys Maycock, the WILB's day care representative, voiced similar concerns, based on her busy schedule of visiting and inspecting new centres throughout the summer and fall of 1967. In Maycock's view, most centres' problems usually boiled down to financial practicalities. The centres that provided the highest-quality care, she informed her supervisors, were for-profit centres that did not qualify for subsidized spaces and thus remained inaccessible to those who most needed their services.[72] Other centres faced similar problems as Marpole. Victoria's Centennial Day Care Centre, for example, the first in the capital city to be part of the PPP Plan, operated below capacity and was thus running a deficit.[73] Even those with high attendance rates faced shortfalls that seemed impossible to make up. Deryck Thomson, the executive director of Family Services of Greater Vancouver, explained to senior provincial officials that their centres had budgeted responsibly and spent carefully but that they would be unable to continue without funding commitments from the provincial government. Fees and subsidies in several of their centres were maximized, he assured the province, but the "present subsidy levels are inadequate to close the gap between the cost of the service and parent fees." Thomson also responded to accusations that these centres were catering to parents who simply wanted to access cheap day care to increase their already high incomes. In "every instance," he argued, "it has been properly determined that the child in question needs day care. In every instance, the parents or parent are expected to pay what they can afford based upon an assessment of family income at the point of intake."[74] Thomson thus joined the growing chorus of day care advocates who insisted that it was not mismanagement or freeloading parents who undermined the success of day care programs but, rather, insufficient funding from the provincial government.

Besides budgetary concerns, other problems plagued start-up centres in the city. Some day cares had trouble obtaining a licence. The Riley Park Community Association in Vancouver, for example, was told that "parks are no place for day care centres."[75] Others faced opposition from the community, seemingly based on a "not in my backyard" mentality that reflected the ongoing stigma around day care and the undesirable families who used them. At Fraserview United Church in East Vancouver, a group of neighbours organized to oppose the granting of a day care licence. Although a kindergarten with an attendance of thirty-five children already operated in the church, these neighbours argued that the increased activity around the day care would infringe on their right for "peace and quiet." "People are always saying hello and goodbye and slamming car doors," one neighbour complained, and the new day care would mean noise "from day to night." The thirty neighbours who came out in support of the day care as a "badly needed service" for working mothers received less attention in the press, but their views prevailed and Fraserview was granted a temporary licence.[76]

This accumulation of problems led the UCS to declare by the fall of 1967 that the day care situation in the province had devolved from "moderately encouraging" to "urgent and explosive."[77] Although each centre had its own unique challenges, Marpole was the fulcrum of the debate about the provincial government's role in, and responsibility towards, day care centres. Provincial officials were eager to pin Marpole's troubles on something other than their own inadequate financial commitments, and they sent Maycock to investigate. Maycock found much fault with Marpole's operations. She noted "out of control" children and undertrained staff and voiced suspicions that the centre was undercharging parents, especially middle-class parents who could afford more than the standard fee. It was perfectly reasonable, Maycock argued, to expect those parents – here she singled out "two women doctors" whose children were in day care – to pay the full amount of what it actually cost to keep a child in day care for one week, an amount she estimated at $80-$100 rather than the $12.50 maximum that the centre charged. She accused the UCS Advisory Committee on Day Care of sacrificing good care and responsible financial management in favour of "the getting of more funds." The only thing "urgent and explosive" about the Marpole situation, Maycock concluded, was their lack of skill in "public relations."[78]

At an 8 December 1967 meeting that illustrated the degree to which the relationship between the advisory committee and the province had deteriorated, the committee defended itself against Maycock's allegations. There were no doctors' children at Marpole, committee member Emily Campbell declared, and Maycock's unrealistic expectations about staff-children ratios would mean leaning heavily on volunteer labour. Since the UCS kept statistics about Marpole's client base and the provincial government did not, Campbell was able to demonstrate that the centre was serving only families whom the provincial government would surely consider "deserving," among them three single mothers who earned $200-$380 per month, children who had been recommended by psychiatrists because of "extra stresses within the family group," and several two-parent families with low incomes ranging from $381-$650 monthly.[79] The average parent fee on the sliding scale hovered around $10 per week per child.[80] These quarrels over Marpole's account books had important implications. The committee declared that without "major revision in the subsidy arrangements," closure was inevitable.[81] Since it was the resource- and expertise-rich demonstration project, Marpole's shutdown would reflect a broader failure of the provincial government's first experiment in day care policy.

A small increase in government funding in April 1968 did little to quell Marpole Day Care Centre's troubles.[82] Instead, the disputes evolved into a much wider-ranging political battle about day care. The inadequacies of the provincial program gained increasing press attention, with newspapers reporting that among the "most urgent" welfare needs was the "creation of child day-care centres – government-operated institutions providing supervision at a uniformly high level, freeing young mothers to find jobs."[83] The backroom meetings between welfare bureaucrats and UCS committee members became public confrontations between politicians, with Norm

Levi, the New Democratic Party member of the legislative assembly (Vancouver South), taking the role of day care defender and supporter of the UCS and the Marpole Area Council. Levi accused Dan Campbell, minister of welfare, of being "indifferen[t] to day care needs" and suggested the provincial government's unwillingness to reform subsidies would mean "the inevitable extinction of all day care."[84] For his part, Minister Campbell remained unsympathetic to Marpole's plight and insisted that they had brought financial misfortune upon themselves. Self-interest and financial mismanagement, Campbell argued, were at the root of Marpole's troubles. "I must point out to you," he wrote to the advisory committee, "that out of the twenty day care centres which have been approved for subsidy since this program was initiated . . . Marpole is the only one reporting severe deficits and continuing inability to operate with the present subsidies."[85]

Pleas for help from other day care centres throughout the province suggested that Campbell may have been misinformed. In Victoria, the Centennial Day Care Centre reported a budget shortfall of more than $10,000 in 1967. While its staffing, programming, and facility costs totalled $15,785, the revenue generated from parent fees and subsidies did not reach $6,000.[86] The financial troubles at Chatham Day Care in Prince Rupert demonstrated the flaws in the subsidy system even more clearly. Families from all three subsidy plans attended Chatham, but the "Schedule B" families – those of "sub-marginal income" who were eligible for a $2 daily subsidy – were the most worrisome. Subsidies were not nearly enough to supplement the parent fees, which were set quite low according to the parents' ability to pay. In the absence of an increase to Schedule B subsidies, the committee declared, their only other option was to increase parent fees, which would result in an outcome desirable to no one (least of all the government) – parents "will stop being self-supporting and take Welfare."

The Chatham committee also asked, as did other centres, to receive subsidy payments based on a monthly, rather than a daily, attendance record, which would provide a more consistent revenue flow.[87] In Vancouver, the Strathcona day care committee (which operated the Strathcona Nursery School) also drew attention to their inability to provide effective services:

> Current provincial subsidies do help programs if the maximum fee is charged, but only if the better-off families can afford such fees. New centres trying to offer service to everyone regardless of income have been unable to establish such programs with the current subsidies.[88]

The available dimensions of government support, the Strathcona council argued, had a limited impact that did not extend to those who most needed it.

Facing pressure from all sides, and especially from Levi, Minister Campbell announced in March 1968 that the government would undertake a review of subsidy levels.[89] This announcement, however, seemed a half-hearted attempt to appease some of the controversy. For the most part, Campbell remained unsympathetic to the plight of day care centres and keen to shift the blame away from the government. He continued to accuse the UCS of failing to operate in good faith to ensure the success of the Marpole project. He suggested, for example, that they withdraw voluntary funds, thereby deliberately increasing the expectation for public funding.[90] According to Minister Campbell, the private sector, not the public sector, was failing in its responsibilities towards working mothers and their children.

"What, then, is day care?"

At the very least, the announcement of a provincial review gave the Advisory Committee on Day Care yet another opportunity to outline their position on day care. Their July 1968 report, however, read more like an ultimatum than a series of recommendations: if the government was unwilling to improve the quality of day care services, the committee would resign. As Emily Campbell explained, the members of the committee felt like they had been working in vain. They had met regularly for two years to discuss problems and solutions, they had "talked to groups, prepared briefs, raised money," and they attempted to provide constructive solutions while absorbing much of the "discontent and frustration" with day care policy. Despite the committee's efforts, however, day care in the greater Vancouver area (and elsewhere) remained "in a state of confusion." The government had not established an "overall plan for starting new centres" or any "clear policy on subsidies."[91] The relative failure of day care services, the committee argued, could be boiled down to a lack of administrative direction and leadership. The appointment of a single bureaucrat to oversee the entire provincial day care program, equipped with the "training, authority, and staff to do the job," would go a long way towards putting the province on the right track.[92] So too would a complete overhaul of the subsidy system, including enrollment-based payments, subsidization of staff salaries, and increased payments to centres and homes.[93]

Through a series of meetings in the late summer, the government paid lip service to the advisory committee's demands. Rickinson admitted that the attendance-based subsidy had been "a complete failure as a method of financing," and the government tentatively committed to hiring a day care director for the Vancouver area. There were also some indications that Rickinson would consider providing "conditional grants" to start-up centres.[94] When no concrete action was forthcoming by October, however, the advisory committee submitted its resignation to the UCS Board of Directors. As one committee member explained, the resignation was an act of protest designed to draw attention to the "appalling confusion" in provincial day care policy: "Dan Campbell doesn't buy day care. He has just dug his heels in ... We are alarmed that the government is doing nothing to increase the budget for day care needs."[95]

For his part, Minister Campbell maintained indifference towards the fate of the UCS Advisory Committee on Day Care. "If the day care advisory committee ... feels inclined to resign," he declared, "that is their responsibility." Campbell continued to insist that the blame for day care failures lay not with the provincial government but, rather, with the centres that failed to "practice budgetary constraint."[96] When Campbell announced a series of reforms in November 1968, including subsidy extensions to private centres and to more low-income families, he suggested that they were necessary in part to clean up the mess created by the UCS and other mismanaged centres. He agreed, for example, to cover Marpole's 1968 deficit, which had reached almost $9,000 by the end of the year.[97] These reforms were, as Campbell suggested, an "enlargement" of the provincial day care program in that they included broader subsidy coverage, but he was also quick to remind everyone that subsidies were still confined to those who were "economically disadvantaged ... Those who can afford to pay the full fee [will] be expected to do so."[98]

In many ways, the back-and-forth debate during the summer and fall of 1968 represents the beginning of British Columbia's version of what Mahon has called the "never-ending story" of day care struggles.[99] Each side in the battle about day care funding and policy had become entrenched. While the provincial government deflected responsibility for day care beyond the targeted subsidies, advocates and providers became deeply dissatisfied and frustrated with the government's unwillingness to take meaningful policy action. Day care providers, community groups, and local agencies such as the UCS and the advisory committee (whose resignation had not been accepted by the UCS board) argued that the government's piecemeal reforms did not address any fundamental flaws in the system. The lack of start-up funding hindered the creation of new day care spaces, and the extension of subsidies was accompanied by a new means test that was "offensive to the dignity of parents" as well as a "regression to past methods" of welfare policy.[100] Furthermore, as Emily Campbell pointed out, the failure of the province to provide day care spaces was bad economic policy. One day care space cost somewhere between $75 and $122 per child per month, while the costs of care for a child in the custody of the welfare department could run close to $800 monthly. Providing day care was "vastly less expensive than the cost of rebuilding lives after not providing the services," Campbell argued.[101]

By the end of the decade, it was clear that the most prominent theme in the "never-ending story," even more than haggling over funding, was a philosophical difference over the meaning and purpose of publicly funded child care in BC society. Was day care meant to be an anti-poverty measure only for poor mothers? Or should it be a service to which all women should have access should they so choose? The Business and Professional Women's Club of British Columbia was one organization that released a report making a case for the latter. Certainly, they argued, day care services were important for "encourag[ing] husbandless mothers to become self-supporting," thereby reducing mothers' claims on social assistance and lowering taxes overall. Children would also benefit from safe, healthy, and supportive care. But publicly funded day care services, the club insisted, had become something much more than a service for disadvantaged mothers and children:

> Since becoming enfranchised, women have advanced rapidly and progressively into equal rights with men for jobs and remuneration if they are qualified. Women take great pride in the security of being able to earn their own living or in supporting their dependents.
>
> It is a fact that never again can we keep all women at home. We cannot take away the privilege of working outside the home from women anymore than we can take back their franchise, nor anymore than we can take back unions from working people or social assistance from the needy.[102]

The advisory committee, the broader UCS, and their supporters made similar arguments, although they did not go so far as to suggest that day care be universally available. "Certainly, the parent who can afford to do so should pay up to the full cost of the service," the committee said, but they insisted that the existing subsidy program excluded thousands of deserving children and parents. Extreme poverty was not the only reason why a family sought access to day care; "employment, study, health, or the particular need of the child himself" were also valid situations in which a subsidy should be granted.[103]

Minister Dan Campbell, Sadler, and Rickinson remained unswayed by these campaigns, holding fast to their position that day care was a welfare program for poor families. Campbell, for one, took "great exception" to the advisory committee's insistence that all children should have access to day care, regardless of family income:

> This was not the original intention of government support of day care centres. The Committee was advised that the policy of government was to support day care centres which were provided for children of social allowance families and marginal income groups where mothers were being rehabilitated, either through part-time employment or taking training fitting them for employment.[104]

There was no room in Campbell's vision of day care services for mothers who considered it their right to choose to work outside the home.

This ideological impasse was highlighted once again at a day care symposium hosted by the University Women's Club at the University of British Columbia in March 1969. Criticism of the particular failures of government policy was a central theme of the symposium, but so too was the question of the purpose of day care in a modern society. Panellists included representatives from the government, from the community of day care operators, and from interested citizens. Victor Belknap, the superintendent of neglected children, spoke on behalf of the provincial government, and his exchanges with Behesti (of the advisory committee) and Deryck Thomson (of Family Service Centres), in particular, highlighted the unbridgeable gap between what working families wanted and needed and what the government was willing to provide.[105] Although Belknap was targeted, as elsewhere repeatedly by frustrated child care advocates, he stood firm in relating the priorities of the provincial government with respect to the provision of day care. First, he said, the government was responsible to protect the safety of children in day care centres and homes through the standards and regulations of the WILB. The second priority was to serve families on social assistance and, third, to "recognize the role of prevention of social problems which operates intrinsically in good Day Care operations." When asked, Belknap stated explicitly that the provincial government considered that day care "would continue for some time to be a residual program," housed in the newly renamed Department of Rehabilitation and Social Improvement, a title that Premier Bennett considered better reflected the government's approach to social programs.[106]

The symposium's keynote speaker, Barbara Chisholm, the executive director of Victoria Day Care Services in Toronto, brought the alternative reading of the day to the table. Day care was not just a rehabilitative service, Chisholm argued, but was crucial to the development of a healthy citizenry and the rights of all family members, especially mothers. She pointed out the "double standard" to which working mothers were held: "On one hand, society looks at the mother on welfare and says she shouldn't be a public drag; on the other hand, if she is working, it says she should be home taking care of her children."[107]

Provincial policy, Chisholm suggested, was built around the "myths" of motherhood, of which there were several. The most damaging was that all women were instinctually programmed to be good mothers and that separation equalled deprivation. As Chisholm pointed out, mothers were held to impossible standards of "the virtue of self-reliance and independence," with no acknowledgement of the reality for most working mothers. High-quality, affordable day care was "a must," she concluded, and not just because children and social welfare recipients deserved it but, rather, because working mothers were entitled to a service that recognized and supported their right to earn an income. Other panellists drew attention to related implications, including the dismal wages of day care workers and the attitudes of men and fathers towards day care.[108]

As these political debates played out in Vancouver and Victoria, groups around the province continued to struggle with the practical challenges of keeping a day care centre running. In Port Edward, the Women's Auxiliary of the United Fishermen and Allied Workers' Union requested provincial funding for the child care centre for the mothers working in Nelson Brothers Fisheries, since they expected a budget shortfall of $2,300.[109] Similar appeals came from community groups in towns from Quesnel to Courtenay.[110] The government's responses ranged from promising to look into the matter, to tentative offers to raise subsidy levels on a per-case basis, to an outright denial of responsibility. In Port Edward, Sadler suggested that Nelson Brothers was "basically responsible for the day care need" since the company was the one that most needed the mothers' labour.[111]

As the 1960s drew to a close, British Columbia's day care scene was one of frustration and dissatisfaction. Although the number of day care centres had increased in number – as of October 1969, there were forty-eight licensed day care centres in British Columbia for three to five year olds, representing 1,306 spaces – their operation remained "chaotic" and their "finances uncertain."[112] The supply of licensed spaces did not come close to the demand, resulting in a number of "bootleg" day care centres and family homes operating without licenses, whose health and safety standards were beyond regulatory control.[113] There was still no provision in the *Welfare Institutions Licensing Act* to allow centre-based care for children under the age of three.[114] Subsidies remained inadequate, despite small tweaks to the amounts and means test in 1969.[115] Even Maycock, the WILB official responsible for day care, characterized the day care situation as "from the sublime to the ridiculous."[116] As the turn of the decade approached, the state of day care affairs inspired renewed efforts to take stock of the relative failures of initial day care programming and to make sense of what was needed.

Well into the 1960s, calls for enhanced day care services in British Columbia were countered with threats about the destruction of "family life due to women ... going back to work."[117] Policy-makers may have recognized the presence of mothers in the 1960s labour force, but this recognition did not necessarily translate into wholesale acceptance. Despite statistics that were beginning to suggest otherwise, working motherhood was still not considered a "normal" part of middle-class family life. Neither was working mothers' need for day care. Instead, the province's first venture into day care subsidization was imprinted with an ideological adherence to the gendered division of labour in the work and the home as well as the long-standing view that working motherhood indicated a family in crisis needing state support to get back to "normal."

The absence of labour voices in 1960s day care debates is revealing. This was true at the level of policy-making; the provincial Department of Labour was virtually silent on day care throughout the 1960s. However, it was also true among organized labour. The BC Federation of Labour, for example, would not weigh in on the issue of working mothers' access to day care until 1973.[118] British Columbia was not unique in this respect. Joan Sangster points out that in the 1950s and 1960s labour activists across the country largely "accepted the gendered division of labour as natural and inevitable" and, thus, when they supported working women's rights, did so in a way that "endorsed a shared vision of women as temporary, secondary, and decorative workers."[119] The notion of worker-citizenship – and, crucially, the social benefits that derived from worker-citizenship – remained out of reach for working mothers. At the same time, the assumption that women held primary responsibility for child care followed them into the labour force. Using their influence to call for state provision of child care, which also smacked of communism, was not on the agenda for organized labour before the late 1960s.[120]

Instead, day care was left to welfare bureaucrats. Subsidies were offered to mothers who were obligated to work because of economic need or family breakdown, mothers whose wage earning indicated a commitment to preventing long-term dependency on social assistance. The first efforts at government-sponsored day care reinforced deeply held patterns of welfarist intervention in the lives of mothers. As the BC women's movement grew in strength, however, women's rights activists offered an alternative vision for provincial day care policy, one premised upon a version of social citizenship for working mothers on par with that of male breadwinners.

5

"Talkin' Day Care Blues": Feminist Child Care Battles in the 1960s and 1970s

It's February 1st 1973
We're all here in Vancouver BC
There's a bunch of women all sittin' here
Trying to make the situation clear
About – daycare – 'cause there ain't no daycare
There's money been promised for you and me
But there ain't no money for the under threes
My kids are fine and they ain't no bore
And they can't help it if they're under three
They're 2½ and 1⅓ and its [sic] about time their voice was heard
About daycare – 'cause there ain't no day care
You see on August 30th '72
The people of BC – that's me and you
We all went down to the polling stations
And we didn't give the Socreds congratulations
We voted them out. And we voted in
The Socialist hoards by a wide margin –
That's the NDP for you and me
But there's a lot of folks can't pay the fee
For daycare – and there ain't no daycare . . .

Opening verses of "Talkin' Day Care Blues," written by the Child Care Occupation Forces during the February 1973 sit-in at the day care information office in Vancouver. Source: Simon Fraser University Archives, Doc. F-111-7-1-23, *Childcare/Daycare, 1973-81.*

Perhaps more than any other time during the twentieth century, the early 1970s marked a moment when the potential existed to radically transform the meaning of public responsibility for child care. Challenges to the welfare orientation of day care, so firmly established in the 1960s, emerged from the so-called second-wave feminist movement that swept across British Columbia and the rest of Canada. Working both separately and in alliance with each other, feminist and welfare rights groups and individuals insisted that public day care was necessary for the restructuring of work and caregiving that would erase women's inequality in the home and the labour force. Activists and advocates called for the inclusion of a universal day care program as part of a fully realized version of social citizenship for working mothers.

The feminist-inspired battles of the late 1960s and early 1970s signalled important shifts in the politics of work, motherhood, and social policy in twentieth-century British Columbia. These shifts were certainly not cut and dried nor were they borne out of wholesale consensus from within the women's movement. The meanings and values assigned to mothers' wage work and their caregiving work, and the ways in which those activities should be supported by the state, were matters of impassioned debate among the various women who identified as feminist in the 1970s, just as they had been for at least the six decades prior. But while maternalist campaigns for social policy still existed – the Wages for Housework movement was one example of this – they were, to a large extent, sidelined in the 1960s and 1970s relative to the central focus, in both policy and activism, on women's rights as workers. The "concept of worker-citizenship had taken root" in the post-war Canadian welfare state, as Annis May Timpson explains, and the challenge was how to fit women into that category.[1] Debates about how to secure women's independence, equality, and social rights, therefore, were understood as being inseparable from their wage earning. A high-quality, accessible, affordable child care program was one solution among many that feminists put forward as strategies to secure working mothers' rights, especially for single, low-income, and social assistance mothers but including all mothers who needed and wanted to work.[2]

Child care, and the state's responsibility to provide it, was an issue woven throughout the many layers and versions of feminism, many of them differentiated by class, that comprised the "second-wave" movement in Vancouver – a period that Joan Sangster suggests is perhaps better described as an "upsurge in [the] current" of twentieth-century feminism.[3] Feminist organizers on Simon Fraser University's (SFU) "radical campus" offered a highly visible challenge to prevailing attitudes towards day care in British

Columbia.[4] Their child care co-operative drew attention not only to the shortage of day care spaces for working and student mothers but also to the capitalist, patriarchal social order that impeded gender equality in the family and the workplace. As campus feminists began to move "down the hill" into Vancouver, their efforts overlapped with the welfare rights activists who had long been engaged in their own battles with welfare officials about the inadequacy of provincial day care subsidies. This overlap between New Left feminism and welfare rights was the source of much of the early 1970s child care movement's energy, strength, and optimism. The movement's high point came in 1973 with the occupation of the government's day care offices, which gave rise to the protest song that opens this chapter. Along the way, liberal feminist organizations and labour groups declared their support for a universal day care program that would ensure women's equality with men in the public sphere.

In the United States, Deborah Dinner argues, campaigns for rights-based child care in the 1960s and 1970s led diverse groups of feminists to identify "shared policy interests" and to form coalitions. "Different activists," Dinner suggests,

> emphasized childcare's potential to facilitate middle-class women's entry into the workforce, liberate women from the oppression of the patriarchal family, enable welfare recipients' economic autonomy, free children from constraints of social convention, and empower minority communities.[5]

The story was much the same in British Columbia. In summary, the early 1970s represented a period of remarkable feminist-led consensus about the need for more government support for high-quality day care and for the involvement of mothers and parents in program development. Their successes were limited. Activists of all stripes consistently ran up against politicians and bureaucrats firmly opposed to spending money on programs they considered "social experiments or frills."[6] However, thanks to their efforts, the multiple dimensions of child care, and the multiple reasons "why we need" day care, as the Vancouver Status of Women's newspaper put it, had earned a permanent place on the provincial political agenda.[7] For some of these groups, like the SFU socialist feminists, public and collective responsibility for child care supported the broader goal of ungendering caregiving and work, thus liberating women to pursue and achieve a fully realized citizenship. For others, like the welfare rights feminists in More Opportunities for Mothers (MOMs), day care was needed simply to give struggling single mothers the freedom to work towards economic independence. For mainstream groups, worker-citizenship for women was the goal. Together, however, these grassroots efforts had the common goal of pulling day care out of its welfarist orientation. Together, these groups challenged the limited version of social citizenship that linked day care to poor women's obligation to work and made day care an issue central to the recognition of women's social rights.

National Context

British Columbia's day care battles in the late 1960s and early 1970s were very much part of a national story. Child care, along with issues of reproductive rights, education, and the varieties of legal and political gender discrimination, became part of women's rights agendas across the country thanks largely to the Royal Commission on the Status of Women (RCSW), which was appointed by Liberal Prime Minister Lester Pearson in 1967. The seven commissioners, led by Florence Bird, were asked to "inquire into and report upon the status of women in Canada, and to recommend what steps may be taken by the Federal Government to ensure for women equal opportunities with men in all aspects of Canadian society."[8] Pearson's instructions reflected a preoccupation with women in the paid labour force and particularly married women, not least because while their numbers were growing, married women were also "clustered in low status clerical, sales and secretarial positions and, as a result, earned significantly less than men." The federal government recognized how important female workers had become to the national economy, and officials were also under pressure from human rights movements to eliminate workplace discrimination.[9]

For six months, commissioners travelled to hear testimony from women's organizations and individuals and collected about 1,000 individual submissions. In every corner of the country, women's hearings and briefs revealed

> [the] fissures, contradictions, and stress points they sensed between constructions of women's economic needs and their actual material predicament, between idealized stay-at-home domesticity and the reality that more women were going out to work, between the expectations placed on "good" mothers and the constraints of the double day.[10]

Women's views on working motherhood and child care, in other words, varied widely. Timpson has analyzed the range of opinions and policy recommendations contained within the RCSW submissions. For a significant number of respondents, Timpson found, women's equality depended on the public provision of "non-maternal" child care, with policy solutions that ranged from tax relief for working mothers' child care costs, to the creation of more day care spaces, to the establishment of a national day care program.[11] Alternatively, Timpson also identified a number of submissions that resisted this liberal feminist interpretation of equality and worried about the "devaluation of motherhood" that public child care represented. These submissions, Timpson observes, "called on Commissioners to recognize women's caring work in the home" through provisions for part-time employment and generous family allowances.[12]

In their report, which was released in 1970, the commissioners incorporated as much as possible the principle that "women should be free to choose whether or not to take employment outside their homes" and made recommendations, including a new system of tax credits, that would make it easier for mothers to remain home to care for their children.[13] However, to a much greater extent, a public system of child care was their focus. What was needed, the commissioners said, was a national day care act to replace the "inappropriate," welfare-oriented *Canada Assistance Plan (CAP)* provisions.[14] "For the federal government to fail to proceed with a specific child-care programme, removed from welfare legislation of a more general nature," the commissioners said, "would be to deny the claim which Canadian women have made for concrete assistance in the burden of responsibility which they have been compelled to carry."[15] The crucial message of the 1970 RCSW report, Timpson argues, was that it "legitimiz[ed] women's right to worker-citizenship."[16] Moreover, commissioners acknowledged that gender equality could not be achieved simply by treating male and female workers identically. Instead, women were entitled to rights-based social benefits that recognized their distinct responsibility for reproduction and child rearing.

In the aftermath of the RCSW report, there were tangible, if ultimately unsubstantial, changes to day care policy discussions in Ottawa. Prime Minister Pierre Trudeau established the Interdepartmental Committee on the Status of Women, which contained several senior female public servants who had been intimately involved with the RCSW as members of committee's mainstream feminist groups.[17] A national plan for day care was on the RCSW's agenda, though it was assigned to the working group on family life and community services, not the working group on women's economic participation, a decision that Timpson argues had long-term repercussions for the marginalization of day care policy.[18] There were also concerted efforts taken to gauge the status of day care across the country: what provincial day care legislation existed; how many day cares were there in each province; and how were they regulated? How extensive, exactly, were day care shortages and how could more spaces be created? Over 350 people, including parents, day care operators, politicians, and public servants, explored these questions at a national day care conference held in Ottawa in June 1971.[19] The Canadian Council of Social Development's 1972 report on day care was another effort to consolidate information about programs, legislation, and facilities across the country as a starting point for enhanced policy-making.[20] Also in 1972, the federal government recognized that it had at least some responsibility for day care when it established the Child Care Programs Division, housed in the Department of National Health and Welfare. Day care, in other words, had arrived on the federal political agenda, where it would be assured a contested place for years to come.

Perhaps the most important effect of the RCSW, however, was that it provided a platform and agenda for women's rights interpretations of public child care. Questions of earning and caring were still contentious (and sometimes divisive) issues within the different varieties of feminist movements, but the RCSW's report signalled a new, very public direction for advocates based on a basic consensus: child care policy was not just about the rehabilitation of poor families. Instead, it was an issue of intrinsic importance to women as social and economic citizens. Leading liberal feminist organizations, including the National Action Committee on the Status of Women, which was established to maintain pressure for the implementation of the commission's recommendations, indicated their strong support for a national day care program on these grounds.[21] But these "relatively elite" actors were not the only ones assembling their forces for day care battles. The RCSW had "energized the whole spectrum of the women's movement" across the country. Toronto was the centre of much of this action (or at least the focus of attention from historians), but British Columbia was also home to grassroots feminist groups, many of them with liberationist goals, that worked to transform the terms of the day care debates beginning in the late 1960s.[22]

More Than Just Babysitting

Vancouver was a locus of activity for the revitalized feminist movement in Canada, and, as in other urban centres such as Toronto and Montreal, university campuses were the initial source of much of this activist energy. In Vancouver's case, this energy originated in large part at SFU, the so-called "radical campus."[23] In the late 1960s, the student movement at SFU was involved in battles around internal issues, such as the "democratization of the university," as well as external issues such as "racism, imperialism, and war." Furthermore, the university was "in an almost continuous state of crisis" for three years, while students, faculty, and administration clashed over university admissions policies, governance, and programs, especially in the Department of Political Science, Sociology, and Anthropology (a battle that ultimately ended with the dissolution of the department).[24]

Many women were frustrated with their own unequal status within the New Left student movement as well as with the lack of attention paid to women's issues by male leaders. However, they were also influenced deeply by the "thought-expanding perspectives" of the New Left, particularly around the different analyses of oppression. The early women's movement at SFU, as elsewhere in Canada, was thus "a challenge to the decade's New Left as well as something that grew organically out of it," as Bryan Palmer suggests.[25] Facing resistance from their "male comrades" and feeling an increased sense of their shared struggles as women, a group of women in 1968 established the SFU Feminine Action League, which was renamed the SFU Women's Caucus shortly afterwards.[26] In their fights against women's subordination on campus and in broader society, student feminists joined with faculty members such as Maggie Benston, the author of the essay that helped ignite the New Left feminist spark, "The Political Economy of Women's Liberation."[27]

For this "vanguard" of feminists at SFU, child care was a premier issue. The story of feminist day care politics began in the spring of 1968. Amidst the campus-wide disputes about university governance, a group of students occupied a boardroom to protest the actions of administrators. Initially a statement against faculty privilege, education student Gini Yorke proposed that the occupation could also be used to politicize the lack of child care on campus. The occupiers agreed and turned the boardroom into an ad hoc child care centre. They were eventually forced to vacate the room, but the university administration could not dampen the momentum that had developed around the need for child care on campus. A group of students, most of them women and many of them mothers, seized the southwest corner of the student lounge and cafeteria on the second floor of the academic quadrangle and declared that they were using the space to establish a child care co-operative.

The co-operative received widespread attention and support from across campus. The Student Society granted $500, which organizers used to purchase toys and equipment. A significant number of students, staff, and faculty lent their support to the venture by donating toys, food, and time and volunteering to lead outings and activities for the children. Through the summer of 1968, co-op members cared for an average of thirty children per day and a total of sixty different children. Mothers provided most of the care; they set up a system whereby each member, in return for the care of their children, was required to contribute a half-day of caregiving per week, in addition to a weekly $1 fee for snacks and milk.[28]

Although co-operative child care was not new to British Columbia, the idea that it could be a vehicle for women's liberation was.[29] Feminists elsewhere in Canada, particularly on university campuses, were engaged in the same types of experiments. At the University of Toronto, a group of women and men formed the Campus Community Day Care Centre (CCDCC) in a building on St. George Campus in the fall of 1969, a co-operative venture that one organizer explained was meant to "break down the nuclear family" and the gender roles upon which it was built.[30] When the university threatened the CCDCC with eviction in March 1970, parents, staff, faculty, and supporters of the day care occupied the senate chamber. The group won the right to stay in their space, and they were awarded some financial support for renovations to bring the centre up to licensing standards. In their struggle, the Toronto feminists highlighted the need for an "egalitarian and democratic" model in the social organization of care.[31] As one organizer explained, "if you didn't have child care, then how could women have equality?"[32]

Likewise, for the women who spearheaded the SFU co-operative, collective child rearing was about much more than meeting practical needs.[33] Instead, the co-operative represented a new way to organize communities and families that counteracted the stifling inequalities created by a patriarchal and capitalist society. "We reject," they declared, "the definition of the co-op as just a baby-sitting agency and see it as a genuine social movement."[34] "An extended family has been formed," one spokesperson explained, "freeing each mother for part of each day from individual responsibility for the child."[35] Indeed, the group called themselves the SFU Co-operative Family or simply the Family. Mothers' use of the co-operative allowed them to study, work, and pursue their own interests – to participate, in other words, in all aspects of society as a rights-bearing citizen. The co-op organizers also encouraged the wives of male students, faculty, and staff to join since "the time spent with the Family is time away from the neurosis-causing boredom and vacuity of the home." "It was a way out," another pamphlet declared, "a way for women ... to become independent, their own person first, and not just somebody's mother."[36] The breaking down of gender roles applied to the children as well since an opposition to hierarchy and authority was central to New Left organizing. Children wore gender-neutral clothes, took part in gender-neutral play, and were treated like "people" rather than "property." The Family parents were clearly proud of one three year old, who, when scolded by a "pompous university official" for peeing on the sidewalk, promptly told the official to "fuck off." In another instance, parents decided to accept the donation of a toy fort and soldiers from a supportive community member only on the condition that such a "war-like" gift be referred to as a "peace-keeping mission."[37]

Through the summer and into the early fall, the Family insisted on preserving the grassroots and parent-driven nature of their project. In their view, the best way to ensure women's inclusion as fully participating citizens in public and private life was not through the reform of "impersonal institutions" and state structures but, rather, through informal organizations responsive to the needs of the group. Eventually, however, they had to concede the inevitability of government intervention. For one thing, they could not escape the web of bureaucratic requirements created by the provincial Welfare Institutions Licensing Board and the university administration. The corner of the lounge where the co-operative was located did not have kitchen facilities, access to outside play areas, a dedicated washroom, nor a phone, and the university would not provide access to those things unless the child care program was licensed. A licence would also make them eligible for government grants, which would allow them to update and expand their facilities and materials.

Along with these practical concerns, it was also becoming increasingly clear that the co-operative was unsustainable for many mothers. Though they lamented the abandonment of the ideological commitment to co-operation, the reality was that many women (and men) were juggling school, work, and parenting and did not have the time nor the energy to take on extra unpaid care work during the day. Co-operatives worked in theory, but only for a relatively exclusive middle-class group of mothers and children:

> The strength and weakness of parent co-ops is that they place the burden of organizing facilities on the parents. In a growing number of families, both parents work an eight-hour day, often at very tiring jobs and simply do not have the time to participate actively in the day care centre. One result of demanding the day care centres be parent co-operatives would be that the people most in need of day care services – working parents – would be the last to obtain them.[38]

As a licensed day care, the co-operative would qualify lower-income mothers for provincial subsidies and allow the group to hire trained child care workers, thus making their services more accessible to more people. University administrators also indicated their support for licensing, afraid of the public relations storm that these "tense and most crusadish" women could raise if they forced the closure of the co-op.[39] The decision was made to move towards a more formal institutional structure. With the support of provincial licensing officer Gladys Maycock, the co-operative secured a small amount of government funding and hired Emily Campbell, formerly a member of the United Community Services (UCS) Advisory Committee on Day Care, as a co-ordinator. Through the next several years, Campbell worked with the university administration to acquire a more permanent space, and by 1973 the Burnaby Mountain Day Care Society had incorporated and moved into portable trailers, where licensed, subsidized child care was available to all campus mothers and families.[40] Campbell, a faculty member at the University of British Columbia (UBC), also consulted and worked closely with that campus' day care council, which initiated and co-ordinated three day care centres: Acadia Day Care Centre, University Kindercare, and the Campus Nursery Co-operative, the first centre in British Columbia granted a licence for the care of under-three year olds.[41]

Ultimately, the campus child care co-op experiment was not a long-term solution for most families. But for many feminists, the relative failure of the co-op model was beside the point. Above all, they argued, the action at SFU highlighted the cumbersome and stifling nature of the provincial day care bureaucracy. "While it's really encouraging to see people coming together to solve common-people needs," a group of BC feminists wrote, "it's also infuriating to see, again and again, that they *have* to do it all alone."[42] For many of the women involved, the co-operative represented a jumping-off point for a larger, feminist child care movement in the city and the province. "What we want," the co-op mothers explained,

> is day care that will help people BE with their kids and not just away from them; that will fill the gap between the kind of institutional (i.e. professional and standardized) centres we have now and the traditional nuclear family unit of mother-father-child; that is part of building a new definition of community, an extension of the family, a social sharing of child care responsibilities.[43]

In an important sense, then, the SFU Family reoriented child care activism towards the broader goals of women's liberation and citizenship rights and, in doing so, offered a reconceptualized system of public child care in British Columbia.

By 1969, the SFU Women's Caucus had begun to look beyond campus towards the problems and barriers facing women in the wider Lower Mainland community. Beginning with off-campus meetings, the SFU group eventually moved "down the hill" in August 1969 and became the Vancouver Women's Caucus (VWC), with a permanent downtown office.[44] Containing currents of both socialist and radical feminist thought, the VWC became part of a lively feminist domain that included consciousness-raising groups, feminist unions, and the Women's Bookstore on Davie Street. The VWC published the newspaper *The Pedestal*, and in 1970 they were responsible for perhaps the best-known undertaking of second-wave feminism, the Abortion Caravan.[45] Alongside access to birth control, abortion, and freedom from domestic violence and rape, the VWC took up day care as one of its principal targets in the quest for women's liberation.[46] In their day care "manifesto," they called for more child care centres in every neighbourhood in the city, at every place of work, and on every college and university campus. Central to the provision of good day care, they said, was a high level of parent and family involvement. The caucus' position stemmed from an analysis of the "mystique" of motherhood at the root of women's oppression, which they described as

> the powerful idea that we belong at home with the children, that we deserve less because we should not be out working in the first place, that we are hard-bitten and unfeminine if we want anything but the mother's role and above all, that the children will suffer, will be warped, will grow up into criminals and monsters if we are not there with them at every moment.[47]

Overcoming the motherhood mystique, the caucus insisted, required a fundamental shift in society's attitudes towards working mothers. It also required social resources – such as universal day care – that were offered in recognition of women's right to work, their right to equality in the home, their right to autonomy and independence, and their right "to seek fulfillment . . . as a full human being."[48] These pronouncements provided the ideological backdrop for the development of more concrete day care initiatives in the city.

Welfare Rights, Feminism, and Day Care

In the diverse milieu that defined the late 1960s and early 1970s in Vancouver, feminist thought and action began to overlap with the city's well-organized welfare rights movement. Groups such as the Unemployed Citizens Welfare Improvement Council (UCWIC) and the Vancouver Welfare Rights Organization were campaigning for higher social assistance rates, decent and affordable housing, and health and dental benefits for welfare recipients. They also criticized the subtly (and sometimes overtly) pervasive attitudes that characterized the treatment of welfare recipients and demanded more respect from welfare agencies as well as the inclusion of their members on management and policy-making boards.[49] As the influence of feminist thought and action spread throughout the city, these welfare rights groups began to incorporate into their activism an attention to the feminized nature of poverty. The UCWIC, the more militant of the two groups, publicly declared its support for the demands of the VWC and other groups working for the "legal, political and social rights and economic independence" of women.[50] Its members created alliances and partnerships with feminist groups to protest unequal social assistance rates for women, which, they pointed out, were made even more disproportionate by the fact that women more often had dependents to support. The UCWIC worked with the Women's Liberation Alliance, for example, on a brief to the provincial government that showed that women's average welfare rate was $116.87 compared to men's $124.21.[51]

Feminist welfare rights activists pointed to many reasons why women had a harder time than men breaking free from the cycle of poverty and welfare dependency, including, for instance, unequal job opportunities, lack of power in labour negotiations, and low wages. They also insisted that unaffordable and inaccessible day care was one of the biggest barriers to women's independence. Indeed, government investigations revealed as much. One report noted that of the 24,000 welfare cases in Vancouver as of December 1971, about one-third were "possible employables," "capable of supporting themselves." The women in this category cited a lack of access to day care as among their biggest stumbling blocks.[52] Welfare mothers' advocates called on the provincial government to increase capital funding, relax licensing regulations, and run awareness campaigns to educate social assistance recipients about their access to day care subsidies.[53]

One group, in particular, embodied the overlap between feminist and welfare rights organizing and made day care the centrepiece of its efforts on behalf of welfare mothers. MOMs was founded in 1968 by a group of six mothers who lived in the same public housing project. Long-standing frustrations with the provincial social assistance program inspired them to organize to find ways to "tackle the barriers" for mothers who felt "trapped" on social assistance. With the help of well-known community organizer Margaret Mitchell, MOMs developed a training program for mothers that was intended to give them work experience and on-the-job training, equipping and preparing them for labour force participation. MOMs worked with supportive community agencies, most of them volunteer-based and non-profit firms, to create work placements for mothers.[54] The program was popular because of the opportunity it gave mothers to improve their chances of finding permanent employment, but, for many mothers, such placements were impossible without access to reliable day care.

Mitchell, a passionate advocate for welfare mothers as well as a savvy political operator, invited both Grace McCarthy, a Social Credit member of the legislative assembly (MLA), and Grace MacInnis, by this time NDP member of parliament (MP) for Vancouver-Kingsway, to a meeting with MOMs leaders, the heads of the city's welfare and housing programs, and a sampling of private family agencies in the city who had been trying to set up day care services. MacInnis was well known as a supporter of government day care services going back to the Second World War, but McCarthy, a "particularly right-wing" member of the Social Credit government, seemed an odd choice as an ally for day care activists.[55] Nevertheless, Mitchell and MOMs saw McCarthy, one of the few female Social Credit MLAs, as a potential supporter and hoped that under the watchful gaze of these two senior politicians, welfare officials would take action. Some initial action was encouraging: the city social services department, for example, offered support to a child care centre established in a donated Lutheran church space run by volunteers from the National Council of Jewish Women.[56]

Encouraged by this evidence that "institutional change" was possible, Mitchell and MOMs decided to expand their efforts.[57] They moved into offices on Commercial Drive and sought out partnerships with other non-profit community agencies willing to provide placements for mothers. MOMs' work quickly gained the attention of senior city welfare officials, who approved of work-based solutions to chronic welfare dependency. The city was so impressed, in fact, that officials wanted to apply the same model to all welfare recipients, not just mothers. As a result, under the guidance of city administrators, MOMs morphed into the Vancouver Opportunities Program (VOP), which was also known as the Vancouver Incentive Program. Like MOMs, the VOP remained primarily a women's program: two-thirds of its client base was women, who made up the majority of the city's 5,000 single-parent welfare recipients.[58] The city's Welfare and Rehabilitation Department oversaw the VOP's operations and provided the program with funding, which the city received from the province's *CAP* disbursements, although the day-to-day administration of the program remained at arm's length from the municipal government. Those who participated in the program received a monthly honorarium of $50, later raised to $100. Through the VOP, mothers were able to gain work experience in schools, libraries, community information centres, food co-operatives, tenant and welfare rights offices, self-help programs, and a range of other community agencies – placements in which they would achieve "self-growth and the attainment of a measure of independence and self-support," the hope being that such experiences would lead to permanent jobs.[59]

Although the expansion of the VOP was encouraging, the problem of inadequate day care remained. For many mothers, VOP opportunities were meaningless without access to affordable child care. One city official bluntly explained that "the problems of child care in Vancouver have been the foremost problems faced by Welfare Recipients who wish to take part in the Incentive Program we offer."[60] Mothers and their advocates reported that the only child care to be found was temporary, expensive, or, in the case of one mother who walked "10 blocks to her baby-sitter with a 2 yr. old and a 10 mth. old," inconvenient. This mother had requested help in purchasing a double stroller for her children, but her city social worker was reluctant to help. "It's a wonder," a member of the Vancouver Welfare Rights Organization suggested, "this woman is still motivated to work even with the [Welfare and Rehabilitation] Dept. against her. But, as she says, she cannot live without the extra $100.00 she earns a month."[61]

Eventually, pressure from VOP organizers compelled the city to authorize a monthly $25 "babysitting allowance" as well as the promise to make more of an effort to educate mothers about their eligibility for provincial day care subsidies. While this allowance helped during the six-month VOP placement, many mothers were once again left scrambling for child care at the end of their program. Of the VOP graduates who sought to move into permanent paid work, 20 percent cited "reasons of small children" as their biggest barrier to employment.[62] The cumbersome provincial day care bureaucracy compounded the problem. VOP personnel repeatedly appealed to senior provincial officials that "no one knows what to do with us, or can tell us how to correctly fill out our forms" – forms that were required to be approved for a day care subsidy. "We require babysitters in our homes, some of us have to take our children out to babysitters, some are in out-of-school day care centres, and others have babysitters after school," VOP women explained. "Do we therefore tick everything in sight?"[63] Moreover, not every type of child care was covered. Centre-based care for children under the age of three remained unlicensable and thus ineligible for subsidy coverage, a gap that continued to strike many mothers as among the most outdated of the government's policies.

Inadequate day care become such a difficult obstacle for VOP clients that administrators decided to use a portion of the staff salary budget to hire a day care organizer, Betsy Wood. With the needs of working mothers as her top priority, Wood did not overly concern herself with licensing regulations as she set about establishing day care facilities in the low-income neighbourhoods where most VOP mothers resided. Her efforts resulted in Grandview Terrace Day Care and South Hill Day Care, both located in East Vancouver. Neither centre met the provincially mandated space and safety standards that Wood considered arbitrary and cumbersome. To the great consternation of licensing officials, Wood also indicated that she intended to care for children under three years of age, especially those whose older siblings attended the centres. Although Wood got "hassled . . . a lot," she considered her deliberate flouting of the rules to be an important political statement about government unresponsiveness.[64] By the early 1970s, Wood was one voice among many in a chorus of frustration that highlighted policy shortcomings as well as the flawed ideological context in which policy was made.

A Growing Movement

Other day care centres around the province were confronting the same red tape as Betsy Wood, impeding their efforts to provide more and better day care. In Victoria, the Jiminy Cricket Day Care, established in 1967, had to reduce staff salaries and increase parent fees in 1971 after they depleted their budget on renovations and programming changes they considered unnecessary, but without which Family and Children's Services (Victoria's administering agency for provincial policy) threatened to revoke their licence.[65] In Williams Lake, the Department of Social Welfare declined to replace the funding of a day care centre that was unexpectedly denied a Local Initiatives Programme grant – an important source of federal funding for physical improvements to day care centres for a short period in the early 1970s – despite evidence that a day care centre would have allowed several Aboriginal mothers to participate in Canada Manpower job training designed to get them off of welfare.[66] In North Vancouver, welfare officials deemed that the Novaco Day Care was relying too heavily on subsidies and not on parent fees, and the centre was forced to enrol more children and cancel their lunch program, against the wishes of overburdened staff.[67] This growing litany of complaints painted a province-wide picture of a provincial welfare administration doing more to discourage than to encourage high-quality and accessible day care.

With more and more parents, day care providers, and feminist activists willing to speak out, the prohibition against licensing for under-three centres emerged as one of the most fiercely contested aspects of provincial policy. Home-based services remained the only option for mothers who needed subsidized care for their infants and toddlers, but the family day care system was coming under increased feminist scrutiny. A report from the Child Care and Day Care Study Group in the summer of 1971 argued that children in these homes often received no more than substandard custodial care, for reasons that were beyond the caregivers' control.[68] The report noted that day care mothers were isolated and exploited by the provincial system of child care. Caregiving mothers bore the hidden costs of child care; they effectively "donated" their homes "to the system" and shouldered the costs of food, toys, and equipment, yet the subsidies for home-based care were lower than those available for centre-based care. Furthermore, support systems and training were not made available to caregivers since, as the report pointed out, they were considered "mothers, not workers."[69] Since their job "satisfie[d] an emotional loyalty to an anachronistic mystique," namely that of the devoted stay-at-home mother, the family day care system essentially allowed the provincial government to look like they were assuming responsibility for child care without actually challenging the gendered division of labour.[70] The study group recommended phasing out the family day care system altogether and replacing it with state-funded, parent-involved group care, with trained workers who were treated fairly and equitably, reflecting the value of the service they provided to society.

British Columbia's mainstream feminist groups also contributed a number of studies, reports, and calls to action around the multiple inadequacies of the child care system. The Vancouver Status of Women Council considered day care to be one of its "highest priorities" in the creation of a "human rights state."[71] In its view, the creation of social rights and entitlements such as day care, equal pay, divorce reform, and education and health care reform were the best paths to gender equity, although they also recognized the limits of state action. State reforms were not possible, an article in its newspaper *Kinesis* pointed out, until the "twin ideologies of 'Mother's place, in the home' and 'Day care, an evil to be avoided'" were overcome, which had to happen on a deeper societal level.[72] The Status of Women Action and Co-ordinating Council espoused similar views in a brief to senior provincial officials. "What women want," the council explained, was that "child care be considered a bold instrument of social policy to care for, protect and develop Canadian children."[73] Beyond simply criticizing the failings of policy mechanics, groups such as this one emphasized what they considered the fundamental flaw of the provincial day care program: that it was classified as a welfare service. Such an approach, they reiterated, "perpetuate[d] the notion that day care exists [only] for families who have in some way failed their family responsibility."[74]

Labour feminists also weighed in. The BC Federation of Labour Women's Rights Committee surveyed a group of working women and found that one-third of them had "at some time or another turned down a promotion, a raise in pay or a better paying job because they were unable to make suitable arrangements for the care of their children." Many more working women, and especially women who were new immigrants without extensive social networks, were stuck in a position whereby they earned just enough to make them ineligible for low-income subsidies, but their "exorbitant" child care fees wiped out any financial advantage to be gained through working. The Vancouver Status of Women would make a similar point in their 1974 study *Immigrant Women in the Labour Force*, which found that many mothers left work altogether because of the expense (or lack) of child care, throwing them back into a state of dependency.[75] This "tragic and frustrating" structural inequality could be reversed, labour feminists urged, with universal twenty-four-hour, seven-day-a-week child care that would also allow women to work higher-paying night shifts.[76]

It became difficult for provincial politicians and bureaucrats to ignore the avalanche of day care grievances. In mid-1971, E.R. Rickinson, the deputy minister of rehabilitation and social improvement, attempted to buy some time by ordering a complete review of provincial programs, from subsidy rates, to licensing regulations, to the on-the-ground circumstances of supply and demand.[77] The recommendations that resulted, made public in March 1972, did more to aggravate the day care community than to appease their concerns. Emily Campbell, fresh from her battles with Marpole Day Care Centre and overseeing the SFU child care co-op, put together the Ad Hoc Committee on Day Care of Greater Vancouver and organized a "Day Care Fair" at UBC in April, where parents and advocates could air their grievances.[78] Over 200 parents, teachers, educators, labour representatives, businessmen, administrators, students, and interested citizens gathered to share their stories and propose solutions. The Day Care Fair resulted in three resolutions, which were by then becoming very familiar: (1) that government devote attention to hiring and training "competent staff for co-ordination and consultation of day care services"; (2) that more capital be provided to help with start-up costs; and (3) that services be expanded and created to meet real community needs, among them under-three licensed centres.[79]

In the face of all of this pressure, the Social Credit government remained firmly attached to the status quo: only the "bare minimum" in terms of welfare spending.[80] Officials in the welfare department continued to insist that "the primary aim of the policy was to meet the needs of the single parent." At a meeting between provincial and municipal welfare officials in the spring of 1972,

> Mr. Bingham [an official in the social welfare department] suggested the main criteria was rehabilitation of parents – the person who needs to work to maintain his independence, the family with one parent incapacitated, the breadwinner obtaining vocational training. The case where employment of both parents still left the family income very low was also raised as a probably justifiable situation.[81]

"The family which has a high debt structure merely because of excessive spending on luxuries," as T.D. Bingham characterized the majority of day care users, were not a public responsibility.[82]

"Listen to the day care rumblings..."

After several years of Social Credit unresponsiveness, child care advocates sensed a reason for optimism as the 1972 provincial election approached. The election campaign provided a platform for a province-wide discussion about public responsibility for child care, and advocates thought they had found a sympathetic ally in New Democratic Party (NDP) leader Dave Barrett, a former social worker. While Social Credit politicians continued to warn about the dangers of "Soviet-style" day care, Barrett at least appeared to take the arguments of advocates seriously. He promised a "rational, sensible, child welfare program in this province," one built around a system of "government-supported daycare centres under the department of health." Barrett stopped short of proclaiming day care a necessary emancipatory tool for all women – "the first priority," he insisted, "is for those on welfare and low paid working groups" – but he nevertheless seemed to offer a more hopeful approach to provincial day care services.[83]

BC electors voted in an NDP majority government at the end of August 1972, putting an end to a twenty-year Social Credit reign. Within a few months, Barrett installed Norm Levi, long an outspoken advocate for day care from the opposition benches, as the new minister of rehabilitation and social improvement.[84] Day care was high on Levi's agenda. The centrepiece of his new day care initiatives, announced late in the fall of 1972, was a set of reforms known as "New Day Care." As Levi explained, New Day Care accomplished three goals: it increased availability of spaces, it gave parents more choices, and it eliminated the complicated administrative structures that "hinder peoples' attempts to obtain government services."[85] In an attempt to streamline administration, all day care policy and programs would be routed through a new provincial day care information office in Vancouver and satellite offices throughout the province.[86] Perhaps the most significant aspect of New Day Care was the creation of one-time grants of up to $20,000 for groups who needed help with centre renovations and improvements, in part to replace the funds that were no longer available since the federal Local Initiatives Programme had been cancelled. There were other reforms, too, including subsidy increases, the distribution of subsidies on a monthly rather than a daily basis, and the phasing out of a three-tier subsidy system to one determined solely on the basis of income and the number of family members – the intrusive means test and interview process were eliminated.[87] Levi's administration also eventually got involved with the construction of "pre-fab" buildings, purchased by the provincial government and leased to local organizations in co-operation with municipalities, in an effort to increase the number of spaces. The training, education, and professionalization of day care staff also received significant attention under Levi's leadership.[88]

In the immediate aftermath of the election, the response from the day care community was cautious optimism. "If this program is tied to a swift and efficient administration," the UCS said, "it could remarkably increase the supply of good quality day care resources in the community."[89] When the scope of the NDP plan became apparent, however, many advocates pointed out that the reforms essentially amounted to an infusion of funding into programs that otherwise remained unchanged. Furthermore, some of the advocates' most specific demands were overlooked. The government made no indication of licensing for under-three centres, let alone any discussion of universality. Levi continued to insist that family day care was preferable for children under three years of age, a position that did not seem to mesh with what working mothers throughout the city were saying.

The UBC Day Care Council released the results of a survey in the fall of 1972 in which more than 90 percent of working mothers who responded were dissatisfied with the quality of child care in the city and especially with what was available for children under three.[90] Another report from the UCS indicated that even with Levi's reforms, fewer than 10 percent of the children under six of working mothers in the greater Vancouver area would be served by the provincial day care program.[91] More broadly, the feminist campaigns for social rights were dealt a blow when Barrett refused to create a Ministry of Women's Rights, a recommendation of the NDP Women's Committee. Barrett explained that he believed in "human rights, not women's rights, because human rights include the rights of both women and men."[92] This view did not leave much room for the creation of programs that recognized women's distinct struggles for equality as workers and mothers. Groups such as the UBC Day Care Council, the UCS, and Vancouver Status of Women expressed renewed frustration through the fall of 1972.

Betsy Wood, the VOP day care organizer, was especially vocal in her criticism of New Day Care. Nothing in the proposed reforms, she insisted, made things any easier for the mothers and staff of Grandview Terrace and South Hill Day Cares. In the meantime, her insistence on allowing children under the age of three to attend had resulted in the province's threats to close the centres. Wood, "tired, angry, and depressed" over her dealings with health and welfare bureaucrats, warned Barrett in January 1973 to "listen to the child care rumblings because they are powerful, people believed, the need is there ... and now the N.D.P. is the stumbling block in the way of human progress."[93]

On 1 February 1973, at the opening of the new provincial day care information centre – one of the key initiatives of New Day Care – a group of women and parents who were involved with Grandview Terrace and South Hill Day Cares gathered to express their long-standing grievances. Although originally intended simply as a rally and protest, as one participant recalled, "someone asked if it was a sit-in, so it became a sit-in." With that, the Child Care Occupation Forces were born.[94] A group of mothers, along with their children, occupied the day care office and essentially transformed it into their own community child care information centre, complete with changing tables on the desks of bureaucrats. "We've been forced to take this action," they argued, "because it is the only way open to the community for genuinely participating in the government's decision-making on day care." It was abundantly clear, they pointed out, that the NDP government had no intention of following through on their campaign promises on day care.[95]

The occupied building on West 10th Avenue became a hive of activity during the eleven-day sit-in. Between caring for the children and composing protest songs – "Talkin' Day Care Blues" – the occupiers put together a detailed and comprehensive list of policy demands. The promise to look into twenty-four-hour care had not been taken seriously, they argued, and under-three group care seemed no longer to be on the government's agenda. The red tape created by licensing regulations was an exercise in "absurdity"; there was more support for the problematic family day care system than there was for centre-based care; and nothing was being done to support community and parent participation. "Changes in rhetoric," they concluded, "are not producing changes in the program."[96] Moreover, the occupiers used the publicity generated by their actions to frame day care as an issue of women's liberation. Adequate day care was not just about

Figure 5 Protestors at the occupation of the Provincial Day Care Information Centre in Vancouver, 2 February 1973.

Credit: Photograph: Dan Scott. Courtesy of the *Vancouver Sun*.

children's interests, they said, but also about creating equal opportunities in the labour force for British Columbia's working women and not just for those whose work was a financial necessity. Half of the mothers doing paid work in Vancouver did so as a choice, according to a UCS report, and those mothers deserved day care too.[97] Beyond simply providing a "stop-gap charity service," social agencies should "be helping mothers and other working women to organize to secure better wages and time off to create and run cooperative child care themselves."[98]

As support from other child care groups flooded in, the forces began to outline their specific demands.[99] At the top of the list was a meeting with Levi and the ministers of health (Dennis Cocke) and education (Eileen Dailly). The three ministers along with five backbenchers agreed to meet with the occupiers within forty-eight hours of the start of the sit-in. The meeting was not productive. The only "concrete" result was Levi's request that the group write "3 one-to-two page proposals outlining its demands more specifically." Within a day or two, occupiers had put forward their three points. First, they proposed a one-year pilot project for a community-based under-three centre. Their second demand was for government-funded community organizers to oversee and support parent initiatives. Finally, and not surprisingly, they called for more funding and the relaxation of licensing regulations.[100]

The health minister did not attend the second meeting, and, though Levi appeared, he was not "receptive" to the proposals. For the occupiers, this lack of reception indicated that the government was not negotiating "in good faith." Furthermore, Levi would not allow the observers (the press and other interested parties) into this second meeting. The only proposal that he was willing to discuss in any detail was the one that dealt with funding, although his concessions went only so far as to offer to arrange a meeting with the civil servants responsible for such issues. The occupiers grew increasingly frustrated, and "insisted that Levi give us an answer on our first proposal [regarding the under-three pilot project] by the following Monday."[101]

In a press release given a week later, Levi announced that the government was not interested in supporting the pilot project. His grounds were that "no group without sufficient, recognized training would be permitted to ignore the licensing regulations per se." His words seemed especially harsh to the occupiers, among them Betsy Wood and other "highly recognized, innovative day care supervisors" who had a long history in Vancouver's day care scene. Levi tried to soften the blow by announcing a small payment to Grandview Terrace and South Hill Day Cares, and he promised to begin investigations into a revamped subsidy program. He indicated, however, that the government would not budge on issues around licensing regulations despite protestors' insistence that "archaic" rules discouraged many parent-run centres.[102] Faced with government intransigence, the occupation essentially fizzled out. In the end, while the feminist-inspired occupation may have changed the public conversation about day care, it did little to effect change in terms of policy and programming. The government held to the position that their support of day care was appropriate only insofar as welfare families and single mothers needed it and that for children under three "in-home day care" was the best and cheapest approach.[103]

"'Cuz There Ain't No Daycare"

Despite its limited results, the occupation generated a certain degree of energy and enthusiasm in the ranks of British Columbia's feminist child care advocates. Not long after the sit-in, members of the Vancouver Women's Caucus released '*Cuz There Ain't No Daycare (or Almost None She Said)*, a wide-ranging book that contained practical tips about setting up day cares as well as feminist essays about the need for universal care. *'Cuz There Ain't No Daycare* represented the culmination of several years of advocacy efforts and offered, yet again, a vision for future policy directions. Alongside its step-by-step instructions for dealing with the provincial licensing bureaucracy and its analysis of subsidy reforms, the book provided a forum for the synthesis of critiques from welfare rights activists, feminist groups, parents, and day care practitioners. Its publication amounted to the clearest articulation of the ideological underpinnings that explained the early 1970s child care movement in the province. Day care, the authors wrote, was "not . . . a way for women to forego child care responsibilities but . . . a way for women to have children and not 'end' every other part of their lives . . . a way for mothers to continue to grow themselves so that they have something of themselves left to give to society."[104] Day care, they said, should not be wielded as a regulatory tool for poor families but should be provided as a necessary and normal part of a well-functioning society, one in which men and women shared equality in paid work as well as in caring work. *'Cuz There Ain't No Day Care*'s central message was that women had the right to pursue satisfaction and independence through participation in the public sphere but that they did not have to "abandon" motherhood in order to do so. A universal day care system, it argued, shaped and directed with input from mothers, was a long overdue ingredient of women's full social citizenship.[105]

The occupation and the release of *'Cuz There Ain't No Daycare* also solidified a feeling of community among day care lobbyists. Thanks to undertakings such as the occupation, there was a sense among a growing number of advocates of a common purpose and a "commonality of interest," one that needed to be fostered over the long term. To ensure this sense of continuity and optimism, a group of parents, organizers, and day care workers came together in the summer of 1973 as the Child Care Federation.[106] With a membership initially drawn from day care societies from West Point Grey, South Hill, Kitsilano, and Surrey, along with centres from the Neighbourhood Services Association, their mandate was to encourage "communication and mutual support among child care groups" and to act as "a vehicle for putting collective pressure on the government to improve child care conditions."[107] About eighty people attended the first federation meeting, and with the help of a grant from the UCS, the group was able to establish a permanent office in Vancouver. Subcommittees were formed to focus on funding, day care centre design, and government engagement. The federation's first concerted advocacy efforts ensured that parents and day care providers had a voice in changes to licensing regulations in 1973. Another subcommittee dedicated its efforts to publishing and distributing *Ragamuffin* (later known as *Growing Pains*), a newsletter that provided a forum for debate and information sharing for all British Columbians with a vested interest in child care.

As the middle of the decade approached, then, the child care lobby in British Columbia maintained a sense of vitality and optimism. Much of that energy no doubt had to do with the somewhat improving day care policy landscape in British Columbia. There were certainly ongoing frustrations with the government's direction – the sit-ins and persistent lobbying were evidence of this dissatisfaction. But there was also a sense that reforms were possible under an NDP administration and that more fundamental changes to the public provision of child care were on the horizon. Between 1972 and 1974, the numbers seemed to suggest as much: the number of children in subsidized day care increased by more than 350 percent between September 1972 and December 1973 under New Day Care, and over the same time period almost 100 new day care centres were licensed or in the process of being licensed.[108] By the summer of 1974, the number of subsidized spaces in the province had increased sixfold from 1972.[109] In Vancouver, this number included several centres that had begun to accept children under the age of three.[110] Day care providers received another boost in the spring of 1974 when Levi established the Vancouver Resource Board (VRB) and, elsewhere in the province, community resource boards. Reporting directly to the

Department of Human Resources, the boards represented a new decentralized delivery mechanism for social services at the community level, the idea being that services should be determined through grassroots engagement and consultation. In each community, boards were "responsible for community needs, establishing priorities and operating or contracting for programmes other than statutory ones."[111] In Vancouver, the VRB replaced the Children's Aid Society and Catholic Children's Aid Society and, therefore, became responsible for the delivery of family and child welfare services. It also absorbed many of the responsibilities of the city's social service department.[112] Child care programs, both the maintenance of existing ones such as those run by the Neighbourhood Services Association as well as the creation of new ones, were on the roster of the VRB's new responsibilities after this administrative overhaul, a fact that organizations such as the UCS met with hopeful anticipation.[113] By the fall of 1974, Levi's department had overseen the establishment of several day cares throughout the Lower Mainland in partnership with the VRB, and several city councillors were exerting pressure on the province to go even further.[114]

These reforms, however, represented "small improvements" rather than "major feminist change."[115] At the end of the NDP's first term, day care remained firmly lodged in the welfare bureaucracy, targeted at social assistance families and those with the lowest incomes. The character of child care policy remained much the same as it had since subsidies were introduced within the *CAP* programming in the 1960s. The distribution of subsidies was done using the voucher system, which for many was linked directly to the stigmatizing elements of welfare. Day care was still the responsibility of the social welfare department, where it was a "preventive social service" for families who were "experiencing serious social problems."[116] Moreover, provincial officials suggested that they had no option but to link day care to the employment of low-income and welfare mothers because of the pervading ideas about work and respectability. While they could recognize a need to "accept that many mothers should be encouraged to remain at home with their children," the "wide-spread public confusion that associates negative feelings about employment with all [social assistance] recipients" held sway over policy-making.[117] The feminist upheaval of the early 1970s had added new meaning to the contested landscape of child care politics, but the state continued to treat day care as a tool for the enforcement of the work ethic in poor and low-income families.

The feminist-inspired day care advocacy of the late 1960s and early 1970s offered a profoundly different reading of public responsibility for the care of working mothers' children than that which had defined social policy in the previous five decades. The demands of child care advocates in this brief period spoke to something more than simply better welfare policy. They called for a realignment of women's relationship to the workplace and the family. A complete and meaningful version of working mothers' social citizenship, advocates said, included a universal, twenty-four-hour, parent-involved day care system that allowed for women's full and equal participation in the workforce, that did not alienate women from their caring role but supplemented it, and that made the rearing of a child a collective responsibility in recognition of the value of care work to society.

The efforts of campus child care co-operatives, the welfare rights feminists in MOMs, and the range of day care practitioners and families willing to engage the state in pursuit of a better deal for working mothers and their children resulted, to be sure, in positive changes. A relatively sympathetic NDP government introduced incremental increases in funding, improved subsidy rates, and provided more child care spaces. Ultimately, none of these reforms actually moved policy towards feminists' vision of a child care system that offered women equality and liberation at work and at home. As a result of their efforts, however, public responsibility for child care was ensured a permanent – and permanently contested – place on the provincial and national policy agendas. Their vision for a fully realized version of social citizenship for working mothers endured for the next several decades and continues today.

6 "The feeling lingers that day care just isn't nice": Provincial and National Child Care Politics since the Mid-1970s

Since the 1970s, working mothers have become a normal part of Canadian family life. For over forty or so years, their numbers have steadily increased to the point that by 2010 69 percent of mothers with a youngest child up to two years of age were in the labour force. For those whose youngest child was between three and five years old, this rate increased to 75 percent. In British Columbia, 60 percent of children under the age of sixteen had a mother who was in the labour force.[1] To some extent at least, these changing family forms have been accompanied by a greater cultural acceptance of working motherhood. Critics continue to denounce selfish working mothers – "please don't go to work, Mommy," one *Vancouver Sun* writer titled her investigation into working motherhood in 1998 – but for every dramatic warning about neglected children, mothers and their advocates have pushed back against fears that were "40 years out of date." As one mother declared,

> women work for the same reasons men do: financial reward, personal satisfaction, professional challenge, to enjoy peer relationships and to be fully engaged in life ... It's time to get comfortable with the fact many of us are not feeling at all guilty, and are downright happy to be in the workforce.[2]

Despite this transformation of cultural attitudes, not to mention the statistical significance of working motherhood, child care policy has not kept up. In a 2008 study, UNICEF put Canada in last place, tied with Ireland, in a ranking of the child care systems of twenty-five countries in the Organisation for Economic Co-operation and Development. Of the ten benchmarks deemed crucial for a quality early childhood care and education system, Canada achieved only one: at least 50 percent of staff in accredited services are "educated with relevant qualifications." (Sweden achieved all ten benchmarks; Iceland, Denmark, Finland, France, and Norway each achieved eight.[3])At the provincial and local levels, the country's poor record on child care translates into a chronic shortage of spaces, crises of affordability, and targeted provincial programs that often result in two-tiered child care systems.

In other words, despite the dramatic change in the scope of working motherhood since the 1970s, child care policy in the ensuing forty years has been a story of continuity rather than change. While the details around the edges of child care policy have been adjusted somewhat, the core principles of the policy have remained the same. Child care subsidies are offered to low-income families within a welfare paradigm, there are varying degrees of granting support for child care centres, and governments have consistently stayed away from any serious suggestion of creating comprehensive, high-quality programs. To be sure, there were brief flashes of promise. Provincially, a universal system seemed possible during the administrations of the New Democratic Party (NDP) in the early 1990s and again at the turn of the millennium. In the federal arena, optimism about a universal program peaked in the late 1980s and then again in 2006. None of these plans were realized. Instead, a succession of federal governments since the 1970s have dealt with child care as a taxation reform issue, and provincial governments have approached child care through piecemeal welfare reforms.

The battles and reforms in British Columbia, as well as within the national context, contain direct echoes of debates that have been embedded into the child care landscape since the 1910s. Is child care a public or a private responsibility? What kinds of mothers should be working for pay? Is it better to require poor and "needy" mothers to go to work or to support them to stay home with their young children? What role does child care play in gender equity and welfare policies? The gender- and class-based uneasiness around mothers' work and caregiving was consistently at the centre of a child care politics that remained as contested as ever, although new threads of meaning, including debates about early learning and "investable" children, have also become a big part of the story in the new millennium.

Since the feminist-inspired lobbies of the early 1970s, shifting coalitions of activists, child care providers, sympathetic politicians, and parents have worked to keep high-quality, affordable, accessible, and even universal child care on the political agenda. BC advocates have had to negotiate a political culture characterized by "polarization between parties and party ideas" and dramatic shifts between left- and right-leaning governments.[4] They also have had to work within the context of federal child care programs and funding promises, which had a direct bearing on provincial policy-making. Along the way, working mothers and their supporters have struggled to have their voices heard, to maintain a decent standard of living, and to ensure that their children had access to quality care.

"Driven Apart": The Middle to Late 1970s

In her important study of post-war child care policy, Annis May Timpson argues that as federal policy evolved from the 1970s onwards questions of child care and early childhood education were "driven apart" from the issue of women's employment equality. Despite the best efforts of feminist activists (and some federal bureaucrats) to frame child care as a women's rights issue, Timpson argues, a range of forces contributed to the growing distance between the fight for more and better child care, on the one hand, and the push for women's equal opportunities in the male-dominated labour force on the other.[5] Campaigns for child care were often waged alongside and within battles for child development, child welfare, and early learning programs rather than being put forward as an issue of working women's choices and rights. Timpson traces key moments in the 1970s, 1980s, and 1990s that illustrated this driving apart, both in terms of advocacy efforts and policy-making. At the 1982 National Day Care Conference in Winnipeg, for example, advocates focused on a universal child care program as an issue of children's development and educational opportunities. The question of women's employment equality was an issue left to the women's movement and to the labour movement, which did not always foreground universal child care.[6] As Timpson points out, the federal government's approach to child care, contained in royal commissions, studies, and policy decisions, mirrored this split.

Applied to the BC context, Timpson's analysis goes a long way to explaining why child care advocacy in the province seemed to decline after the enthusiasm of the early 1970s. By the middle of the decade, there was a marked slippage between child care advocacy and feminism that contributed to waning energy in the day care fight. This is not to say that child care lobbying disappeared entirely. Certainly, organizations such as the Child Care Federation and their allies maintained pressure on the provincial government to improve the quality and quantity of day care. In 1975, for example, the federation organized a well-publicized rally in Victoria to protest the cancellation of South Hill Day Care's hot lunch program, and later that year they protested franchised day care or "Kentucky Fried Day Care." A range of voices and organizations continued to fight for improvements in funding and licensing.[7] There were indications, however, that the Child Care Federation and others were conceding the feminist ideological battles over child care. Instead of framing their advocacy in terms of women's liberation or liberal feminist reform efforts, they began to focus on the piecemeal, tangible changes to existing programs. "We all seem," a federation spokesperson explained, "to have moved past the stage of active criticism of Government policies (lack of policies) to the realization that the time has come now for constructive suggestion as to the direction for child care."[8]

Developments in the BC Federation of Women (BCFW) suggest a similar disconnect. Founded in 1974, the BCFW's original policy statement included a commitment to "the creation of a high-quality, non-sexist, 24 hour a day childcare, available and accessible to all children from infancy onwards, in all parts of the province."[9] The Child Care Interest Group was charged with working towards this goal. Under the leadership of Ellen Frank, the interest group remained relatively active in 1975, even hosting a child care conference in Vancouver. A group of enthusiastic women and men publicized the BCFW's child care message through public events, publications and leaflets, and organizational support for parent-run day cares.[10] However, the child care group enjoyed only a brief period of support. Before long, Frank announced that the "child care Interest group is in *DESPERATE*!!! need of new energy. In other words, NO NEW ENERGY – NO SUBCOMMITTEE!!!! [sic]."[11] Child care did not remain near the top of the BCFW's priority list. By January 1976, the BCFW admitted that the "committee appears to be defunct in spite of Ellen's tremendous efforts to keep it going."[12] By the 1979 annual convention, there was no mention at all of child care policy discussions. Other issues had taken priority in the feminist movement, including abortion, rape, sexual harassment, and women and unions.[13]

There were other signs of the fragmentation of women's rights organizations and child care advocacy by the middle and late 1970s. While groups such as the Child Care Federation, the Coalition to Improve Day Care Services, and, later, the BC Day Care Action Coalition lobbied for increased funding and more day care spaces, they did so with rhetoric that focused on the educational, developmental, and anti-poverty benefits for children.[14] "The care of children is the rule of thumb, not the well-being of parents as such," declared yet another ad hoc day care committee in a report commissioned by Vancouver city councillor Darlene Marzari in 1977, although they admitted that "the system works best when both children's and mothers' needs are met."[15] To be sure, there were still groups concerned with employment equity who remained devoted to the fight for universal child care. For example, the Service, Office and Retail Workers' Union of Canada (SORWUC), an independent, socialist feminist union with roots in the Vancouver Women's Caucus Working Women's Association and which organized day care workers at several centres throughout the Lower Mainland in the mid-1970s, included free parent-controlled child care among its list of policy demands that also included community-controlled schools and health services, price and rent controls, and the end to discrimination in hiring, wages, and promotions. SORWUC's focus was on the status, wages, and benefits of child care workers, but such labour battles were also embedded in an analysis of the larger feminist purposes of child care. However, even for groups like SORWUC, there was a sense by the later 1970s that lobbying for government action on child care was increasingly futile. Instead, SORWUC focused on advancing their cause by piecemeal changes through collective bargaining (and, in March 1976, a one-day strike of child care workers).[16]

Frustration and disappointment with a new provincial government no doubt contributed to this advocacy gap and overall dampened lobbying efforts. After three relatively optimistic years under Dave Barrett's NDP government, the Social Credit party was returned to power in 1975. Led by Premier Bill Bennett, the Social Credit administration was suspicious of women-led initiatives and had a "deep loathing for the welfare state."[17] Bennett set the tone for the relationship between his government and women's rights advocates when he cut the women's program budget and eliminated the office of the provincial co-ordinator of the status of women. Women reacted swiftly and loudly. Four hundred women's groups from around the province gathered in Victoria for "Women Rally for Action" and presented Bennett with a list of eighty-five demands. However, the premier reacted largely with indifference, telling one group from the South Okanagan that he was "unaware" of their day needs in Kelowna.[18] Bennett's response to the rally was indicative of his broader suspicion of those with "feministic [sic] viewpoints," which, combined with his disdain for "welfare bums," served to undermine provincial child care programs.[19]

Human Resources Minister Bill Vander Zalm introduced a series of reforms that amounted to an erosion of the progress, however limited, that had been made during the NDP years. Vander Zalm was particularly worried about ensuring that subsidies were fully cost shared through the *Canada Assistance Plan* (*CAP*), and so he narrowed eligibility requirements to include only the most "needy" families – a marked reversal from the NDP, which had been pushing federal officials to expand their cost-sharing provisions so that day care did not develop only "as a program for the poor."[20] Families in which both parents were attending school, for example, were made ineligible for subsidization in 1977.[21] These and other restrictions meant that the numbers of children receiving subsidized care declined sharply in the first five years of the Social Credit administration, from 11,878 children subsidized at the end of 1975 to 7,986 children in 1980.[22]

A shortage of high-quality child care spaces was also a growing concern. Thanks to Vander Zalm's decision to cancel the capital granting program, there were fewer new spaces created and existing ones became harder to maintain. The 1978 announcement that the Ministry of Human Resources was "ceas[ing] administration" of six day care centres in Vancouver, which the province operated in partnership with the Vancouver Resource Board, further threatened the viability of spaces in high-need areas. "All day care centres in the province are run privately or by societies," Vander Zalm explained, "and that's the way it should be."[23] The government was more than content to let family day cares provide the majority of subsidized services in the province, even though reports indicated that a reliance on home-based services often led to irregular and inadequate care.[24]

These reforms, along with the lifting of a fee ceiling that day care operators were allowed to charge, translated into serious affordability problems for parents.[25] Many families could not absorb the higher fees, and for some two-parent families it was more financially prudent for one parent to stay home, usually the lower-earning mother.[26] As a result, by the end of the 1970s, day care facilities around the province began to report alarming vacancy rates, making it even harder for them to maintain the revenue stream required for their operation.[27] The Nanaimo Children's Day Care Centre, for example, expressed its "grave concern" over low enrolment because "parents are short of money, and can find cheaper, if less desirable, care for their children elsewhere."[28] In Castlegar, Port Hardy, Terrace, and other locations around the province, child care providers and parent boards wrote to provincial officials requesting increases to subsidy rates so that parents could afford to enrol and re-enrol their children in their centres.[29] Emily Campbell of Simon Fraser University's Child Care Society laid it out even more clearly. "At the subsidized level of $140 per month [for group day care]," she told Vander Zalm, "a centre can only manage if that centre is fully enrolled and fulfills the following conditions: no rent, no utilities, low salaries, no insurance, no outings and no bad debts." To meet the real costs of providing good care, she argued, the subsidy should be closer to $170 per month per child.[30]

Provincial officials had their own explanation for high fees and vacancies: high unemployment rates, union demands for increased staff wages, the expense of providing care for under-three year olds (in the few pilot projects throughout the province), and the continued stonewalling by the federal government over *CAP* cost sharing.[31] In the 1977 report commissioned by Marzari, author Ruth Chisholm agreed that mothers' unemployment was part of the problem. But a more serious impediment, Chisholm argued, was the newly stringent requirements that parents had to meet in order to qualify for a subsidy. Mothers were asked to provide documentation, receipts, statements of income, and more – a bureaucratic quagmire and one closely associated with the stigmatizing receipt of welfare, which many wanted to avoid. Chisholm also revealed a general "disenchantment" with day care, especially in group centres. Mothers told her that they were opting for in-home care or family day care because it was less of a hassle when unexpected circumstances, such as sickness or travel, inevitably arose.[32]

By the early 1980s, the effects of the Social Credit "restraint agenda" were starkly apparent. Day care centres around the province were bombarding the Ministry of Human Resources with pleas for capital grants, operating funds, boosts to the subsidy rate, and supplements for the wages of their chronically underpaid – and, in some cases, newly unionized – staff.[33] Many were in a similar situation as the Grandview Terrace Day Care in East Vancouver, which "lurche[d] along precariously from month to month ... without a penny to spare."[34] The province, however, consistently took the position that day care services were fundamentally not a public responsibility. Vander Zalm insisted that the financial health of day care centres was not the government's business and that injection of public money into these centres would create "inequitable programs," lack of accountability, and inefficient and time-consuming administration. "Our system," he argued, "is established to subsidize parents and not centres."[35] It was business as usual under the new human resources minister, Grace McCarthy, who was appointed in 1981. Under her oversight, day care subsidies inched upwards, hitting $200 in 1981, but the cost of running a centre rose at the same time, leaving parents and centres in the same financial crunch as before.[36] McCarthy explained that the best place for all of these issues to be worked out was in "the marketplace."[37] Not only, then, was child care even further removed from any consideration of women's social rights as workers, but its status as a public service was also increasingly called into question.

Debating Welfare and Day Care, Work and Motherhood

Although its prominence within the mainstream women's movement may have faded by the late 1970s, child care remained on the public agenda thanks to the complex dynamics of welfare politics: the gendered, classed, and racialized dimensions of working mothers' rights and obligations as the recipients of public support. Access to day care continued to be a key issue in debates about whether and how to get mothers off of social assistance. Mothers involved in the Vancouver Opportunities Program summed up their ongoing frustrations:

> If you can find a babysitter who charges under 75 cents an hour or anyone who will do day care for under $4.00 a day, please let us know. We have to give our sitters your cheque plus money out of our V.O.P. cheque or welfare cheque or we don't have a sitter. Please, we want to join the work force again, and we want to be able to hold our heads up in society once again. *Why are you making it so hard for us*, when we're trying to better ourselves and get off Social Assistance etc?[38]

A significant policy change soon after the Social Credit party was elected ensured that day care remained a crucial hinge in the politics of welfare reform. In 1976, the government introduced the *Guaranteed Available Income for Need Act* (*GAIN Act*), under which day care subsidies (and the sporadically offered capital and operating grants) were administered as part of the spectrum of "rehabilitation and support services."[39] This decision was nothing new, of course, but the Social Credit government's restraint agenda lent a particular cast to the distribution of subsidies. Across the board, officials were concerned with cutting down on the number of welfare recipients by weeding out the "employables" and by targeting new "services related to employment and training."[40]

The "employability" of welfare recipients raised significant questions about the thousands of women who were served by the *GAIN Act* and especially the 20,000 or so who were single mothers.[41] Were women with young children, especially those who were lone parents, employable? What did the government, and the public more broadly, consider to be "work"? Did mothers have access to jobs that would help them achieve economic independence? The answer to these questions became even more contentious after a series of welfare reforms in late 1981. Single parents with one child over six months of age or with two children over twelve years of age were reclassified as "employable" and had their income assistance payments reduced.[42] This change was based on the expectation that single parents, most of them mothers, should be working towards self-sufficiency and independence rather than remaining dependent upon the state.[43] Ironically, Grace McCarthy harnessed some feminist rhetoric to justify this policy, explaining that women who stay at home were "a thing of the past."[44]

As many observers pointed out, however, there was a fundamental flaw with this new classification of single mothers as "employables." "Why," one reporter asked, "is the ministry of human resources implementing a program to put thousands of single parents in the work force while at the same time providing funding for only 1,000 day care spaces?" McCarthy insisted that those affected by welfare reclassification would be entering the workforce "at a staggered rate over several years" and that day care needs would be met in the meantime by private and parent-run services.[45] Reports and evidence on the ground, however, suggested the problem was worse than McCarthy realized or was willing to admit. The Vancouver Council of Women found that the need for day care and nursery school "far exceed[ed] current supply" in most areas of the city, especially for under-three year olds.[46] A study by the United Way of the Lower Mainland revealed year-long waiting lists in Vancouver and spots for only one child out of eighteen.[47] In the year prior to 1981, 177 day care centres in British Columbia had closed down.[48] In many cases, municipal governments and school boards tried to pick up the slack, with mixed results. In Penticton, Houston, Burns Lake, Kitimat, and Williams Lake, for example, city councils provided small grants to centres or offered them free or reduced rents and leases or tax breaks. In South Cariboo, Courtenay, and Abbotsford, among others, school boards tried to lighten the load of day care organizations by lending before- and after-school space or making empty classrooms available for daytime care.[49] Despite these efforts, the availability, cost, and quality of child care services remained a serious problem for many mothers who faced being pushed off of social assistance and into the labour force.

For others, these welfare cutbacks raised a more fundamental question. Why was mothers' caregiving labour not given the social supports and protections it deserved? Groups such as the Vancouver Welfare Rights Coalition, the Downtown Eastside Residents Association, and the BC Federation of Anti-Poverty Groups resented what they perceived to be the underlying assumption of the "employability" focus: that their domestic and caregiving work was not considered an important contribution to society. As McCarthy's welfare reforms rolled out, many single mothers angrily insisted that they were already doing valuable work caring for their children. Some went so far as to frame their stay-at-home motherhood as a right, one deserving of state compensation.[50]

These kinds of comments must be set in the context of the Wages for Housework movement that emerged in the late 1970s out of divisions within the feminist movement about the politics of motherhood. Wages for Housework adherents took exception to the second-wave feminist emphasis on waged work as the only path to "liberation" and equality and argued that domestic and caring labour should be considered equally as empowering – an argument that was reminiscent of the maternalist campaigns from earlier in the century.[51] Though not all BC mothers and organizations identified explicitly with the Wages for Housework movement, their objections to job-focused welfare reforms were rooted in the same rhetoric and ideology. In their 1980 report, the Skeena Terrace Welfare Rights Committee took offence to the government's assumption that getting mothers off welfare was equated with getting them to "do something useful." The authors of the report insisted:

> Most of us are already working, although in unpaid jobs within the home. A recent estimate states that if women were paid for all the work they do in the home at labour market prices, they would be earning approximately $40,000 per year. We are both angry and appalled at a recent Ministry report that advocated that women be forced into the labour market.[52]

This was a contentious idea, both within and outside of the feminist movement. Not everyone agreed that "subsidizing needy mothers to stay home to raise their children" was the best course of action, because it sent the "degrading" message that women were not "worth much," according to the low value typically assigned to feminine caretaking labour.[53] For groups such as Skeena Terrace, though, the inadequacy of day care services was a critical factor informing their insistence on caregiving-based welfare provision. Again and again, low-income mothers pointed out that even as welfare officials promoted self-sufficiency, the province was taking little action on improving day care. Should she be forced to take a low-paying job, one mother asked, "where am I going to find someone who will be as good a mother as I am to [my daughter]?"[54] Moreover, as the Skeena Terrace mothers pointed out, the gender biases built into work programs hindered their ability to actually achieve independence through wage work. The ministry provided job training programs to help mothers get off welfare but only in the form of vocational programs "approved under the Individual Opportunity Plan."[55] Their training options were limited to "domestics, child-care workers or office workers" – low-paying jobs with minimal job opportunities. "We are discouraged from exploring many jobs that might be appealing both from a personal and a monetary point of view," the mothers protested.[56]

The debates about welfare and work became more complicated by the assumptions built into racial difference. Mothers who were not white were subject to questions about the nature of their "contributions" to society in much the same way that poor and low-income white women were. This was particularly true of women who had immigrated to British Columbia, which in 1970s Vancouver primarily meant mothers of Chinese, Portuguese, Italian, East Indian, and Greek backgrounds.[57] Commentators in British Columbia focused largely on immigrant mothers, but it is also important to note that the kinds of work with which they were concerned was no doubt also performed by indigenous women, although the historical record is mostly silent in this regard. Historians, though, have begun to explore the paid work of indigenous women in the post-war years, and in many respects their observations overlap with the work experiences of immigrant women. When it came to "'raced' labour," Carol Williams points out, "prescriptions of femininity were judiciously 'relaxed'" because of assumptions that such women's paid work was a necessary antidote to poverty and dependency. Moreover, these women were needed to do the jobs considered undesirable by other workers, particularly low-paid domestic service, clerical, and factory work.[58] Lest they become a "wasted and destroyed human resource," in other words, immigrant and racialized mothers were expected to participate in wage work – a far cry, of course, from prevailing expectations about middle-class white women, whose paid work was considered selfish and neglectful.[59]

These marginalized mothers' struggle to access day care was considered a serious problem. In fact, Darlene Marzari suggested that the city's day care vacancy problem in the late 1970s could be traced to immigrant mothers' loss of subsidies under more restrictive eligibility requirements.[60] Ruth Chisholm's 1977 report confirmed Marzari's suspicions. Chisholm found a "greater reluctance" to provide subsidies to immigrant families, including foreign students, because welfare officials insisted that "respons[ibility] for their needs," child care included, fell to their sponsor families rather than to the government.[61] While they were expected to be "contributing" members of society through labour force participation, immigrant and racialized mothers were expected to do so without relying on public resources. Chisholm's report also identified a number of other race- and ethnicity-based hurdles that impeded access to child care. For one, bureaucratic machinations discouraged newly immigrated mothers from applying for a subsidy. This was not a new problem. Women's groups and day care operators for several years had been drawing attention to the cultural obstacles that hampered access to public child care support. As one report to Norm Levi in the early 1970s pointed out, many families were "totally unaware" that they could have day care costs subsidized. In some cases, mothers assumed that only centre-based care was eligible for a subsidy, not realizing that they could use subsidized in-home and family day care. For those who did apply, language and communication issues made wading into the "two or three month ordeal with repeated bureaucratic demands of forms, letter, etc" an intimidating process that required the use of interpreters. Furthermore, many mothers worried about effective communication with day care providers and "felt that their children would not receive the care which was harmonious with the cultural values of the family."[62] Others were reluctant to get involved in day care centres because of the expectation that they sit on parent boards, responsibilities that presented an onerous time commitment for working families.[63]

Advocates' focus on the particular challenges of immigrant, non-white, poor, and low-income mothers was necessary and understandable since their child care needs were so pressing. However, highlighting the class- and race-based dimensions of child care politics also had an unintended consequence. This focus helped to reinforce the cultural stereotypes around "needy" families as well as day care's alignment with welfare and anti-poverty measures. The degree to which this association was ingrained in the public consciousness was evident in public opinion surveys from the late 1970s and 1980s, which consistently revealed a widespread negative perception of any kind of non-maternal child care because it was considered a service for poor, failed, and one-parent families. Survey respondents supported government-supported child care for truly needy families but insisted that a universal child care program was a misuse of taxpayers' money. In a 1977 survey of 1,000 British Columbians, 8 percent favoured free, universal day care and only another 11 percent were in favour of government subsidies "regardless of family need."[64] A 1981 Prince George task force plumbed even deeper into public attitudes towards day care. Where the state did play a role, respondents said, child care services needed to be closely monitored to ensure that they were not misused or abused by selfish mothers who were not actually in need and instead "living beyond their means."[65] A significant proportion of the BC public, therefore, continued to insist that day care, as a facet of social assistance, needed to be policed according to mothers' marital status, their work ethic, and the nature of their contributions to society.

Beyond the context of welfare reform, British Columbia's day care debates continued to be informed by a broad distrust and disapproval of any woman who combined paid work and motherhood, regardless of circumstance. "The feeling lingers that day care just isn't nice," according to a 1977 *Vancouver Sun* article. "It's a threat to the home."[66] "We worry," another reporter noted, "our tax dollars are squandered on the children of women who must go to work or go on welfare; on children of divorced, deserted, or widowed mothers or fathers; on children of the unwed parent."[67] Commentators feared that providing government day care services to some mothers, no matter how needy, would lead all mothers to expect child care support and thus feel entitled to move into the paid work force. "Children are the responsibility of the *Parents* not the state," as one Prince George citizen insisted. According to another, the issue was simple: "We should not be supporting working mothers."[68]

However, many observers sensed an opening. Something had shifted by the late 1970s, thanks to the rising numbers of working mothers and efforts of feminist activists. This fear of family breakdown ran up against a "new social attitude" that had firmly staked its claim on the political landscape – "that the right to work is no longer solely a male privilege."[69] As a result, there was a greater societal willingness to view child care as a legitimate public service. One report suggested that public opinion had altered course enough that "a government with foresight and imagination" might successfully implement "experimental projects" in child care beyond simply low-income subsidies. Selling such a project, the report's author, Paul Koenig, cautioned, would have to rely on safe and familiar political motivations, including reducing juvenile delinquency, crime, and psychological difficulties as well as "increased discipline and work adjustment."[70] But these justifications opened the door to more comprehensive services, for which mothers and their supporters continued to advocate. "How about some licensed group Day Care for 2 year olds?" one Prince George mother asked. Another suggested facilities "which meet the needs of children with special requirements." Others called for day care for shift workers. "It is growing increasingly difficult," one mother explained, "to meet one's basic commitments in these inflationary days. A second parent working part-time is becoming a necessity not a luxury."[71] The persistence of these mothers ensured that attention to BC child care ramped up alongside national politics in the 1980s and 1990s.

Flirting with Universality: Provincial Politics in a National Context, 1980s–2000s

Feminist advocates across the country had invested a lot of hope in the recommendations of the Royal Commission on the Status of Women. The report's call for a national day care program was a coup for those, including the National Action Committee on the Status of Women (NAC), who considered child care integral to gender equity. The NAC experienced internal divisions – how much to support profit versus non-profit day care, for example – but child care nonetheless remained a key issue for the organization through the 1970s.[72] For the NAC and others, the Liberal government's approach to child care under Pierre Trudeau was disappointing. Trudeau was reluctant to tackle child care head on for a number of reasons, among them the basic reality that "Canadians remained ambivalent about the public provision of child care."[73] His administration was also wary of the complicated federal-provincial negotiations required of any child care policy and reluctant to interfere with an area of provincial jurisdiction. Content to keep federal fiscal responsibility for child care within the framework of the *CAP*, Trudeau instead introduced the child care expense deduction (CCED) in 1971, which allowed parents to deduct a portion of child care expenses from their taxable income.[74] The child tax credit followed in 1978 in part to address the limitations of the CCED, among them the fact that the deduction did not easily apply to low-income families who often relied on unregulated, and therefore unclaimable, care. The tax credit was also meant to compensate for cuts to family allowances.[75] As Rianne Mahon has argued, despite the best efforts of "state feminists" throughout the 1970s, they were unable to "wrest control of the issue from the social policy bureaucracy, which had a distinct welfarist orientation."[76]

While child care was an important if divisive issue within the women's movement throughout the 1970s, the early 1980s marked the emergence of distinct child care advocacy organizations at both the national and provincial levels. The Canadian Council on Social Development held its second national day care conference in Winnipeg in 1982, where social agencies, child care providers, women's groups, and others "launch[ed] their demand that child care should become a universal social program."[77] Two organizations emerged out of the conference to further these goals: the Canadian Child Care Federation, a network for early childhood educators, and the Canadian Day Care Advocacy Association (CDCAA). In British Columbia, a new spark of advocacy energy was provided by a gathering of day care workers, parents, and community organizers who met in 1981 at Douglas College and agreed to work together towards improved working conditions and wages for day care workers, lobbying the government for more funding, and pushing for better administrative oversight of day care programs. Their efforts arose out of a concern about the "effects of the [Social Credit] restraint program on child care services in British Columbia."[78] British Columbia's reinvigorated child care movement was represented by the creation of the BC Day Care Action Coalition and the Western Family Day Care Association.[79] Since child care was a battle that had to be fought on two fronts, British Columbia's provincial organizations often worked closely with national groups.

Advocacy resources from around the country were mobilized several times throughout the 1980s, thanks to a series of commissions and task forces undertaken out of Ottawa. The first was the Task Force on Child Care. In 1984, the CDCAA, along with the NAC and the NDP, called for a national examination of child care policy, hoping to capitalize on the positive attention to women's issues that was being generated thanks to events such as the 1984 leaders' debate.[80] Trudeau was amenable, and later that year he appointed a task force to be chaired by Katie Cooke. The task force was asked to examine and assess both federal and provincial child care services, along with paid parental leave, and to make recommendations to Judy Erola, the minister responsible for the status of women, about the federal government's role in developing a "system of quality child care in Canada."[81] After an extensive series of consultations, hearings, surveys, reports, and research projects, Cooke's team reported in 1986 with fifty-three major recommendations. The centrepiece, though, was the call for "complementary systems of child care and parental leave that are as comprehensive, accessible and competent as our systems of health care and education."[82] For Cooke, this meant a national, universal child care program cost-shared between the federal government and the provinces. Adding fuel to the fire was the report by the Royal Commission on Equality in Employment (RCEE), which was chaired by Rosalie Abella and released in 1984.[83] Abella identified a national day care program as among the top requirements, Timpson explains, to "allow women the fullest opportunity to exercise their potential for worker-citizenship."[84]

In the meantime, however, Trudeau's Liberals had been replaced by the Conservatives under Brian Mulroney. Mulroney was not keen to take his cues from Trudeau-appointed commissions, and so to pre-empt the recommendations he was expecting from Cooke, he appointed his own Parliamentary Special Committee on Child Care. The Mulroney committee's position was clear. "A universal day-care system," the report insisted, "is not the solution to the problem."[85] Mulroney did admit, however, that there was a problem, and he pushed forward with his own plan that he dubbed the "National Strategy" on child care. Its main feature was the introduction in July 1988 of Bill C-144, the *Canada Child Care Act*. Should the act pass, the federal government would share operational costs for child care spaces and take on 75 percent of capital costs. So as not to encroach on provincial jurisdiction, complete control over regulation and licensing would remain with the provinces.[86]

British Columbians were among the chorus of advocacy voices who voiced frustration and dissatisfaction with federal policies during the 1980s and particularly with Mulroney's National Strategy. After the optimism generated by the Cooke report, lobbyists were disappointed with the plans that simply amounted to reforms within the same tax-relief framework – a set of "band-aid recommendations" that were "misguided and inadequate."[87] The NAC and the CDCAA argued that the plan would result in less money for child care in the long run since it placed a cap on spending that did not exist with the *CAP*.[88] Penny Coates, the president of the CDCAA who was also the spokesperson for the BC Day Care Action Coalition, maintained that the National Strategy would have very little positive impact for "people looking for child care in B.C."[89] The bill itself was inadequate, she argued, but so was the take-up of effective reforms at the provincial level. The BC Ministry of Social Services and Housing, which by then had responsibility for administering the subsidy program, made overtures towards "enhancing" the current program should funds become available, but Coates and others were not convinced by the vague promises.[90] Citing fiscal restraint, Mulroney's government abandoned most aspects of the National Strategy and the introduction of Bill C-144, instead turning their attention to issues of child poverty.[91]

The efforts of advocates in the 1980s, however, had longer reverberations in British Columbia. As political scientist Cheryl Collier argues, the closing years of the decade were marked by a shifting consciousness towards women's issues in the province, thanks largely to the mobilization of child care groups. The Social Credit government had long been ignoring day care in the name of financial restraint, but "disaffected women voters" were an increasing cause of concern for Premier Bill Vander Zalm leading up to the 1991 election, especially since day care advocates had come together in a more co-ordinated and cohesive body – the Westcoast Child Care Resource Centre – which included the BC Day Care Action Coalition, the Western Family Day Care Association, and five other education and child services organizations.[92] Day care reforms became part of Vander Zalm's agenda in the late 1980s and into the 1990s. In 1989, he increased funding to virtually all parts of child care programming, including a 15 percent increase in subsidies and matching grants for non-profit centres. Between 1989-90 and 1990-91, ministry spending on day care grew from $291,088 to more than $1.5 million.[93] He moved forward even more aggressively in 1990 by appointing a nineteen-member task force on child care, which was prompted by concern about his electoral fortunes as well as a desire to address the cumbersome bureaucracy that impeded effective reforms.[94]

The task force's investigations over the course of several months highlighted both long-standing and new concerns, which they outlined in their 1991 report *Showing We Care*.[95] The need for licensed group care for under-three year olds, seven-day-a-week centres, and improved after-school services emerged as top priorities. The task force also noted that British Columbians were increasingly concerned about the training, wages, and benefits of child care workers. Running throughout these and other recommendations were repeated calls for more funding, in the form of subsidies, spaces, and support for mothers who wished to stay home with their children. *Showing We Care* drew particular attention to the lack of administrative co-ordination, which was complicated by the *CAP* provisions, and so it recommended that the Social Credit party create one provincial child care authority – ministry, council, or otherwise – that could deliver "an adequately funded, comprehensive, high quality child care system that is accessible and affordable to British Columbia families."[96]

Before they had a chance to respond to *Showing We Care*, the Social Credit government was defeated in the October 1991 election. The new NDP government under Mike Harcourt was, however, receptive to many of its recommendations. In fact, Harcourt's election ushered in a relatively promising period with respect to child care, a period that advocates characterized as having "high levels of feminist consciousness."[97] A series of funding infusions and reforms were buttressed by a symbolically important administrative overhaul. Harcourt created the Ministry of Women's Equality and assigned it responsibility for "developing an overall policy framework for child care." This responsibility included oversight of operational and capital grants, day care subsidies, and a wage supplement for child care workers.[98] Besides providing more policy co-ordination, making these things the responsibility of the Ministry of Women's Equality signalled a shift away from thinking about child care as a welfare service. Instead, access to high-quality child care was positioned alongside other programs meant to address "women's opportunities and choices – in their homes, in their workplaces and in their communities."[99] Ministry officials explicitly acknowledged throughout the early 1990s that affordable and accessible child care was a crucial plank of women's full citizenship rights, especially for female-headed one-parent families. Child care, they noted, was the "single greatest barrier" facing mothers and parents "who want to get education and training, or find and keep a job to support their families."[100]

Harcourt backed up these symbolic actions with concrete reforms. He appointed a Provincial Child Care Council and an inter-ministerial child care team and increased funding to subsidies. By 1996, the subsidy budget had almost doubled from 1991.[101] The number of children in subsidized care grew to 30,000, and funding was made available to First Nations children in on-reserve child care programs. The government made a $5 million allocation to supplement the wages of low-paid workers in non-profit centres. British Columbia became the first province to negotiate a four-year, $32 million cost-sharing agreement with the federal government to "test new ways of managing, delivering, and funding child care." This strategic initiative resulted in the development of pilot projects such as one-stop access centres around the province, which provided information on training, licensing, and subsidies and which supported improvements in "multicultural, rural, seasonal and emergency care."[102]

In the mid-1990s, Harcourt moved to overhaul the delivery of welfare services, including child care. He introduced the *BC Benefits Act*, which was designed to replace the *GAIN Act*.[103] The *BC Benefits (Child Care) Act* was one of the four main prongs of this overhaul, along with a new focus on job training and employability, an increase to the minimum wage, and improved disability benefits.[104] The Ministry of Women's Equality supported the introduction of the act as it offered a chance to "[remove] child care from the welfare system and [reinforce] child care as a key part of the Province's work to renew the social safety net."[105] However, under the new framework, the nature of discussions and approaches to child care in the province changed perceptibly. Instead of concerning women's equality and employment equity, child care became an issue of "the health, safety and well-being of children."[106] This child-centred, rather than woman-centred, approach was reinforced in early 1997 when child care programs and their almost $200 million budget were transferred to the Ministry for Children and Families. Under the new NDP premier, Glen Clark, who replaced Harcourt in 1996, women's issues were "less visible" and less well supported.[107] By the later 1990s, any sort of fundamental change to British Columbia's child care policy was a victim of this disinterest in women's issues and the restructuring of social service delivery writ large.

The brief dip in British Columbia's child care rollercoaster, however, was not as dramatic as the freefall that began at the federal level in the 1990s. The "hollowing out" of the welfare state, which had been occurring since the late 1970s, reached its peak in 1996 with the Canada Health and Social Transfer (CHST), which replaced the *CAP*.[108] All aspects of the welfare state were affected by this restructuring. The CHST amounted to an overall reduction in social spending, and, in transferring money to the provinces in a condition-free consolidated grant, it also represented a significant shift in spending power and prioritization to the provinces. Child care and other women's services that enjoyed tenuous public support were made most "vulnerable" by the CHST.[109] The Liberal government, for example, abandoned the promise it had made in 1993 to increase the number of child care spaces, instead "deferring to provincial control." The CHST was also part of a broader retreat in spending in favour of tax breaks and benefits, such as the introduction of the National Child Benefit in 1998, which served to "individualize the state's relationship with poor families and their children."[110] Nationally, then, child care, like many other social and welfare services, was pushed off the public agenda and into the realm of responsibility the government assumed was the domain of markets, communities, and families.

British Columbia's child care programs certainly felt the effects of federal restructuring, but the NDP governments of the 1990s helped to ensure that child care funding and space creation were not as severely reduced in British Columbia as they were in other provinces by the end of the decade. Despite Clark's turn away from child care as a women's issue, the amount of money spent on child care in British Columbia continued to rise and at a much higher rate than elsewhere in the country, save for Québec. Between 1992 and 2001, the number of regulated spaces in British Columbia increased by 70 percent, a dramatically higher proportion than in any other province (again, save for Québec). During the same span of years, spending on regulated child care increased by 150 percent.[111] This relative commitment to

Provincial and National Child Care Politics since the Mid-1970s 171

child care spending throughout the 1990s set the stage for Ujjal Dosanjh's government, which moved to radically transform BC child care into the new millennium.

In early 1999, a strike among workers in the community services sector called into question the status of day care workers as public sector employees. Workers from eighteen child care programs participated in the strike, although their entitlement to wage supplements comparable to other social service workers was cast into doubt throughout the negotiations. The strike and its aftermath highlighted the continuing uneasiness about the value and purpose of child care. For advocates, the strike highlighted the need for a common voice when dealing with the government.[112] In March 1999, six provincial organizations came together as the Child Care Advocacy Forum. With a united front and a steady source of funding, the forum brought renewed attention to the province's child care crisis and helped to "convince the NDP to push forward with the pro-feminist [child care] agenda."[113]

The Child Care Advocacy Forum was deeply involved in consultations set up by welfare officials, particularly in the dialogues around a discussion paper commissioned by Moe Sihota, the minister of social development and economic security. "Building a Better Future for British Columbia's Kids" was an acknowledgment of the ongoing and serious problem with child care in the province. According to a 1997 survey, one-third of respondents indicated that "child care-related issues interfered with their ability to either seek employment, remain in the paid labour market, or pursue education or training."[114] Sihota invited British Columbians to share their stories and to offer suggestions for better policy-making. Based on an overwhelming first wave of responses, an interim report was released in January 2000, and further consultations were undertaken. The final report, *Child Care for British Columbia*, was based on the input of more than 10,000 British Columbians.[115] It revealed a clear consensus: 94 percent of respondents "saw child care as an urgent issue." These respondents also indicated their belief that responsibility for alleviating the child care crisis and for providing more resources and support to public programs of all kinds lay with the federal and provincial governments.[116]

Based on recent historical patterns, advocates were concerned that *Child Care for British Columbia* would not lead to anything substantial. The plans that Premier Ujjal Dosanjh announced, though, were a cause for optimism. In fact, they amounted to the "most progressive child care policy that anyone in BC, or Canada outside of Quebec for that matter, had yet experienced."[117] First, the government introduced a before- and after-school program for children from Grades 1-12, at a cost of $7 per day and $14 for school holidays (down from an average of $12 and $23, respectively).[118] The first phase of the plan also included funding for new spaces for these programs. The school-aged program was implemented on 1 January 2001 and represented 15,000 spaces.

Premier Dosanjh embarked on the even more ambitious second phase of the $400 million plan in the run-up to the June 2001 election. Along with the creation of thousands of new child care spaces, he began to lay the groundwork for a publicly funded child care system – only the second in the country, after Québec.[119] Advocates enthusiastically celebrated this plan as a "huge victory."[120] The implementation of the program was outlined in the *Child Care BC Act*, which was proclaimed in March 2001.[121] The act set out a four-year plan that would eventually result in publicly funded care for infants and children aged three to five in licensed family and group day care centres throughout the province.

All of this momentum came to a screeching halt, however, when the NDP was defeated in the June 2001 election. The new Liberal government immediately put the plans for a publicly funded child care system on hold and cancelled the $14-a-day out-of-school program. Member of the Legislative Assembly Bill Bennett explained that the program was financially unsustainable and that the Liberals did not "feel obligated to continue" because "this was an NDP program and NDP legislation."[122] Besides scrapping the plans for universal access, the next few years also saw reductions in spending on subsidies, and the cessation of funding to services such as the one-stop access services and child care resource and referral programs.[123] Parents, child care providers, and advocates were understandably discouraged. Evidence indicated that the Liberal reforms to child care services had a damaging impact on working families' ability to access child care. In 2003, 57 percent of child care providers surveyed reported that they had fewer subsidized children in their program, 31 percent had increased their fees, and 49 percent had decreased enrolment largely because "low and moderate income families" could no longer afford to put their children in care.[124]

The Dosanjh administration was the closest that British Columbia has (yet) come to implementing a universal child care program. In the absence of meaningful provincial reforms in the first decade of the new millennium, advocates, day care workers, and parents instead pinned their hopes on the federal government. There was some cause for optimism. In 2003, the federal government, three territories, and nine of the provinces (excluding

Québec) signed the *Multilateral Framework on Early Childhood Learning and Care*, which included $900 million in transfers to the provinces for enhanced programming for children under the age of six as well as $35 million for Aboriginal child care programs.[125] The agreement represented, as Martha Friendly and Susan Prentice have noted, the first time since the Second World War that the federal government earmarked funding specifically for child care programs. Following the signing of the framework, the Liberal government promised to implement a universal early childhood education and care program, which they called "Foundations." As 2006 dawned, the federal government was "closer than it ever had been" to a national child care program.[126] BC advocates expected that well over $600 million in federal funding would flow into the province over five years "to support the goals of the agreement" and described themselves as "hopeful" that a national child care system was on the horizon.[127]

All of those plans were put on hold, however, with the election of Stephen Harper's Conservative government in 2006. In place of a national child care program, the Conservatives introduced the Universal Child Care Benefit (UCCB), which gave parents a $100 monthly allowance for each child under six years of age. This policy direction was informed by Harper's commitment to parent "choice" and individual responsibility and by his aversion to the unwieldy bureaucracy that a public system would necessitate.[128] As critics point out, however, the UCCB is a sorely inadequate benefit to parents, which masks a child care system suffering from "chronic neglect."[129] By the end of the first decade of the new millennium, the broad trends are troubling: the rates of space expansion and increases to public funding have slowed, parents' fees have become unmanageable, and for-profit care, often of low quality, has been expanding at a greater rate than non-profit care.[130] The diminished capacity of public child care programs has continued to take place within a retreating and restructuring welfare state. It is a "paradigm shift," Paul Kershaw argues, "in which federal and provincial governments identified a reduced role for the state in welfare provision." Beginning in the 1990s and continuing today, the making (or not making) of social policy is defined by a neo-liberal emphasis on individual responsibility, narrowly targeted programs, and the off-loading of responsibility for social services to "families, the voluntary sector, and especially the market."[131] The claims that social citizens are able to make on the state are disappearing en masse, the effects of which are particularly troubling for women and working mothers who need child care.

Uncertainty in the New Millennium

As of 2012, British Columbia's child care policy consists of five prongs, including the income-based child care subsidy program, the child care operating funding program (available to licensed group and family providers), the child care resource and referral program (which provides support, resources, and referral services in offices around the province), the Early Childhood Educator Registry (responsible for the licensure of educators and assistants), and a small capital funding grants program.[132] Public support for child care services, in other words, looks much the same as it has since 1966: subsidies for low-income parents and irregular grants to privately operated child care centres. The policy rut over the past few decades has resulted in troubling circumstances for British Columbia's working families. Within Canada, BC families' access to child care is among the most expensive and hard to come by. According to 2010 numbers, fewer than one in five BC children up to the age of twelve have access to a regulated child care space of any kind.[133] Furthermore, BC families face one of the country's worst affordability crises. Median monthly child care fees in British Columbia in 2012 were $1,047 for full-time infant care and $907 and $761, respectively, for toddlers and three to five year olds.[134] The maximum subsidy that parents could claim was just over $600.[135] The problem was especially acute in Vancouver, where families could pay up to $14,000 a year for the care of one two year old in a licensed child care facility.[136]

The current state of BC child care is the product of a decades-long entrenchment of ideas about gender and class, work and caregiving, welfare and motherhood. It is still informed by assumptions that "normal" families should deal with their child care needs privately and that public support should be reserved for struggling, low-income families. There are still analysts who insist, for example, that, despite dramatic changes in family and workplace composition, child care is a "discretionary" or "special" expense for most Canadian families, not part of the average costs of raising children.[137] Child care subsidies for poor and low-income mothers are considered a necessary evil, one that is the responsibility of the Ministry of Children and Family Development, alongside other programs that "promote and develop the capacity of families and communities to care for and protect vulnerable children and youth."[138]

In British Columbia and around the country, child care advocacy groups continue to offer alternatives to the broad trends in spending, space creation, and fee increases that have defined a worsening child care system in recent years. But, as Susan Prentice points out, the case for child care has been "reframed" leading into the twenty-first century. In their recognition that the gendered imbalance in caregiving and labour force participation was at the root of inattention to child care, feminist child care advocates through the 1960s, 1970s, and into the 1980s ensured that child care was a women's issue. This feminist framing of child care is much less likely in recent years. For some advocates, this may be a strategic lobbying decision – an effort to gain sympathy from politicians and public servants in a political climate shaped largely by rightward turns in governments.[139] Divisions within, and the fragmentation of, feminist movements may also help explain the dwindling of this women-centred framework. There have been disagreements in the national advocacy scene, for example, about the degree to which child care services should be based in the community or provided by the state.[140] Whatever the reason, the result is the same: "mothers' needs," not to mention their rights, "are being written out of the central purpose of child care."[141] This scenario has often been very explicit in British Columbia. In negotiations around the *Child Care BC Act*, for example, activist Sandra Griffin declared that a universal child care program was "beyond a feminist issue now."[142]

Similarly, the 1991 *Showing We Care* report called for "recognition of child care" not as a "women's issue" but, rather, as a family issue and as a children's issue.[143] This call speaks to another of the emergent child care frameworks from recent years. "The child," as Alexandra Dobrowolsky and Jane Jenson argue, "has come to occupy central stage" in debates about "appropriate state action, about new rights, about where 'to invest,' and about how to modernize social models."[144] Instead of being a woman's right, child care is now primarily framed as an issue of children's interests and rights, particularly through the language of early learning and care. This shift was influenced by academic research into child development, behaviour, and success, research that was considered publicly and politically palatable in terms of "selling" early childhood programs to the public. The 2003 multilateral framework, for example, had an explicit focus on learning and care.[145] To be sure, this framework has led to favourable policy directions, including British Columbia's decision in 2010 to provide full-day kindergarten to all children. There is still a disconnect, however, between educationally oriented goals and care-oriented goals in public policy, the legacy of class-based differences between the two approaches over the course of the twentieth century. Administratively, this disconnect is reflected in kindergarten's home in the Ministry of Education, separate from child care programs.

Related to this children-focused framework is what Prentice calls the "business case and its association of childcare with prosperity."[146] Many of the most recent high-profile voices in support of child care have emphasized the long-term benefits of "investing" in all children and particularly in children from disadvantaged families. Rianne Mahon has identified this notion as part of a broader turn towards "inclusive liberalism" in the making of Canadian social policy, by which she means an emphasis on "social investment designed to 'empower individuals to take their place in markets and civil society,'" particularly when those individuals are children.[147] As such, included among the chorus of pro-child care voices in recent years are individuals and groups that are unfamiliar players in the child care advocacy scene, including "business leaders, bankers, economists, and middle-of-the-road politicians."[148] In the first years of the twenty-first century, calls for improved child care services have come from economists in the Royal Bank of Canada and Toronto-Dominion Bank as well as from the governor of the Bank of Canada.[149] The crux of the Toronto-Dominion Bank's Craig Alexander's argument, for example, is the potential for early childhood care and learning to "unlock the potential of individuals" through education and "skills development" at an early age. This action, Alexander says, can "help reduce poverty, address skills shortages, improve productivity and innovation, and a host of other national priorities," leading to a healthier economy overall.[150] Alexander's economic analysis builds on reports such as Gordon Cleveland and Michael Krashinsky's *The Benefits and Costs of Good Child Care*. Released in 1998, this report argues that "for every dollar spent" on a comprehensive child care program, "approximately two dollars worth of benefits are generated for children and their parents." In the long run, Cleveland and Krashinsky argue, it is simply a good "Industrial and educational strategy" to invest in the "human capital" of young children.[151]

BC advocates have recently made efforts to bring together many of these frameworks to make the case for child care based on multiple rationales. A remarkably united advocacy front emerged in 2010 with the release of the first edition of the *Community Plan for a Public System of Integrated Care and Learning* or simply the "$10-a-day plan," based on its most prominent feature.[152] The two major advocacy groups in the province, the Coalition of Child Care Advocates of British Columbia (CCCABC) and the Early Childhood Educators of British Columbia (ECEBC) are the co-authors of the report. The $10-a-day plan is based on principles long-established in the advocacy movement, most notably universal access. Families who earn less than $40,000 annually would have free access to publicly funded care, according to the plan, and children from other families would be able to access licensed, high-quality care for $10 per day or $7 for part-time care. The plan also calls for administrative control over the child care program by the Ministry of Education, suggesting that the principle of universality in the public education system needs to be extended to preschool-aged children.

The CCCABC and the ECEBC (and the many endorsers of the plan) make their case on multiple levels. The plan's potential to reduce child and family poverty is foregrounded, as is its many benefits to children's development and learning.[153] A careful economic analysis was done, with the conclusion that for every dollar invested in $10-a-day care, the province will see a return of $2.54.[154] And with an emphasis on parent choice through a range of centre- and home-based services, supporters also emphasize that the plan will have positive effects on women's labour force participation and their ability to balance work and family life – simply put, that high quality child care is essential to women's equality.[155] As Tammy Findlay points out, the community-based aspect of the plan serves to offset some of the effects of neo-liberal welfare state retrenchment. Building on the recent Vancouver model of local non-profit child care centres housed in park board or city facilities, not to mention the models of co-operative child care from the 1960s and 1970s, the plan calls for the participatory and decentralized provision of child care across the province, and it has the potential to foster more social inclusion among traditionally marginalized groups.[156]

The $10-a-day plan has received endorsements from the business community, unions, politicians, community and service agencies, school districts, and municipalities, but the provincial Liberal government has so far kept its distance from the plan. As of early 2013, the Christie Clark government promised more funding for the creation of child care spaces and, taking its cues from the federal government, the introduction of a $55-per-month tax credit. There remains, in other words, a sizable gap between government policy, which continues to slot child care into residual and targeted services and frames it as an issue of personal responsibility, and the visions proposed by mothers, families, and advocates. The future of child care in British Columbia remains uncertain.

Conclusion

Why has there never been universally accessible, affordable, high-quality public child care in British Columbia or in the rest of Canada? This study suggests that the answer to this question lies in a fundamental discomfort around working motherhood. Measured against the gendered ideals of family life, a working mother was a "problem." The "solutions" offered by public programs reflected the uneasiness inherent in working mothers' relationships to their families, the labour market, and the state. In one sense part of a welfare paradigm designed around women's stay-at-home dependency, working mothers also had to navigate the expectations of welfare programs that assigned them, as the heads of poor, low-income, and otherwise marginalized families, the responsibility of preserving the work ethic and maintaining their families' independence. Compelled to work for economic reasons and to prove their deservedness for public assistance, working mothers were nonetheless denied any type of protection or support to put them on an even playing field with male worker-citizens. As a result, comprehensive public child care, one of the "gender-encompassing social rights" required for the recognition of women's fully realized citizenship, was never a serious possibility.[1] Instead, British Columbia's child care policy has consistently been welfare-oriented, reserved for the "neediest" families and, from the state's perspective, better left to private and market sources.

Welfare regime theorists such as Rianne Mahon and Susan Phillips argue that BC child care policies have been firmly embedded in the development of a liberal welfare regime, one defined by limited public supports targeted to low-income families. They point in particular to the subsidy programs under the *Canada Assistance Plan* of the 1960s as a moment when the "liberal bias" in child care coalesced and has since "proved difficult to throw off."[2] However, the forces that carved out that residual path for BC child care can be traced in patterns of policy-making established well before the 1960s. Beginning with the Vancouver City Crèche in the 1910s, state-sponsored child care programs operated at the margins of public welfare as residual programs, if they were offered at all. Both provincial and municipal governments preferred to let working mothers arrange for their own child care needs through family, neighbours, and private social agencies, since they were reluctant to allocate resources to policies that might undermine the male-breadwinner/female-homemaker family ideal. If the state needed to step in to support families, according to this line of reasoning, it should be done in such a way as to maintain a mother's connection to the home – as mothers' pensions did, in theory – or to compensate male breadwinners for their loss of a family wage. The suggestion of any sort of universal, publicly funded care programs for working mothers was clearly in conflict with this welfare logic that pervaded much of twentieth-century British Columbia.

Yet if child care was not appropriate for "normal" families, it was considered a necessary evil for some. Governments were willing to provide targeted child care services to working-class and working poor families that were considered to have suffered some sort of family breakdown. Providing assistance in the form of child care was thought to be the best way to keep those families off the relief rolls, to preserve their work ethic, and to allow the family to preserve some semblance of self-sufficiency – even if that meant the family's breadwinner was the mother. At the same time, those mothers could fill much-needed, low-paid roles in the labour force. However, rather than being a source of social rights, mothers' work signalled family crisis: poverty, desertion, single motherhood, or the like. The various iterations of public child care that developed in response to these situations were therefore conceived as temporary stopgap measures on the road to the restoration of "normal" family life. They were not designed to recognize a mother's right to work nor her right to equality within the labour force.

Working Mothers and the Child Care Dilemma offers a welfare history with remarkably constant themes throughout the twentieth century. The construction of social citizenship's boundaries was based on gendered and class-based notions about what kinds of mothers should work and for what reasons. But it is also a story about the deeply contested meanings of child care held and debated by British Columbians over the same time period. As the century unfolded, child care controversies emerged from diverse political and societal contexts, including early-century social reform and a domestic servant shortage; the introduction of mothers' pensions and the preoccupation with male unemployment; the labour requirements of a society at war; the "discovery" of poverty and the construction of a welfare state; feminist debates about women's rights as workers and mothers; working motherhood as the new "normal"; and the ongoing controversies about how best to support all women's choices and entitlements in a welfare state that was being undermined and restructured. Along the way, child care politics were infused with ever-changing currents of thought in early childhood development and education. In all of these moments, advocates, feminists, mothers, families, child care providers, politicians, and others consistently challenged governments' and welfare agencies' narrow definitions of child care, in effect offering a "departure from the liberal mold" within which child care policies were embedded.[3]

Some, like the Vancouver social agencies of the 1950s and the child development experts of the later decades of the century, argued that child care represented an investment in a democratic and educated future citizenry. Others, like the women's liberationists of the 1960s and 1970s, argued that collective, community-based child care was the first step to eliminating the patriarchy. And at virtually all moments in the twentieth century, but especially since the Second World War, there were voices insisting that child care was a woman's right. For the crèche mothers, for mothers receiving pensions and social assistance, for feminists and welfare rights activists, the work that mothers did in the labour force – as well as the work they performed caring for their families – signalled their status as productive, contributing citizens. In this framing, public support for the child was a necessary component of social citizenship that gave all women access to economic autonomy and the ability to make choices about how to balance being both mothers and workers.

This rights-based vision for child care remains on the public agenda in the twenty-first century, thanks to committed advocacy efforts. In their campaigns for high-quality, accessible, and affordable child care, these advocates continue to draw attention to the ways that families have changed, the growing gap between the costs of child care and the subsidies available to offset those costs, the worrying trend towards private and for-profit child care services that often lead to compromises in quality, and the low pay and high turnover of qualified child care staff. The only way to forestall this dwindling child care capacity, advocates argue, is public investment in a comprehensive system.[4] In making their case, child care advocacy organizations such as the Coalition of Child Care Advocates of British Columbia have allied with anti-poverty groups (the BC Poverty Reduction Coalition, for example), associations of early childhood educators (such as the Early Childhood Educators of British Columbia), and child advocacy organizations (such as First Call: BC Child and Youth Advocacy Coalition) and received support from politicians (mostly on the left) and even business leaders. Child care is now seen as a family issue, a children's issue, and an economic issue. These frameworks for understanding child care have no doubt led to important advocacy gains, but they are also troubling for those who recognize that feminist analysis is crucial to understanding why child care has been so inadequate and why a universal system is so important. As Susan Prentice says, the reframing of child care in these directions "sidesteps gender injustice and thus may act as a brake on social equity and feminist mobilization."[5]

For Prentice and others, abandoning the feminist framework for child care runs the risk of ignoring the root of today's inadequate child care policy: a long-entrenched legacy of social policy-making in the twentieth century, one built upon the unequal relations of gender. Welfare policies were premised upon the central figure of a male breadwinner worker-citizen who was entitled to state protection and support in times of justifiable need, with women and children entitled to support only as the dependents of male breadwinners. A working-class or middle-class woman who worked because her family needed the income, a poverty-stricken mother trying to keep her family together, or a mother who chose to work because she found it personally fulfilling was not granted the full rights of social citizenship in the welfare state. Her access to social benefits was, at best, conditional and partial. Constructing a model of social citizenship that includes women as well as men (and children), advocates argue, requires recognizing that social rights are not gender neutral and that if policies such as universal child care are to be considered a serious possibility, we have to start with the principle that gender-differentiated social rights are necessary for equal citizenship.

Many contemporary scholars and observers make the case that a feminist framework is more important than ever in an age of welfare state restructuring. The boundaries of social citizenship have been shrinking, and inclusion within those boundaries has been made especially difficult for women (and for some women more than others).[6] This is part of a pattern that Ann Shola Orloff calls a "farewell to maternalism" in favour of "employment for all," which has intensified since the 1990s.[7] Federal and provincial governments have introduced neo-liberal welfare state reforms that, with their focus on privatization of services and personal responsibility, have reinforced the association between citizenship rights and attachment to the workforce. However, the particular social rights needed to promote and support women's labour force participation have gone largely ignored. As Mahon says, the logic of "gender sameness" underlies this social policy retrenchment, as have the realities of gender inequalities in the labour market.[8] In the American context, the cancellation of Aid to Families with Dependent Children in 1996, which disproportionately applied to poor black women, promoted independence but did (and does) not take into account the inadequacies of child care systems, not to mention the racism and sexism that make it difficult for women to find jobs that allow them to support their families.[9]

Recent changes to social assistance in British Columbia have similar consequences. Margaret Little and Lynne Marks have analyzed these reforms, which essentially amount to restricted eligibility based on labour force criteria. The goal of welfare officials is to reduce welfare dependency, thereby allowing them to cut spending. In order to receive assistance, one must demonstrate that he or she has looked for a job. In some cases, proof of working and earning in previous years is required. Single parents with children older than three are considered employable. These are policies that assume "that welfare recipients can find work if they really need to," as Little and Marks argue.[10] As they point out, these reforms ignore the "invisible barriers that make it very difficult for [women] to get and keep jobs," including time spent caregiving and, perhaps most of all, the lack of access to affordable, high-quality, flexible child care.[11]

The dilemmas of working motherhood, in other words, remain deeply embedded in welfare reform. As a result, scholars have continually asked about the nature of a "woman-friendly" state, a question raised by Helga Hernes in 1987.[12] In some form or another, this question of "woman friendliness" imbues most feminist analyses of the welfare state. Scholars debate whether welfare programs offer empowerment to women or whether it simply reproduces their dependence on a patriarchal state rather than a male breadwinner. Others point out that in their relationships with welfare officials, women are subject to moral, sexual, and physical regulation.[13] Some scholars, though, emphasize the opportunities that welfare programs have created for women, especially when those women are viewed as active agents in their relationship with the state. It has provided mothers with steady (if limited) incomes after divorce or desertion, it has offered women the chance for employment, and it has provided women with a range of benefits such as wage protection, freedom from discrimination, and the securing of reproductive rights.[14]

Hernes's question of woman friendliness also compels us to ask about worker-citizenship and mother-citizenship. Is a women-friendly state one that buttresses women's complete access to worker-citizenship – one that allows women, in other words, to participate in the wage labour force on the same terms as men? In order to create such a state, universal child care is necessary, as is generous maternity/parental leave, flexible work arrangements, the recognition that the often part-time, temporary, or otherwise "irregular" work of mothers should not disqualify them from the social rights typically linked to male breadwinner work.[15] Observers often point to Sweden as the "archetype" of this kind of woman-friendly welfare state. The Swedish state provides low-cost child care and paid parental leave, women are employed at high levels and with good wages, and working hours are relatively low, better allowing for a satisfactory workplace-home balance.[16]

Even the Swedish model, however, has its limitations, including a persistently gender-segregated labour force that sees women disproportionately represented in lower-paying occupations. Commentators also point to other drawbacks of policies that promote mothers' wage earning: though they may attain equality in the wage labour force, they still put in a "double day" through domestic and caregiving tasks at home.[17] Emphasizing wage work as the pinnacle of participation and empowerment, furthermore, serves to devalue caregiving work, reproducing long-held patterns at the root of women's oppression. For others, then, a women-friendly state is one that is not so focused on women's opportunities within the paradigm of worker-citizenship but, rather, one that values, recognizes, and compensates caregiving work. Social programs in this kind of state, in other words, would regard care as being as important as wage earning. This is not, of course, a new idea but one that harkens back to mothers' pensions and Wages for Housework, and historians have shown that certain women have been advocating along these lines for a long time. The early twentieth-century working-class women studied by Emily Abel, for example, "struggle[d] to be able to care" for their families and resisted the charity workers' insistence that their "rehabilitation" was to be found through wage work.[18]

These ideals are still present in contemporary policy proposals towards creating a women-friendly state. Building on Nancy Fraser's idea of the "universalization of care," scholars and advocates suggest the need to assign value to caregiving and to implement policy levers that would break down the divide between the traditionally masculine public sphere of wage earning and the traditionally feminine private sphere of caregiving.[19] As Paul Kershaw puts it, such policies would reject the "one-sided workerist vision of social inclusion" and citizenship.[20] More specifically, this might include policy reforms such as making access to social assistance dependent not only on labour market participation but also on time spent providing care for children or elderly or disabled family members. It could also mean, for another example, providing non-contributory pensions for all or providing some sort of "care allowance."[21]

In this vein, Kershaw proposes a set of policy reforms that he calls carefair, based on the idea that we need to remake social citizenship to mean someone who is "neither wholly a labour force participant nor only an unpaid caregiver, but a citizen who interweaves both roles."[22] Crucially, Kershaw argues, this citizenship must include both women and men. He offers a series of concrete changes that would work towards this goal: governments should make parental leave more generous and extended to include self-employed and part-time workers; pensions should operate on the same principles; employment standards should be reformed so that fewer hours qualify as full-time work; and, of course, greater public commitment to child care would be required. These reforms would also help to ensure that women of colour, immigrant women, and Aboriginal women, who are often disproportionately represented in low-paid and precarious work, have access to the social supports that would allow them to balance work and care and to maintain autonomy.[23] Of course, Kershaw points out, carefair requires "cultural norms about masculinity, fatherhood, motherhood, and employment [to] evolve to endorse male caregiving as a valuable practice on par with other citizenry pursuits that enjoy more social status for men." However, sending a clear message about the importance of caregiving through policy reforms, he argues, will "nudge men to make more socially responsible and equitable choices about caregiving."[24]

Current social policy directions, and proposals such as Kershaw's to reform them, arise out of a long historical trajectory of debate, negotiation, and experimentation. Both making and challenging child care policy, in other words, requires historical context. In British Columbia and across Canada, the current state of child care policy as well as the broader determination of the particular contours of a women-friendly state suggest the need for even more historical investigation into the meanings and purposes of child care, the cultural values assigned to work and motherhood, and women's relationships to the state. This is particularly true when it comes to differences across race and class lines. To take seriously the claims that caregiving needs to be formalized through state compensation, for example, we need to know more about if and how understandings and approaches to caregiving work in indigenous communities and among immigrant women and women of colour in British Columbia and Canada is different from the normative middle-class white experience. These kinds of questions can take their cues from historical work such as Linda Gordon's, which reveals that minority women in the United States often had "different welfare priorities" than white women.[25] The legacy of racist child welfare practices such as the "60s scoop," for example, not to mention the history of institutionalization in residential schools, inform much different meanings around non-maternal child care in indigenous families in British Columbia.[26] These historical factors need to be more deeply explored in order to be taken seriously in contemporary policy-making.

The twenty-first century's racialized politics of child care labour also point to the need for more historical investigation. Today, many child care observers point out that Canada's "crisis of care" is being met by the live-in caregiver (LCP) program, one of the federal government's temporary foreign worker programs.[27] Introduced in 1991, the LCP allows foreign-born caregivers, today mostly women from the Philippines, to work for families as a way to earn permanent residency status after twenty-four months of work. Families who hire live-in caregivers must provide suitable accommodations and can employ caregivers only for child care or elderly caregiving.[28] That the LCP has become Canada's de facto child care system suggests the need to examine the racial and class dynamics of who has provided child care for mothers who were in the labour market and how the low status assigned to caregiving as an occupation contributes to the inequalities between women. Although the LCP is held up by the federal government as a shining "example of access to membership in Canadian society," organizations of live-in caregivers and their advocates point out that the caregivers live and work in exploitative and vulnerable conditions: long hours, unpaid overtime, lack of privacy, long separations from their own families, and low pay.[29] The LCP, as Rachel Brickner and Christine Straehle note, highlights "the crisis of caring labour, in which women joining the paid workforce simply replace their unpaid domestic labour with the paid labour of socially and politically invisible migrant women."[30] This situation was certainly true in the past as well, but we know little about the women who worked as caregivers in British Columbia and Canada. The perceived incompatibility of wage work and caregiving for some women and not for others was informed by historical patterns of race- and class-based discrimination, but there is still much to be learned about who provided paid child care. Who, for example, were the women who worked in the day care centres? Who worked as nannies and in-home caregivers for the working mothers who did not have access to group centres? How do the racial dynamics of the historical child care labour force contribute to the continual undervaluing of caregiving labour today and to the low status and pay afforded child care workers even as defenders of the family touted the "priceless" value of motherhood?

The politics of child care in the twenty-first century is a complex and often-contradictory tangle of both long-established and new meanings. Child care is framed as an incentive to get low-income mothers into the work force; as an anti-poverty strategy; as an invasive government program that undermines the sacred role of mothers; as a women's right; as an investment in children; and as sound long-term economic policy. After one hundred years of debates, though, the multi-dimensional and fundamental uneasiness around working motherhood remains embedded in child care politics. Working mothers have long been an uncomfortable fit inside the boundaries of social citizenship. The framework through which a public child care system could be achieved, then, requires a vision of social citizenship that does not position working mothers as outsiders but, rather – in their combination of wage earning and caregiving, in the value they provide to their families, and in their workplaces, their communities, and society – the model upon which the construction of social citizenship is based.

Notes

Introduction
1. "Editorial," *Victoria Daily Times*, 10 April 1920, 4.
2. *Victoria Daily Times*, 9 April 1920, 1; *Victoria Daily Times*, 14 January 1919, 1. *Mothers' Pensions Act*, SBC 1920, c. 61.
3. *Victoria Daily Times*, 10 April 1920, 4.
4. "Editorial," *Vancouver Province*, 15 March 1944, 4.
5. *Victoria Daily Colonist*, 15 July 1967, 19.
6. "Childcare's Not about Funds, but About Caring," *The Province*, 15 March 2013; Martha Friendly et al., *Early Childhood Care and Education in Canada 2012* (Toronto: Childcare Resource and Research Unit, 2013), 63.
7. *Victoria Daily Times*, 8 July 1965, 21. Emphasis in original.
8. Letter to the Editor, *Victoria Daily Times*, 5 January 1922, 4.
9. *Victoria Daily Times*, 8 July 1965, 21; *Vancouver Sun*, 8 March 1969, 14.
10. Shelley Fralic, "Do We Owe Anyone a Living?" *Vancouver Sun*, 17 December 2001, A13.
11. *Victoria Daily Colonist*, 10 April 1920, 1, 3.
12. In its original context, "crèche" refers to the charitable daytime care for children under two years of age, a service first established in France in the mid-nineteenth century. The Vancouver City Crèche was a service that provided care during the day for the children of working mothers and not just infants. Similar services around North America were more often called day nurseries. As Larry Prochner notes, though, several such institutions retained the name crèche, though they "bore little resemblance" to the older French institutions. See Larry Prochner, *A History of Early Childhood Education in Canada, Australia, and New Zealand* (Vancouver: UBC Press, 2009), 90–92.

13 Susan Prentice, "High Stakes: The 'Investable' Child and the Economic Reframing of Childcare," *Signs: Journal of Women in Culture and Society* 34, 3 (2009): 687.
14 Prentice, "High Stakes," 687. For a recent report that makes this business case, see Craig Alexander and Dina Ignjatovic, *Early Childhood Education Has Widespread and Long Lasting Benefits*, TD Economics Special Report (27 November 2012). See also Gordon Cleveland and Michael Krashinsky, *The Benefits and Costs of Good Child Care: The Economic Rationale for Public Investment in Young Children* (Toronto: Childcare Resource and Research Unit, University of Toronto, 1998).
15 Judith Shklar, *American Citizenship: The Quest for Inclusion* (Cambridge, MA: Harvard University Press, 1991), 98–99.
16 Nancy Christie, *Engendering the State: Family, Work, and Welfare in Canada* (Toronto: University of Toronto Press, 2000).
17 Alice Kessler-Harris, *In Pursuit of Equity: Women, Men, and the Quest for Economic Citizenship in Twentieth-Century America* (Madison, NY: Oxford University Press, 2001), 11.
18 "Wages for Housework" campaigners, who were part of second-wave feminism, resented the association between waged work and women's "liberation" and instead sought to have the value of housework and caregiving recognized.
19 Sonya Michel, *Children's Interests / Mothers' Rights: The Shaping of America's Child Care Policy* (New Haven, CT: Yale University Press, 1999), 7.
20 Cynthia Comacchio, "'A Postscript for Father': Defining a New Fatherhood in Interwar Canada," *Canadian Historical Review* 78, 3 (September 1997): 392; Cynthia Comacchio, *The Infinite Bonds of Family: Domesticity in Canada, 1850–1940* (Toronto: University of Toronto Press, 1999); Neil Sutherland, *Children in English-Canadian Society: Framing the Twentieth-Century Consensus* (Waterloo, ON: Wilfrid Laurier University Press, 2000); Ruth Frager and Carmela Patrias, *Discounted Labour: Women Workers in Canada, 1870–1939* (Toronto: University of Toronto Press, 2005); Joan Sangster, *Transforming Labour: Women and Work in Postwar Canada* (Toronto: University of Toronto Press, 2010).
21 T.H. Marshall, "Citizenship and Social Class," in *Class, Citizenship, and Social Development: Essays by T.H. Marshall* (Westport, CT: Greenwood Press, 1964), 72.
22 Rianne Mahon, "Child Care As Citizenship Right? Toronto in the 1970s and 1980s," *Canadian Historical Review* 86, 2 (June 2005): 285–315.
23 Michel, *Children's Interests / Mothers' Rights*, 2 [emphasis in original]. Gender critiques of Marshall include Nancy Fraser and Linda Gordon, "Contract versus Charity: Why Is There No Social Citizenship in the United States?" *Socialist Review* 22, 3 (July-September 1992): 45–67; Barbara Hobson, "Feminist Strategies and Gendered Discourses in Welfare States: Married Women's Right to Work in the United States and Sweden," in *Mothers of a New World: Maternalist Politics and the Origins of Welfare States*, ed. Seth Koven and Sonya Michel (New York: Routledge, 1993); Carol Pateman, "The Patriarchal

Welfare State," in *Democracy and the Welfare State*, ed. Amy Gutman (Princeton, NJ: Princeton University Press, 1988).

24 Alexandra Z. Dobrowolsky and Jane Jenson, "Shifting Representations of Citizenship: Canadian Politics of 'Women' and 'Children,' *Social Politics* 11, 2 (Summer 2004): 158; Ann Shola Orloff, "Gendering the Comparative Analysis of Welfare States: An Unfinished Agenda," *Sociological Theory* 27, 3 (September 2009): 317–19, 334.

25 Lara Campbell, *Respectable Citizens: Gender, Family, and Unemployment in Ontario's Great Depression* (Toronto: University of Toronto Press, 2009), 11; Maria Bucur, "Gender and Citizenship: Difference and Power in the Modern State," *Journal of Women's History* 20, 4 (2008): 160–70.

26 Warren Magnusson, "The Local State in Canada: Theoretical Perspectives," *Canadian Public Administration* 28, 4 (1985): 575–99. See also Janine Brodie, "The Social in Social Citizenship," in *Recasting the Social in Citizenship*, ed. Engin F. Isin (Toronto: University of Toronto Press, 2008); and the articles in the collection by Robert Adamoski, Dorothy E. Chunn, and Robert Menzies, eds., *Contesting Canadian Citizenship: Historical Readings* (Peterborough, ON: Broadview Press, 2002).

27 Jane Jenson, "Representations of Gender: Policies to 'Protect' Women Workers and Infants in France and the United States," in *Women, the State, and Welfare*, ed. Linda Gordon (Madison, WI: University of Wisconsin Press, 1990), 152. Gender analyses are among the most recent approaches to studying the welfare state. Previous studies have argued that the origins of welfare states can be found in functionalist explanations, in state- and bureaucracy-centred analyses, in comparative studies of political culture, or in analyses of class conflict. For a useful overview of these approaches, see James Struthers, *The Limits of Affluence: Welfare in Ontario* (Toronto: University of Toronto Press and Ontario Historical Studies Series, 1994), 3–18; Alvin Finkel, *Social Policy and Practice in Canada: A History* (Waterloo, ON: Wilfrid Laurier University Press, 2006), 1–14. Studies of women and the welfare state began to emerge in the 1980s as a reaction to these "gender-blind" historical analyses. See Alvin Finkel, "Changing the Story: Gender Enters the History of the Welfare State," *Tijdschrift Voor Sociale Geschiedenis* 22, 1 (1996): 67–81.

28 Christie, *Engendering the State*; Finkel, *Social Policy and Practice*. For an important American study, see Linda Gordon, *Pitied but Not Entitled: Single Mothers and the History of Welfare, 1890–1935* (New York: Free Press, 1994).

29 For example, Gillian Creese, "Sexuality Equality and the Minimum Wage in British Columbia," *Journal of Canadian Studies / Revue d'Etudes Canadiennes* 26, 4 (Winter 1991–92): 120–40; Ruth Roach Pierson, "Gender and the Unemployment Insurance Debates in Canada, 1934–1940," *Labour / Le Travail* 25 (Spring 1990): 77–103.

30 Finkel, "Changing the Story," 71; Barbara Nelson, "The Origins of the Two-Channel Welfare State: Workmen's Compensation and Mothers' Aid," in Gordon, *Women, the State, and Welfare*, 123–51; Margaret Jane Hillyard Little, *No Car, No Radio, No Liquor Permit: The Moral Regulation of Single Mothers in Ontario, 1920–1997* (Toronto: Oxford University Press, 1998); James Struthers,

"'In the Interests of the Children': Mothers' Allowances and the Origins of Income Security in Ontario, 1917–1930," in *Social Fabric or Patchwork Quilt: The Development of Social Policy in Canada*, ed. Raymond Blake and Jeffrey A. Keshen (Peterborough, ON: Broadview Press, 2006); Veronica Strong-Boag, "'Wages for Housework': Mothers' Allowances and the Beginnings of Social Security in Canada," *Journal of Canadian Studies / Revue d'Etudes Canadiennes* 14, 1 (Spring 1979): 24–34; Joanne Goodwin, *Gender and the Politics of Welfare Reform: Mothers' Pensions in Chicago* (Chicago: University of Chicago Press, 1997).

31 Mimi Abramovitz, *Regulating the Lives of Women: Social Welfare Policy from Colonial Times to the Present* (Boston: South End Press, 1996).

32 Ann Porter, *Gendered States: Women, Unemployment Insurance, and the Political Economy of the Welfare State in Canada, 1945–1997* (Toronto: University of Toronto Press, 2003).

33 James Struthers, *No Fault of Their Own: Unemployment and the Canadian Welfare State* (Toronto: University of Toronto Press, 1983); P.E. Bryden, *Planners and Politicians: Liberal Politics and Social Policy, 1957–1968* (Montreal and Kingston: McGill-Queen's University Press, 1997); Raymond Blake, *From Rights to Needs: A History of Family Allowances in Canada* (Vancouver: UBC Press, 2009); Little, *No Car, No Radio*; Struthers, *The Limits of Affluence*.

34 Michel, *Children's Interests / Mothers' Rights*, 3, 8.

35 See, for example, Larry Prochner, "A History of Early Education and Child Care in Canada, 1820–1966," in *Early Childhood Care and Education in Canada*, ed. Larry Prochner and Nina Howe (Vancouver: UBC Press, 2000), 45–51; Finkel, *Social Policy and Practice in Canada*, 70–76. More focused studies of some of these institutions include Larry W. Prochner, "Themes in the History of Day Care: A Case Study of the West End Crèche, Toronto, 1909–1939," PhD dissertation, University of Toronto, 1994; Wendy J. Atkin, "Playing Together as Canadians: Historical Lessons from the West End Crèche," in *Changing Child Care: Five Decades of Child Care Advocacy and Policy in Canada*, ed. Susan Prentice (Halifax: Fernwood Publishing, 2001); and Christina Simmons, "'Helping the Poorer Sisters': The Women of the Jost Mission, Halifax, 1905–1945," *Acadiensis* 14, 1 (Autumn 1994): 3–27. General histories of day care in Canada include Donna Varga, *Constructing the Child: A History of Canadian Day Care* (Toronto: James Lorimer, 1997); and the collection by Kathleen Gallagher Ross, ed., *Good Day Care: Fighting for It, Getting It, Keeping It* (Toronto: Women's Press, 1978).

36 See, for example, Diane Purvey and Christopher Walmsley, eds., *Child and Family Welfare in British Columbia: A History* (Calgary: Detselig Enterprises, 2005).

37 Alvin Finkel, "Even the Little Children Cooperated: Family Strategies, Childcare Discourse, and Social Welfare Debates 1945–1975," *Labour/Le Travail* 36 (Fall 1995): 91–118; Rianne Mahon, "The Never-Ending Story: The Struggle for Universal Child Care Policy in the 1970s," *Canadian Historical Review* 81, 4 (December 2000): 582–622. *Canada Assistance Plan*, RSC 1966–67, c. C-45.

38 Susan Prentice, "Workers, Mothers, Reds: Toronto's Postwar Day Care Fight," *Studies in Political Economy* 30 (Autumn 1989): 115–41; Mahon, "Child Care as Citizenship Right"; Suzanne Morton, "From Infant Homes to Day Care: Child Care in Halifax," in *Mothers of the Municipality: Women, Work, and Social Policy in Post-1945 Halifax*, ed. Judith Fingard and Janet Guildford (Toronto: University of Toronto Press, 2005); Tom Langford, *Alberta's Day Care Controversy: From 1908 to 2009 and Beyond* (Edmonton: Athabasca University Press, 2010); Prentice, *Changing Child Care*.

39 Jane Jenson, "Against the Current: Child Care and Family Policy in Quebec," in *Child Care Policy at the Crossroads: Gender and Welfare State Restructuring*, ed. Sonya Michel and Rianne Mahon (New York: Routledge, 2002), 310–11; Patrizia Albanese, "Small Town, Big Benefits: The Ripple Effect of $7/day Child Care," *Canadian Review of Sociology and Anthropology* 43, 2 (2006): 130; Jocelyne Tougas, "What We Can Learn from the Quebec Experience," in *Our Children's Future: Child Care Policy in Canada*, ed. Gordon Cleveland and Douglas Krashinsky (Toronto: University of Toronto Press, 2001), 92–93; Micheline Lalonde-Graton, *Des salles d'asile aux centres de la petite enfance: La petite histoire des services de garde au Québec* (Sainte-Foy, QC: Presses de l'Université du Québec, 2002).

40 Annis May Timpson, *Driven Apart: Women's Employment Equality and Child Care in Canadian Public Policy* (Vancouver: UBC Press, 2001). Other works on Canadian child care that emerge from political economy, law, and sociology – most of them relatively contemporary – include Cheryl Collier, "Governments and Women's Movements: Explaining Child Care and Anti-Violence Policy in Ontario and British Columbia, 1970–2000," PhD dissertation, University of Toronto, 2006; Dobrowolsky and Jenson, "Shifting Representations of Citizenship"; and Lene Madsen, "Citizen, Worker, Mother: Canadian Women's Claims to Parental Leave and Childcare," *Canadian Journal of Family Law* 11 (2002): 11–74. There is no Canadian study that offers the equivalent of Sonya Michel, *Children's Interests / Mothers' Rights* nor, for the post-war period, Emilie Stoltzfus, *Citizen, Mother, Worker: Debating Public Responsibility for Child Care after the Second World War* (Chapel Hill, NC: University of North Carolina Press, 2003).

41 Gøsta Esping-Andersen, *The Three Worlds of Welfare Capitalism* (Cambridge: Polity Press, 1990), 26–27. In conservative-corporatist welfare states, the "preservation of status differentials" predominated, as did the preservation of traditional family forms, and so the "redistributive impact" of the state was negligible. Social democratic regimes "pursued a welfare state that would promote an equality of the highest standards, not an equality of minimal needs as was pursued elsewhere."

42 Rianne Mahon, "Gender and Welfare State Restructuring: Through the Lens of Child Care," in Michel and Mahon, *Child Care Policy at the Crossroads*, 1–27; Julia S. O'Connor, Ann Shola Orloff, and Sheila Shaver, *States, Markets, Families: Gender, Liberalism and Social Policy in Australia, Canada, Great Britain and the United States* (Cambridge: Cambridge University Press, 1999);

Rianne Mahon and Susan Phillips, "Dual Earner Families Caught in a Liberal Welfare Regime? The Politics of Child Care Policy in Canada," in Michel and Mahon, *Child Care Policy at the Crossroads*, 191–218; Kimberly J. Morgan, *Working Mothers and the Welfare State: Religion and the Politics of Work-Family Policies in Western Europe and the United States* (Stanford, CT: Stanford University Press, 2006); Tammy Findlay, "Provincial Child Care: Gender Regimes and Social Citizenship in Canada," paper presented at the Annual Meeting of the Canadian Political Science Association, University of Victoria, 4 June 2013.

43 Mahon, "Gender and Welfare State Restructuring," 6.
44 Kimberley J. Morgan, "Child Care and the Liberal Welfare Regime: A Review Essay," *Review of Policy Research* 20, 4 (December 2003): 747.
45 Rianne Mahon et al., "Convergent Care Regimes? Childcare Arrangements in Australia, Canada, Finland and Sweden," *Journal of European Social Policy* 22, 4 (2012): 428; Rianne Mahon, "Varieties of Liberalism: Canadian Social Policy from the 'Golden Age' to the Present," *Social Policy and Administration* 42, 4 (August 2008): 342–61.
46 One example of the trend towards provincial comparisons is Kelly Pasolli and Lisa Young, "Comparing Child Care Policy in the Canadian Provinces," paper presented to the Annual Meeting of the Canadian Political Science Association, University of Alberta, 12–15 June 2012.
47 Collier, "Governments and Women's Movements," 107–10.
48 Ruth Lister, "Dilemmas in Engendering Citizenship," in *Gender and Citizenship in Transition*, ed. Barbara Hobson (New York: Routledge, 2000), 49.
49 Lister, "Dilemmas," 53. Sonya Michel calls this the "limits of maternalism." Sonya Michel, "The Limits of Maternalism: Policies toward American Wage-Earning Mothers during the Progressive Era," in Koven and Michel, *Mothers of a New World*, 277–320.
50 Mahon, "Gender and Welfare State Restructuring," 4. For an introduction to this debate in the sociological literature, see Mary Daly and Katherine Rake, *Gender and the Welfare State: Care, Work and Welfare in Europe and the US* (Cambridge: Polity Press, 2003); Helga Maria Hernes, *Welfare State and Women Power: Essays in State Feminism* (Oslo, Norway: Norwegian University Press, 1987); Jane Lewis, "Gender and the Development of Welfare Regimes," *Journal of European Social Policy* 2, 3 (1992): 159–73; Orloff, "Gendering the Comparative Analysis of Welfare States," 317–43.
51 Paul Kershaw, *Carefair: Rethinking the Responsibilities and Rights of Citizenship* (Vancouver: UBC Press, 2005), 4.
52 Nelson, "The Origins of the Two-Channel Welfare State."
53 Nancy Fraser and Linda Gordon, "A Genealogy of Dependency: Tracing a Keyword of the US Welfare State," *Signs* 19, 2 (Winter 1994): 320–23.
54 Margaret Hillyard Little, "Claiming a Unique Place: The Introduction of Mothers' Pensions in BC," *BC Studies* 105–6 (Spring/Summer 1995): 80–102.
55 Finkel, *Social Policy and Practice*, 203.
56 Findlay, "Provincial Child Care," 7.

57 Struthers, *No Fault of Their Own.*
58 Christie, *Engendering the State*, 4.
59 Eileen Boris, "What About the Working of the Working Mother?" *Journal of Women's History* 5, 2 (Fall 1993): 104–9.
60 Jeanne Fay, "The 'Right Kind' of Single Mothers: Nova Scotia's Regulation of Women on Social Assistance, 1956–77," in *Mothers of the Municipality: Women, Work, and Social Policy in Post-1945 Halifax*, ed. Judith Fingard and Janet Guildford (Toronto: University of Toronto Press, 2005); Eileen Boris and S.J. Kleinberg, "Mothers and Other Workers: (Re)conceiving Labor, Maternalism, and the State," *Journal of Women's History* 15, 3 (Autumn 2003): 104; Gwendolyn Mink, "The Lady and the Tramp: Gender, Race, and the Origins of the American Welfare State," in Gordon, *Women, the State, and Welfare*, 92–122; Goodwin, *Gender and the Politics of Welfare Reform*; Annalise Orleck, *Storming Caesar's Palace: How Black Mothers Fought Their Own War on Poverty* (Boston: Beacon Press, 2005); Gwendolyn Mink, *Welfare's End* (Ithaca, NY: Cornell University Press, 2002).
61 Little, "Claiming a Unique Place"; Little, *No Car, No Radio.*
62 Sangster, *Transforming Labour*, 199–232.
63 Struthers, "'In the Interests of the Children,'" 68. For a further discussion on the class-based origins of the welfare state, see Alvin Finkel, "The State of Writing on the Welfare State: What's Class Got to Do with It?" *Labour/Le Travail* 54 (Fall 2004): 151–74.
64 Joy Parr, *The Gender of Breadwinners: Women, Men, and Change in Two Industrial Towns, 1880–1950* (Toronto: University of Toronto Press, 1998).
65 Stoltzfus, *Citizen, Mother, Worker*, 6.
66 See Ruth K. Abbott and R.A. Young, "Cynical and Deliberate Manipulation? Child Care and the Reserve Army of Female Labour in Canada," *Journal of Canadian Studies / Revue d'Etudes Canadiennes* 24, 2 (1989): 22–38.
67 Campbell, *Respectable Citizens*, 18. Shirley Tillotson's work on women's resistance to tax regulations is another interesting example of "women's political and economic agency that allowed them to cope in an unfair world that, from their disadvantaged world, they could not change." Shirley Tillotson, "Relations of Extraction: Taxation and Women's Citizenship in the Maritimes," *Making Up the State: Women in Twentieth-Century Atlantic Canada*, ed. Janet Guildford and Suzanne Morton (Fredericton, NB: Acadiensis Press, 2010), 109. See also Shirley Tillotson, "Citizen Participation in the Welfare State: An Experiment," *Canadian Historical Review* 75, 4 (1994): 511–42.
68 Linda Gordon makes the important point that much of the recent historiography of women and welfare emphasizes the ways in which working with/in the state offers opportunities for women, not just oppression. Linda Gordon, "The New Feminist Scholarship on the Welfare State," in Gordon, *Women, the State and Welfare*, 9–35.
69 Susan Prentice, "Changing Child Care: Looking Back, Moving Forward," in Prentice, *Changing Child Care*, 20.
70 Mahon, "Gender and Welfare State Restructuring."

71 Prochner, "A History of Early Education and Child Care," 22–23; Larry Prochner, *A History of Early Childhood Education*.
72 Prochner, "A History of Early Education and Child Care," 28.
73 Loren Lind and Susan Prentice, *Their Rightful Place: An Essay on Children, Families and Childcare in Canada* (Toronto: Our Schools/Our Selves Education Foundation, 1992), 92.
74 Diane Barbara Purvey, "Alexandra Orphanage and Families in Crisis in Vancouver, 1892–1928," in Purvey and Walmsley, *Child and Family Welfare in British Columbia*, 53–75.
75 Prochner, "A History of Early Education and Child Care," 23–27.
76 Ibid., 43.
77 Ibid., 51; Robert Adamoski, "The Child-The Citizen-The Nation: The Rhetoric and Experience of Wardship in Early Twentieth-Century British Columbia," in Adamoski, Chunn, and Menzies, *Contesting Canadian Citizenship*, 315–36.
78 Varga, *Constructing the Child*, chapters 3, 4, 5. Penney Clark, Mona Gleason, and Stephen Petrina, "Preschools for Science: The Child Study Centre at the University of British Columbia, 1960–1997," *History of Education Quarterly* 52, 1 (February 2012): 29–61.
79 Atkin, "Playing Together as Canadians," 31; Varga, *Constructing the Child*, 88–94.
80 The *WDNA* came into effect through Order in Council P.C. 6242, 20 July 1942. See "Memorandum of Agreement...between His Majesty the King, in the right of the Dominion of Canada...and His Majesty the King, in the right of the Province...," Library and Archives Canada (LAC), RG 27, v. 609, file 6-52-1 pt. 1.
81 Prochner, "A History of Early Education and Child Care," 54.
82 Larry Prochner, "'Share Their Care Mrs. Warworker': Wartime Day Nurseries in Ontario and Quebec, 1942–1945," *Canadian Journal of Research in Early Childhood Education* 5, 1 (1996): 115–26.
83 Gillian Weiss, "An Essential Year for the Child: The Kindergarten in British Columbia," in *Schooling and Society in Twentieth Century British Columbia*, ed. J. Donald Wilson and David C. Jones (Calgary: Detselig Enterprises, 1980), 146.
84 Prentice, "Workers, Mothers, Reds."
85 Lind and Prentice, *Their Rightful Place*, 95.
86 Varga, *Constructing the Child*, 47.
87 Clark, Gleason, and Petrina, "Preschools for Science," 36.
88 Weiss, "An Essential Year for the Child."
89 Prochner, "A History of Early Education and Child Care," 38; Clark, Gleason, and Petrina, "Preschools for Science," 54.
90 Prochner, "A History of Early Education and Child Care," 55.
91 Canadian policy was influenced by Project Head Start in the United States in 1965. Varga, *Constructing the Child*, 115.
92 Prentice, "High Stakes."
93 Linda A. White, "Trends in Child Care/Early Childhood Education/Early Childhood Development Policy in Canada and the United States," *American Review of Canadian Studies* (Winter 2004): 666, 670–71.

94 *Fact Sheet 1 for BC Parents: What the Plan Means for Families*, prepared by the Coalition of Child Care Advocates of British Columbia and Early Childhood Educators of British Columbia as part of the Community Plan for a Public System of Integrated Early Care and Learning, 4th edition (July 2013).
95 Martha Friendly and Susan Prentice, *About Canada: Childcare* (Black Point, NS: Fernwood Publishing, 2009), 114.
96 Pamela Nuttall Nason and Pam Whitty, "Bringing action research to the curriculum development process," *Educational Action Research* 15, 2 (June 2007): 271–81.
97 Findlay, "Provincial Child Care," 4.
98 Prentice, "High Stakes."
99 Kelly Pasolli, "Child Care Advocacy in Alberta," BA thesis, University of Lethbridge, 2010.
100 Discussions of working mothers' private child care arrangements often appear, however briefly, in histories of women and families. See, for example, Elizabeth Rose, *A Mother's Job: The History of Day Care, 1890–1960* (New York: Oxford University Press, 1999), 49–55; Magda Fahrni, *Household Politics: Montreal Families and Postwar Reconstruction* (Toronto: University of Toronto Press, 2005), 57–60.

Chapter 1: "A proper independent spirit"

This chapter was originally published as "'A Proper Independent Spirit': Working Mothers and the Vancouver City Crèche, 1909–1920," *BC Studies* 173 (Spring 2012): 69–95.

1 "Tots May Play While Mothers Toil," *Vancouver Sun*, 4 April 1912; "The Creche," *Vancouver Sun*, 26 April 1912; "Head of the New Creche," *Vancouver Province*, 10 July 1914; "Here Is a Home Where Kiddies Are Always Welcome: Creche Is Doing Noble Work in Caring for Children," *Vancouver Sun*, 12 October 1912; "The Creche," *Vancouver Daily World*, 5 February 1913. The latter article noted that members of the St. Andrew's Circle of King's Daughters provided volunteer kindergarten teachers.
2 Vancouver City Crèche, *Register Book 1912–19*, City of Vancouver Archives (CVA), Add MSS 124, 511-G-3, file 1.
3 Allan Irving, "The Development of a Provincial Welfare State: British Columbia 1900–1939," in *The "Benevolent" State: The Growth of Welfare in Canada*, ed. Allan Moscovitch and Jim Albert (Toronto: Garamond Press, 1987); Robert Adamoski, "Their Duties towards the Children: Citizenship and the Practice of Child Rescue in Early Twentieth Century British Columbia," PhD dissertation, Simon Fraser University, 1995; Gillian Creese, "The Politics of Dependence: Women, Work and Unemployment in the Vancouver Labour Movement before World War II," in *British Columbia Reconsidered: Essays on Women*, ed. Gillian Creese and Veronica Strong-Boag (Vancouver: Press Gang Publishers, 1992); Margaret Hillyard Little, "Claiming a Unique Place: The Introduction of Mothers' Pensions in BC," *BC Studies* 105–6 (Spring/Summer 1995): 80–102; Megan Davies, "'Services Rendered, Rearing Children for the State': Mothers' Pensions in British Columbia," in *Not Just Pin Money: Selected Essays on the History of Women's Work in British Columbia*, ed. B. Latham and

R. Pazdro (Victoria: Camosun College Press, 1984); Kenneth A. Venables, "The Making of Protective Labour Legislation in British Columbia: The 1912 Royal Commission on Labour and Its Aftermath," MA thesis, Simon Fraser University, 1996.

4 Diane L. Matters, "Public Welfare Vancouver Style," *Journal of Canadian Studies / Revue d'Etudes Canadiennes* 14, 1 (Spring 1979): 3.

5 Seth Koven and Sonya Michel, "Introduction: 'Mother Worlds,'" in *Mothers of a New World: Maternalist Politics and the Origins of Welfare States*, ed. Seth Koven and Sonya Michel (New York: Routledge, 1993).

6 James Struthers, *No Fault of Their Own: Unemployment and the Canadian Welfare State, 1914–1941* (Toronto: University of Toronto Press, 1983); Nancy Christie, *Engendering the State: Family, Work, and Welfare in Canada* (Toronto: University of Toronto Press, 2000).

7 Elsie Gregory MacGill, *My Mother the Judge: A Biography of Judge Helen Gregory MacGill* (Toronto: Ryerson Press, 1955), 130.

8 Elizabeth Norcross, "Mary Ellen Smith: The Right Woman in the Right Place at the Right Time," in Latham and Pazdro, *Not Just Pin Money*, 357–64.

9 *Henderson's City of Vancouver Directory* (Vancouver: Henderson's Publishing Company, 1909).

10 T.E. Aikins does not appear in the city directories around 1909.

11 Wendy Mitchinson, "Early Women's Organizations and Social Reform: Prelude to the Welfare State," in Moscovitch and Albert, *The "Benevolent" State*, 77–92.

12 MacGill, *My Mother the Judge*, 130–34; Adamoski, "Their Duties towards the Children," especially chapter 3.

13 Christina Simmons, "'Helping the Poorer Sisters': The Women of the Jost Mission, Halifax, 1905–1945," *Acadiensis* 14, 1 (Autumn 1994): 3–27.

14 Larry W. Prochner, "Themes in the History of Day Care: A Case Study of the West End Crèche, Toronto, 1909–1939," PhD dissertation, University of Toronto, 1994; Wendy J. Atkin, "Playing Together as Canadians: Historical Lessons from the West End Crèche," in *Changing Child Care: Five Decades of Child Care Advocacy and Policy in Canada*, ed. Susan Prentice (Halifax: Fernwood Publishing, 2001).

15 Donna Varga, *Constructing the Child: A History of Canadian Day Care* (Toronto: James Lorimer, 1997), 20.

16 See, for example, *Victoria Daily Colonist*, 25 October 1913, 7; *Victoria Daily Colonist*, 18 October 1913, 8; *Victoria Daily Colonist*, 17 October 1913, 10.

17 Gillian Weiss, in her thorough study of Vancouver's clubwomen, argues: "The activities of the churches at this time no doubt served to enhance the climate of social reform within which women's clubs operated and no doubt some women were strongly influenced by their own personal religious convictions but there is no evidence that the women's clubs studied were one of the major media through which they worked." See Gillian Weiss, "'As Women and As Citizens': Clubwomen in Vancouver, 1910–1928," PhD dissertation, University of British Columbia, 1983, 255. For insight into British Columbia's "irreligiousity," see Lynne Marks, "'Leaving God Behind When They Crossed the

Rocky Mountains': Exploring Unbelief in Turn-of-the-Century British Columbia," in *Household Counts: Canadian Households and Families in 1901*, ed. Peter Baskerville and Eric W. Sager (Toronto: University of Toronto Press, 2007).

18 Weiss, "'As Women and As Citizens'"; Margaret Jane Hillyard Little, *No Car, No Radio, No Liquor Permit: The Moral Regulation of Single Mothers in Ontario, 1920-1997* (Toronto: Oxford University Press, 1998), 26. Though historians have debated the distinction between "maternalism" and "feminism," Weiss argues that the rationale behind Vancouver's clubwomen's activities is best described as maternal feminism. On this issue, see Molly Ladd-Taylor, *Mother-Work: Women, Child Welfare, and the State, 1890-1930* (Urbana, IL: University of Illinois Press, 1994).

19 Weiss, "'As Women and As Citizens,'" 142-44; Creese, "The Politics of Dependence," 364-90.

20 Statistics Canada, *Rural and Urban Population of Canada, by Province and Sex, 1911*, http://www65.statcan.gc.ca/acyb02/1917/acyb02_191700849a-eng.htm.

21 Lorraine Brown, "Domestic Service in British Columbia, 1850-1914," MA thesis, University of Victoria, 1995, 22-31.

22 Robin John Anderson, "Domestic Service: The YWCA and Women's Employment Agencies in Vancouver, 1898-1915," *Histoire Sociale/Social History* 25, 50 (November 1992), 311. See also Eric W. Sager, "The Transformation of the Canadian Domestic Servant, 1897-1931," *Social Science History* 31, 4 (Winter 2007): 509-37.

23 Robert A.J. McDonald, "Working Class Vancouver, 1886-1914: Urbanism and Class in British Columbia," in *Vancouver Past: Essays in Social History*, ed. Robert A.J. McDonald and Jean Barman (Vancouver: UBC Press, 1986), 42-43; Venables, "The Making of Protective Labour Legislation," 36-38. Women comprised 9.6 percent of Vancouver's manufacturing workforce.

24 Lilian Nelson, "Vancouver's Early Days and the Development of Her Social Services," paper given at the annual meeting of the Social Workers' Club, 18 May 1934, CVA, PAM 1935-53.

25 *Victoria Daily Colonist*, 14 November 1907, 6.

26 National Council of Women of Canada, *Annual Report* (Toronto, 1907), 66. Cited in Anderson, "Domestic Service," 313. See also Robert A.J. McDonald, *Making Vancouver: Class, Status, and Social Boundaries, 1863-1913* (Vancouver: UBC Press, 1996), 99.

27 Sager, "The Transformation of the Canadian Domestic Servant," 526-27.

28 Brown, "Domestic Service in British Columbia," 78-81.

29 Jean Mann et al., *Women Lead the Way: A History of the University Women's Club of Vancouver, 1907-2007* (Vancouver: Ray Hignell Services, 2007), 12.

30 Anderson, "Domestic Service," 313.

31 Patricia Roy, *A White Man's Province: British Columbia Politicians and Chinese and Japanese Immigrants, 1858-1914* (Vancouver: UBC Press, 1989), 180.

32 Nelson, "Vancouver's Early Days," 20.

33 Roy, *A White Man's Province*, 180.

34 Patricia Roy and John Herd Thompson, *British Columbia: Land of Promises* (Don Mills, ON: Oxford University Press, 2005), 91; Roy, *A White Man's Province*, 185–226.
35 *Vancouver Daily World*, 3 February 1913, 9; Nelson, "Vancouver's Early Days," 20.
36 Brown, "Domestic Service," 75–77.
37 Anderson, "Domestic Service," 310–11.
38 Nelson, "Vancouver's Early Days," 20.
39 Vancouver City Council, Meeting of the Finance Committee, *Minutes*, 3 November 1911, CVA, City Council and Office of the City Clerks fonds, series 33, volume 18, 376.
40 *Census of Canada 1901*, Table 1; *Census of Canada 1911*, Table 7; McDonald, *Making Vancouver*, xii-xv.
41 Matters, "Public Welfare Vancouver Style," 3.
42 See the Finding Aid for City Social Service Department fonds, Associated Charities of Vancouver, CVA, PR 447.
43 Associated Charities, *Minutes of Annual Meeting*, 5 February 1912, CVA, PR 447, Minute Book 1912–14, 106-A-1, file 6.
44 Associated Charities, *Case Book 1909*, CVA, PR 447, 106-A-1, file 3.
45 Vancouver City Council, *Minutes*, 19 January 1912, CVA, City Council and Office of the City Clerks fonds, series 31, volume 18, 478.
46 Associated Charities, *Minutes of 29 February 1912 Meeting*, CVA, PR 447, Minute Book 1912–14, 106-A-1, file 6.
47 Rev. J.K. Unsworth Obituary, *The Province*, 17 December 1938; Irene Howard, *The Struggle for Social Justice in British Columbia: Helena Gutteridge, the Unknown Reformer* (Vancouver: UBC Press, 1992), 108.
48 MacDonald, for example, testified extensively before the Royal Commission on Labour in 1913. See BC Royal Commission on Labour, Vancouver, 12 March 1913, British Columbia Archives (BCA), GR 0684, box 2, file 1.
49 The crèche committee consisted of: Mrs. Lillian Forbes MacDonald (regent of the Imperial Order Daughters of the Empire's (IODE) Richard McBride Chapter), Mrs. J.K. Unsworth (first vice-regent), Mrs. McAlpine (the wife of a doctor), Mrs. F.C. Wade, Mrs. P. Donnelly (whose husband was the president and manager of Canadian Financiers), Mrs. N.C. Kydd, Mrs. M. McBeath (the wife of alderman and future mayor Malcolm McBeath), Mrs. William M. Barnard (whose husband was a jewelry manufacturer at Henry Birk and Sons), Mrs. C.F. Campbell (whose husband was a partner in the law firm Campbell and Singer), Mrs. H.W. Baker (wife of the president of Northern Securities), Mrs. A.E. Short (whose husband owned a real estate and insurance firm), and Mrs. R. Charles Stoddard. Information taken from Membership Lists 1912–13, IODE, Richard McBride/Valcartier Camp Chapter, CVA, Add MSS 556, 566-A-6, file 4; and *Henderson's City of Vancouver Directory* (1912). Members of the city's Health Board also had voting privileges on the crèche committee. Vancouver City Council, *Minutes of the Meeting of the Health Committee*, 9 February 1912, CVA, City Council and Office of the City Clerk fonds, series 31, volume 18, 522.

50 MacGill, *My Mother the Judge*, 129–30; *Vancouver Women's Building, Diary and Directory*, CVA, PAM 1938-16. In 1926, the Vancouver Women's Building organization erected a building perfectly suited to their purposes.
51 Chuck Davis, *The Greater Vancouver Book: An Urban Encyclopedia* (Surrey, BC: Linkman Press, 1997).
52 *Vancouver Daily World*, 5 February 1913, 9. Some sources indicate that the mothers also had to pay a $1 yearly membership fee to use the crèche. Associated Charities, *Minutes of 6 January 1913 Meeting*, CVA, PR 447, "Minutes 1912–14," 106-A-1, file 6.
53 *Vancouver Sun*, 26 April 1912, 6, 11.
54 *Vancouver Sun*, 12 October 1912, 7; *Vancouver Daily World*, 5 February 1913, 9.
55 *The Province*, 25 April 1912, 25.
56 *Vancouver Sun*, 26 April 1912, 6, 11.
57 *Vancouver Daily World*, 5 February 1913, 9.
58 *Vancouver Sun*, 12 October 1912, 7.
59 "The Creche," *The Province*, 27 November 1912; Vancouver City Crèche, *Register Book 1912–19*, CVA, Add MSS 124, 511-G-3, file 1.
60 Associated Charities, *Minutes*, 28 November 1912, CVA, PR 447, "Minutes 1912–14," 106-A-1, file 6.
61 *The Province*, 27 November 1912, 6; *Vancouver Sun*, 4 December 1912, 6.
62 Vancouver City Council, *Minutes*, 2 December 1912, CVA, City Council and Office of the City Clerk fonds, series 31, volume 19, 185, 248.
63 *The Province*, 10 July 1914, 8.
64 Ibid. Paul earned $60 per month, and she had two assistants who each earned $35 per month.
65 Lilian Nelson obituary, *The Province*, 17 September 1960.
66 Jean Barman, *The West beyond the West: A History of British Columbia* (Toronto: University of Toronto Press, 2007), 195.
67 Roy and Thompson, *Land of Promises*, 102–11. For other works that address cycles of economic boom and bust in British Columbia in the 1910s and effects on the labour market, see Barman, *The West beyond the West*, 189–251; McDonald, "Working Class Vancouver," 33–69; Robert A.J. McDonald, "Victoria, Vancouver, and the Economic Development of British Columbia, 1886–1914," in *British Columbia: Historical Readings*, ed. W. Peter Ward and Robert A.J. McDonald (Vancouver: Douglas and McIntyre, 1981).
68 "Everything Hideous for Vancouver's Out-of-Works," *British Columbia Federationist*, 10 April 1914.
69 Barman, *The West beyond the West*, 217–18; Canada, *The Labour Gazette* (Ottawa: Department of Labour, August 1914), 190. Gutteridge wrote *The Labour Gazette*'s Vancouver entry.
70 "Workless Women Hold a Mass Meeting," *British Columbia Federationist*, 25 September 1914.

71　Canada, *The Labour Gazette* (Ottawa: Department of Labour, November 1914).
72　Vancouver Trades and Labour Council (VTLC), *Minutes*, 15 October 1914, University of British Columbia Rare Books and Special Collections (UBCRBSC), *Minutes of Regular Meetings*, 1912–16, VTLC fonds, box 16.4.
73　"How Women Handle Unemployment Problems," *British Columbia Federationist*, 19 February 1915; "Women Organize an Unemployment League," *British Columbia Federationist*, 9 October 1914. The Women's Employment League is well documented in Howard, *The Struggle for Social Justice*.
74　"Mothers, Children, and Deserted Wives," *British Columbia Federationist*, 30 October 1914.
75　Desmond Morton, *Fight or Pay: Soldiers' Families in the Great War* (Vancouver: UBC Press, 2004), 190–91.
76　VTLC, *Minutes*, 18 February 1915, UBCRBSC, "Minutes of Regular Meetings, 1912–16," VTLC fonds, box 16.4.
77　Morton, *Fight or Pay*, 190–91.
78　*British Columbia Federationist*, 19 February 1915, 1; "The Man's Problem That Needs Solving," *British Columbia Federationist*, 16 October 1914, 1.
79　Gutteridge, *The Struggle for Social Justice*, 105.
80　*Analysis of Families Receiving Relief*, 1915 Relief Officer, CVA, PR 20, 13-C-2, file 1. In March 1915, the *Labour Gazette* reported that 600-700 of approximately 1,900 relief listings were families.
81　The Employment and Relief Association operated through 1914 and included representatives from city council, Relief Officer George Ireland, the Trades and Labour Council, the Board of Trade, clergymen, the Victorian Order of Nurses, and various benevolent organizations. The city council's Relief Committee also existed at the same time. Both relied on the management of Relief Officer George Ireland. With the creation of a new department, relief structures were consolidated. Matters, "Public Welfare, Vancouver Style," 3.
82　"Appeal Is Made for Day Nursery," *Victoria Daily Colonist*, 17 October 1913, 10.
83　Anderson, "Domestic Service," 330.
84　*British Columbia Federationist*, 19 February 1915, 1. The remaining placements were for stenographers, dressmakers, office workers, clerks, waitresses, chambermaids, and a few teachers and nurses.
85　*British Columbia Federationist*, 16 April 1915, 1.
86　*Vancouver Sun*, 31 October 1916, 10.
87　McDonald, "Working Class Vancouver," 42; *British Columbia Federationist*, 25 September 1914.
88　*The Province*, 26 March 1917, 8.
89　Matters, "Public Welfare Vancouver Style," 5.
90　I would like to thank Shirley Tillotson for her input regarding these ideas.
91　*Vancouver Daily World*, 22 January 1917, 10.
92　*Vancouver Daily World*, 2 June 1917, 15.
93　*Vancouver Daily World*, 22 January 1917, 10.
94　*The Province*, 26 March 1917, 8.

95 City of Vancouver, *Annual Report of the Medical Health Officer*, 1913–16, CVA, City Publications Collection, PDS 11. The number of days of care grew from 7,322 to 9,140.
96 Vancouver City Crèche, *Register Book 1912–19*, CVA, Add MSS 124, 511-G-3, file 1.
97 Ibid.
98 Ibid. These are from 1912. A more systematic analysis is not possible because the entries are quite inconsistent and, in some cases, left almost entirely blank. By far the majority of cases must be classified as "unknown." As per the CVA's confidentiality agreement, the names of these families have been changed.
99 Vancouver City Crèche, *Register Book 1912–19*, CVA, Add MSS 124, 511-G-3, file 1.
100 Ibid.
101 Diane Barbara Purvey, "Alexandra Orphanage and Families in Crisis in Vancouver, 1892–1928," in *Child and Family Welfare in British Columbia: A History*, ed. Diane Purvey and Christopher Walmsley (Calgary: Detselig Enterprises, 2007).
102 *British Columbia Federationist*, 9 October 1914, 1; *British Columbia Federationist*, 25 September 1914, 1.
103 Vancouver City Crèche, *Register Book 1912–19*, CVA, Add MSS 124, 511-G-3, file 1. There is an example of this occurring in April 1913.
104 Vancouver City Council, *Minutes of the Relief Committee*, 12 July 1915, CVA, City Council and Office of the City Clerk fonds, series 33, volume 20, 662.
105 *Vancouver Sun*, 12 October 1912, 7.
106 Roy and Thompson, *Land of Promises*, 107–8.
107 Creese, "The Politics of Dependence," 374–75. Women were first employed as munitions workers in 1917 for the Vancouver Engineering Company. See *British Columbia Federationist*, 26 January 1917, 1.
108 "Creche Proves Very Expensive," *Vancouver Daily World*, 13 January 1917.
109 See, for example, *Victoria Daily Colonist*, 4 March 1917, 8; *Victoria Daily Colonist*, 11 January 1918, 10; *Victoria Daily Colonist*, 18 January 1918, 7; *Victoria Daily Colonist*, 18 January 1918, 8; Victoria Children's Aid Society, *Minutes of 8 July and 12 August 1914 Meeting*, Records Book, 1912–1917, BCA, MS 0431, box 1.
110 *The Province*, 26 October 1916, 8.
111 *The Province*, 6 February 1917, 11; *Vancouver Daily World*, 6 February 1917, 8.
112 *Vancouver Sun*, 31 October 1916, 10.
113 *Vancouver Daily World*, 25 January 1917, 9; *The Province*, 6 February 1917, 11.
114 *The Province*, 6 February 1917, 11.
115 Adamoski, "Their Duties towards the Children," 118–19.
116 Andrew Jones and Leonard Rutman, *In the Children's Aid: J.J. Kelso and Child Welfare in Ontario* (Toronto: University of Toronto Press, 1981), 51.
117 *Vancouver Daily World*, 13 January 1917, 23.
118 *Vancouver Daily World*, 25 January 1917, 9.
119 *Vancouver Sun*, 30 January 1917, 12.
120 Ibid.
121 See Koven and Michel, "Introduction," 1–33.

122 Little, "Claiming a Unique Place," 81.
123 Gillian Creese, "Sexual Equality and the Minimum Wage in British Columbia," *Journal of Canadian Studies / Revue d'Etudes Canadiennes* 26, 4 (Winter 1991–92): 125. Male minimum wage legislation was passed in 1926.
124 See Gutteridge, *The Struggle for Social Justice*, 104–35; Marie Campbell, "Sexism in British Columbia Trade Unions, 1900–1920," in *In Her Own Right: Selected Essays on Women's History in British Columbia*, ed. Cathy Kess and Barbara Latham (Victoria: Camosun College Press, 1980).
125 The mothers' pension commission was officially called the BC Commission on Health Insurance. *Report of the Hearing of the Health Insurance Commission*, Nelson, BC, 13 December 1919, BCA, GR 0706.
126 Ibid.
127 *Report of the Hearing of the Health Insurance Commission*, Vancouver, BC, 20 January 1920, BCA, GR 0706.
128 Christie, *Engendering the State*, 145–47.
129 Matters, "Public Welfare Vancouver Style," 8.
130 Relief Officer, *Crèche Report*, 2 January 1929 to 16 January 1929, CVA, City Council and Office of the City Clerk fonds, series 20, 14-F-5, file 5.
131 Relief Officer, *Crèche Reports*, 1918–29, CVA, City Council and Office of the City Clerk fonds, series 20; Vancouver Day Nursery Association, *Annual Report*, 1932–33, UBCRBSC.

Chapter 2: "Self help is to be encouraged to the fullest extent"

1 *Victoria Daily Colonist*, 9 December 1921, 4; *Victoria Daily Times*, 5 January 1922, 7; *Victoria Daily Colonist*, 10 January 1922, 4; *Victoria Daily Colonist*, 11 January 1922, 6.
2 *Victoria Daily Colonist*, 9 December 1921, 4.
3 *Victoria Daily Times*, 5 January 1922, 4. This was a letter from a "Mother of Five."
4 *Victoria Daily Colonist*, 19 January 1922, 6.
5 Victoria Children's Aid Society, *Minutes*, 11 January 1922, British Columbia Archives (BCA), MS 0431, box 1.
6 *Mothers' Pensions Act*, SBC 1920, c. 61.
7 A discussion of the notion of "good" dependency can be found in Nancy Fraser and Linda Gordon, "A Genealogy of Dependency: Tracing a Keyword of the US Welfare State," *Signs* 19, 2 (Winter 1994): 319–20.
8 Margaret Hillyard Little, "Claiming a Unique Place: The Introduction of Mothers' Pensions in BC," *BC Studies* 105–6 (Spring/Summer 1995): 167–69. The other study that focuses exclusively on BC mothers' pensions is Megan Davies, "'Services Rendered, Rearing Children for the State': Mothers' Pensions in British Columbia," in *Not Just Pin Money: Selected Essays on the History of Women's Work in British Columbia*, ed. B. Latham and R. Pazdro (Victoria: Camosun College Press, 1984).
9 Elizabeth Rose, *A Mother's Job: The History of Day Care, 1890–1960* (New York: Oxford University Press, 1999), 73.

10 Allan Irving, "The Development of a Provincial Welfare State: British Columbia 1900–1939," in *The "Benevolent" State: The Growth of Welfare in Canada*, ed. Allan Moscovitch and Jim Albert (Toronto: Garamond Press, 1987).

11 Charlotte Whitton, *Report of Miss Charlotte Whitton, Executive Director of the Canadian Council on Child and Family Welfare, on Mothers' Pensions and Social Service Work in the Province of British Columbia*, prepared for the Honourable S.L. Howe, Provincial Secretary (Victoria, 1 December 1931) [a full version of this report is available in the British Columbia Legislative Library].

12 Joanne Goodwin, *Gender and the Politics of Welfare Reform: Mothers' Pensions in Chicago* (Chicago: University of Chicago Press, 1997), 7.

13 Lara Campbell, *Respectable Citizens: Gender, Family, and Unemployment in Ontario's Great Depression* (Toronto: University of Toronto Press, 2009), 58.

14 *Victoria Daily Times*, 14 January 1919, 1; *Victoria Daily Times*, 15 January 1919, 18.

15 Seth Koven and Sonya Michel, "Introduction: 'Mother Worlds,'" in *Mothers of a New World: Maternalist Politics and the Origins of Welfare States*, ed. Seth Koven and Sonya Michel (New York: Routledge, 1993), 4. Major studies of mothers' pensions in the United States include Goodwin, *Gender and the Politics of Welfare Reform* and Theda Skocpol, *Protecting Soldiers and Mothers: The Political Origins of Social Policy in the United States* (Cambridge, MA: Harvard University Press, 1992).

16 Koven and Michel, "Introduction," 2 [emphasis in the original].

17 Barbara Nelson, "The Origins of the Two-Channel Welfare State: Workmen's Compensation and Mothers' Aid," in *Women, the State, and Welfare*, ed. Linda Gordon (Madison, WI: University of Wisconsin Press, 1990).

18 James Struthers, "'In the Interests of the Children': Mothers' Allowances and the Origins of Income Security in Ontario, 1917–1930," in *Social Fabric or Patchwork Quilt: The Development of Social Policy in Canada*, ed. Raymond B. Blake and Jeffrey A. Keshen (Peterborough, ON: Broadview Press, 2006), 81. See also Margaret Jane Hillyard Little, *No Car, No Radio, No Liquor Permit: The Moral Regulation of Single Mothers in Ontario, 1920–1997* (Toronto: Oxford University Press, 1998); Veronica Strong-Boag, "'Wages for Housework': Mothers' Allowances and the Beginnings of Social Security in Canada," *Journal of Canadian Studies / Revue d'Etudes Canadiennes* 14, 1 (Spring 1979): 24–34.

19 Little, "Claiming a Unique Place."

20 Ibid., 167–69.

21 Elizabeth Norcross, "Mary Ellen Smith: The Right Woman at the Right Place at the Right Time," in Latham and Pazdro, *Not Just Pin Money*, 357–64.

22 Lyn Gough, *As Wise As Serpents, 1883–1939: Five Women and an Organization That Changed British Columbia* (Victoria, BC: Swan Lake Publishing, 1988).

23 *British Columbia Federationist*, 30 October 1914; Vancouver Trades and Labour Council (VTLC), *Minutes of Regular Meetings, 1912–16*, 8 February 1915, University of British Columbia Rare Books and Special Collections (UBCRBSC), VTLC fonds, box 16.4.

24 VTLC, *Minutes of Regular Meetings, 1912–16*, 21 August 1913, UBCRBSC, VTLC fonds, box 16.4.
25 VTLC, *Minutes of Regular Meetings, 1912–16*, 15 October 1914, UBCRBSC, VTLC fonds, box 16.4.
26 British Columbia, *First Annual Reports of the Superintendent of Neglected Children and Mothers' Pensions for the Year Ending November 30th, 1920*, reprinted in *Sessional Papers of the Province of British Columbia* (Victoria: King's Printer, 1921). This report also contains a complete listing of the organizations and individuals that were part of the delegations.
27 *Victoria Daily Colonist*, 22 March 1918, 11.
28 The commission actually released an earlier, separate report on mothers' pensions, leaving aside the question of state health insurance for a later date.
29 Royal Commission on Health Insurance (1919–21), *Report on Mothers' Pensions*, 22 March 1920, 2, BCA, GR 0706, box 1, file 1.
30 BC Commission on Health Insurance (1919–21), *Proceedings*, Princeton Hearings, Reverend Robert Herbison, 8 December 1919, BCA, GR 0706, box 1, file 3 [*Proceedings 1919–21*].
31 *Proceedings 1919–21*, Revelstoke Hearings, Mrs. S.G. Robbins, Women's Canadian Club, 6 January 1920, BCA, GR 0706, box 1, file 3.
32 *Proceedings 1919–21*, Vancouver Hearings, Mrs. Lillian Nelson, 20 January 1920, BCA, GR 0706, box 1, file 4; *Proceedings 1919–21*, Victoria Hearings, Mrs. William Grant (Maria), 13 January 1920, BCA, GR 0706, box 1, file 3.
33 Speech by the Honourable J.D. MacLean on the Second Reading of the Bill Providing for Pensions for Mothers, BCA, GR 0344, box 1, file 2.
34 *Proceedings 1919–21*, Nanaimo Hearings, Joseph Dickson, 12 January 1920, BCA, GR 0706, box 1, file 3.
35 "Another View of Mothers' Pensions," *Victoria Daily Times*, 1 May 1920, 23.
36 Royal Commission on Health Insurance, *Report on Mothers' Pensions*, 3.
37 *Proceedings 1919–21*, Prince Rupert Hearings, Edith Booth, 31 December 1919, BCA, GR 0706, box 1, file 3. See also the testimony of *Proceedings 1919–21*, Fernie Hearings, W. Robson, Gladstone Local Union of United Mine Workers, 10 December 1919, BCA, GR 0706, box 1, file 3.
38 *Proceedings 1919–21*, Vancouver Hearings, Jack Kavanagh, 20 January 1920, BCA, GR 0706, box 1, file 4. For a discussion of Kavanagh and other "socialist radicals" in the VTLC after 1917, see Irene Howard, *The Struggle for Social Justice in British Columbia: Helena Gutteridge, the Unknown Reformer* (Vancouver: UBC Press, 1992), 127.
39 Sonya Michel, "The Limits of Maternalism: Policies toward American Wage-Earning Mothers during the Progressive Era," in Koven and Michel, *Mothers of a New World*, 277–320.
40 *Act to Provide Pensions for Mothers*, SBC 1920, c. 61.
41 *Victoria Daily Colonist*, 10 April 1920, 1.
42 British Columbia, *Mothers' Pensions Board Annual Reports* (Victoria: King's Printer, 1922–44).
43 Little, "Claiming a Unique Place," 99.

Notes to Pages 57–59

44 *Victoria Daily Times*, 21 August 1920, 6 ; *Victoria Daily Times*, 30 September 1920, 8.
45 *Victoria Daily Times*, 13 August 1920, 1.
46 Royal Commission on Health Insurance, *Report on Mothers' Pensions*, 12–13.
47 *Victoria Daily Colonist*, 16 September 1920, 5.
48 *An Act to Amend the Mothers' Pensions Act*, SBC 1921, c. 43.
49 *Victoria Daily Colonist*, 23 October 1921, 4.
50 *Victoria Daily Times*, 31 March 1921, 6.
51 Mrs. Alicia Smith, Letter to Editor, *Victoria Daily Colonist*, 1 November 1921, 4; Mrs. May Wize, Letter to the Editor, *Victoria Daily Colonist*, 4 November 1921, 4; Mrs. Montague Williams, Letter to the Editor, *Victoria Daily Colonist*, 6 November 1921, 27.
52 *Victoria Daily Times*, 31 March 1921, 6.
53 *Victoria Daily Times*, 11 November 1922, 28.
54 British Columbia, *Annual Report Made under the Mothers' Pensions Act for the Year Ending September 30, 1922* (Victoria: King's Printer, 1923). The permanent appointment of a woman to the Mothers' Pensions Board became a controversial issue in 1924–25. Both the New Era League (NEL) and the Civilian Pensioned Mothers Association (CPMA), an organization to provide charitable assistance to struggling pensioned mothers, were concerned to get one of their own appointed to the Mothers' Pensions Board. The NEL pushed particularly hard on this issue and wanted the Mothers' Pensions Board completely separated from the Workmen's Compensation Board (WCB) and constituting at least two women (Susie Lane Clark and another NEL member). The CPMA simply wanted their president, Barbara Chippendale, appointed to the already-existing Mothers' Pensions Board. Both groups were disappointed by the government's decision in December 1924 to appoint Miss Margaret Sutherland, president of the Women's Liberal Association, to the board. Chippendale felt the appointment was a "great blow" to her personally, for she had assumed she was the favoured appointee of the government (as opposed to the women of a "certain league," undoubtedly the NEL). Susie Lane Clark was also dismayed at Sutherland's appointment. Clark conceded she was "no doubt a very estimable and capable person" but felt she was "not fitted for the position, because as a single women [sic], she has not the intuitional knowledge which belongs to a women [sic] who is a wife or mother, and must be embarrassed in the nature of the discussion which of necessity must come in the business of the Board." Correspondence between E.S. Winn, J. Morton, and J. Fulton of the CPMA, 1922, BCA, GR 0441, box 227, file 8; Correspondence between J. Fulton and J. Morton, 1923, BCA, GR 0441, box 235, file 9; Correspondence between B. Chippendale/J. Fulton, E.S. Winn, and Premier Oliver, 1924, BCA, GR 0441, box 242, file 8.
55 E.S. Winn to Attorney-General Manson, 14 February 1925, BCA, GR 1323, reel B2320. According to Winn, it was only fair that mothers' pension amounts were on par with WCB payments. Interestingly, even though many more mothers' pensions were granted throughout the mid-1920s, the amount the province spent on workmen's compensation payouts to "dependents of

deceased workmen" was higher overall. See British Columbia, *Workmen's Compensation Board Annual Reports* (Victoria: King's Printer, 1924–30).
56   Speech by the Honourable J.D. MacLean on the Second Reading of the Bill Providing for Pensions for Mothers, BCA, GR 0344, box 1, file 2.
57   M.C.C. to J.D. MacLean, 5 February 1921, BCA, GR 0344, box 1, file 2. A similar example is found in J.A.B. to J.D. MacLean, 13 August 1920, BCA, GR 0344, box 1, file 2.
58   *Victoria Daily Colonist*, 8 November 1921, 4.
59   E.S. Winn to Premier Oliver, 10 November 1925, BCA, GR 0441, box 250, file 14.
60   *Victoria Daily Colonist*, 20 October 1921, 4; *Victoria Daily Times*, 19 October 1921, 13.
61   Correspondence between Mrs. W, Premier Oliver, and E.S. Winn, 1922, BCA, GR 0441, box 227, file 8. Other senior officials repeatedly expressed similar sentiments. See, for example, A. McNabb (Mothers' Pensions Board Secretary) to R.H. Pooley (Attorney-General), 24 December 1928, BCA, GR 1323, reel B2320.
62   Correspondence between G. Pyke, J. Morton, and MPP George Hanes, June–July 1923, BCA, GR 0441, box 235, file 9. At one point, Pyke identified the age beyond which a mother might be incapable of supporting a child through work as forty-five.
63   Correspondence between G. Pyke and J. Morton (Secretary to Premier Oliver), 1923, BCA, GR 0441, box 235, file 9; Correspondence between Mr. S, Premier MacLean, and E.S. Winn, 1927, BCA, GR 0441, box 267, file 6.
64   *Victoria Daily Times*, 19 October 1921, 13.
65   British Columbia, *Annual Report Made under the Mothers' Pensions Act for the Year Ending September 30, 1922* (Victoria: King's Printer, 1923), 2.
66   James Struthers, *"No Fault of Their Own": Unemployment and the Canadian Welfare State, 1914–1941* (Toronto: University of Toronto Press, 1983), 6–7.
67   British Columbia, *Annual Report Made under the Mothers' Pensions Act for the Year Ending September 30 1929* (Victoria: King's Printer, 1930), 1.
68   British Columbia, *Annual Report of the Department of Labour for the Year Ending December 31st 1920* (Victoria: King's Printer, 1921). Minimum wage rates varied by industry. Mercantile workers earned a minimum of $51 per month, while those in the fishing industry were entitled to at least $62 per month, the highest minimum wage rate for women. Office, telephone, and telegraph operators also had high minimum wages at $60 monthly in 1920.
69   Correspondence between G. Pyke and J. Morton, 1923, BCA, GR 0441, box 235, file 9. Other senior officials echoed this sentiment. See E.S. Winn to A.M. Manson, 7 November 1922, BCA, GR 1323, reel B02211; McNabb to Pooley, 24 December 1928, BCA GR 1323, reel B02320.
70   G. Pyke to J. Farris, 6 April 1921, BCA, GR 1323, reel B02211.
71   G. Pyke to A.M. Johnson (Deputy Attorney-General), 4 April 1921, BCA, GR 1323, reel B02211.
72   David Brankin (Superintendent of Neglected Children) to J. Farris, 24 March 1922, BCA, GR 1323, reel B02211.

73 See British Columbia, *Annual Report(s) Made under the Mothers' Pensions Act* (for the years ending 1922–30) (Victoria: King's Printer, 1923–31).
74 Jean Barman, *The West beyond the West: A History of British Columbia* (Toronto: University of Toronto Press, 2007), 268.
75 British Columbia, *Report of the Committee Appointed by the Government to Investigate the Finances of British Columbia* (Victoria: King's Printer, 1932). The report was commonly known as the *Kidd Report*. The Kidd commission was chaired by George Kidd, the former president of the BC Electric Company. See ibid., 268–71.
76 Christopher Walmsley, "The British Columbia Child Welfare Survey (1927): A Policy Narrative of Children's Needs," in *Child and Family Welfare in British Columbia: A History*, ed. Diane Purvey and Christopher Walmsley (Calgary: Detselig Enterprises, 2005).
77 Nancy Christie, *Engendering the State: Family, Work, and Welfare in Canada* (Toronto: University of Toronto Press, 2000), 168.
78 See Catherine Mary Ulmer, "The Report on Unemployment and Relief in Western Canada, 1932: Charlotte Whitton, R.B. Bennett and the Federal Response to Relief," MA thesis, University of Victoria, 2009.
79 Christie, *Engendering the State*, 167–73; James Struthers, "A Profession in Crisis: Charlotte Whitton and Canadian Social Work in the 1930s," *Canadian Historical Review* 62, 2 (June 1981): 169–85; Patricia Rooke and R.L. Schnell, *No Bleeding Heart: Charlotte Whitton, A Feminist on the Right* (Vancouver: UBC Press, 1987).
80 The government employed a "field staff" of six to look after mothers' pensions, all of whom were women. Mrs. F.H. Murrie (appointed in 1922, a Scottish-born social worker, widowed with one son); Mrs. Laura Edwards (appointed 1920, widowed with no children, formerly of the Catholic Children's Aid Society); Mrs. O.J. Taylor (appointed 1927, widowed with no children, trained as a nurse); Mrs. Daisy Thompson (appointed 1921, widowed, a trained nurse with experience in the Medicine Hat, AB, Relief Department); Mrs. Amy G. Mowbrat (appointed 1924, married with two teenage children, husband a retired bank manager); and Mrs. Henrietta St. John (appointed 1927, married, husband was "totally disabled," formerly a visitor of the Board of Pensions in Ottawa). Each of these women was responsible for anywhere from 150 to 300 cases.
81 Whitton, *Report on Mothers' Pensions*, 44–46.
82 In the case of Mrs. M, for example, an investigator encouraged her to divorce her husband since, as a divorced woman, she would be considered under the discretionary clause of the act, and investigators assured her that "assistance could be paid when the divorce had been secured." If they had been doing their jobs properly, Whitton argued, investigators would have recognized that Mrs. M's case was not for the consideration of pension administrators but, rather, belonged under the *Deserted Wives Maintenance Act, 1901*, 1 Edw. VII, c.18, where her husband would have been forced to provide support. Whitton, *Report on Mothers' Pensions*, 144–45.

83 Whitton, *Report on Mothers' Pensions*, 174.
84 British Columbia, *Annual Report(s) Made under the Mothers' Pensions Act* (for the years ending 1922–30) (Victoria: King's Printer, 1923–31).
85 Whitton, *Report on Mothers' Pensions*, 67.
86 Ibid., 77.
87 Ibid., 71.
88 Ibid., 62.
89 Ibid., 204.
90 For example, a mother with one child who had equity in property and no rent to pay might qualify for as little as $15 per month. Other potential sources of support that Whitton said investigators needed to be aware of were military pensions, WCB payments, or family members collecting old age pensions. Whitton, *Report on Mothers' Pensions*, 150.
91 Ibid., 87.
92 Ibid., 90.
93 Sometimes she went so far as to suggest that legal action be allowed "for maintenance against older children in a position to assist, and who refuse to do so." Such an action would be allowed under the 1922 *Parents' Maintenance Act*, SBC 1922, c. 57. Whitton, *Report on Mothers' Pensions*, 208.
94 Whitton, *Report on Mothers' Pensions*, 100.
95 Ibid., 172.
96 Moral regulation was a common feature of mothers' pensions administrations across Canada. For the best treatment of this subject, see Little, *No Car, No Radio*.
97 Whitton, *Report on Mothers' Pensions*, 81.
98 Ibid., 83–85.
99 Ibid., 124, 209. She suggests this for women who received insurance payouts too, suggesting they should hand over their earnings to the state, which would then disperse it monthly along with the pension.
100 Ibid., 209.
101 Ibid., 202.
102 British Columbia, *Report and Financial Statement Made under the Mothers' Pensions Act for the Year April 1st 1932 to March 31st 1933* (Victoria: King's Printer, 1933).
103 Ibid. Such as "illness on the part of the mother or child" or "another child in the home over the age of sixteen in ill health."
104 *Victoria Daily Times*, 8 November 1932, 7; *The Province*, 26 September 1932, 16; *The Province*, 16 September 1932, 9.
105 *Victoria Daily Times*, 24 March 1932, 6; *The Province*, 22 March 1932, 1.
106 E.S. Winn to R.H. Pooley, 16 March 1931, BCA, GR 1323, reel B02321.
107 *Victoria Daily Times*, 14 October 1933, 7; *Victoria Daily Colonist*, 21 March 1931, 1; *Vancouver Sun*, 4 February 1932, 1.
108 *The Province*, 4 April 1933, 5, 7.
109 Christie, *Engendering the State*, 172.
110 Harry Cassidy is quoted in ibid., 177.

111 British Columbia, *Report and Financial Statement Made under the Mothers' Pensions Act for the Year April 1st 1934 to March 31st 1935* (Victoria: King's Printer, 1935).
112 *Victoria Daily Times*, 23 March 1933, 1.
113 G. Davidson to Mother, 20 October 1934, BCA, GR 1323, reel B2320.
114 British Columbia, Superintendent of Welfare, *Annual Report on the Administration of the Mothers' Pensions Act of the Province of British Columbia 1936–1937* (Victoria: King's Printer, 1937).
115 Mothers' Pensions Advisory Board (MPAB), *Minutes*, 10 May 1937, 28 September 1937, and 14 March 1938, BCA, GR 0496, box 26, file 9. The MPAB was created as part of 1936 reforms to mothers' pensions legislation, a short-lived effort to improve the program before it was displaced even further into the realm of relief. Most significantly, the province reassumed full financial responsibility for the pensions. Other amendments stipulated that the husband had to have been disabled in British Columbia, increased the allowed property value to $2,500, granted pensions to native British women even if they married an "alien," and granted some money ($7.50) to a mother if she had a disabled husband living with her. Members of the MPAB included Dr. Olga Jardine (past president of University Women's Club and president of the Local Council of Women), Dr. George F. Davidson (chair), Mrs. W.R.F. Richmond, Mrs. F.W Smelts (who had worked with the Vancouver City Crèche), and Mr. Robert Bone. Jardine became chair in 1939. *Victoria Daily Times*, 12 August 1936, 1; *Victoria Daily Times*, 19 June 1939, 11. On job training in the Depression, see Heidi MacDonald, "Maritime Women, the Great Depression, and the Dominion-Provincial Youth Training Program," in *Making Up the State: Women in Twentieth-Century Atlantic Canada*, ed. Janet Guildford and Suzanne Morton (Fredericton, NB: Acadiensis Press, 2010).
116 MPAB, *Minutes*, 28 September 1940, BCA, GR 0496, box 26, file 9.
117 Christie, *Engendering the State*, 169.
118 British Columbia, *Report and Financial Statement Made under the Mothers' Pensions Act for the Year April 1st 1935 to March 31st 1936* (Victoria: King's Printer, 1936), 2.
119 Whitton, *Report on Mothers' Pensions*, 71.
120 Eric W. Sager, "Women in the Industrial Labour Force: Evidence for British Columbia, 1921–53," *BC Studies* 149 (Spring 2006): 45–47, 56. See also Veronica Strong-Boag, "The Girl of the New Day: Canadian Working Women in the 1920s," *Labour/Le Travail* 4 (1979): 131–64; Bettina Bradbury, *Working Families: Age, Gender, and Daily Survival in Industrializing Montreal* (Toronto: University of Toronto Press, 2007), 169–70. Lara Campbell reminds us, however, that the steady rates of women's employment should not obscure the extent of women's unemployment. Mothers and young women looking for jobs were often not recorded as unemployed but, rather, as "dependents." Campbell, *Respectable Citizens*, 45.
121 British Columbia, *Annual Reports of the Department of Labour* (Victoria: King's Printer, 1925–40).

122 Correspondence between Mrs. C and J. Morton, 1928, BCA, GR 0441, box 277, file 10.
123 Sager, "Women in the Industrial Labour Force," 48. For a debate about reactions to married women in the labour force and the degree to which that was explained by concepts of economic justice versus gender norms, see Alice Kessler-Harris, "Gender Ideology in Historical Reconstruction: A Case Study from the 1930s," *Gender and History* 1, 1 (Spring 1989): 31–49; Margaret Hobbs, "Rethinking Antifeminism in the 1930s: Gender Crisis or Workplace Justice? A Response to Alice Kessler-Harris," *Gender and History* 5, 1 (Spring 1993): 4–15.
124 British Columbia, *Annual Report of the Department of Labour* (Victoria: King's Printer, 1935), K41.
125 Alvin Finkel, *Social Policy and Practice in Canada: A History* (Waterloo, ON: Wilfrid Laurier University Press, 2006), 120.
126 Christie, *Engendering the State*, 246. This point is persuasively made by a number of other studies as well, including Campbell, *Respectable Citizens*, 58; Ruth Roach Pierson, "Gender and the Unemployment Insurance Debates in Canada, 1934–1940," *Labour/Le Travail* 25 (Spring 1990): 77–103. Gender, work, family, and welfare in the Depression era are also explored in the following studies: Margaret Hobbs, "Gendering Work and Welfare: Women's Relationship to Wage-Work and Social Policy in Canada during the Great Depression," PhD dissertation, University of Toronto, 1994; Joan Sangster, *Earning Respect: The Lives of Working Women in Small-Town Ontario, 1920–1960* (Toronto: University of Toronto Press, 1995); James Struthers, *The Limits of Affluence: Welfare in Ontario, 1920–1970* (Toronto: University of Toronto Press, 1994); Christie, *Engendering the State*; Denyse Baillargeon, *Making Do: Women, Family and Home in Montreal during the Great Depression* (Waterloo, ON: Wilfrid Laurier University Press, 1999); Katrina Srigley, *Breadwinning Daughters: Young Working Women in a Depression-Era City, 1929–1939* (Toronto: University of Toronto Press, 2010).
127 Finkel, *Social Policy and Practice in Canada*, 121.
128 Pierson, "Gender and the Unemployment Insurance Debates."
129 *Mothers' Allowances Act*, SBC 1937, c. 53.
130 Whitton, *Report on Mothers' Pensions*, 177–78.
131 Gillian Creese, "The Politics of Dependence: Women, Work and Unemployment in the Vancouver Labour Movement before World War II," in *British Columbia Reconsidered: Essays on Women*, ed. Gillian Creese and Veronica Strong-Boag (Vancouver: Press Gang Publishers, 1992), 372; Irene Howard, "The Mothers' Council of Vancouver: Holding the Fort for the Unemployed, 1935–1938," *Vancouver Past: Essays in Social History*, ed. Robert A.J. McDonald and Jean Barman (Vancouver: UBC Press, 1986).
132 *Victoria Daily Times*, 26 February 1935, 7; *Vancouver Sun*, 26 February 1935, 9; Susan Walsh, "The Peacock and the Guinea Hen: Political Profiles of Dorothy Gretchen Steeves and Grace MacInnis," in Creese and Strong-Boag, *British Columbia Reconsidered*, 73–89; Margaret Hobbs, "Equality and Difference:

Feminism and the Defence of Women Workers during the Great Depression," *Labour/Le Travail* 32 (Fall 1993), 208; Sangster, *Earning Respect*, 78-79.
133 See, for example, Correspondence between Mrs. R and Premier Oliver, 1927, BCA, GR 0441, box 267, file 6; Correspondence between Mrs. B and J. Morton, 1923, BCA, GR 0441, box 235, file 9; Correspondence between Mrs. D and Premier Oliver, 1924, BCA, GR 0441, box 242, file 8. For a careful analysis of working-class expressions of citizenship in Ontario, see Campbell, *Respectable Citizens*.
134 Correspondence between Mrs. A and Premier Oliver, 1926, BCA, GR 0441, box 258, file 9.
135 Correspondence between Mrs. S (friend of Mrs. N) and Premier Oliver, 1922, BCA, GR 0441, box 227, file 8; Correspondence between Mr. E (friend of Mrs. H) and Premier Oliver, 1926, BCA, GR 0441, box 258, file 9.
136 Vancouver Day Nursery Association, *Annual Report*, 1933, UBCRBSC, HV 862 V2A1, 1932 to 1945.
137 Vancouver Day Nursery Association, *Annual Report*, 1936 and 1937, UBCRBSC, HV 862 V2A1 1932 to 1945.
138 Michel, *Children's Interests/Mothers' Rights*, 3.
139 Patricia Vandebelt Schulz, "Day Care in Canada: 1850-1962," in *Good Day Care: Fighting for It, Getting It, Keeping It*, ed. Kathleen Gallagher Ross (Toronto: Women's Press, 1978), 146; Donna Varga, *Constructing the Child: A History of Canadian Day Care* (Toronto: James Lorimer, 1997), 13-14.

Chapter 3: "It takes real mothers and real homes to make real children"

1 The *WDNA* came into effect through Order in Council P.C. 6242, 20 July 1942. See "Memorandum of Agreement...between His Majesty the King, in the right of the Dominion of Canada...and His Majesty the King, in the right of the Province...," Library and Archives Canada (LAC), RG 27, v. 609, file 6-52-1 pt. 1.
2 Ruth Roach Pierson, *"They're Still Women After All": The Second World War and Canadian Womanhood* (Toronto: McClelland and Stewart, 1986), especially chapter 1; Jennifer Stephen, *Pick One Intelligent Girl: Employability, Domesticity, and the Gendering of Canada's Welfare State, 1939-1947* (Toronto: University of Toronto Press, 2007), 18, 25-29.
3 British Columbia, *Annual Report of the Department of Labour 1941* (Victoria: King's Printer, 1941), I52.
4 British Columbia, *Annual Report of the Department of Labour 1942* (Victoria: King's Printer, 1942), F54.
5 Eric W. Sager, "Women in the Industrial Labour Force: Evidence for British Columbia, 1921-53," *BC Studies* 149 (Spring 2006): 46.
6 British Columbia, *Annual Report of the Department of Labour* (Victoria: King's Printer, 1939-45).
7 Pierson, *"They're Still Women,"* 50.
8 Ibid., 50-51.
9 Ibid., 51.

10 *Victoria Daily Colonist*, 3 July 1943, 6.
11 Pierson, "*They're Still Women,*" 51.
12 Tom Langford, *Alberta's Day Care Controversy: From 1980 to 2009 and Beyond* (Edmonton: Athabasca University Press, 2011), 20–21.
13 Larry Prochner and Nina Howe, "The Wartime Child Care Centres in Canada and Great Britain: The Sixtieth Anniversary," *Canadian Children* 26, 2 (Fall 2001): 21.
14 Susan Prentice, "Workers, Mothers, Reds: Toronto's Postwar Day Care Fight," *Studies in Political Economy* 30 (Autumn 1989): 116–17. See also Patricia Schulz, "Daycare in Canada: 1850–1962," in *Good Day Care: Fighting for It, Getting It, Keeping It*, ed. Kathleen Gallagher Ross (Toronto: Women's Press, 1978), 150.
15 I. Harvey to F. Eaton, 27 June 1942, British Columbia Archives (BCA), GR 0883, box 18, file 17.
16 F. Eaton to I. Harvey, 2 July 1942, BCA, GR 0883, box 18, file 17; Memorandum of Agreement between Dominion Government and Province of Ontario, 1942, BCA, GR 0883, box 18, file 17.
17 I. Harvey to R. Dalgleish (Tacoma Family Welfare Association), 3 August 1942, and R. Dalgleish to I. Harvey, 25 July 1942, BCA, GR 0883, box 18, file 17.
18 I. Harvey to A.E. Parker (note: in official correspondence, Mrs. G.C. Parker), 6 April 1942, Library and Archives Canada (LAC), MG 28 I 10, volume 49, file 448a.
19 L. Holland to A.E. Parker, 27 March 1942, LAC, MG 28 I 10, volume 49, file 448a.
20 F. Barr to A.E. Parker, 23 March 1942, LAC, MG 28 I 10, volume 49, file 448a; M. Bradford to A.E. Parker, 8 April 1942, LAC, MG 28 I 10, volume 49, file 448a.
21 L. Holland to A.E. Parker, 27 March 1942, LAC, MG 28 I 10, volume 49, file 448a.
22 British Columbia, *Annual Report of the Department of Labour 1942* (Victoria: King's Printer, 1942), F55.
23 Vancouver Day Nursery Association (VDNA), *Annual Report 1941*, University of British Columbia Rare Books and Special Collections (UBCRBSC), HV 862 V2A1, 1932 to 1945.
24 Vancouver Day Nursery Association, *Annual Report 1942*, UBCRBSC, HV 862 V2A1, 1932 to 1945.
25 Bradford to Parker, 8 April 1942.
26 Details about 1941 numbers are in M. Bradford to A.E. Parker, 8 April 1942; VDNA, *Annual Report 1941*.
27 I. Harvey to R. Dalgleish, 3 August 1942.
28 L. Holland to A.E. Parker, 27 March 1942.
29 *Vancouver Sun*, 1 December 1942, 6.
30 See Megan Davies, "Welfare Amazons or Handmaidens of the State?: Welfare Field Workers in Rural BC, 1935–42," in *Child and Family Welfare in BC: A History*, ed. Diane Purvey and Christopher Walmsley (Calgary: Detselig Enterprises, 2005).
31 M. York to I. Harvey, 6 October 1942, BCA, GR 0883, box 18, file 17.

Notes to Pages 82–86

32 Mrs. J. Kisell to Superintendent of Neglected Children, 2 November 1942, BCA, GR 0883, box 18, file 17.
33 B. Holt to Z. Collins, 28 September 1943, BCA, GR 0883, box 18, file 17.
34 I. Harvey to M. York, 8 October 1942, BCA, GR 0883, box 18, file 17.
35 B. Holt to Z. Collins, 28 September 1943. Though apparently Holt ran into problems with the Parent-Teacher's Association, who thought that any kind of child care system should go well beyond custodial care. Their plan, essentially, was to force all children of working mothers (or otherwise "neglected") into PTA-sponsored child care, where they would receive lessons in "habit training and character building." As Holt told Harvey, "it took a great deal of talking to have some of the members realize that the working parent of a child was the one to decide whether they would Place a child in a Foster Home or not." Evidently, the PTA members thought they could "impose Foster Home care on the workers."
36 The debate was also heated in Kelowna, where women were increasingly being employed for fruit-picking jobs. There were tentative inquiries into day nurseries, but no real action. Regional Supervisor to Mrs. E. Pringle (Deputy Inspector of Welfare Institutions), 12 July 1943, BCA, GR 0883, box 18, file 17.
37 I. Harvey to M. York, 8 October 1942, BCA, GR 0883, box 18, file 17.
38 Zella Collins, *Married Women in Employment: Port Alberni and Alberni*, 25 October 1942, BCA, GR 2738, box 1, file 2.
39 Ibid.
40 M. Bradford to A.E. Parker, 8 April 1942.
41 *Vancouver Sun*, 1 December 1942, 6.
42 Gillian Weiss, "An Essential Year for the Child: The Kindergarten in British Columbia," in *Schooling and Society in Twentieth Century British Columbia*, ed. J. Donald Wilson and David C. Jones (Calgary: Detselig Enterprises, 1980), 144.
43 Ben Isitt, *Militant Minority: British Columbia Workers and the Rise of a New Left, 1948–1972* (Toronto: University of Toronto Press, 2011), 24–25; Susan Walsh, "Equality, Emancipation, and a More Just World: Leading Women in the B.C. CCF," MA thesis, Simon Fraser University, 1984, 54, 77.
44 Walsh, "Equality, Emancipation, and a More Just World," 132; Connie Carter and Eileen Daoust, "From Home to House: Women in the BC Legislature," in *Not Just Pin Money: Selected Essays on the History of Women's Work in British Columbia*, ed. Barbara K. Latham and Roberta J. Pazdro (Victoria: Camosun College Press, 1984), 395.
45 *Women, Dry Those Tears* is undated, but it was published in Victoria during the war years. It is reprinted in Beth Light and Ruth Roach Pierson, *No Easy Road: Women in Canada 1920s to 1960s* (Toronto: New Hogtown Press, 1990), 373–77.
46 *Victoria Daily Colonist*, 3 July 1943, 6.
47 Weiss, "An Essential Year for the Child," 145.
48 Walsh, "Equality, Emancipation, and a More Just World," 170, 187.
49 Quoted in Ann Farrell, *Grace MacInnis: A Story of Love and Integrity* (Markham, ON: Fitzhenry and Whiteside, 1994), 264–65.

50 Walsh, "Equality, Emancipation, and a More Just World," 188.
51 *Victoria Daily Colonist*, 3 July 1943, 6; Joan Sangster, *Dreams of Equality: Women on the Canadian Left, 1920–1950* (Toronto: McClelland and Stewart, 1989), 174–77.
52 *Victoria Daily Times*, 12 February 1944, 11.
53 *The Province*, 14 December 1943, 12.
54 *Vancouver Sun*, 12 February 1944, 13. Point Grey was an upper middle-class riding in Vancouver.
55 *Vancouver Sun*, 5 February 1944, 30.
56 Ibid., 40.
57 *Victoria Daily Colonist*, 4 March 1943, 1.
58 *Victoria Daily Times*, 5 February 1944, 5. See also *Vancouver Sun*, 5 February 1944, 30; *The Province*, 5 February 1944, 6; *The Province*, 26 February 1944, 6; *The Province*, 15 March 1944, 4.
59 *The Province*, 3 March 1944, 4.
60 Prentice, "Workers, Mothers, Reds," 120.
61 Mary Frank Macfarlane, "A Survey of Pre-School Centres in Vancouver," MSW thesis, University of British Columbia, 1949, 7.
62 Ibid., 6–7.
63 Ibid., 5.
64 Irene Howard, "The Mother's Council of Vancouver: Holding the Fort for the Unemployed," in *Vancouver Past: Essays in Social History*, ed. Robert A.J. McDonald and Jean Barman (Vancouver: UBC Press), 267–68, 286.
65 Macfarlane, "A Survey of Pre-School Centres," 8.
66 Ibid., 8–9.
67 *The Province*, 20 August 1943, 5; *The Province*, 7 September 1943, 22.
68 Zella Collins, *Report Prepared for the Council of Social Agencies Re War Time Day Nurseries*, 18 August 1943, LAC, MG 28 I 10, volume 49, file 448d.
69 Ibid.
70 *Vancouver Sun*, 9 August 1943, 2; E. Stanway Scanlon to Alderman G. Miller, 30 July 1943, City of Vancouver Archives (CVA), City Social Service Department fonds, PR 449, 106-A-5, folder 13.
71 Donald Granville Stewart, "Strathcona Nursery School: Its Contributions for Working Mothers," MA thesis, University of British Columbia, 1956, 8.
72 Z. Collins to W.R. Bone (City Social Service Department), 14 August 1943, CVA, City Social Service Department fonds, PR 449, 106-A-5, folder 13.
73 City Clerk to W.R. Bone, 20 August 1943, CVA, City Social Service Department fonds, PR 449, 106-A-5, folder 13.
74 Collins, *Report Prepared for the Council of Social Agencies*.
75 *The Province*, 30 July 1943.
76 Collins, *Report Prepared for the Council of Social Agencies*.
77 *Victoria Daily Colonist*, 3 December 1943, 2. This representation to Pearson included representatives from the Vancouver Council of Social Agencies, the James Bay Wartime Housing Centre, the Trades and Labor Council, the Parent-Teachers Association, the Mothers' Union, the Joint Labor Conference, the

Co-operative Commonwealth Federation, the Labor-Progressive party, the Business and Professional Women's Club, and the University Women's Club.
78 *Victoria Daily Colonist*, 30 October 1943, 6.
79 *Victoria Daily Times*, 3 December 1943, 6.
80 *Victoria Daily Colonist*, 30 October 1943, 6; Weiss, "An Essential Year for the Child," 148.
81 Quoted in Gail Cuthbert Brandt, "'Pigeon-Holed and Forgotten': The Work of the Subcommittee on the Post-War Problems of Women, 1943," *Histoire Sociale/Social History* 15, 29 (May 1982): 247. As Brandt explains, the participation of women in the post-war labour force, furthermore, was "dependent upon the achievement of postwar prosperity."
82 Brandt, "Pigeon-Holed and Forgotten," 253.
83 Ibid., 249.
84 Stephen, *Pick One Intelligent Girl*, 202–3. For the most thorough discussion of the post-war return to gender norms, see Ruth Roach Pierson, *They're Still Women After All*. Jeff Keshen sees more evidence of progress with respect to women's place in immediate post–Second World War society, though still located within the continued persistence of gender stereotypes. Jeff Keshen, "Revisiting Canada's Civilian Women during World War II," *Social History/Histoire Sociale* 30, 60 (1997): 239–66.
85 Nancy Christie, *Engendering the State: Family, Work, and Welfare in Canada* (Toronto: University of Toronto Press, 2000), 251.
86 Stephen, *Pick One Intelligent Girl*, 174–77.
87 *An Act Respecting Day Nurseries*, SO 1946, 10 Geo. VI, c. 17.
88 Prentice, "Workers, Mothers, Reds," 121–26; Susan Prentice, "Reds, Mothers, Militants: A History of the Postwar Daycare Campaigns in Toronto," PhD thesis, York University, 1993.
89 *The Province*, 5 February 1944, 6.
90 *The Province*, 26 February 1944, 6.
91 Stephen, *Pick One Intelligent Girl*, 202–3; Veronica Strong-Boag, "Canada's Wage-Earning Wives and the Construction of the Middle-Class," *Journal of Canadian Studies / Revue d'Etudes Canadiennes* 29, 3 (Fall 1994): 5.
92 *Vancouver Sun*, 1 December 1942, 6.
93 *Vancouver Sun*, 23 February 1944, 13; *The Province*, 23 February 1944, 15.
94 Prentice, "Workers, Mothers, Reds," 120.
95 *The Province*, 21 February 1944, 7; *Vancouver Sun*, 21 March 1944, 12; *The Province*, 21 March 1944, 9; *The Province*, 15 April 1944, 16.
96 *Vancouver Sun*, 14 April 1944, 11.
97 *Vancouver Sun*, 3 March 1944, 4.
98 *The Province*, 14 April 1944, 14.
99 *The Province*, 17 May 1944, 4.
100 Ibid.
101 Weiss, "An Essential Year for the Child," 144.
102 *The Province*, 4 March 1944, 10.

103 *Vancouver Sun*, 29 March 1944. While kindergartens were private institutions, their operation was regulated by the provincial government. School boards had been authorized since 1922 to establish kindergartens, but none had done so. See Weiss, "An Essential Year for the Child," 147. The act which governed public education in BC at the time was *An Act Respecting Public Schools*, SBC 1872, no. 16.
104 Weiss, "An Essential Year for the Child," 148.
105 *Vancouver Sun*, 25 February 1944, 6.
106 *Victoria Daily Colonist*, 22 June 1944, 5.
107 Weiss, "An Essential Year for the Child," 11–16.
108 *Welfare Institutions Licensing Act*, SBC, RS 1947, c. 78.
109 British Columbia, *Annual Report of the Social Welfare Branch of the Department of Health and Welfare for the Year Ended March 31st 1948* (Victoria: King's Printer, 1948). The Welfare Institutions Licensing Board (WILB) was made up of the provincial health officer or his deputy, the superintendent of child welfare, and three other civil servants. The WILB was initially the responsibility of the provincial secretary, was shifted to the Department of Health and Welfare in 1950, and then to the Department of Social Welfare in 1960 (and Health became a separate department).
110 Sandra Griffin et al., "Canadian Child Care in Context: Perspectives from the Provinces and Territories: British Columbia Report," in *Canadian National Child Care Study*, ed. Alan Pence (Ottawa: Department of Health and Welfare, 1992), 22–23. The other area in which the provincial government was more actively involved in the 1950s was preschool teacher training (24–25).
111 British Columbia, *Annual Report of the Social Welfare Branch of the Department of Health and Welfare for the Year Ended March 31st 1952* (Victoria: Queen's Printer, 1952), W96.
112 Alvin Finkel, "Even the Little Children Cooperated: Family Strategies, Childcare Discourse, and Social Welfare Debates 1945–1975," *Labour/Le Travail* 36 (Fall 1995): 94.
113 VDNA, *Annual Report of Executive Secretary for the Year 1945*, UBCRBSC, HV 862 V2A1, 1932 to 1945.
114 Foster Day Care Association of Vancouver, *Annual Report, 1955*, UBCRBSC, SPAM Collection.
115 British Columbia, *Public Welfare in British Columbia, 1954* (Victoria: Queen's Printer, 1954), J97.
116 The Strathcona Nursery School was still being run as a private organization, with funding from the Community Chest as well as Alexandra Neighbourhood Activities. Stewart, "Strathcona Nursery School," 5, 10–11, 8, 55–57, 88.
117 *The Province*, 16 June 1949, 42. This was the response given by Edna Page, the deputy superintendent of welfare, to Mrs. H, who wanted to establish a day nursery but was denied licensing because she did not have a social work diploma.
118 British Columbia, *Public Welfare in British Columbia 1953* (Victoria: Queen's Printer, 1953), U93. Emphasis in original.
119 Ibid.

120 For an article that argues for the utility of the reserve army of labour thesis, see Ronnie Leah, "Women's Labour Force Participation and Day Care Cutbacks in Ontario," *Atlantis* 7 (1981): 36–44. See also Ruth K. Abbott and R.A. Young, "Cynical and Deliberate Manipulation? Child Care and the Reserve Army of Female Labour in Canada," *Journal of Canadian Studies / Revue d'Etudes Canadiennes* 24, 2 (1989): 22–38. Abbott and Young challenge the simple "reserve army" thesis, instead arguing that mothers represent a "latent" labour reserve – that is, their presence in the labour force (encouraged through child care provision) is better explained by the fact that they are considered cheap labour, not just their simple presence or absence in certain jobs.

Chapter 4: "The working mother is here to stay"

1 Women's Bureau, Department of Labour, *Working Mothers and Their Child Care Arrangements* (Ottawa: Queen's Printer, 1970).
2 Alvin Finkel, *Social Policy and Practice in Canada: A History* (Waterloo, ON: Wilfrid Laurier Press, 2006), 205.
3 British Columbia, *Public Welfare Services in British Columbia, 1956* (Victoria: Queen's Printer, 1956), T102.
4 Jean Barman, *The West beyond the West: A History of British Columbia* (Toronto: University of Toronto Press, 1991), 270–89.
5 Cheryl Collier, "Governments and Women's Movements: Explaining Child Care and Anti-Violence Policy in Ontario and British Columbia, 1970–2000," PhD dissertation, University of Toronto, 2006, 116.
6 *Canada Assistance Plan*, RSC 1966–67, c. C-45.
7 Similar programs were set up in other provinces. See, for example, James Struthers, *The Limits of Affluence: Welfare in Ontario* (Toronto: University of Toronto Press and Ontario Historical Studies Series, 1994), 242–43; Tom Langford, *Alberta's Day Care Controversy: From 1908 to 2009 and Beyond* (Edmonton: Athabasca University Press, 2010).
8 Martha Friendly and Susan Prentice, *About Canada: Childcare* (Black Point, NS: Fernwood Publishing, 2009), 75.
9 Joan Sangster, *Transforming Labour: Women and Work in Postwar Canada* (Toronto: University of Toronto Press, 2010), 50–51. See also Veronica Strong-Boag, "Canada's Wage-Earning Wives and the Construction of the Middle Class, 1945–60," *Journal of Canadian Studies / Revue d'Etudes Canadiennes* 29, 3 (1994): 5–25; Joan Sangster, *Earning Respect: The Lives of Working Women in Small-Town Ontario, 1920–1960* (Toronto: University of Toronto Press, 1995), chapter 8.
10 Rianne Mahon, "The Never-Ending Story: The Struggle for Universal Child Care Policy in the 1970s," *Canadian Historical Review* 81, 4 (December 2000): 593.
11 Canadian Council on Social Development (CCSD), *Day Care: Report of a National Study* (Ottawa: CCSD, January 1972), 8.
12 British Columbia, *Department of Labour Annual Reports* (Victoria: Queen's Printer, 1962–67). In 1962, women made up 26 percent of the total labour force; in 1963, 28 percent; in 1964, 29 percent; in 1965, 30 percent; in 1966, 30 percent; and in 1967, 31 percent. See Mahon, "The Never-Ending Story," 590.
13 Women's Bureau, *Working Mothers and Their Child-Care Arrangements*, 37.

14 Sangster, *Transforming Labour*, 19.
15 Women's Bureau, *Working Mothers and Their Child-Care Arrangements*, 39. For 12 percent of children, their mothers worked only during school hours; 4 percent of the children of working mothers were cared for by mothers at their jobs (that is, as a boarding housekeeper or foster home mother).
16 Women's Bureau, *Working Mothers and Their Child-Care Arrangements*, 41.
17 On the Royal Commission of Education, see Gillian Weiss, "An Essential Year for the Child: The Kindergarten in British Columbia," in *Schooling and Society in Twentieth Century British Columbia*, ed. J. Donald Wilson and David C. Jones (Calgary: Detselig Enterprises, 1980), 154.
18 British Columbia, *Department of Social Welfare Report for the Year Ended March 31st 1960* (Victoria: Queen's Printer, 1960), L86.
19 British Columbia, *Social Welfare Branch* and *Department of Social Welfare Annual Reports* (Victoria: Queen's Printer, 1956–65).
20 Foster Day Care Association of Vancouver, *Annual Report*, 1955, University of British Columbia Rare Books and Special Collections, SPAM Collection.
21 British Columbia, *Department of Social Welfare Report for the Year Ended March 31 1962* (Victoria: Queen's Printer, 1962), K87.
22 Advisory Committee on Day Care, United Community Services, *Day Care Services*, 16 July 1968, British Columbia Archives (BCA), GR 0135, box 2, file 18.
23 *A Brief on the Urgent Needs in Child Welfare Services in British Columbia*, 13 September 1965, BCA, GR 0128, box 8, file 72. This brief was submitted by a "Delegation Representing a Group of Independent Citizens."
24 Michael Wheeler, *A Report on Needed Research in Welfare in British Columbia*, March 1961, BCA, GR 0128, box 8, file 71. Wheeler would go on to write the CCSD's report on day care in 1972.
25 Community Chest and Councils of the Greater Vancouver Area, Welfare and Recreation Council, *Report on Day Care Needs* (June 1965) [the UBCRBSC contains a copy of this report].
26 Community Chest, *Report on Day Care Needs*, 1.
27 Ibid., ii.
28 Ibid., i.
29 The report identified ten small-scale private day care centres, along with several foster day homes. Seven of the homes that provided care were not licensed. According to the report, these services were able to meet 10 percent of the need for child care.
30 Community Chest, *Report on Day Care Needs*, 20. Statistics are located throughout the report.
31 See, for example, Board of Directors, Gordon Neighbourhood House to W.D. Black, 10 December 1965, BCA, GR 0128, box 13, file 138; Minister of Social Welfare to J.A.C. Grant (President, Alexandra Community Activities), 29 December 1965, BCA, GR 0128, box 13, file 138.
32 E.R. Rickinson, *Memo Re: Meeting in Honourable Black's Office*, 17 December 1965, BCA, GR 0128, box 10, file 92.
33 Community Chest, *Report on Day Care Needs*, iii-iv.

34 Ibid., 8–9.
35 Michael Clague et al., *Reforming Human Services: The Experience of the Community Resource Boards in BC* (Vancouver: UBC Press, 1984), 13. *Social Assistance Act*, SBC 1945, c. 62.
36 Clague et al., *Reforming Human Services*, 18.
37 Ibid., 13–14.
38 Struthers, *Limits of Affluence*, 211.
39 Quoted in Struthers, *Limits of Affluence*, 234.
40 Struthers, *Limits of Affluence*, 232.
41 Finkel, *Social Policy and Practice in Canada*, 258–60. 69. One percent of female single-parent homes were living in poverty, compared to 21.2 percent of all families. These are 1975 national statistics. As Finkel points out, Prime Minister Pearson estimated that 200,000 women would be added to "the rolls of those receiving a federal contribution." On the issue of the feminization of poverty, see Diana Pearce, "Welfare Is Not for Women: Why the War on Poverty Cannot Conquer the Feminization of Poverty," in *Women, the State, and Welfare*, ed. Linda Gordon (Madison, WI: University of Wisconsin Press, 1990); Wendy McKeen, *Money in Their Own Name: The Feminist Voice in Poverty Debate in Canada, 1970–1995* (Toronto: University of Toronto Press, 2004), especially chapter 3.
42 At that time, there were fewer than 300 mothers' allowances cases in the province. Most mothers since 1945 had been helped through social allowances since the regulations of that program were broader and less prohibitive. With regard to the statistics, the Department of Social Welfare classified social assistance recipients according to "heads of families," "singles," and "dependents." Wives and children made up the dependents category. Within the heads of families category, reports only rarely distinguished between "one-parent families" and "two-parents families" and even then did not specify whether the family head was male or female. The clearest glimpse we get at the proportions of single mothers came in 1965 and 1967, when the department's annual reports stated that one-parent families made up "one quarter" and "23 percent" of family cases – and it seems the reader is meant to assume those family heads were mothers. British Columbia, *Department of Social Welfare Annual Reports* (Victoria: Queen's Printer, 1967 and 1969). See *An Act to provide for Mothers' Allowances and to repeal the "Mothers' Pensions Act,"* SBC 1937, no. 18.
43 British Columbia, *Department of Social Welfare Annual Report for the Year Ending March 31st 1965* (Victoria: Queen's Printer, 1965), G37.
44 Women's Bureau, Department of Labour, *Day Care Services for Children of Working Mothers* (Ottawa: Queen's Printer, 1964).
45 Mahon, "The Never-Ending Story," 593. See also Annis May Timpson, *Driven Apart: Women's Employment Equality and Child Care in Canadian Public Policy* (Vancouver: UBC Press, 2001), 18–20.
46 Community Chest and Councils of the Greater Vancouver area, *Proposals for the Federal/Provincial Conference on Poverty and Opportunity,* 8 December

1965, BCA, GR 0128, box 3, file 29. A "homemaker-housekeeper" service was one popular anti-poverty strategy recommended by several welfare groups. This service provided help for social assistance recipients who could not do their own cleaning, cooking, laundry, or other domestic tasks because of illness, disability, or injury. It could also provide "baby-sitting" services for working mothers. There was talk about turning these services into public programs with the help of *CAP* (n 6) funds. See the correspondence in BCA, GR 0128, box 5, file 41. See also J.S. White, "Issues in Social Policy," speech given at the Community Funds and Councils of Canada Staff Development Institute, Geneva Park, ON, 23 March 1968, BCA, GR 0135, box 2, file "Canadian Welfare Council, Correspondence," 67–68.

47 Mahon, "The Never-Ending Story."
48 British Columbia, *Department of Social Welfare Annual Report for the Year Ending March 31st 1967* (Victoria: Queen's Printer, 1967), H17.
49 See Michael Krashinsky, *Day Care and Public Policy in Ontario* (Toronto: Ontario Economic Council by University of Toronto Press, 1977), 20–21.
50 J.A. Sadler (Assistant Deputy Minister of Social Welfare), *Circular Letter to All Municipalities and Officials of the Department of Social Welfare*, 7 November 1968, BCA, GR 0135, box 2, file 18.
51 T.D. Bingham (Superintendent of Child Welfare) to J.A. Sadler, *Memo Re: Day Care*, 23 January 1967, BCA, GR 0135, box 2, file 18.
52 Sadler, *Circular Letter to All Municipalities and Officials*; *Victoria Daily Times*, 19 July 1967, 39.
53 *Victoria Daily Times*, 13 January 1967, 32; *Victoria Colonist*, 22 June 1967, 23; *Victoria Daily Times*, 22 June 1967, 2.
54 *Victoria Daily Times*, 22 February 1967, 26.
55 *Victoria Daily Times*, 22 February 1967, 26. *Victoria Daily Times*, 17 February 1968, 27; *Vancouver Sun*, 27 July 1968, 14; *Vancouver Sun*, 8 March 1969, 14; *The Province*, 30 September 1967, 41.
56 *Victoria Daily Colonist*, 13 January 1967, 21.
57 *Victoria Daily Times*, 15 July 1967, 23; *Victoria Colonist*, 15 July 1967, 19; *Victoria Colonist*, 16 July 1967, 6.
58 *Victoria Daily Times*, 19 July 1967, 39; *Victoria Colonist*, 13 January 1967, 21.
59 British Columbia, *Department of Social Welfare Annual Reports* (Victoria: Queen's Printer, 1967–70).
60 *Information on Day Care for Mr. R. R. Loffmark prepared by Marpole Area Council (UCS), Day Care Committee*, 31 October 1967, BCA, GR 0135, box 2, file 19.
61 United Community Services of the Greater Vancouver Area, *Report on Preschool Enrichment Programmes*, April 1968, BCA, GR 0135, box 2, file 19.
62 Letter from V. Biernes (President of UCS) to D. Campbell (Minister of Social Welfare), 13 June 1968, BCA GR 0135, box 2, file 18.
63 *Advisory Committee on Day Care*, n.d. [c. January 1967], BCA, GR 0135, box 2, file 18.
64 Provincial officials were also keen to ensure that the United Community Services (UCS) did not abandon their commitments to day care, thinking that the

Notes to Pages 112–18

provincial government would pick up the slack. By the time *CAP* funding was announced, Sadler had secured a commitment from the UCS that "they would endeavour to put more resources into these services and would not withdraw any voluntary funds because of government participation." Letter from V. Biernes (President of UCS) to D. Campbell (Minister of Social Welfare), 13 June 1968, BCA GR 0135, box 2, file 18.

65 A description of the plan can be found in Minister of Social Welfare, *Press Release*, 7 November 1968, BCA, GR 0135, box 2, file 18.
66 Marpole Area Committee on Day Care, *Progress Report*, 13 February 1967, BCA, GR 0135, box 2, file 19; *The Province*, 30 September 1967, 41. The Marpole neighbourhood is in south-central Vancouver, along the northern edge of the Fraser River.
67 D. Behesti to D. Campbell, February 1967, BCA, GR 0135, box 2, file 19.
68 UCS, *The Expansion of Day Care Services: Statement of the Advisory Committee on Day Care*, November 1967, BCA, GR 0135, box 2, file 19.
69 Ibid., Appendix A: Marpole Day Care Centre: Budget vs. Actual.
70 Ibid.
71 Ibid.
72 G. Maycock to T.D. Bingham, 22 September 1967, BCA, GR 0135, box 2, file 19. Maycock dealt with inquiries from several centres in the greater Vancouver area and from as far away as Vernon. See, for example, Mrs. R. Merriman (Okanagan Valley Pre-School Education Association) to D. Campbell, 14 June 1967, BCA, GR 0135, box 2, file 19; M. Clark (Day Care Centre Board, the Church of St. John the Divine) to D. Campbell, 21 July 1967, BCA, GR 0135, box 2, file 19.
73 D.G. Homer (Executive Director, Greater Victoria Community Welfare Council) to E.R. Rickinson, 20 June 1967, BCA, GR 0135, box 2, file 19.
74 D. Thomson to J.A. Sadler, 31 October 1967, BCA, GR 0135, box 2, file 19.
75 *Vancouver Sun*, 13 October 1967, 16.
76 *Vancouver Sun*, 5 July 1968, 10.
77 UCS, *The Expansion of Day Care Services*, 1.
78 G. Maycock to T.D. Bingham, 24 November 1967, BCA, GR 0135, box 2, file 19.
79 For comparison, the one single father who used the centre earned $540 per month.
80 E. Campbell to G. McCarthy, 2 April 1968, BCA, GR 0135, box 2, file 19.
81 Mrs. D.M Stewart to D. Behesti, 15 January 1968, BCA, GR 0135, box 2, file 19.
82 J. Sexton to D. Campbell, 6 April 1968, BCA, GR 0135, box 2, file 18.
83 *The Province*, 20 January 1968, 5.
84 *Vancouver Sun*, 13 December 1968, 26.
85 D. Campbell to E. Campbell, 30 January 1968, BCA, GR 0135, box 2, file 19.
86 Centennial Day Care, Victoria, *Budget*, 1967, GR 0135, box 2, file 18.
87 H.W. Harding (Treasurer, Chatham Day Care Centre) to Hon. W.H. Murray, 8 March 1968, BCA, GR 0135, box 2, file 19. There is some indication that the government did in fact approve an increase in Schedule B subsidies to

Chatham, at least temporarily. D. Campbell to H.W. Harding, 8 April 1968, BCA, GR 0135, box 2, file 19.
88 M.S. Wark (Chairman, Strathcona Area Council) to E. Wolfe (MLA) and D. Campbell, 21 February 1968, BCA, GR 0135, box 2, file 19.
89 D. Campbell to E. Wolfe, 20 March 1968, BCA, GR 0135, box 2, file 19.
90 The example that Campbell gave was the Alexandra Neighbourhood Services Association in Vancouver, which considered cancelling a planned opening of a day care centre because the UCS could not commit to supporting their operational costs. The day care centre went ahead, largely because of private donations. From the Alexandra Neighbourhood Services Association's view, however, their hope was not that the UCS would support them but, rather, that "the Provincial Government would meet with basic operating costs." E.J. Helm (Executive Director, Alexandra Neighbourhood Services Association) to E.R. Rickinson, 12 July 1968; E.R. Rickinson to E.J. Helm, 25 July 1968; E.J. Helm to E.R. Rickinson, 31 October 1968, all documents in BCA, GR 0135, box 2, file 18.
91 UCS Advisory Committee on Day Care, *Day Care Services*, 16 July 1968, BCA, GR 0135, box 2, file 18. The other gap in government policy was "a clear guide for teacher's training programs."
92 E. Campbell, *Presentation to the Welfare Institutions Licensing Board*, 13 June 1968, BCA, GR 0135, box 2, file 18.
93 UCS Advisory Committee on Day Care, *Day Care Services*.
94 UCS, *Report on Special Meeting on Day Care*, 21 August 1968, BCA, GR 0135, box 2, file 18.
95 *Vancouver Sun*, 23 October 1968, 26; E. Campbell, *Presentation to the Welfare Institutions Licensing Board*.
96 D. Campbell to V. Biernes (in official correspondence, Mrs. A.D.), 22 November 1968, BCA, GR 0135, box 2, file 18.
97 Minister of Social Welfare, *Press Release*; V. Biernes to G.K. Moreton (President, Family Service Centres), 13 November 1968, BCA, GR 0365, box 2, file 10; V. Belknap to E.R. Rickinson, *Memo Re: Marpole Day Care Centre*, 17 February 1969, BCA, GR 0365, box 2, file 10.
98 Minister of Social Welfare, *Press Release*.
99 Mahon, "The Never-Ending Story," 583.
100 J.A. Sadler to M. Egan (Director, Social Planning, City of Vancouver), 28 November 1968, BCA, GR 0135, box 2, file 18; J.A. Duncan (President, Kitsilano Area Council, UCS) to D. Campbell, 10 February 1969, BCA, GR 0365, box 2, file 10; V. Biernes to D. Campbell, 25 October 1968, BCA, GR 0135, box 2, file 18.
101 E. Campbell, *Presentation to the Welfare Institutions Licensing Board*.
102 Business and Professional Women's Clubs of British Columbia and Yukon, *Brief on Need for Starting Grants for Child Day Care Centres*, report presented to D. Campbell, 1968 [on file in the BC Legislative Library].
103 UCS Advisory Committee on Day Care, *Day Care Services*.
104 R.A. Sadler to E.R. Rickinson, *Memo Re: Day Care Centres*, 23 August 1968, BCA, GR 0135, box 2, file 18.

105 Other panellists included early childhood education experts and academics. R. Pestell (Day Care Symposium Committee) to V. Belknap, 28 February 1969, BCA, GR 0365, box 2, file 10.
106 *Vancouver Sun*, 29 March 1969, 32; *A Symposium on Day Care*, 28 March 1969, BCA, GR 0365, box 2, file 10. D. Campbell to Mrs. A, 16 June 1969, BCA, GR 0365, box 2, file 10; Clague et al., *Reforming Human Services*, 25.
107 *A Symposium on Day Care.*
108 Ibid.
109 J. Taselaar (Board of Directors Port Edward Day Care Centre) to R. Loffmark, 1 May 1969, BCA, GR 0365, box 2, file 10; M. McLean (Secretary, Central Council Women's Auxiliaries to the United Fishermen and Allied Workers' Union) to R. Loffmark, 22 April 1969, GR 0365, box 2, file 10. This included a year-round day care centre for three to five year olds in the community hall as well as a nursery for under-threes during canning season.
110 E.R. Rickinson to A. Mulder, 16 July 1969, BCA, GR 365, box 2, file 10; E.R. Rickinson to Mrs. P, 10 November 1969, BCA, GR 0365, box 2, file 10.
111 R.A. Sadler to H.W. Murray, 3 July 1969, BCA, GR 0365, box 2, file 10; V. Belknap to E.R. Rickinson, *Memo Re: Gordon House Day Care Centre, Vancouver*, 2 June 1969, BCA, GR 0365, box 2, file 10.
112 *Vancouver Sun*, 7 October 1968, 29; *British Columbia Licensed Group Day Care Centres for Three to Five Year Old Children*, October 1969, BCA, GR 0365, box 2, file 10.
113 *Vancouver Sun*, 5 October 1968, 29; *Vancouver Sun*, 7 October 1968, 29; *Vancouver Sun*, 8 October 1968, 30.
114 *Welfare Institutions Licensing Act*, RSBC 1961, c. 66.
115 For more details, see N.S. Brooke (Supervisor, Social Assistance and Rehabilitation Division, Department of Social Welfare) to E.R. Rickinson, *Memo Re: Day Care-Homemaker Application Form*, 15 May 1969, BCA, GR 0365, box 2, file 10.
116 *Vancouver Sun*, 8 October 1968, 30.
117 *Victoria Daily Times*, 8 July 1965, 21.
118 BC Federation of Labour, *Submission of the Committee on Women's Rights to the Minister of Human Resources on Child Care Requirements* (BC Federation of Labour Committee on Women's Rights, 1973) [on file in the BC Legislative Library].
119 Sangster, *Transforming Labour*, 51.
120 Ibid., 80; Susan Prentice, "Workers, Mothers, Reds: Toronto's Postwar Day Care Fight," *Studies in Political Economy* 30 (Autumn 1989): 115–41.

Chapter 5: "Talkin' Day Care Blues"

1 Annis May Timpson, "Royal Commissions as Sites of Resistance: Women's Challenges on Child Care in the Royal Commission on the Status of Women," *International Journal of Canadian Studies / Revue d'Etudes Canadiennes* 20 (Fall 1999): 125.
2 In other words, child care politics were embedded in the fundamental reordering of dependency that defined post-war welfare states. See Nancy Fraser

and Linda Gordon, "A Genealogy of Dependency: Tracing a Keyword of the U.S. Welfare State," *Signs* 19, 2 (Winter 1994): 324.
3 Joan Sangster, "Radical Ruptures: Feminism, Labor, and the Left in the Long Sixties in Canada," *American Review of Canadian Studies* 40, 1 (March 2010): 13.
4 Hugh Johnston, *Radical Campus: Making Simon Fraser University* (Vancouver: Douglas and McIntyre, 2005).
5 Deborah Dinner, "The Universal Childcare Debate: Rights Mobilization, Social Policy, and the Dynamics of Feminist Activism, 1966–1974," *Law and History Review* 28, 3 (August 2010): 579.
6 Cheryl Collier, "Governments and Women's Movements: Explaining Child Care and Anti-Violence Policy in Ontario and British Columbia, 1970–2000," PhD dissertation, University of Toronto, 2006, 116.
7 *Kinesis*, January 1974, 2.
8 Florence Bird, *Report of the Royal Commission on the Status of Women in Canada* (Ottawa: Information Canada, September 1970), vii.
9 Timpson, "Royal Commissions as Sites of Resistance," 125.
10 Joan Sangster, "Invoking Experience as Evidence," *Canadian Historical Review* 92, 1 (March 2011): 150.
11 Timpson, "Royal Commissions as Sites of Resistance," 133–35.
12 Ibid., 139, 136.
13 Bird, *Report of the Royal Commission*, xii; Timpson, "Royal Commissions as Sites of Resistance," 140.
14 *Canada Assistance Plan*, RSC 1966–67, C. C-45.
15 Bird, *Report of the Royal Commission*, 270.
16 Annis May Timpson, *Driven Apart: Women's Employment Equality and Child Care in Canadian Public Policy* (Vancouver: UBC Press, 2001), 53.
17 Rianne Mahon, "The Never-Ending Story: The Struggle for Universal Child Care Policy in the 1970s," *Canadian Historical Review* 81, 4 (December 2000): 582–622.
18 Timpson, *Driven Apart*, 55–56.
19 Canadian Council on Social Development (CCSD), *Proceedings: Canadian Conference on Day Care, June 20–23, 1971* (Ottawa: CCSD and Department of Health and Welfare, January 1972).
20 CCSD, *Day Care: Report of a National Study* (Ottawa: CCSD, 1972).
21 See Nancy Adamson et al., *Feminist Organizing for Change: The Contemporary Women's Movement in Canada* (Toronto: Oxford University Press, 1988), 46–47; Timpson, *Driven Apart*, 67–68; Vappu Tyyskä, *The Politics of Caring and the Welfare State: The Impact of the Women's Movement on Child Care Policy in Canada and Finland, 1960–1990* (Helsinki, Finland: Suomalainen Tiedeakatemia, 1995), 133–35.
22 Dinner, "Universal Childcare Debate," 582; Tyyskä, *The Politics of Caring and the Welfare State*, 133. As Dinner points out, however, these national, elite groups are the ones who have received the most scholarly attention. See, for example, in Canada: Alvin Finkel, "Even the Little Children Cooperated: Family Strategies, Childcare Discourse, and Social Welfare Debates 1945–1975,"

Labour/Le Travail 36 (Fall 1995): 91–118; Mahon, "The Never-Ending Story." In the United States: Sonya Michel, *Children's Interests/Mothers' Rights: The Shaping of America's Child Care Policy* (New Haven, CT: Yale University Press, 1999); Emilie Stoltzfus, *Citizen, Mother, Worker: Debating Public Responsibility for Child Care after the Second World War* (Chapel Hill, NC: University of North Carolina Press, 2003). With the exception of Susan Prentice's and Wendy Atkin's studies of Toronto, little attention has been paid to grassroots efforts of second-wave feminists with respect to child care. Susan Prentice, "Workers, Mothers, Reds: Toronto's Postwar Daycare Fight," *Studies in Political Economy* 30 (Autumn 1989): 115–41; Wendy Atkin, "'Babies of the World Unite': The Early Day-Care Movement and Family Formation in the 1970s," in *Family Matters: Papers in Post-Confederation Canadian Family History*, ed. Lori Chambers and Edgar-Andre Montigny (Toronto: Canadian Scholars' Press, 1998); Rianne Mahon, "Challenging National Regimes from Below: Toronto Child-Care Politics," *Politics and Gender* 3 (2007): 57.

23   Johnston, *Radical Campus*, 52.

24   Roberta Lexier, "How Did the Women's Liberation Movement Emerge from the Sixties Student Movements: The Case of Simon Fraser University," *Women and Social Movements in America, 1600–2000* 13, 2 (Fall 2009).

25   Bryan Palmer, *Canada's 1960s: The Ironies of Identity in a Rebellious Era* (Toronto: University of Toronto Press, 2008), 301.

26   Lexier, "How Did the Women's Liberation Movement Emerge."

27   Margaret Benston, "The Political Economy of Women's Liberation," *Monthly Review* 21 (September 1969): 13–27. See Palmer, *Canada's 1960s*, 297–99.

28   The story of Simon Fraser University's (SFU) family co-operative can be found in Marcy Cohen et al., *'Cuz There Ain't No Daycare (or Almost None She Said)* (Vancouver: Press Gang Publishers, 1973), 20. *The Peak*, the campus student newspaper, also reported extensively on the co-op. See, for example, *The Peak*, 21 May 1968.

29   Since 1945, the Association of Co-operative Play Groups had been operating in Vancouver, and on Vancouver Island an organization of co-operative pre-schools was established in the late 1940s. These playgroup organizations, though, were not about providing essential day-time care for working mothers. Rather, they were designed to give middle-class housewives a break during the day and to provide their children with a chance to socialize with others. Canadian Co-operative Association, *Child Care Co-operatives in Canada 2007: A Research Report* (prepared for the Co-operatives Secretariat and Human Resources and Social Development Canada in conjunction with the Co-operatives Secretariat, March 2007), 10–11.

30   Judy Rebick, *Ten Thousand Roses: The Making of a Feminist Revolution* (Toronto: Penguin Canada, 2005), 61.

31   Mahon, "Challenging National Regimes," 63; Atkin, "'Babies of the World Unite!'"; Jason Ellis, "'This is not a medieval university attended by celibate clergy': Contesting the University of Toronto's First Daycare Sit-in," unpublished paper, York University, May 2005 [on file with the author].

32   Rebick, *Ten Thousand Roses*, 65.

33 Although that was certainly an important motivation, given the number of mature students with families enrolled at SFU.
34 *The Peak*, 21 May 1969, 6.
35 Cohen et al., *'Cuz There Ain't No Daycare*, 20.
36 Ibid.
37 *The Peak*, 29 July 1970, 5.
38 Barb Cameron et al., *The Day Care Book* (Toronto: Canadian Women's Educational Press), Simon Fraser University Archives (SFUA), F-111-7-1-23, "Childcare/Daycare, 1973–81," 17.
39 Memo to President K. Strand, SFUA, F-149-1-1-0-1, "Early development, 1968–98." (note: as per SFUA access restrictions, identifiable information from this file has been removed).
40 In April 1977, the construction of an entirely new building for child care was completed. This is the current Child Care Centre on the SFU campus.
41 *The Ubyssey*, 9 February 1971.
42 Cohen et al., *'Cuz There Ain't No Day Care*, 13. Emphasis in original.
43 Ibid., 26.
44 Ian Milligan, "Coming off the Mountain: Forging an Outward-Looking New Left at Simon Fraser University," *BC Studies* 171 (Autumn 2011): 69–91.
45 Frances Wasserlein, "An Arrow Aimed at the Heart: The Vancouver Women's Caucus and the Abortion Caravan of 1970," MA thesis, Simon Fraser University, 1990; Christabelle Sethna, "Clandestine Operations: The Vancouver Women's Caucus, the Abortion Caravan, and the RCMP," *Canadian Historical Review* 90, 3 (September 2009): 466–69.
46 Dominique Clement, "'I Believe in Human Rights, Not Women's Rights': Women and the Human Rights State, 1969–1984," *Radical History Review* 101 (Spring 2008): 115–16.
47 Melody Kilian (Women's Caucus), "Day Care Manifesto," n.d., University of British Columbia Rare Books and Special Collections (UBCRBSC), SPAM 27572.
48 Ibid., 1. See also *The Pedestal*, July 1970, 3; *The Pedestal*, Fall 1969, 4.
49 The Unemployed Citizens Welfare Improvement Council (UCWIC), especially, was explicitly militant in approach. "The dispossessed people of Vancouver," it declared, "can unite and obtain their individual rights and to create a democratic and militant union to improve upon those rights." With the Vancouver Welfare Rights Organization, the UCWIC staged a series of protests and demonstrations in the summer of 1971 to oppose proposed changes to welfare rates and administration. The very nature of public assistance, they said, denied the "fundamental rights of birth" and undermined the dignity, autonomy, and independence of welfare recipients in British Columbia. "Unemployed Citizens Welfare Improvement Council Newsletter," and *Report to the Health and Welfare Committee of the Vancouver City Council from the Unemployed Citizens Welfare Improvement Council, 12 August 1971*, British Columbia Archives (BCA), GR 2921, box 10, file "Special Projects."

50 UCWIC, "Our Stand," in *The Voice of the Unemployed*, c. summer 1971, BCA, GR 2921, box 10, file "Special Projects."
51 Women's Liberation Alliance, *Brief Submitted to the Standing Committee of Council on Health and Welfare*, 22 December 1971, BCA, GR 2921, box 10, file "Social Allowance Rates."
52 Art Phillips, *Brief to Standing Committee on Health and Welfare*, 23 December 1971, BCA, GR 2921, box 10, file "Social Allowance Rates."
53 *The Pedestal*, July 1970, 3.
54 *Vancouver Opportunities Program*, 30 August 1973, and City of Vancouver Welfare and Rehabilitation Department, *Recipients of Opportunities Incentive Allowance*, December 1973, BCA, GR 2921, box 10, file "Vancouver Opportunities Program v. V."
55 Collier, "Governments and Women's Movements," 116.
56 Margaret Mitchell, *No Laughing Matter: Adventure, Activism, and Politics* (Vancouver: Granville Island Publishing, 2008), 74–75.
57 Ibid.
58 Male heads of families could participate if they were "not readily placeable in employment." W.N. Boyd (City of Vancouver Welfare and Rehabilitation Department) to Alderman Rankin, *Memo Re: Vancouver Opportunities Program*, 18 October 1973, BCA, GR 2921, box 10, file "Vancouver Opportunities Program v. V." The Vancouver Opportunities Programme (VOP) also served people on Handicapped Persons Income Assistance. The single-parent figure came from United Community Services (UCS), Social Policy and Research Department, *The Economics of Day Care* (Vancouver: UCS, 1973), iii, UBCRBSC, Social Work BC Collection, P1012269.
59 *Vancouver Opportunities Program*, 30 August 1973, BCA, GR 2921, box 10, file "Vancouver Opportunities Program v. V"; N. Levi to M. Mitchell, 7 March 1974, BCA, GR 2921, box 10, file "Vancouver Opportunities Program – Day Care."
60 Correspondence between W.N. Boyd and T.D. Bingham, July 1972, BCA, GR 2921, box 4, file "Day Care Services – Child Welfare."
61 Mrs. D (of the Lower Mainland Welfare Rights Organization) to N. Levi, 3 October 1973, BCA, GR 2921, box 10, file "Welfare Rights Organization – Lower Mainland."
62 City of Vancouver Welfare and Rehabilitation Department, *Recipients of Opportunities Incentive Allowance*, December 1973, BCA, GR 2921, box 10, file "Vancouver Opportunities Program v. V." The majority – 60 percent – did not enter into paid work because of "health reasons."
63 VOP Personnel to N. Levi, 26 September 1973, BCA, GR 2921, box 10, file "Vancouver Opportunities Program vol. V."
64 *Growing Pains*, December 1974.
65 A. Patterson (Jiminy Cricket) to W. Cownden (Family and Children's Service), 7 March 1972, BCA, GR 0746, box 1, file 18.
66 Mrs. A.G. to A. Fraser (MLA Cariboo), 3 March 1972; R.A. Sadler to Mrs. A.G., 8 March 1972, BCA, GR 0746, box 1, file 18.

67 Mrs. G (Novaco) to G. Maycock, 19 July 1972; M.E. (Novaco) to J.C. Ellingham, 10 August 1972; J.C. Ellingham to M. Egan, 16 August 1972; J.C. Ellingham to Mr. D (Novaco), 8 September 1972, all in BCA, GR 0746, box 1, file 19.
68 *Opportunities for Youth Projects: Vancouver Community Co-operative Child Care and Day Care Study*, A Brief on Day Care for Children under 3 Years, presented to the Community Care Facilities Board, 15 September 1971, SFUA, F-111-7-1-22, file "Childcare/Daycare 1970–78."
69 Ibid., 6, 14.
70 Ibid., 15.
71 Clement, "'I Believe in Human Rights,'" 114.
72 *Kinesis*, January 1974, 2.
73 Status of Women Action and Co-ordinating Council of BC to Community Care Facilities Licensing Board, 5 January 1971, BCA, GR 0746, box 1, file 18.
74 Collier, "Governments and Women's Movements," 150–51.
75 Vancouver Status of Women and YWCA, *Immigrant Women in the Labour Force*, report to Norman Levi, n.d., BCA, GR 0363, box 12, file 10.
76 BC Federation of Labour, *Submission of the Committee on Women's Rights to the Minister of Human Resources on Child Care Requirements* (BC Federation of Labour Committee on Women's Rights, 1973).
77 E.R. Rickinson to T.D. Bingham, 7 May 1971, BCA, GR 0746, box 1, file 17.
78 E. Campbell to Mayor T. Campbell, 10 March 1972; and C.A. Soong to Mayor Campbell, 12 June 1972, both in BCA, GR 2921, box 4, file "Day Care Services – Child Welfare."
79 Day Care Secretary to Premier Bennett, 15 April 1972; and P.A. Gagliardi to E. Wolfe (MLA), 29 June 1972, BCA, GR 0746, box 1, file 18.
80 Collier, "Governments and Women's Movements," 116.
81 J.C. Ellingham, *Record of Meeting of Lower Mainland and Municipal Administrators at Victoria*, 29 March 1972, BCA, GR 0746, box 1, file 18. At the meeting were J.C. Ellingham, T.D. Bingham, and several others.
82 Ibid.
83 *Vancouver Sun*, 8 August 1972, clipping from the file SFUA, F-111-7-1-22, "Childcare/Daycare, 1970–78."
84 Collier, "Governments and Women's Movements," 125.
85 Premier's Office, Press Release, 13 December 1972, BCA, GR 0746, box 1, file 19.
86 *Vancouver Sun*, 28 March 1973. R.A. Sadler, *Serial Letter No. 425–342 – Addendum*, 5 October 1972, BCA, GR 0746, box 1, file 19.
87 Premier's Office, Press Release, 13 December 1972, BCA, GR 0746, box 1, file 19.
88 In May 1973, Levi called together a group of representatives from colleges, day cares, and the provincial government to talk about what kind of training/education requirements should be made available and required of day care staff. In large part, this was due to pressure from day care workers themselves, who (along with their feminist allies) were tired of the low pay and long hours that defined their undervalued work. They wanted to increase the status of day care work through more formal training, which would help to challenge the common perception that day care work was "more a hobby than a career." The

workshop resulted in the striking of an ad hoc committee, which was supposed to limit its investigation to training and education questions. The committee took it upon itself to expand its mandate and instead released a comprehensive report outlining the "priority of needs" for day care services, calling for locally based decision making about what kinds of day care services should be provided and, closest to their original mandate, outlining a "career ladder." Though a fairly conservative report – the committee did not even touch on the issue of licensing for under-three year olds – like the others before it, this committee's recommendations fell on deaf ears. Early Childhood Education College Committee, *Child Development: A Proposal for The Regional Colleges of British Columbia*, June 1972; R.J. Burnam, *Memo Re: Canada Manpower – Special Job Finding Service for Day Care Personnel*, 1 August 1973, BCA, GR 0746, box 3, file 35; George Wellwood, *Report of Day Care Conference*, 9 May 1973, BCA, GR 2667, box 1, file "Ad Hoc Committee"; *Report of Ad Hoc Committee on Care for Children 0–5*, presented to N. Levi, 1 June 1973, BCA, GR 2667, box 1, file "Ad Hoc Committee." For more about the professionalization of day care workers, including unionization, see the entire file at BCA, GR 2667, box 1, file "Ad Hoc Committee"; H. Polowy (Professor, UBC) to N. Levi, 21 November 1973, BCA, GR 2667, box 1, file "Ad Hoc Committee."

89 UCS, *The Economics of Day Care*, 2.
90 *Ragamuffin*, October 1974; University Daycare Council, University of British Columbia, *Childcare and the Provincial Government*, 6 November 1972, SFUA, F-111-7-1-22, "Childcare/Daycare 1970–78"; UCS, *The Economics of Day Care*.
91 UCS, *The Economics of Day Care*, 9. This report outlined an alternative plan for a fee schedule, based on a progressive fee structure rather than on an income test.
92 Cited in Clement, "'I Believe in Human Rights,'" 116.
93 B. Wood to D. Cocke (Minister of Health Services and Hospital Insurance) and C.W. Gorby, 4 January 1973, SFUA, F-111-7-1-22, "Childcare/Daycare 1970–78"; B. Wood to D. Barrett, 26 January 1973, SFUA, F-111-7-1-22, "Childcare/Daycare 1970–78."
94 *Growing Pains*, December 1974.
95 *Every parent has a right to daycare*, n.d. [c. February 1973], SFUA, F-111-7-2-5, "Childcare Occupation Forces, 1973."
96 Ibid.
97 UCS, *The Economics of Day Care*, 8.
98 Cohen et al., *'Cuz There Ain't No Day Care*, 35.
99 See, for example, UBC Day Care Council, Press Release, 7 February 1973, SFUA, F-111-7-1-22, "Childcare/Daycare 1970–78."
100 Childcare Occupation Forces, *Proposal Number One, Proposal No. 2*, and *Proposal No. 3*, Press Release, February 1973, SFUA, F-111-7-2-5.
101 Childcare Occupation Forces, Press Release, 13 March 1973, SFUA, F-111-7-2-5.
102 Cohen et al., *'Cuz There Ain't No Day Care*, 2–3; Childcare Occupation Forces, Press Release, 15 March 1973.

103 *Ragamuffin*, October 1974.
104 Cohen et al., *'Cuz There Ain't No Day Care*, 9.
105 Ibid., 6–9.
106 *Growing Pains*, December 1974.
107 Ibid.
108 British Columbia, *Services for People: Annual Report of the Department of Human Resources 1973* (Victoria: Queen's Printer, 1973), 19. Subsidized programs included group day care, family day care, kindergartens, playschools, and services for special needs children.
109 This is from a Human Resource Department booklet called *Creative Guide to Developing a Daycare Centre*, 1974, BCA, GR 0363, box 3, file 11.
110 *Kinesis*, January 1974, 1.
111 "Resource Boards Get Go Ahead," *Integration News: Department of Human Resources* 1, 2 (February 1974), in BCA, GR 0363, box 3, file 5.
112 N. Levi to Dr. S. Segal (President, Children's Aid Society of Vancouver), 24 January 1974, BCA, GR 0363, box 3, file 8. See also Michael Clague et al., *Reforming Human Services: The Experience of the Community Resource Boards in BC* (Vancouver: UBC Press, 1984).
113 M. Dahl to Mr. N. Helm (Executive Director, Neighbourhood Services Association), 3 August 1973, BCA, GR 0363, box 3, file 12; United Community Services of the Greater Vancouver Area, News Release, 19 October 1973, BCA, GR 0363, box 9, file 7.
114 *The Province*, 15 October 1974, 8; D. Marzari to M. Phelps, 18 March 1974, BCA, GR 0363, box 3, file 12.
115 Collier, "Governments and Women's Movements," 216.
116 British Columbia, *Services for People: Annual Report of the Department of Human Resources 1973* (Victoria: Queen's Printer, 1973), 21.
117 British Columbia, *Annual Report of the Department of Rehabilitation and Social Improvement 1972* (Victoria: Queen's Printer, 1972), N40.

Chapter 6: "The feeling lingers that day care just isn't nice"

1 Jane Beach and Martha Friendly, *The State of Early Childhood Education and Care in Canada 2010: Trends and Analysis* (Toronto: Childcare Resource and Research Unit, February 2013), 3–4.
2 Karen Gram, "Please don't go to work, Mommy," *Vancouver Sun*, 23 October 1998, B6; Nita Joy, "Working Mothers Can Also Be Positive Role Models," *Vancouver Sun*, 28 October 1998, A16.
3 UNICEF, *The Child Care Transition, Innocenti Report Card 8* (Florence, Italy: UNICEF Innocenti Research Centre, 2008).
4 Cheryl Collier, "Governments and Women's Movements: Explaining Child Care and Anti-Violence Policy in Ontario and British Columbia, 1970–2000," PhD dissertation, University of Toronto, 2006, 107.
5 Annis May Timpson, *Driven Apart: Women's Employment Equity and Child Care in Canadian Public Policy* (Vancouver: UBC Press, 2001).
6 Ibid., 90–92.

7   *Growing Pains*, April 1975; *Growing Pains*, n.d. (but probably Summer 1975); *South Hill Child Care Centre Statement of Purpose*, 1975, and Ellen Frank, *Now What?*, Simon Fraser University Archives (SFUA), F-82-4-0-6; *The Province*, 18 April 1975, 1; *Growing Pains*, December 1975; *Western Voice*, 7 May 1975, 3; *Franchised Day-Care or the Kentucky-Fried Children Special*, n.d. (estimated approximately December 1975), British Columbia Archives (BCA), GR 2667, box 1, file "Regulations – Standards and Guidelines"; D.S.S. Marshall, for the United Community Services of the Greater Vancouver Area, *Issues in Day Care in Greater Vancouver*, December 1973, University of British Columbia Rare Books and Special Collections (UBCRBSC), Social Work BC Collection, P1001974.

8   Child Care Federation, *Childcare News and the Red Tape Rag*, 1974, SFUA, F-111-7-1-23.

9   British Columbia Federation of Women, *Constitution and Policy Handbook*, volume III, 1977, SFUA, F-82-2-0-3.

10 *Growing Pains*, December 1975; *BCFW – Childcare Interest Group, 1975*, SFUA, F-82-2-0-4. Concern emerged from the conference that the parent-driven day cares "just aren't working out."

11 *Growing Pains*, September 1975. Emphasis in original.

12 Standing Committee of the BC Federation of Women, *Minutes*, 31 January 1976, SFUA, F-82-2-0-4.

13 British Columbia Federation of Women, *1978 Convention: Schedule of Workshops*, SFUA, F-82-2-0-4.

14 Collier, "Governments and Women's Movements," 151.

15 Ad Hoc Committee on the Status of Day Care [Ruth Chisholm], *Day Care: 1977: A Report* (Vancouver: Vancouver Resources Board, June 1977), 13. Emily Campbell was also on this committee.

16 Julia Smith, "An 'Entirely Different' Kind of Union: The Service, Office, and Retail Workers' Union of Canada (SORWUC), 1972–1986," *Labour/Le Travail* 73 (Spring 2014): 23–65. For a discussion of union efforts to ensure women's equality with respect to their reproductive capacities, see Joan Sangster, "Debating Maternity Rights: Pacific Western Airlines and Flight Attendants' Struggle to 'Fly Pregnant' in the 1970s," in *Work on Trial: Canadian Labour Law Struggles*, ed. Judy Fudge and Eric Tucker (Toronto: Irwin Law, 2010). For more on the gender politics of the labour movement, see Meg Luxton, "Feminism as Class Act: Working-Class Feminism and the Women's Movement in Canada," *Labour/Le Travail* 48 (Fall 2001): 63–88; and Pamela Sugiman, *Labour's Dilemma: The Gender Politics of Auto Workers in Canada, 1937–1979* (Toronto: University of Toronto Press, 1994). There was little indication in British Columbia that male-dominated unions gave much attention to "women's issues." See Gillian Creese, "Gendering Collective Bargaining: From Men's Rights to Women's Issues," *Canadian Review of Sociology and Anthropology* 33, 4 (November 1996): 437–56.

17 Collier, "Governments and Women's Movements," 117. Collier refers in this discussion to Allen Garr's description of Bennett. See Allen Garr, *Tough*

Guy: Bill Bennett and the Taking of British Columbia (Toronto: Key Porter Books, 1985).
18 *Vancouver Sun*, 22 March 1976, 1.
19 Collier, "Governments and Women's Movements," 121, 117.
20 British Columbia, *Services for People: Annual Report of the Department of Human Resources 1974* (Victoria: Queen's Printer, 1974). *Canada Assistance Plan*, RSC 1966-67, C. C-45.
21 *Vancouver Sun*, 12 September 1977, 29.
22 British Columbia, *Services for People: Annual Report of the Department of Human Resources 1975* (Victoria: Queen's Printer, 1975); British Columbia, *Annual Report of the Ministry of Human Resources 1980* (Victoria: Queen's Printer, 1980).
23 *Vancouver Sun*, 3 July 1978, C1. The Social Credit government also abolished the Vancouver Resource Board and the Community Resource Boards.
24 Colleen A. Carr, *A Pilot Study of Family Day Care in BC*, April 1976, UBCRBSC, P1035385. Between 1975 and 1980, the proportion of children who received subsidized centre-based care also declined – the highest proportion shifted to family day care.
25 British Columbia, *Services for People: Annual Report of the Department of Human Resources, 1976* (Victoria: Queen's Printer, 1976), V37. Day care operators were allowed to charge parents a fee that was above the maximum subsidy rate.
26 *Vancouver Sun*, 12 September 1977, 29.
27 *Vancouver Sun*, 3 February 1977, 9.
28 K. Knott (President, Nanaimo Children's Daycare Society) to Mayor Ney and Members of City Council, 11 October 1977, BCA, GR 1421, reel B06278.
29 N. Mutch to Honourable W. Vander Zalm, 3 October 1978, BCA, GR 1421, reel B06278; B. Bryant (Social Worker, Child Day Care, Family and Children's Services) to M. Dahl (Deputy Manager, Family and Children's Services), 20 December 1977, BCA, GR 1421, reel B06278; S. Hammond to W. Vander Zalm, 17 April 1978, BCA, GR 1421, reel B06278.
30 E. Campbell to W. Vander Zalm 15 December 1977, BCA, GR 1421, reel B06278.
31 British Columbia, *Services for People: Annual Report of the Department of Human Resources, 1975* (Victoria: Queen's Printer, 1975), M38-39.
32 *The Province*, 4 March 1977, 26. The report that is referenced in this article is Ad Hoc Committee [Chisholm], *Day Care: 1977: A Report*.
33 "Day Care: As Need Increases, the Crunch Hits the Centres," *Vancouver Sun*, 24 November 1981, B6.
34 "Daycare Faces Crisis as Dollars Run Out," *Vancouver Sun*, 7 August 1981, B1.
35 W. Vander Zalm to E. Campbell, 23 November 1977, BCA, GR 1421, reel B06278.
36 *Vancouver Sun*, 28 March 1981.
37 Quoted in Collier, "Governments and Women's Movements," 222.

38 VOP Personnel to N. Levi, 26 September 1973, BCA, GR 2921, box 10, file "Vancouver Opportunities Program v. V." Emphasis in original.
39 *Guaranteed Available Income for Need Act*, RSBC 1979, c. 158 [*GAIN Act*].
40 British Columbia, *Services for People: Ministry of Human Resources Annual Report, 1985–86* (Victoria: Queen's Printer, 1986).
41 "Welfare Moms Speak Out," *Vancouver Sun*, 24 November 1981, B1.
42 Ibid. The payments were reduced for a four-month period, at which time their case was reviewed.
43 British Columbia, *Services for People: Annual Report of the Ministry of Human Resources, 1981* (Victoria: Queen's Printer, 1981).
44 "Welfare Moms Speak Out," B1.
45 "Day Care Denial from McCarthy," *Vancouver Sun*, 24 November 1981, B1.
46 Pat Duffy Hutcheon, *Vancouver Council of Women Study on Day Care and Nursery School Needs and Services in Vancouver City* (Vancouver: Vancouver Council of Women, 1981).
47 Social Planning and Research Department, *Responsible Day Care: The Coming of Age of an Essential Community Service* (Vancouver: United Way of the Lower Mainland, January 1981), 19. The Study Advisory Committee included Emily Campbell, Darlene Marzari, and a couple of others.
48 "Day Care Denial from McCarthy," B1.
49 Prince George Child Care Advisory, *Day Care in Prince George: Mayor's Task Force Report*, May 1982, 26–32, UBCRBSC, Social Work Collection, P1001312.
50 "But McCarthy's Mind Is Still Firmly Made Up," *Vancouver Sun*, 24 November 1981, B1.
51 Lynne Marks and Margaret Little, "Discourses of Motherhood and Second Wave Women's Movements in English Canada," paper presented at the Canadian Historical Association's annual meeting, Fredericton, 31 May 2011.
52 Skeena Terrace Welfare Rights Committee, *Welfare Position Paper*, 1980, UBCRBSC, Social Work Collection, P1625102.
53 Eileen Morris, "Who Will Mind the Children?" *Homemaker's Magazine*, October 1977, 116.
54 "Welfare Moms Speak Out," B1.
55 "Welfare: The System That 'Prevents Getting a Degree,'" *Vancouver Sun*, 24 November 1981, B5.
56 Skeena Terrace Welfare Rights Committee, "Welfare Position Paper."
57 Vancouver Status of Women and the Young Women's Christian Association (YWCA), *Immigrant Women in the Labour Force: Report to The Honourable Norman Levi, Minister of Human Resources*, July 1974, BCA, GRG 0363, box 12, file 10. For an interesting study of Punjabi working women in the Skeena region, see Kamala Elizabeth Nayar, *The Punjabis in British Columbia: Location, Labour, First Nations, and Multiculturalism* (Montreal and Kingston: McGill-Queen's University Press, 2012), chapter 5.
58 Carol Williams, "Introduction," in *Indigenous Women and Work: From Labor to Activism*, ed. Carol Williams (Urbana, IL: University of Illinois Press, 2012),

11; Mary Jane Logan McCallum, *Indigenous Women, Work, and History: 1940–1980* (Winnipeg: University of Manitoba Press, 2014); Joan Sangster, *Transforming Labour: Women and Work in Postwar Canada* (Toronto: University of Toronto Press, 2010), 199–232.
59 Vancouver Status of Women and the YWCA, *Immigrant Women in the Labour Force*.
60 *The Province*, 18 December 1976, 25.
61 Ibid.
62 Vancouver Status of Women and the YWCA, *Immigrant Women in the Labour Force*.
63 R. McLean (Director, St. Andrew's Day Nursery) to N. Levi, 27 March 1974, BCA, GR 0363, box 3, file 12. Furthermore, Ruth MacLean told Norm Levi that these were things that should be the responsibility of government, not unloaded onto working parents in the guise of "parent involvement."
64 Trevor B. Proverbs and Daniel J. Koenig, Department of Human Resources, *Social Services for Children: The Public Speaks* (Victoria: Elector Concern and Satisfaction Surveys, 1977), 52–53.
65 Prince George Child Care Advisory, *Day Care in Prince George*, 53–54.
66 *Vancouver Sun*, 12 September 1977, 29.
67 Morris, "Who Will Mind the Children?" 114.
68 Prince George Child Care Advisory, *Day Care in Prince George*, 53–54. Emphasis in original.
69 Morris, "Who Will Mind the Children?" 116.
70 Proverbs and Koenig, *Social Services for Children*, 71.
71 Prince George Child Care Advisory, *Day Care in Prince George*, 53–54.
72 Vappu Tyyskä, *The Politics of Caring and the Welfare State: The Impact of the Women's Movement on Child Care Policy in Canada and Finland, 1960–1990* (Helsinki, Finland: Suomalainen Tiedeakatemia, 1995), 130–35.
73 Timpson, *Driven Apart*, 67.
74 Ibid., 65. Section 63 of the *Income Tax Act*, RSC 1985, c. 1, specifies that single parents and low-income parents can deduct up to $1,000 from taxable income for child care expenses incurred because they were working, in school, doing research, or in training.
75 Timpson, *Driven Apart*, 64–65; Rebecca Kelley Scherer, "Federal Child Care Policy Development: From World War II to 2000," in *Changing Child Care: Five Decades of Child Care Advocacy and Policy in Canada*, ed. Susan Prentice (Halifax: Fernwood Publishing, 2001), 190.
76 Rianne Mahon, "The Never-Ending Story: The Struggle for Universal Child Care Policy in the 1970s," *Canadian Historical Review* 81, 4 (December 2000): 584.
77 Timpson, *Driven Apart*, 89.
78 Sandra Griffin et al., "Canadian Child Care in Context: Perspectives from the Provinces and Territories: British Columbia Report," in *Canadian National Child Care Study*, ed. Alan Pence (Ottawa: Department of Health and Welfare, 1992), 30–31.

79 Collier, "Governments and Women's Movements," 152–53.
80 Tyyskä, *The Politics of Caring and the Welfare State*, 139.
81 Katie Cooke, *Report of the Task Force on Child Care* (Ottawa: Status of Women Canada, 1986), xxiii. See also Judy Rebick, *Ten Thousand Roses: The Making of Feminist Revolution* (Toronto: Penguin Canada, 2005), chapter 5.
82 Cooke, *Report of the Task Force on Child Care*, 373.
83 Rosalie Silberman Abella, *Equality in Employment: A Royal Commission Report* (Ottawa: Commission on Equality in Employment, 1984).
84 Timpson, *Driven Apart*, 124.
85 Martha Friendly, *It was twenty years ago today . . . March 8, 1986*, Childcare Resource and Research Unit Briefing Note, 3 March 2006, http://www.childcarecanada.org/sites/default/files/BNtwentyyears.pdf.
86 The National Strategy also included an increase in tax deductions and benefits as well as the creation of the Child Care Initiatives Fund, which was designed to enhance child care services for shift workers, special needs children, and services for Aboriginal children.
87 Scherer, "Federal Child Care Policy," 192; Kim Bolan and Gillian Shaw, "Day-Care Report Receives Roasting," *Vancouver Sun*, 31 March 1987, B7.
88 "Child-Care Plan a Sham, Critics Say," *Vancouver Sun*, 16 February 1988, A6. Advocates were also angry that the bill allowed for the sharing of costs in commercial child care centres, a provision they felt undermined their central goal of a universal, publicly funded system. Timpson, *Driven Apart*, 153–54.
89 Shelley Fralic, "Day-Care Dollars Don't Mean Much Here," *Vancouver Sun*, 30 July 1988, B9; Volkart, Carol, "Child-Care Legislation Rapped by Coalition," *Vancouver Sun*, 30 September 1988, G5. It is worth noting, however, that there were submissions from British Columbia to Brian Mulroney's Parliamentary Special Committee that voiced opposition to any kind of "government daycare." "I think it is very important for mothers to stay home and raise their own children whenever possible," insisted one Kelowna mother. "How else will their values and morals be taught to the next generation?" Her views were not uncommon. See "Submission no. 2489," Kelowna, 29 May 1986, *Submissions to the Task Force on Child Care*, volume 1 (Canada: Task Force on Child Care, 1984–86).
90 British Columbia, *Services to People: Ministry of Social Services and Housing Annual Report, 1987–88* (Victoria: Queen's Printer, 1988).
91 Alexandra Dobrowolsky and Jane Jenson, "Shifting Representations of Citizenship: Canadian Politics of 'Women' and 'Children,'" *Social Politics* 11, 2 (2004): 167.
92 Collier, "Governments and Women's Movements," 122–23, 223–24, 152–53.
93 British Columbia, *Services to People: Ministry of Social Services and Housing Annual Report 1989–90*, and *1990–91* (Victoria: Queen's Printer, 1990 and 1991).
94 Day care policy in 1990 amounted to an ad hoc concoction of programs, with responsibility for various aspects of child care provision housed in at least six different ministries. The Ministry of Social Services and Housing carried most of the load. It oversaw the subsidy program still administered through the

GAIN Act. BC Task Force on Child Care, *Showing We Care: A Child Care Strategy for the 1990s* (Victoria: BC Task Force on Child Care, 1991), 12.
95 Ibid.
96 BC Task Force on Child Care, *Showing We Care*, 21.
97 Collier, "Governments and Women's Movements," 226. Harcourt's commitment to gender equality extended beyond child care, in fact. His election platform included significant attention to women's health, reproductive rights, domestic abuse, and pay equity. Valerie Casselton, "Equality for Women Pledged If New Democrats Take Power," *Vancouver Sun*, 1 November 1990, B1.
98 British Columbia, *Annual Report, Ministry of Women's Equality, 1993-94* (Victoria: Queen's Printer, 1994); British Columbia, *Annual Report, Ministry of Women's Equality, 1994-95* (Victoria: Queen's Printer, 1995).
99 British Columbia, *Annual Report, Ministry of Women's Equality, 1993-94*.
100 British Columbia, *Annual Report, Ministry of Women's Equality, 1992-93* (Victoria: Queen's Printer, 1993).
101 British Columbia, *Annual Report, Ministry of Women's Equality, 1996-97* and *1997-98* (Victoria: Queen's Printer, 1997 and 1998).
102 Collier, "Governments and Women's Movements," 226; Alicia Priest, "Subsidy of $5 million for child-care workers receives mixed reviews," *Vancouver Sun*, 29 January 1994, B10; British Columbia, *Annual Report, Ministry of Women's Equality, 1995/96* (Victoria: Queen's Printer, 1996).
103 *BC Benefits (Child Care) Act*, RSBC 1996, c. 26.
104 Mike Harcourt, "Welfare reform began in BC," *Vancouver Sun*, 23 November 2001, A23.
105 British Columbia, *Annual Report, Ministry of Women's Equality, 1996/97* and *1997/98*.
106 Ibid.
107 Collier, "Governments and Women's Movements," 131.
108 *Canada Health and Social Transfer Regulations*, SOR/2007-303, s. 44.
109 Patricia M. Evans and Gerda R. Wekerle, "The Shifting Terrain of Women's Welfare: Theory, Discourse, and Activism," in *Women and the Canadian Welfare State: Challenges and Change*, ed. Patricia M. Evans and Gerda R. Wekerle (Toronto: University of Toronto Press, 1997), 5-7.
110 Susan Prentice, "Less, Worse and More Expensive: Childcare in an Era of Deficit Reduction," *Journal of Canadian Studies / Revue d'Etudes Canadiennes* 34, 2 (June 1999), 145.
111 Martha Friendly et al., *Early Childhood Care and Education in Canada 2001* (Toronto: Childcare Resource and Research Unit, 10 February 2003), table 29 and table 32.
112 Since the early 1990s, child care workers had been included in the Community Social Services Employers Association (CSSEA), which was the recommendation of the Korbin Commission of Inquiry into the Public Service and Public Sector. As part of the CSSEA, child care workers were eligible for wage supplements. In 1998, the CSSEA began negotiations on behalf of four unions for increases in wages and benefits. As part of these negotiations, the government

began to "isolate child care" from other CSSEA workers. Child care workers went on strike with other CSSEA members when negotiations broke down. The Munroe settlement, which ended the strike in May 1999, separated child care workers from other social services workers, with the result that "CSSEA, [the Public Sector Employer's Council,] and the funding ministries agree[d] to explore the complexities of wage/benefit increases for child care workers." Child Care Advocacy Forum, *Child Care Sector and Low Wage Redress: A Brief History*, October 2000, http://www.wstcoast.org/pdf/CCAF_history_web.pdf, 75–76. See also "Striking Social Service Workers Rally in Protest," *Victoria Times Colonist*, 25 March 1999, B1; "Community Services Brace for Job Action," *Vancouver Sun*, 12 March 1999, B7.

113 Coalition of Child Care Advocates of British Columbia; BC Association of Child Care Employers; Early Childhood Educators of British Columbia; School Age Child Care Association of British Columbia; Western Canada Family Child Care Association of British Columbia; West Coast Child Care Resource Centre.

114 British Columbia, Ministry of Social Development and Economic Security, *Child Care for British Columbia* (Victoria: Ministry of Social Development and Economic Security, May 2000), 2.

115 Ibid.

116 British Columbia, Ministry of Social Development and Economic Security, *Child Care for British Columbia*, 4.

117 Collier, "Governments and Women's Movements," 229.

118 "B.C. Moves toward Universal Day Care Funded by Taxpayers," *Vancouver Sun*, 6 June 2000, A1.

119 Mark Hume, "BC Premier Woos Voters with $400M in childcare," *National Post*, 9 January 2001.

120 Child Care Advocacy Forum, "We Kept Our Eyes on the Prize – And It Worked!" n.d., http://www.wstcoast.org/pdf/CCAF_history_web.pdf, 61.

121 *Child Care BC Act*, SBC 2001, c. 4.

122 Gerry Warner, "Local Child Care Providers Blast B.C. Government," *Kimberley Daily Bulletin*, 20 August 2001.

123 Child Care Advocacy Forum, *Child Care Advocacy Forum Reaffirms Common Vision and Agenda*, March 2002, http://www.wstcoast.org/pdf/CCAF_history_web.pdf, 129–32.

124 Child Care Advocacy Forum, *Where Are the Children?* 10 February 2003, http://www.wstcoast.org/pdf/CCAF_history_web.pdf, 143.

125 Government of Canada, *Multilateral Framework on Early Childhood Learning and Care*, March 2003, http://www.ecd-elcc.ca/eng/elcc/about.shtml.

126 Martha Friendly and Susan Prentice, *About Canada: Childcare* (Halifax: Fernwood Publishing, 2009), 83–84.

127 First Call: BC Child and Youth Advocacy Coalition, *An Open Letter to the Education Community: End the Divide between Early Learning and Care*, November 2005, http://www.firstcallbc.org/pdfs/EarlyChildhood/1-education%20community.pdf.

128 Kristin Goff, "Child Care Cheques Sent out but Young Child Supplement Gets Axed," *Vancouver Sun*, 21 July 2006, A6.
129 Friendly and Prentice, *About Canada*, 1.
130 Martha Friendly and Jane Beach, *The State of Early Childhood Education and Care in Canada 2010: Trends and Analysis* (Toronto: Childcare Resource and Research Unit, 5 February 2013), 2–3.
131 Paul Kershaw, *Carefair: Rethinking the Responsibilities and Rights of Citizenship* (Vancouver: UBC Press, 2005), 3–4.
132 British Columbia, Ministry of Children and Family Development, *Child Care Programs and Services 2010–11 Report*, http://www.mcf.gov.bc.ca/childcare/pdfs/child_care_programs_services_report_2010_2011.pdf.
133 Friendly and Beach, *The State of Early Childhood Education and Care in Canada 2010*.
134 Coalition of Child Care Advocates of British Columbia, *The Current Child Care Context in BC*, http://www.cccabc.bc.ca/plan/wp-content/uploads/2013/05/BCisFailing.pdf.
135 Martha Friendly et al., *Early Childhood Education and Care in Canada 2012* (Toronto: Childcare Resource and Research Unit, 28 August 2013), 16.
136 BC Government and Service Employees' Union, *Can't Afford Child Care*, cantaffordchildcare.ca.
137 Christopher A. Sarlo, *The Cost of Raising Children* (Vancouver: Fraser Institute, 2013), 2, 40.
138 This is the stated purpose of the Ministry of Children and Family Development: British Columbia, *Ministry of Children and Family Development*, http://www.gov.bc.ca/mcf/ (accessed 5 November 2014). See British Columbia, Ministry of Children and Family Development, *Child Care Programs and Services 2010–11 Report*.
139 See, for example, Kelly Pasolli, "Child Care Advocacy in Alberta," BA Honours thesis, University of Lethbridge, 2010.
140 See Tammy Findlay, "Gendering the Governance of Child Care: State, Community and Nancy Fraser's Étatism," paper presented at the 2012 Annual Meeting of the Canadian Political Science Association, Concordia University, 1–3 June 2010 [cited with permission].
141 Prentice, "High Stakes," 702.
142 Cited in Collier, "Governments and Women's Movements," 231.
143 BC Task Force in Child Care, *Showing We Care*, 77.
144 Dobrowolsky and Jenson, "Shifting Representations," 174.
145 Linda A. White, "Trends in Child Care/Early Childhood Education/Early Childhood Development Policy in Canada and the United States," *American Review of Canadian Studies* (Winter 2004): 672.
146 Prentice, "High Stakes," 687.
147 Rianne Mahon, "Varieties of Liberalism: Canadian Social Policy from the 'Golden Age' to the Present," *Social Policy and Administration* 42, 4 (August 2008): 345. Mahon is citing D. Craig and D. Porter, "The Third Way and the Third World: Poverty Reduction and Social Inclusion in the Rise of 'Inclusive Liberalism,'" *Review of International Political Economy* 11, 2 (2004): 91.

148 Mahon, "Varieties of Liberalism," 690.
149 Ibid., 688.
150 Craig Alexander and Dina Ignjatovic, *Special Report, TD Economics: Early Childhood Education Has Widespread and Long Lasting Benefits*, 27 November 2012, http://www.td.com/document/PDF/economics/special/di1112_EarlyChildhoodEducation.pdf.
151 Gordon Cleveland and Michael Krashinsky, *The Benefits and Costs of Good Child Care: The Economic Rationale for Public Investment in Young Children: A Policy Study* (University of Toronto, Child Care Resource and Research Unit, 1998), 5, 78.
152 Coalition of Child Care Advocates of BC, *Community Plan for a Public System of Integrated Early Care and Learning* (April 2011), http://www.cccabc.bc.ca/plan/.
153 Ibid., Fact Sheet 4.
154 Ibid., Fact Sheet 2.
155 Ibid., Fact Sheet 3.
156 Though, as Findlay points out, community-based, democratic models also run the risk of relying heavily on women's volunteer labour. The reliance on this model can also create unequal access to services in neighbourhoods with different levels of "social capital." Findlay, "Gendering the Governance of Child Care," 8–9.

Conclusion

1 Alice Kessler-Harris, *In Pursuit of Equity: Women, Men, and the Quest for Economic Citizenship in Twentieth-Century America* (Madison, NY: Oxford University Press, 2001), 13.
2 Rianne Mahon and Susan Phillips, "Dual-Earner Families Caught in a Liberal Welfare Regime? The Politics of Child Care Policy in Canada," in *Child Care Policy at the Crossroads: Gender and Welfare State Restructuring*, ed. Sonya Michel and Rianne Mahon (New York: Routledge, 2002), 210. *Canada Assistance Plan*, RSC 1966–67, C. C-45.
3 Rianne Mahon, "Gender and Welfare State Restructuring: Through the Lens of Child Care," in Michel and Mahon, *Child Care Policy at the Crossroads*, 8.
4 See, for example, Child Care Advocacy Association of Canada, http://www.ccaac.ca.
5 Susan Prentice, "High Stakes: The 'Investable' Child and the Economic Reframing of Childcare," *Signs* 34, 3 (2009): 703.
6 Alexandra Dobrowolsky, "Introduction: Neo-Liberalism and After?" in *Women and Public Policy in Canada: Neo-Liberalism and After?* ed. Alexandra Dobrowolsky (Don Mills, ON: Oxford University Press, 2009), 4.
7 Ann Shola Orloff, "From Maternalism to 'Employment for All': State Policies to Promote Women's Employment across the Affluent Democracies," in *The State after Statism: New State Activities in the Age of Liberalization*, ed. Jonah D. Levy (Boston: Harvard University Press, 2006).
8 Mahon, "Gender and Welfare State Restructuring," 7.

9   See Gwendolyn Mink, *Welfare's End* (Ithaca, NY: Cornell University Press, 2002). See also Teresa L. Amott, "Black Women and AFDC: Making Entitlement out of Necessity," in *Women, the State, and Welfare*, ed. Linda Gordon (Madison, WI: University of Wisconsin Press, 1990).
10 Margaret Little and Lynne Marks, "Ontario and British Columbia Welfare Policy: Variants on a Neoliberal Theme," *Comparative Studies of South Asia, Africa and the Middle East* 30, 2 (2010): 195.
11 Ibid. See also Jane Jenson and Mariette Sineau, "Citizenship in the Era of Welfare State Redesign," in *Who Cares? Women's Work, Childcare, and Welfare State Redesign*, eds. Jane Jenson and Mariette Sineau (Toronto: University of Toronto Press, 2001).
12 Helga Maria Hernes, *Welfare State and Woman Power: Essays in State Feminism* (Oslo, Norway: Norwegian University Press, 1987).
13 For a sustained analysis of how the welfare system reinforces women's subordination, see Mimi Abramowitz, *Regulating the Lives of Women: Social Welfare Policy from Colonial Times to the Present* (Boston: South End Press, 1996).
14 See Frances Fox Piven, "Ideology and the State: Women, Power, and the Welfare State," in Gordon, *Women, the State, and Welfare*, 250–64; Carole Pateman, "The Patriarchal Welfare State," in *Democracy and the Welfare State*, ed. Amy Gutman (Princeton, NJ: Princeton University Press, 1988).
15 See Kimberley J. Morgan, Working Mothers and the Welfare State: Religion and the Politics of Work-Family Policies in Western Europe and the United States (Stanford, CA: Stanford University Press, 2006), 6–7.
16 Orloff, "From Maternalism to 'Employment for All.'" For more international comparisons, see Sonya Michel and Rianne Mahon, eds., *Child Care Policy at the Crossroads: Gender and Welfare State Restructuring* (New York: Routledge, 2002); and Julia S. O'Connor, Ann Shola Orloff, and Sheila Shaver, *States, Markets, Families: Gender, Liberalism and Social Policy in Australia, Canada, Great Britain and the United States* (Cambridge: Cambridge University Press, 1999).
17 See Meg Luxton and Ester Reiter, "Double, Double, Toil and Trouble: Women's Experience of Work and Family in Canada, 1980–1995," in *Women and the Canadian Welfare State: Challenges and Change*, ed. Patricia M. Evans and Gerda R. Wekerle (Toronto: University of Toronto Press, 1997).
18 Emily K. Abel, "Valuing Care: Turn-of-the-Century Conflicts between Charity Workers and Women Clients," *Journal of Women's History* 10, 3 (Autumn 1998): 32.
19 Nancy Fraser, *Justice Interruptus: Critical Reflections on the "Postsocialist" Condition* (New York: Routledge, 1997).
20 Paul Kershaw, *Carefair: Rethinking the Responsibilities and Rights of Citizenship* (Vancouver: UBC Press, 2005), 163.
21 Ruth Lister, *Citizenship: Feminist Perspectives* (New York: New York University Press, 1997), 177.
22 Kershaw, *Carefair*, 138.
23 Ibid., 140–51.
24 Ibid., 155.

25 Linda Gordon, "The New Feminist Scholarship on the Welfare State," in Gordon, *Women, the State, and Welfare*, 25.
26 See, for example, Gord Bruyere, "A Spallumcheen Foster Child," in *Child and Family Welfare in British Columbia: A History*, ed. Diane Purvey and Christopher Walmsley (Calgary: Detselig Enterprises, 2005).
27 See Tammy Findlay, "Provincial Child Care: Gender Regimes and Social Citizenship in Canada," paper presented at the 2013 Annual Meeting of the Canadian Political Science Association, University of Victoria, 4 June 2013 [cited with permission].
28 Rachel K. Brickner and Christine Straehle, "The Missing Link: Gender, Immigration Policy and the Live-in Caregiver Program in Canada," *Policy and Society* 29 (2010): 311. See also Geraldine Pratt, *Families Apart: Migrant Mothers and the Conflicts of Labor and Love* (Minneapolis, MN: University of Minnesota Press, 2012).
29 The number of permits provided for the live-in caregiver program has grown dramatically since 2000. In 2006, there were 21,498 work permits, compared to 5,942 in 2000. Of all temporary foreign workers, nannies are the lowest paid. Brickner and Straehle, "The Missing Link," 313, 315.
30 Ibid., 318.

Bibliography

Archival Sources
British Columbia Archives
GR 0128: Department of Social Welfare Executive Records 1936–66
GR 0135: Department of Social Welfare Executive Records 1966–68
GR 0344: Provincial Secretary Correspondence 1918–26
GR 0363: Community Resource Board Records 1973–77
GR 0365: Social Welfare Department Executive Records 1963–69
GR 0441: Premier's Records 1883–1933
GR 0496: Provincial Secretary Executive Records 1929–47
GR 0684: Royal Commission on Labour 1912–14
GR 0706: Commission on Health Insurance 1919–21
GR 0746: Department of Social Rehabilitation and Social Improvement Executive Records 1966–76
GR 0883: Records with Regard to Child Welfare 1919–63
GR 1323: Attorney-General Correspondence 1902–37
GR 1421: Ministry of Human Resources, Correspondence to the Minister, 1977–80.
GR 2667: Provincial Child Care Facilities Licensing Board Records 1968–79
GR 2738: Neglected Children Case Files 1919–43
GR 2921: Vancouver Resource Board Records 1953–75
MS 0431: Family and Children's Aid Service fonds

Library and Archives Canada
MG 28 I 10 Canadian Council on Social Development fonds
RG 27 Department of Labour fonds

City of Vancouver Archives
City Council and Office of the City Clerk fonds

- Public Records Series 20: Subject Files, including Council Supporting Documents
- Public Records Series 31: Council Minutes
- Public Records Series 33: Standing Committee Minutes

City Social Service Department fonds

- Public Records Series 447: Associated Charities of Vancouver
- Public Records Series 449: Director's Subject Files

City Publications Collection

- PDS 11: Annual Reports of the Medical Health Officer, 1910–36

PAM 1935–53: Lilian Nelson
PAM 1938–16: Vancouver Women's Building Directory
Add. MSS 124: Vancouver City Crèche fonds
Add. MSS 556: Imperial Order Daughters of the Empire, Valcartier Camp Chapter fonds
Major Matthews Collection: Collected Photographs
William Bros. Photographers Collection

Simon Fraser University Archives
F-82: Ellen Frank fonds
F-111: Women's Bookstore Collection
F-149: Simon Fraser University Childcare Society fonds
F-166: Women's Movement Collection (Anne Roberts collector)

University of British Columbia Rare Books and Special Collections
Ad Hoc Committee on the Status of Day Care. *Day Care: 1977: A Report*. Vancouver: Vancouver Resources Board, 1977. P1014562.
Carr, Colleen A. *A Pilot Study of Family Day Care in BC*, April 1976. P1035385.
Cohen, Marcy, Nancy Duggan, Carol Sayre, Barbara Todd, and Nikki Wright. *'Cuz There Ain't No Daycare (or Almost None She Said)*. Vancouver: Press Gang Publishers, 1973.
Foster Day Care Association of Vancouver. *Annual Report*, 1955.
Kilian, Melody. *Day Care Manifesto*. Women's Caucus, n.d. SPAM 27572.
Marshall, David S.S. *Issues in Day Care in Greater Vancouver*. Vancouver: United Community Services of the Greater Vancouver Area, 1973. P1009174.
New Democratic Party of British Columbia. Vancouver-Kingsway Constituency Association fonds 1956–75.
Prince George Child Care Advisory, *Day Care in Prince George: Mayor's Task Force Report*, May 1982. P1001312.
Skeena Terrace Welfare Rights Committee. *Welfare Position Paper*, 1980. P1625102.

United Community Services, Social Policy and Research Department, *The Economics of Day Care*. Vancouver: United Community Services of the Greater Vancouver Area, 1973. P1012269.
Vancouver and District Labour Council fonds 1889–1983.
Vancouver Day Nursery Association. *Annual Report*, 1932–45.

British Columbia Legislative Library
British Columbia Federation of Labour. *Submission of the Committee on Women's Rights to the Minister of Human Resources on Child Care Requirements.* Victoria, 1973.
Business and Professional Women's Clubs of British Columbia and Yukon. *Brief on Need for Starting Grants for Child Day Care Centres.* Report presented to Daniel Campbell, Minister of Social Welfare. Victoria, 1968.
Whitton, Charlotte. *Report of Miss Charlotte Whitton, Executive Director of the Canadian Council on Child and Family Welfare, on Mothers' Pensions and Social Service Work in the Province of British Columbia.* Prepared for the Honourable S.L. Howe, Provincial Secretary. Victoria, 1 December 1931.

Newspapers/Periodicals
British Columbia Federationist
Growing Pains
Homemaker's Magazine
Kimberley Daily Bulletin
Kinesis
National Post
The Peak
The Pedestal
The Province
Ragamuffin
The Ubyssey
Vancouver Daily World
Vancouver Sun
Victoria Daily Colonist
Victoria Daily Times

Web Material
BC Government and Service Employees' Union. *Can't Afford Child Care.* http://cantaffordchildcare.ca.
British Columbia. *Ministry of Children and Family Development.* http://www.gov.bc.ca/mcf/.
Child Care Advocacy Association of Canada. CCAAC Online. http://www.ccaac.ca.
Child Care Advocacy Forum. *Child Care Advocacy Forum, 1999–2010.* http://www.wstcoast.org/pdf/CCAF_history_web.pdf.
Coalition of Child Care Advocates of British Columbia. *Community Plan for a Public System of Integrated Early Care & Learning,* 4th edition, July 2013. http://www.cccabc.bc.ca/plan/Community_Plan_ECL.pdf.

–. *The Current Child Care Context in BC.* http://www.cccabc.bc.ca/plan/wp-content/uploads/2013/05/BCisFailing.pdf.
First Call: BC Child and Youth Advocacy Coalition. *An Open Letter to the Education Community: End the Divide between Early Learning and Care*, November 2005. http://www.firstcallbc.org/pdfs/EarlyChildhood/1-education%20community.pdf.
Government of Canada. *Multilateral Framework on Early Childhood Learning and Care*, March 2003. http://www.ecd-elcc.ca/eng/elcc/about.shtml.
Statistics Canada. *Rural and Urban Population of Canada, by Province and Sex*, 1911. http://www65.statcan.gc.ca/acyb02/1917/acyb02_191700849a-eng.htm.

Other Sources

Abbott, Ruth K., and R.A. Young. "Cynical and Deliberate Manipulation? Child Care and the Reserve Army of Female Labour in Canada." *Journal of Canadian Studies / Revue d'Etudes Canadiennes* 24, 2 (1989): 22–38.
Abel, Emily. "Valuing Care: Turn-of-the-Century Conflicts between Charity Workers and Women Clients." *Journal of Women's History* 10, 3 (Autumn 1998): 32–52.
Abella, Rosalie Silberman. Equality in Employment: A Royal Commission Report. Ottawa: Commission on Equality in Employment, 1984.
Abramovitz, Mimi. *Regulating the Lives of Women: Social Welfare Policy from Colonial Times to the Present.* Boston: South End Press, 1996.
Adamoski, Robert. "The Child-The Citizen-The Nation: The Rhetoric and Experience of Wardship in Early Twentieth-Century British Columbia." In *Contesting Canadian Citizenship: Historical Readings*, ed. Robert Adamoski, Dorothy E. Chunn, and Robert Menzies, 315–36. Peterborough, ON: Broadview Press, 2002.
–. "Their Duties towards the Children: Citizenship and the Practice of Child Rescue in Early Twentieth Century British Columbia." PhD dissertation, Simon Fraser University, 1995.
Adamoski, Robert, Dorothy E. Chunn, and Robert Menzies, eds. *Contesting Canadian Citizenship: Historical Readings.* Peterborough, ON: Broadview Press, 2002.
Adamson, Nancy, Linda Briskin, and Margaret McPhail. *Feminist Organizing for Change: The Contemporary Women's Movement in Canada.* Toronto: Oxford University Press, 1988.
Albanese, Patrizia. "Small Town, Big Benefits: The Ripple Effect of $7/day Child Care." *Canadian Review of Sociology and Anthropology / La Revue Canadienne de Sociologie et d'Anthropologie* 43, 2 (2006): 125–40.
Alexander, Craig, and Dina Ignjatovic. *Early Childhood Education Has Widespread and Long Lasting Benefits.* TD Economics Special Report, 27 November 2012.
Amott, Teresa L. "Black Women and AFDC: Making Entitlement Out of Necessity." In *Women, the State, and Welfare*, ed. Linda Gordon, 280–98. Madison, WI: University of Wisconsin Press, 1990.
Anderson, Robin John. "Domestic Service: The YWCA and Women's Employment Agencies in Vancouver, 1898–1915." *Histoire Sociale / Social History* 25, 50 (November 1992): 307–33.
Atkin, Wendy. "'Babies of the World Unite': The Early Day-Care Movement and Family Formation in the 1970s." In *Family Matters: Papers in Post-Confederation*

Canadian Family History, ed. Lori Chambers and Edgar-Andre Montigny, 57–70. Toronto: Canadian Scholars' Press, 1998.

–. "Playing Together as Canadians: Historical Lessons from the West End Crèche." In *Changing Child Care: Five Decades of Child Care Advocacy and Policy in Canada,* ed. Susan Prentice, 27–38. Halifax: Fernwood Publishing, 2001.

Baillargeon, Denyse. *Making Do: Women, Family and Home in Montreal during the Great Depression.* Waterloo, ON: Wilfrid Laurier University Press, 1999.

Barman, Jean. *The West beyond the West: A History of British Columbia.* Toronto: University of Toronto Press, 2007.

Beach, Jane, and Martha Friendly. *The State of Early Childhood Education and Care in Canada 2010: Trends and Analysis.* Toronto: Childcare Resource and Research Unit, February 2013.

Benston, Margaret. "The Political Economy of Women's Liberation." *Monthly Review* 21 (September 1969): 13–27.

Bird, Florence. *Report of the Royal Commission on the Status of Women in Canada.* Ottawa, September 1970.

Blake, Raymond. *From Rights to Needs: A History of Family Allowances in Canada.* Vancouver: UBC Press, 2009.

Boris, Eileen. "What About the Working of the Working Mother?" *Journal of Women's History* 5, 2 (Fall 1993): 104–9.

Boris, Eileen, and S.J. Kleinberg. "Mothers and Other Workers: (Re)Conceiving Labor, Maternalism, and the State." *Journal of Women's History* 15, 3 (Autumn 2003): 90–117.

Bradbury, Bettina. *Working Families: Age, Gender, and Daily Survival in Industrializing Montreal.* Toronto: University of Toronto Press, 2007.

Brandt, Gail Cuthbert. "'Pigeon-Holed and Forgotten': The Work of the Subcommittee on the Post-War Problems of Women, 1943." *Histoire Sociale / Social History* 15, 29 (May 1982): 239–59.

Brickner, Rachel K., and Christine Straehle. "The Missing Link: Gender, Immigration Policy and the Live-in Caregiver Program in Canada." *Policy and Society* 29, 4 (2010): 309–20.

British Columbia. Department/Ministry of Human Resources. *Services for People: Annual Report of the Department / Ministry of Human Resources,* 1973–86.

–. Department of Labour. *Annual Report,* 1920–67.

–. Department of Social Welfare / Department of Rehabilitation and Social Improvement. *Annual Report,* 1960–72.

–. Legislative Assembly. *Sessional Papers,* 1921.

–. Ministry of Children and Family Development. *Child Care Programs and Services Report,* 2010–11.

–. Ministry of Social Development and Economic Security. *Child Care for British Columbia.* May 2000.

–. Ministry of Social Services and Housing. *Annual Report,* 1987–91.

–. Ministry of Women's Equality. *Annual Report,* 1992–98.

–. Mothers' Pensions Board / Superintendent of Welfare. *Annual Report Made under the Mothers' Pensions Act,* 1922–44.

–. Social Welfare Branch of the Department of Health and Welfare. *Annual Report,* 1948–58.

–. Statutes. *An Act to Amend the Mothers' Pensions Act,* 1921.

–. Statutes. *An Act to Provide Pensions for Mothers,* 1920.

–. Workmen's Compensation Board. *Annual Reports*, 1924–30.
British Columbia Task Force on Child Care. *Showing We Care: A Child Care Strategy for the 90s*. 1991.
Brodie, Janine. "The Social in Social Citizenship." In *Recasting the Social in Citizenship*, ed. Engin F. Isin, 20–43. Toronto: University of Toronto Press, 2008.
Brown, Lorraine. "Domestic Service in British Columbia, 1850–1914." MA thesis, University of Victoria, 1995.
Bruyere, Gord. "A Spallumcheen Foster Child." In *Child and Family Welfare in British Columbia: A History*, ed. Diane Purvey and Christopher Walmsley, 283–94. Calgary: Detselig Enterprises, 2005.
Bryden, P.E. *Planners and Politicians: Liberal Politics and Social Policy, 1957–68*. Montreal and Kingston: McGill-Queen's University Press, 1997.
Bucur, Maria. "Gender and Citizenship: Difference and Power in the Modern State." *Journal of Women's History* 20, 4 (2008): 160–70.
Campbell, Lara. *Respectable Citizens: Gender, Family, and Unemployment in Ontario's Great Depression*. Toronto: University of Toronto Press, 2009.
Campbell, Marie. "Sexism in British Columbia Trade Unions, 1900–1920." In *In Her Own Right: Selected Essays on Women's History in British Columbia*, ed. Cathy Kess and Barbara Latham, 167–86. Victoria: Camosun College Press, 1980.
Canada. Department of Labour. *The Labour Gazette*, 1914–15.
Canadian Co-operative Association. *Child Care Co-operatives in Canada 2007: A Research Report*. Ottawa: Co-operatives Secretariat and Human Resources and Social Development Canada in conjunction with the Co-operatives Secretariat, March 2007.
Canadian Council on Social Development. *Day Care: Report of a National Study*. Ottawa: Canadian Council on Social Development, January 1972.
–. *Proceedings: Canadian Conference on Day Care, June 20–23, 1971*. Ottawa: Canadian Council on Social Development and Department of Health and Welfare, January 1972.
Carter, Connie, and Eileen Daoust. "From Home to House: Women in the BC Legislature." In *Not Just Pin Money: Selected Essays on the History of Women's Work in British Columbia*, ed. Barbara K. Latham and Roberta J. Pazdro, 389–405. Victoria: Camosun College Press, 1984.
Christie, Nancy. *Engendering the State: Family, Work, and Welfare in Canada*. Toronto: University of Toronto Press, 2000.
Clague, Michael et al. *Reforming Human Services: The Experience of The Community Resource Boards in B.C.* Vancouver: UBC Press, 1984.
Clark, Penney, Mona Gleason, and Stephen Petrina. "Preschools for Science: The Child Study Centre at the University of British Columbia, 1960–1997." *History of Education Quarterly* 52, 1 (February 2012): 29–61.
Clement, Dominique. "'I Believe in Human Rights, Not Women's Rights': Women and the Human Rights State, 1969–1984." *Radical History Review* 101 (Spring 2008): 107–29.
Cleveland, Gordon, and Michael Krashinsky. *The Benefits and Costs of Good Child Care: The Economic Rationale for Public Investment in Young Children*. Toronto: Childcare Resource and Research Unit, University of Toronto, 1998.

Collier, Cheryl. "Governments and Women's Movements: Explaining Child Care and Anti-Violence Policy in Ontario and British Columbia, 1970–2000." PhD dissertation, University of Toronto, 2006.

Comacchio, Cynthia. *The Infinite Bonds of Family: Domesticity in Canada, 1850–1940*. Toronto: University of Toronto Press, 1999.

–. "'A Postscript for Father': Defining a New Fatherhood in Interwar Canada." *Canadian Historical Review* 78, 3 (September 1997): 385–408.

Community Chest and Councils of the Greater Vancouver Area, Welfare and Recreation Council. *Report on Day Care Needs*. Vancouver: Community Chest and Councils of the Greater Vancouver Area, June 1965.

Cooke, Katie. *Report of the Task Force on Child Care*. Ottawa: Status of Women Canada, 1986.

Creese, Gillian. "Gendering Collective Bargaining from Men's Rights to Women's Issues." *Canadian Review of Sociology and Anthropology / La Revue Canadienne de Sociologie et d'Anthropologie* 33, 4 (November 1996): 437–56.

–. "The Politics of Dependence: Women, Work and Unemployment in the Vancouver Labour Movement before World War II." In *British Columbia Reconsidered: Essays on Women*, ed. Gillian Creese and Veronica Strong-Boag, 364–90. Vancouver: Press Gang Publishers, 1992.

–. "Sexuality Equality and the Minimum Wage in British Columbia." *Journal of Canadian Studies / Revue d'Etudes Canadiennes* 26, 4 (Winter 1991–92): 120–40.

Daly, Mary, and Katherine Rake. *Gender and the Welfare State: Care, Work and Welfare in Europe and the US*. Cambridge: Polity Press, 2003.

Davies, Megan. "'Services Rendered, Rearing Children for the State': Mothers' Pensions in British Columbia." In *Not Just Pin Money: Selected Essays on the History of Women's Work in British Columbia*, ed. Barbara Latham and Roberta J. Pazdro, 249–63. Victoria: Camosun College Press, 1984.

–. "Welfare Amazons or Handmaidens of the State?: Welfare Field Workers in Rural BC, 1935–42." In *Child and Family Welfare in BC: A History*, ed. Diane Purvey and Chris Walmsley, 195–234. Calgary: Detselig Enterprises, 2006.

Davis, Chuck. *The Greater Vancouver Book: An Urban Encyclopedia*. Surrey, BC: Linkman Press, 1997.

Dinner, Deborah. "The Universal Childcare Debate: Rights Mobilization, Social Policy, and the Dynamics of Feminist Activism, 1966–1974." *Law and History Review* 28, 3 (August 2010): 577–628.

Dobrowolsky, Alexandra. "Introduction: Neo-Liberalism and After?" In *Women and Public Policy in Canada: Neo-Liberalism and After?* ed. Alexandra Dobrowolsky, 1–24. Don Mills, ON: Oxford University Press, 2009.

Dobrowolsky, Alexandra, and Jane Jenson. "Shifting Representations of Citizenship: Canadian Politics of 'Women' and 'Children.'" *Social Politics* 11, 2 (Summer 2004): 154–80.

Ellis, Jason. "'This is not a medieval university attended by celibate clergy'. Contesting the University of Toronto's First Daycare Sit-in." Unpublished paper, York University, May 2005 [on file with the author].

Esping-Andersen, Gosta. *The Three Worlds of Welfare Capitalism*. Cambridge: Polity Press, 1990.

Evans, Patricia M., and Gerda R. Wekerle. "The Shifting Terrain of Women's Welfare: Theory, Discourse, and Activism." In *Women and the Canadian Welfare State: Challenges and Change*, ed. Patricia M. Evans and Gerda R. Wekerle, 3–27. Toronto: University of Toronto Press, 1997.

Fahrni, Magda. *Household Politics: Montreal Families and Postwar Reconstruction*. Toronto: University of Toronto Press, 2005.

Farrell, Ann. *Grace MacInnis: A Story of Love and Integrity*. Markham, ON: Fitzhenry and Whiteside, 1994.

Fay, Jeanne. "The 'Right Kind' of Single Mothers: Nova Scotia's Regulation of Women on Social Assistance, 1956–77." In *Mothers of the Municipality: Women, Work, and Social Policy in Post-1945 Halifax*, ed. Judith Fingard and Janet Guildford, 141–68. Toronto: University of Toronto Press, 2005.

Findlay, Tammy. "Gendering the Governance of Child Care: State, Community and Nancy Fraser's Étatism." Paper presented at the 2012 Annual Meeting of the Canadian Political Science Association, Concordia University, 1–3 June 2010.

–. "Provincial Child Care: Gender Regimes and Social Citizenship in Canada." Paper presented at the 2013 Annual Meeting of the Canadian Political Science Association, University of Victoria, 4 June 2013.

Finkel, Alvin. "Changing the Story: Gender Enters the History of the Welfare State." *Tijdschrift voor Sociale Geschiedenis* 22, 1 (1996): 67–81.

–. "Even the Little Children Cooperated: Family Strategies, Childcare Discourse, and Social Welfare Debates 1945–1975." *Labour / Le Travail* 36 (Fall 1995): 91–118.

–. *Social Policy and Practice in Canada: A History*. Waterloo, ON: Wilfrid Laurier University Press, 2006.

–. "The State of Writing on the Welfare State: What's Class Got to Do with It?" *Labour / Le Travail* 54 (Fall 2004): 151–74.

Frager, Ruth, and Carmela Patrias. *Discounted Labour: Women Workers in Canada, 1870–1939*. Toronto: University of Toronto Press, 2005.

Fraser, Nancy. *Justice Interruptus: Critical Reflections on the "Postsocialist" Condition*. New York: Routledge, 1997.

Fraser, Nancy, and Linda Gordon. "A Genealogy of Dependency: Tracing a Keyword of the U.S. Welfare State." *Signs* 19, 2 (Winter 1994): 309–36.

–. "Contract versus Charity: Why Is There No Social Citizenship in the United States?" *Socialist Review* 22, 3 (July-September 1992): 45–67.

Friendly, Martha. "It was twenty years ago today ... March 8, 1986." Childcare Resource and Research Unit Briefing Note, 8 March 2006.

Friendly, Martha, and Jane Beach. *The State of Early Childhood Education and Care in Canada 2010: Trends and Analysis*. Toronto: Childcare Resource and Research Unit, 5 February 2013.

Friendly, Martha, Jane Beach, and Michelle Turiano. *Early Childhood Care and Education in Canada 2001*. Toronto: Childcare Resource and Research Unit, February 2003.

Friendly, Martha, and Susan Prentice. *About Canada: Childcare*. Black Point, NS: Fernwood Publishing, 2009.

Friendly, Martha, et al. *Early Childhood Education and Care in Canada 2012*. Toronto: Childcare Resource and Research Unit, 28 August 2013.

Garr, Allen. *Tough Guy: Bill Bennett and the Taking of British Columbia*. Toronto: Key Porter Books, 1985.

Goodwin, Joanne. *Gender and the Politics of Welfare Reform: Mothers' Pensions in Chicago*. Chicago: University Chicago Press, 1997.

Gordon, Linda. "The New Feminist Scholarship on the Welfare State." In *Women, the State, and Welfare*, ed. Linda Gordon, 9–35. Madison, WI: University of Wisconsin Press, 1990.

–. *Pitied but Not Entitled: Single Mothers and the History of Welfare, 1890–1935*. New York: Free Press, 1994.

Gough, Lyn. *As Wise As Serpents, 1883–1939: Five Women and an Organization That Changed British Columbia*. Victoria, BC: Swan Lake Publishing, 1988.

Griffin, Sandra, et al. "Canadian Child Care in Context: Perspectives from the Provinces and Territories: British Columbia Report." In *Canadian National Child Care Study*, ed. Alan Pence, 19–37. Ottawa: Department of Health and Welfare, 1992.

Henderson's City of Vancouver Directory. Vancouver: Henderson's Publishing Company, 1909–12.

Hernes, Helga Maria. *Welfare State and Woman Power: Essays in State Feminism*. Oslo, Norway: Norwegian University Press, 1987.

Hobbs, Margaret. "Equality and Difference: Feminism and the Defence of Women Workers during the Great Depression." *Labour / Le Travail* 32 (Fall 1993): 201–23.

–. "Gendering Work and Welfare: Women's Relationship to Wage-Work and Social Policy in Canada during the Great Depression." PhD dissertation, University of Toronto, 1994.

–. "Rethinking Antifeminism in the 1930s: Gender Crisis or Workplace Justice? A Response to Alice Kessler-Harris." *Gender and History* 5, 1 (Spring 1993): 4–15.

Hobson, Barbara. "Feminist Strategies and Gendered Discourses in Welfare States: Married Women's Right to Work in the United States and Sweden." In *Mothers of a New World: Maternalist Politics and the Origins of Welfare States*, ed. Seth Koven and Sonya Michel, 369–429. New York: Routledge, 1993.

Howard, Irene. "The Mothers' Council of Vancouver: Holding the Fort for the Unemployed, 1935–1938." In *Vancouver Past: Essays in Social History*, ed. Robert A.J. McDonald and Jean Barman, 249–87. Vancouver: UBC Press, 1986.

–. *The Struggle for Social Justice in British Columbia: Helena Gutteridge, the Unknown Reformer*. Vancouver: UBC Press, 1992.

Hutcheon, Pat Duffy. *Vancouver Council of Women Study on Day Care and Nursery School Needs and Services in Vancouver City*. Vancouver: Vancouver Council of Women, 1981.

Irving, Allan. "The Development of a Provincial Welfare State: British Columbia 1900–1939." In *The "Benevolent" State: The Growth of Welfare in Canada*, ed. Allan Moscovitch and Jim Albert, 155–74. Toronto: Garamond Press, 1987.

Isitt, Ben. *Militant Minority: British Columbia Workers and the Rise of a New Left, 1948–1972*. Toronto: University of Toronto Press, 2011.

Jenson, Jane. "Against the Current: Child Care and Family Policy in Quebec." In *Child Care Policy at the Crossroads: Gender and Welfare State Restructuring*, ed. Sonya Michel and Rianne Mahon, 309–32. New York: Routledge, 2002.

–. "Representations of Gender: Policies to 'Protect' Women Workers and Infants in France and the United States." In *Women, the State, and Welfare*, ed. Linda Gordon, 152–77. Madison, WI: University of Wisconsin Press, 1990.

–, and Mariette Sineau. "Citizenship in the Era of Welfare State Redesign." In *Who Cares? Women's Work, Childcare, and Welfare State Redesign,* ed. Jane Jenson and Mariette Sineau, 240–65. Toronto: University of Toronto Press, 2001.

Johnston, Hugh. *Radical Campus: Making Simon Fraser University.* Vancouver: Douglas and McIntyre, 2005.

Jones, Andrew, and Leonard Rutman. *In the Children's Aid: J.J. Kelso and Child Welfare in Ontario.* Toronto: University of Toronto Press, 1981.

Kershaw, Paul. *Carefair: Rethinking the Responsibilities and Rights of Citizenship.* Vancouver: UBC Press, 2005.

Keshen, Jeff. "Revisiting Canada's Civilian Women During World War II." *Social History / Histoire Sociale* 30, 60 (1997): 239–66.

Kessler-Harris, Alice. "Gender Ideology in Historical Reconstruction: A Case Study from the 1930s." *Gender and History* 1, 1 (Spring 1989): 31–49.

–. *In Pursuit of Equity: Women, Men, and the Quest for Economic Citizenship in Twentieth-Century America.* Madison, NY: Oxford University Press, 2001.

Koven, Seth, and Sonya Michel. "Introduction: 'Mother Worlds." In *Mothers of a New World: Maternalist Politics and the Origins of Welfare States,* ed. Seth Koven and Sonya Michel, 1–42. New York: Routledge, 1993.

Krashinsky, Michael. *Day Care and Public Policy in Ontario.* Ontario Economic Council by University of Toronto Press, 1977.

Ladd-Taylor, Molly. *Mother-Work: Women, Child Welfare, and the State, 1890-1930.* Urbana, IL: University of Illinois Press, 1994.

Lalonde-Graton, Micheline. *Des salles d'asile aux centres de la petite enfance: La petite histoire des services de garde au Québec.* Sainte-Foy, QC: Presses de l'Université du Québec, 2002.

Langford, Tom. *Alberta's Day Care Controversy: From 1908 to 2009 and Beyond.* Edmonton: Athabasca University Press, 2010.

Leah, Ronnie. "Women's Labour Force Participation and Day Care Cutbacks in Ontario." *Atlantis* (Wolfville, NS) 7 (1981): 36–44.

Lewis, Jane. "Gender and the Development of Welfare Regimes." *Journal of European Social Policy* 2, 3 (1992): 159–73.

Lexier, Roberta. "How Did the Women's Liberation Movement Emerge from the Sixties Student Movements: The Case of Simon Fraser University." *Women and Social Movements in America, 1600-2000* 13, 2 (Fall 2009).

Light, Beth, and Ruth Roach Pierson. *No Easy Road: Women in Canada 1920s to 1960s.* Toronto: New Hogtown Press, 1990.

Lind, Loren, and Susan Prentice. *Their Rightful Place: An Essay on Children, Families and Childcare in Canada.* Toronto: Our Schools / Our Selves Education Foundation, 1992.

Lister, Ruth. *Citizenship: Feminist Perspectives.* New York: New York University Press, 1997.

–. "Dilemmas in Engendering Citizenship." In *Gender and Citizenship in Transition,* ed. Barbara Hobson, 33–83. New York: Routledge, 2000.

Little, Margaret Hillyard. "Claiming a Unique Place: The Introduction of Mothers' Pensions in BC." *BC Studies* 105–6 (Spring/Summer 1995): 80–102.

–. *No Car, No Radio, No Liquor Permit: The Moral Regulation of Single Mothers in Ontario, 1920-1997.* Toronto: Oxford University Press, 1998.

Little, Margaret Hillyard, and Lynne Marks. "Ontario and British Columbia Welfare Policy: Variants on a Neoliberal Theme." *Comparative Studies of South Asia, Africa and the Middle East* 30, 2 (2010): 192–203.

Luxton, Meg. "Feminism as Class Act: Working-Class Feminism and the Women's Movement in Canada." *Labour / Le Travail* 48 (Fall 2001): 63–88.

Luxton, Meg, and Ester Reiter. "Double, Double, Toil and Trouble ... Women's Experience of Work and Family in Canada, 1980–1995." In *Women and the Canadian Welfare State: Challenges and Change*, ed. Patricia M. Evans and Gerda R. Wekerle, 197–221. Toronto: University of Toronto Press, 1997.

MacDonald, Heidi. "Maritime Women, the Great Depression, and the Dominion-Provincial Youth Training Program." In *Making Up the State: Women in Twentieth-Century Atlantic Canada*, ed. Janet Guildford and Suzanne Morton, 131–50. Fredericton, NB: Acadiensis Press, 2010.

Macfarlane, Mary Frank. "A Survey of Pre-School Centres in Vancouver." MSW thesis, University of British Columbia, 1949.

MacGill, Elsie Gregory. *My Mother the Judge: A Biography of Judge Helen Gregory MacGill*. Toronto: Ryerson Press, 1955.

Madsen, Lene. "Citizen, Worker, Mother: Canadian Women's Claims to Parental Leave and Childcare." *Canadian Journal of Family Law* 11 (2002): 11–74.

Magnusson, Warren. "The Local State in Canada: Theoretical Perspectives." *Canadian Public Administration* 28, 4 (Winter 1985): 575–99.

Mahon, Rianne. "Challenging National Regimes from Below: Toronto Child-Care Politics." *Politics and Gender* 3 (2007): 55–78.

–. "Child Care as Citizenship Right? Toronto in the 1970s and 1980s." *Canadian Historical Review* 86, 2 (June 2005): 285–315.

–. "Gender and Welfare State Restructuring: Through the Lens of Child Care." In *Child Care Policy at the Crossroads: Gender and Welfare State Restructuring*, ed. Sonya Michel and Rianne Mahon, 1–27. New York: Routledge, 2002.

–. "The Never-Ending Story: The Struggle for Universal Child Care Policy in the 1970s." *Canadian Historical Review* 81, 4 (December 2000): 582–622.

–. "Varieties of Liberalism: Canadian Social Policy from the 'Golden Age' to the Present." *Social Policy and Administration* 42, 4 (August 2008): 342–61. http://dx.doi.org/10.1111/j.1467-9515.2008.00608.x.

Mahon, Rianne, et al. "Convergent Care Regimes? Childcare arrangements in Australia, Canada, Finland and Sweden." *Journal of European Social Policy* 22, 4 (2012): 419–31.

Mahon, Rianne, and Susan Phillips. "Dual-Earner Families Caught in a Liberal Welfare Regime? The Politics of Child Care Policy in Canada." In *Child Care Policy at the Crossroads: Gender and Welfare State Restructuring*, ed. Sonya Michel and Rianne Mahon, 191–218. New York: Routledge, 2002.

Mann, Jean, Beverley New, and Cathy Barford. *Women Lead the Way: A History of the University Women's Club of Vancouver, 1907–2007*. Vancouver: Ray Hignell Services, 2007.

Marks, Lynne. "'Leaving God Behind When They Crossed the Rocky Mountains': Exploring Unbelief in Turn-of-the-Century British Columbia." In *Household*

Counts: Canadian Households and Families in 1901, ed. Peter Baskerville and Eric W. Sager, 371–404. Toronto: University of Toronto Press, 2007.

Marks, Lynne, and Margaret Little. "Discourses of Motherhood and Second Wave Women's Movements in English Canada." Paper presented at the Canadian Historical Association Annual Meeting, Fredericton, 31 May 2011.

Marshall, T.H. "Citizenship and Social Class." In *Class, Citizenship, and Social Development: Essays by T.H. Marshall*. Westport, CT: Greenwood Press, 1964.

Matters, Diane L. "Public Welfare Vancouver Style." *Journal of Canadian Studies / Revue d'Etudes Canadiennes* 14, 1 (Spring 1979): 3–12.

McCallum, Mary Jane Logan. *Indigenous Women, Work, and History: 1940–1980*. Winnipeg: University of Manitoba Press, 2014.

McDonald, Robert A.J. *Making Vancouver: Class, Status, and Social Boundaries, 1863–1913*. Vancouver: UBC Press, 1996.

–. "Victoria, Vancouver, and the Economic Development of British Columbia, 1886–1914." In *British Columbia: Historical Readings*, ed. W. Peter Ward and Robert A.J. McDonald, 369–95. Vancouver: Douglas and McIntyre, 1981.

–. "Working Class Vancouver, 1886–1914: Urbanism and Class in British Columbia." In *Vancouver Past: Essays in Social History*, ed. Robert A.J. McDonald and Jean Barman, 33–69. Vancouver: UBC Press, 1986.

McKeen, Wendy. *Money in Their Own Name: The Feminist Voice in Poverty Debate in Canada, 1970–1995*. Toronto: University of Toronto Press, 2004.

Michel, Sonya. *Children's Interests / Mothers' Rights: The Shaping of America's Child Care Policy*. New Haven, CT: Yale University Press, 1999.

–. "The Limits of Maternalism: Policies toward American Wage-Earning Mothers during the Progressive Era." In *Mothers of a New World: Maternalist Politics and the Origins of Welfare States*, ed. Seth Koven and Sonya Michel, 277–320. New York: Routledge, 1993.

Michel, Sonya, and Rianne Mahon, eds. *Child Care Policy at the Crossroads: Gender and Welfare State Restructuring*. New York: Routledge, 2002.

Milligan, Ian. "Coming off the Mountain: Forging an Outward-Looking New Left at Simon Fraser University." *BC Studies* 171 (Autumn 2011): 69–91.

Mink, Gwendolyn. "The Lady and the Tramp: Gender, Race, and the Origins of the American Welfare State." In *Women, the State, and Welfare*, ed. Linda Gordon, 92–122. Madison, WI: University of Wisconsin Press, 1990.

–. *Welfare's End*. Ithaca, NY: Cornell University Press, 2002.

Mitchell, Margaret. *No Laughing Matter: Adventure, Activism, and Politics*. Vancouver: Granville Island Publishing, 2008.

Mitchinson, Wendy. "Early Women's Organizations and Social Reform: Prelude to the Welfare State." In *The "Benevolent" State: The Growth of Welfare in Canada*, ed. Allan Moscovitch and Jim Albert, 77–92. Toronto: Garamond Press, 1987.

Morgan, Kimberly J. "Child Care and the Liberal Welfare Regime: A Review Essay." *Review of Policy Research* 20, 4 (December 2003): 743–48.

–. *Working Mothers and the Welfare State: Religion and the Politics of Work-Family Policies in Western Europe and the United States*. Stanford, CA: Stanford University Press, 2006.

Morton, Desmond. *Fight or Pay: Soldiers' Families in the Great War*. Vancouver: UBC Press, 2004.
Morton, Suzanne. "From Infant Homes to Day Care: Child Care in Halifax." In *Mothers of the Municipality: Women, Work, and Social Policy in Post-1945 Halifax*, ed. Judith Fingard and Janet Guildford, 169–88. Toronto: University of Toronto Press, 2005.
Nason, Pamela Nuttall, and Pam Whitty. "Bringing action research to the curriculum development process." *Educational Action Research* 15, 2 (June 2007): 271–81.
Nayar, Kamala Elizabeth. *The Punjabis in British Columbia: Location, Labour, First Nations, and Multiculturalism*. Montreal and Kingston: McGill-Queen's University Press, 2012.
Nelson, Barbara. "The Origins of the Two-Channel Welfare State: Workmen's Compensation and Mothers' Aid." In *Women, the State, and Welfare*, ed. Linda Gordon, 123–51. Madison, WI: University of Wisconsin Press, 1990.
Norcross, Elizabeth. "Mary Ellen Smith: The Right Woman in the Right Place at the Right Time." In *Not Just Pin Money: Selected Essays on the History of Women's Work in British Columbia*, ed. B. Latham and R. Pazdro, 357–64. Victoria: Camosun College Press, 1984.
O'Connor, Julia S., Ann Shola Orloff, and Sheila Shaver. *States, Markets, Families: Gender, Liberalism and Social Policy in Australia, Canada, Great Britain and the United States*. Cambridge: Cambridge University Press, 1999.
Orleck, Annalise. *Storming Caesar's Palace: How Black Mothers Fought Their Own War on Poverty*. Boston: Beacon Press, 2005.
Orloff, Ann Shola. "Gendering the Comparative Analysis of Welfare States: An Unfinished Agenda." *Sociological Theory* 27, 3 (September 2009): 317–19.
–. "From Maternalism to 'Employment for All': State Policies to Promote Women's Employment across the Affluent Democracies." In *The State after Statism: New State Activities in the Age of Liberalization*, ed. Jonah D. Levy, 230–68. Boston: Harvard University Press, 2006.
Palmer, Bryan. *Canada's 1960s: The Ironies of Identity in a Rebellious Era*. Toronto: University of Toronto Press, 2008.
Parr, Joy. *The Gender of Breadwinners: Women, Men, and Change in Two Industrial Towns, 1880–1950*. Toronto: University of Toronto Press, 1998.
Pasolli, Kelly. "Child Care Advocacy in Alberta." Honours thesis, University of Lethbridge, 2010.
Pasolli, Kelly, and Lisa Young. "Comparing Child Care Policy in the Canadian Provinces." Paper presented to the Annual Meeting of the Canadian Political Science Association, University of Alberta, 12–15 June 2012.
Pateman, Carol. "The Patriarchal Welfare State." In *Democracy and the Welfare State*, ed. Amy Gutman, 231–60. Princeton, NJ: Princeton University Press, 1988.
Pearce, Diana. "Welfare Is Not for Women: Why the War on Poverty Cannot Conquer the Feminization of Poverty." In *Women, the State, and Welfare*, ed. Linda Gordon, 265–79. Madison, WI: University of Wisconsin Press, 1990.

Pierson, Ruth Roach. "Gender and the Unemployment Insurance Debates in Canada, 1934–1940." *Labour / Le Travail* 25 (Spring 1990): 77–103.
–. *"They're Still Women After All": The Second World War and Canadian Womanhood*. Toronto: McClelland and Stewart, 1986.
Piven, Frances Fox. "Ideology and the State: Women, Power, and the Welfare State." In *Women, the State, and Welfare*, ed. Linda Gordon, 250–64. Madison, WI: University of Wisconsin Press, 1990.
Porter, Ann. *Gendered States: Women, Unemployment Insurance, and the Political Economy of the Welfare State in Canada, 1945–1997*. Toronto: University of Toronto Press, 2003.
Pratt, Geraldine. *Families Apart: Migrant Mothers and the Conflicts of Labor and Love*. Minneapolis, MN: University of Minnesota Press, 2012.
Prentice, Susan. "Changing Child Care: Looking Back, Moving Forward." In *Changing Child Care: Five Decades of Child Care Advocacy and Policy in Canada*, ed. Susan Prentice, 15–26. Halifax: Fernwood Publishing, 2001.
–. "High Stakes: The 'Investable' Child and the Economic Reframing of Childcare." *Signs: Journal of Women in Culture and Society* 34, 3 (2009): 687–710.
–. "'Kids are Not for Profit': The Politics of Childcare." In *Social Movements / Social Change: The Politics and Practice of Organizing*, ed. Frank Cunningham, Sue Findlay, and Marlene Kadar, 98–128. Toronto: Between the Lines, 1988.
–. "Less, Worse and More Expensive: Childcare in an Era of Deficit Reduction." *Journal of Canadian Studies / Revue d'Etudes Canadiennes* 34, 2 (June 1999): 137–58.
–. "Reds, Mothers, Militants: A History of the Postwar Daycare Campaigns in Toronto." PhD dissertation, York University, 1993.
–. "Workers, Mothers, Reds: Toronto's Postwar Day Care Fight." *Studies in Political Economy* 30 (Autumn 1989): 115–41.
Prochner, Larry. *A History of Early Childhood Education in Canada, Australia, and New Zealand*. Vancouver: UBC Press, 2009.
–. "A History of Early Education and Child Care in Canada, 1820–1966." In *Early Childhood Care and Education in Canada*, ed. Larry Prochner and Nina Howe, 45–51. Vancouver: UBC Press, 2000.
–. "'Share their care Mrs. Warworker': Wartime Day Nurseries in Ontario and Quebec, 1942–1945." *Canadian Journal of Research in Early Childhood Education* 5, 1 (1996): 115–26.
–. "Themes in the History of Day Care: A Case Study of the West End Crèche, Toronto, 1909–1939." PhD dissertation, University of Toronto, 1994.
Prochner, Larry, and Nina Howe. "The Wartime Child Care Centres in Canada and Great Britain: The Sixtieth Anniversary." *Canadian Children* 26, 2 (Fall 2001): 20–27.
Proverbs, Trevor B., and Daniel J. Koenig. Department of Human Resources. *Social Services for Children: The Public Speaks*. Victoria: Elector Concern and Satisfaction Surveys, 1977.
Purvey, Diane Barbara. "Alexandra Orphanage and Families in Crisis in Vancouver, 1892–1928." In *Child and Family Welfare in British Columbia: A History*, ed. Diane Purvey and Christopher Walmsley, 53–75. Calgary: Detselig Enterprises, 2005.
Purvey, Diane Barbara, and Christopher Walmsley, eds. *Child and Family Welfare in British Columbia: A History*. Calgary: Detselig Enterprises, 2005.
Rebick, Judy. *Ten Thousand Roses: The Making of a Feminist Revolution*. Toronto: Penguin Canada, 2005.

Rooke, Patricia, and R.L. Schnell. *No Bleeding Heart: Charlotte Whitton, A Feminist on the Right.* Vancouver: UBC Press, 1987.

Rose, Elizabeth. *A Mother's Job: The History of Day Care, 1890–1960.* New York: Oxford University Press, 1999.

Roy, Patricia. *A White Man's Province: British Columbia Politicians and Chinese and Japanese Immigrants, 1858–1914.* Vancouver: UBC Press, 1989.

Roy, Patricia, and John Herd Thompson. *British Columbia: Land of Promises.* Don Mills, ON: Oxford University Press, 2005.

Sager, Eric W. "The Transformation of the Canadian Domestic Servant, 1871–1983." *Social Science History* 31, 4 (Winter 2007): 509–37.

–. "Women in the Industrial Labour Force: Evidence for British Columbia, 1921–53." *BC Studies* 149 (Spring 2006): 39–62.

Sangster, Joan. "Debating Maternity Rights: Pacific Western Airlines and Flight Attendants' Struggle to 'Fly Pregnant' in the 1970s." In *Work on Trial: Canadian Labour Law Struggles*, ed. Judy Fudge and Eric Tucker, 283–314. Toronto: Irwin Law, 2010.

–. *Dreams of Equality: Women on the Canadian Left, 1920–1950.* Toronto: McClelland and Stewart, 1989.

–. *Earning Respect: The Lives of Working Women in Small-Town Ontario, 1920–1960.* Toronto: University of Toronto Press, 1995.

–. "Invoking Experience as Evidence." *Canadian Historical Review* 92, 1 (March 2011): 135–61.

–. "Radical Ruptures: Feminism, Labor, and the Left in the Long Sixties in Canada." *American Review of Canadian Studies* 40, 1 (March 2010): 1–21.

–. *Transforming Labour: Women and Work in Postwar Canada.* Toronto: University of Toronto Press, 2010.

Sarlo, Christopher. *The Cost of Raising Children.* Vancouver: Fraser Institute, 2013.

Scherer, Rebecca Kelley. "Federal Child Care Policy Development: From World War II to 2000." In *Changing Child Care: Five Decades of Child Care Advocacy and Policy in Canada*, ed. Susan Prentice, 187–200. Halifax: Fernwood Publishing, 2001.

Schulz, Patricia Vandebelt. "Day Care in Canada: 1850–1962." In *Good Day Care: Fighting For It, Getting It, Keeping It*, ed. Kathleen Gallagher Ross, 137–58. Toronto: Women's Press, 1978.

Sethna, Christabelle. "Clandestine Operations: The Vancouver Women's Caucus, the Abortion Caravan, and the RCMP." *Canadian Historical Review* 90, 3 (September 2009): 463–96.

Shklar, Judith. *American Citizenship: The Quest for Inclusion.* Cambridge, MA: Harvard University Press, 1991.

Simmons, Christina. "'Helping the Poorer Sisters': The Women of the Jost Mission, Halifax, 1905–1945." *Acadiensis* 14, 1 (Autumn 1994): 3–27.

Skocpol, Theda. *Protecting Soldiers and Mothers: The Political Origins of Social Policy in the United States.* Cambridge, MA: Harvard University Press, 1992.

Smith, Julia. "An 'Entirely Different' Kind of Union: The Service, Office, and Retail Workers' Union of Canada (SORWUC), 1972–1986." *Labour/Le Travail* 73 (Spring 2014): 23–65.

–. "Organizing the Unorganized: The Service, Office, and Retail Workers' Union of Canada (SORWUC), 1972–1986." MA thesis, Simon Fraser University, 2009.
Social Planning and Research Department, United Way of the Lower Mainland. *Responsible Day Care: The Coming of Age of an Essential Community Service*. Vancouver: United Way of the Lower Mainland, January 1981.
Srigley, Katrina. *Breadwinning Daughters: Young Working Women in a Depression-Era City, 1929–1939*. Toronto: University of Toronto Press, 2010.
Stephen, Jennifer. *Pick One Intelligent Girl: Employability, Domesticity, and the Gendering of Canada's Welfare State, 1939–1947*. Toronto: University of Toronto Press, 2007.
Stewart, Donald Granville. "Strathcona Nursery School: Its Contributions for Working Mothers." MA thesis, University of British Columbia, 1956.
Stoltzfus, Emilie. *Citizen, Mother, Worker: Debating Public Responsibility for Child Care after the Second World War*. Chapel Hill, NC: University of North Carolina Press, 2003.
Strong-Boag, Veronica. "Canada's Wage-Earning Wives and the Construction of the Middle Class, 1945–60." *Journal of Canadian Studies / Revue d'Etudes Canadiennes* 29, 3 (1994): 5–25.
–. "The Girl of the New Day: Canadian Working Women in the 1920s." *Labour / Le Travail* 4 (1979): 131–64.
–. "'Wages for Housework': Mothers' Allowances and the Beginnings of Social Security in Canada." *Journal of Canadian Studies / Revue d'Etudes Canadiennes* 14, 1 (Spring 1979): 24–34.
Struthers, James. "'In the Interests of the Children': Mothers' Allowances and the Origins of Income Security in Ontario, 1917–1930." In *Social Fabric or Patchwork Quilt: The Development of Social Policy in Canada*, ed. Raymond Blake and Jeffrey A. Keshen, 59–87. Peterborough, ON: Broadview Press, 2006.
–. *The Limits of Affluence: Welfare in Ontario*. Toronto: University of Toronto Press and Ontario Historical Studies Series, 1994.
–. *No Fault of Their Own: Unemployment and the Canadian Welfare State*. Toronto: University of Toronto Press, 1983.
–. "A Profession in Crisis: Charlotte Whitton and Canadian Social Work in the 1930s." *Canadian Historical Review* 62, 2 (1981): 169–85.
Sugiman, Pamela. *Labour's Dilemma: The Gender Politics of Auto Workers in Canada, 1937–1979*. Toronto: University of Toronto Press, 1994.
Sutherland, Neil. *Children in English-Canadian Society: Framing the Twentieth-Century Consensus*. Waterloo, ON: Wilfrid Laurier University Press, 2000.
Tillotson, Shirley. "Citizen Participation in the Welfare State: An Experiment." *Canadian Historical Review* 75, 4 (1994): 511–42.
–. "Relations of Extraction: Taxation and Women's Citizenship in the Maritimes." In *Making Up the State: Women in Twentieth-Century Atlantic Canada*, ed. Janet Guildford and Suzanne Morton, 93–109. Fredericton, NB: Acadiensis Press, 2010.
Timpson, Annis May. *Driven Apart: Women's Employment Equality and Child Care in Canadian Public Policy*. Vancouver: UBC Press, 2001.
–. "Royal Commissions as Sites of Resistance: Women's Challenges on Child Care in the Royal Commission on the Status of Women." *International Journal of Canadian Studies* 20 (Fall 1999): 123–48.

Tougas, Jocelyne. "What We Can Learn from the Quebec Experience." In *Our Children's Future: Child Care Policy in Canada*, ed. Gordon Cleveland and Douglas Krashinsky, 92–105. Toronto: University of Toronto Press, 2001.

Tyyskä, Vappu. *The Politics of Caring and the Welfare State: The Impact of the Women's Movement on Child Care Policy in Canada and Finland, 1960–1990*. Helsinki, Finland: Suomalainen Tiedeakatemia, 1995.

Ulmer, Catherine Mary. "The Report on Unemployment and Relief in Western Canada, 1932: Charlotte Whitton, R.B. Bennett and the Federal Response to Relief." MA thesis, University of Victoria, 2009.

UNICEF. *The Child Care Transition: Innocenti Report Card 8*. Florence, Italy: UNICEF Innocenti Research Centre, 2008.

Varga, Donna. *Constructing the Child: A History of Canadian Day Care*. Toronto: James Lorimer, 1997.

Venables, Kenneth A. "The Making of Protective Labour Legislation in British Columbia: The 1912 Royal Commission on Labour and Its Aftermath." MA thesis, Simon Fraser University, 1996.

Vickers, Jill, Pauline Rankin, and Christine Appelle. *Politics As If Women Mattered: A Political Analysis of the National Action Committee on the Status of Women*. Toronto: University of Toronto Press, 1993.

Walmsley, Christopher. "The British Columbia Child Welfare Survey (1927): A Policy Narrative of Children's Needs." In *Child and Family Welfare in British Columbia: A History*, ed. Diane Purvey and Christopher Walmsley, 305–26. Calgary: Detselig Enterprises, 2005.

Walsh, Sue. "Equality, Emancipation, and a More Just World: Leading Women in the B.C. CCF." MA thesis, Simon Fraser University, 1984.

–. "The Peacock and the Guinea Hen: Political Profiles of Dorothy Gretchen Steeves and Grace MacInnis." In *British Columbia Reconsidered: Essays on Women*, ed. Gillian Creese and Veronica Strong-Boag, 73–89. Vancouver: Press Gang Publishers, 1992.

Wasserlein, Frances. "An Arrow Aimed at the Heart: The Vancouver Women's Caucus and the Abortion Caravan of 1970." MA thesis, Simon Fraser University, 1990.

Weiss, Gillian. "An Essential Year for the Child: The Kindergarten in British Columbia." In *Schooling and Society in Twentieth Century British Columbia*, ed. J. Donald Wilson and David C. Jones, 139–61. Calgary: Detselig Enterprises, 1980.

–. "'As Women and As Citizens': Clubwomen in Vancouver, 1910–1928." PhD dissertation, University of British Columbia, 1983.

White, Linda. "Child Care, Women's Labour Market Participation, and Labour Market Policy Effectiveness." *Canadian Public Policy* 27, 4 (2001): 385–405.

–. "Trends in Child Care / Early Childhood Education / Early Childhood Development Policy in Canada and the United States." *American Review of Canadian Studies* 34, 3 (Winter 2004): 665–87.

Williams, Carol. "Introduction." In *Indigenous Women and Work: From Labor to Activism*, ed. Carol Williams, 1–26. Urbana, IL: University of Illinois Press, 2012.

Women's Bureau. Department of Labour. *Day Care Services for Children of Working Mothers*. Ottawa: Queen's Printer, 1964.

–. *Working Mothers and Their Child Care Arrangements*. Ottawa: Queen's Printer, 1970.

Index

Abella, Rosalie, 166
Aboriginal child care programs, 169, 173, 235n86
Aboriginal women, 16, 140, 162, 184, 185. *See also* marginalized women
Act to Provide Pensions for Mothers, 1920, 48–50, 56–62, 70; amendments, 58, 66–68, 209n115; benefits, 58, 61, 64, 67; monitoring of mothers, 57–58, 59, 66, 67; views of Charlotte Whitton on, 63–65, 68. *See also* mothers' pensions
Ad Hoc Committee on Day Care of Greater Vancouver, 142–43
Aikins, Mrs. T.E., 27
Alberta Pacific Lumber Company, 83
Alexandra House Play School (Vancouver), 90–92
Alexandra Orphanage (Vancouver), 41
Asian immigrants: domestic service and, 26, 29–30, 39; exclusion from mothers' pensions, 16, 57
Associated Charities (Vancouver), 32, 35
Associated Charities and Relief committee (Vancouver), 35

Barrett administration, 143–45, 147–48, 149–50, 156
BC Benefits (Child Care) Act, 1996, 169
BC Day Care Action Coalition, 165, 167, 168
BC Federation of Labour, 124, 142
BC Federation of Women (BCFW), 155
Behesti, Dorothy, 113
Belknap, Victor, 122
Bennett, Bill, 172
Bennett (Bill) administration, 156, 157, 158
Bennett (W.A.C.) administration, 101–2, 107–25, 142, 143
Bird, Florence, 129
Blatz, William (Dr.), 20–21, 78–79
boarding establishments, 19, 41, 42
Boeing Limited, 80
Booth, Edith, 56
Bradford, Marjorie, 81
British Columbia. *See* provincial government (BC)
"Building a Better Future for British Columbia's Kids," 171
Burnaby Mountain Day Care Society, 135

Business and Professional Women's Club of British Columbia, 121

Campbell, Dan, 113, 118, 120, 122
Campbell, Emily, 117, 119, 135, 142, 157–58
Campbell administration, 172
Canada: ranking in UNICEF study, 152–53. *See also* federal government
Canada Assistance Plan (CAP), 108, 170; daycare subsidies, 102, 108, 109–10, 130, 157, 158, 168; Vancouver Opportunities Program, 139, 159
Canada Health and Social Transfer (CHST), 170
Canadian Child Care Federation, 166
Canadian Council on Social Development, 78, 131, 154, 165
Canadian Day Care Advocacy Association (CDCAA), 166, 167
Canadian Patriotic Fund, 37–38
Canadian Welfare Council. *See* Canadian Council on Social Development
CAP (Canada Assistance Plan). See Canada Assistance Plan (CAP)
carefair, 184
caregiving work, 9, 14–15, 141, 182, 185–86; unpaid vs paid work, 8, 24, 60, 160–61, 183; valuation of, 14–15, 127, 130, 183–86, 188n18. *See also* day care establishments, staff
caring labour. *See* caregiving work
CCCABC (Coalition of Child Care Advocates of British Columbia), 23, 176–77
CCF (Co-operative Commonwealth Federation), 71, 85–86, 94
CDCAA (Canadian Day Care Advocacy Association), 166, 167
Centennial Day Care Centre (Victoria), 115, 118
Chatham Day Care (Prince Rupert), 118
child care advocacy: growing separation from feminism, 23–24, 154–55, 180–81; left-wing activists, 37, 71, 85–86, 94, 100; maternalist reformers, 27–28, 45, 49, 52–53; 1980s, 165–66, 167–68
Child Care Advocacy Forum, 171
Child Care BC Act, 2001, 172, 175
Child Care for British Columbia, 2000, 171
Child Care and Day Care Study Group, 141
child care expense deductions, 165
Child Care Federation, 149, 154–55
Child Care Occupation Forces, 145–49; photograph, 146; song, 126, 146
child care policies: federal policies, 11–12, 129–31; slow development, 101–2, 104–7, 152–53. *See also Canada Assistance Plan (CAP)*; provincial government (BC)
child care programs: Aboriginal child care programs, 169, 173, 235n86; provincial support for, 168–71. *See also* child care policies; day care establishments; early childhood education; home-based foster day care programs; Welfare Institutions Licensing Board (WILB)
child tax credits, 165
children: under 3 years of age, 19, 103–4, 105–6, 110, 124, 140, 141, 144–45, 147–48, 149; as human capital, 7, 153, 176; rehabilitation of underprivileged children, 44, 92, 93, 102, 104, 106–7, 109, 122, 213n35
Children's Aid Society (Toronto), 44
Children's Aid Society (Vancouver), 44, 89, 111
Children's Aid Society (Victoria), 48, 53
Chinese labourers. *See* Asian immigrants
Chippendale, Barbara, 205n54
Chisholm, Barbara, 123
Chisholm, Ruth, 158, 162–63
CHST (Canada Health and Social Transfer), 170
churches, 111, 196n17
Clark, Susie Lane, 53, 54, 57, 66, 205n54
Clark (Christy) administration, 177

Cleveland, Gordon, 176
Co-operative Commonwealth Federation (CCF), 71, 85–86, 94
co-operative day cares, 127–28, 132–36
Co-operative Play School Association, 97
Coalition of Child Care Advocates of British Columbia (CCCABC), 23, 176–77
Coates, Penny, 167
Cocke, Dennis, 147
Collins, Zella, 83–84
Communist party, 94
Community Plan for a Public System of Integrated Care and Learning ($10-a-day plan), 176–77
community resource boards, 149–50
Consumers' Council of Vancouver, 91, 92
Cooke, Katie, 166
Counselling Services for Mothers Committee, 89
crèches, 19–20, 28, 187n12. *See also* Vancouver City Crèche
'*Cuz There Ain't No Daycare (or Almost None She Said)*, 148–49

Dailly, Eileen, 147
Davidson, George, 78
Dawson School kindergarten, 97
day care: as child-centred issue, 175, 180–81; as mother's right, 93, 105, 121, 123, 127–31, 136, 169, 180–81; parental participation, 133–36, 141, 177; as rehabilitation of the underprivileged child, 44, 92, 93, 102, 104, 106–7, 109, 122, 213n35; stigmatization, 22, 40, 46, 72–73, 105, 116, 163–64; as threat to home and motherhood, 48, 95, 164, 235n89. *See also* day care establishments; work-for-relief
day care establishments: co-operative, 127–28, 132–36; as educational institutions, 20–21, 96–97, 98–99, 100; financial issues, 112–21, 123, 140–41; licensing issues, 116, 140; New Day Care initiative and, 144; spaces, 110, 157, 160, 170, 172, 173, 174; as training grounds, 75, 92, 93, 94; staff, 115, 144, 153, 171, 228n88, 236n112; wartime day nurseries, 21, 75, 90–92. *See also* child care programs; home-based foster day care programs; Vancouver City Crèche
Day Care Information Centre (Vancouver), 145–49
day nurseries. *See* day care establishments
Day Nurseries and Day Care Parents Association (Toronto), 94
demographics: 1911, 29, 31; 1940s, 78, 101, 103; 1960s, 101, 103, 105; 1970s, 103, 145; 2010, 152
Dickson, Joseph, 55
domestic labour, 38–39; societal need for, 26, 28–31, 44, 67, 68–69, 76, 81
Dominion-Provincial Wartime Day Nursery Agreement (WDNA), 21, 74–81, 84, 91, 92, 93, 94–95, 211n1
Dosanjh administration, 171–72

early childhood education, 20, 21–22, 96–97, 100, 154; fusion with practices of care, 22–23, 98–99, 100, 173
Early Childhood Educators of British Columbia (ECEBC), 23, 176–77
Eaton, Fraudena, 69, 78, 79–80, 81, 94; photograph, 79
ECEBC (Early Childhood Educators of British Columbia), 176–77
education. *See* early childhood education
employment opportunities for women: 1900–20, 29, 37, 38–39, 201n107; interwar years, 68–69; Vancouver employment bureaux, 31, 38, 41, 46; World War II, 74, 76–84. *See also* domestic labour; unemployment
Employment and Relief Association (Vancouver), 200n81

family allowances, 94
family day care. *See* home-based foster day care programs

family self-sufficiency, 208n93; ideology of, 61–62, 64–65, 67; role of day care in, 108–9
federal government: *Dominion-Provincial Wartime Day Nursery Agreement* (WDNA), 21, 74–81, 94–95; Harper administration, 173; Local Initiatives Programme, 140; Mulroney administration, 167, 235n89; Pearson administration, 102, 103, 108–10, 129–31, 219n41; taxation reform, 153, 154, 165, 177, 234n74; Trudeau administration, 130, 131, 165, 166; wartime child care initiative, 74–81; welfare reforms, 181–82. *See also Canada Assistance Plan (CAP)*
fees, 78, 91, 142, 157–58, 172, 173, 174; Canada Assistance Plan subsidies and, 110, 114–15, 117, 118; Vancouver City Crèche, 33, 36, 41–42, 199n52
feminism: growing separation from child care advocacy, 23–24, 154–55, 180–81; Harcourt administration and, 168–69; maternalist reformers, 27–28, 45, 49, 52–53; rights-based childcare and, 17–18, 127–29, 141–42, 150–51, 164, 165–66, 175. *See also* gendered inequalities; second-wave feminist movement
First Nations child care programs, 169, 173
foster day care. *See* home-based foster day care programs
Foster Day Care Association, 97–98
franchised day care, 155
Frank, Ellen, 155
Fraserview United Church day care (Vancouver), 116
Friendly Aid Society (Vancouver), 32
Friendly Help Society (Vancouver), 32

GAIN Act, 1976, 159
gendered inequalities, 11, 14; right to labour force participation, 7, 10, 69, 70, 71, 73, 86, 93–94, 121, 154, 156, 164–65, 169, 175; social citizenship and, 10, 14, 181–82; student movements, 132; union views on, 124, 156; wages, 39, 45, 61, 69; welfare, 11, 15, 70, 137, 161–62; working conditions, 17, 50–51, 69, 73, 129–30, 141, 154, 156
Gordon House Play School (Vancouver), 90–92, 95
Gorrie, Kathleen, 95
Grandview Terrace Day Care (Vancouver), 140, 145, 147, 158
Grant, Maria, 53, 55
Greater Victoria Nursery School Association, 92–93
Green, T.C. (Dr.), 54
Growing Pains, 149
Guaranteed Available Income for Need (GAIN) Act, 1976, 159
Gurr, Jane, 111
Gutteridge, Helena, 37, 41, 45, 53

Halifax, 28
Harcourt administration, 168–70, 236n97
Harper administration, 173
Hart administration, 107
Harvey, Isobel, 79–83, 81–84
head taxes, 30
Henry Hudson kindergarten (Vancouver), 97
Herbison, Robert (Rev.), 55
Holland, Laura, 80–82
Holt, Berna, 82
home-based foster day care programs, 19, 44, 46, 72, 80, 82–83, 90, 104; dissatisfaction with, 104–5, 141; licensing, 97–98

immigrants, 16, 19, 52, 185; domestic service, 26, 28, 29; exclusion from mothers' pensions, 49, 52, 57; *Immigrant Women in the Labour Force*, 1974, 142; reluctance to provide day care subsidies for, 162–63. *See also* marginalized women; temporary foreign workers
indigenous women, 16, 140, 162, 184, 185. *See also* marginalized women

Jamieson, Laura, 85–86, 87, 213n45
Japanese workers. *See* Asian immigrants
Jiminy Cricket Day Care (Victoria), 140
Jost Mission (Halifax), 28

Kavanagh, Jack, 56
Kelowna (BC), 213n36
Kelso, J.J., 44
Kershaw, Paul, 184
Kidd, George, 62
Kimberley (BC), 82–83
kindergartens, 9, 18–19, 21–23, 75–76, 96–97, 98, 104, 175–76, 216n103
King, Elizabeth, 66
Koenig, Paul, 164
Krashinsky, Michael, 176

labour unions. *See* unions
Lane, Susie. *See* Clark, Susie Lane
LCP (live-in caregiver program), 185
Lett, Evelyn, 93
Levi, Norm, 117–18, 144, 147–48, 228n88
live-in caregiver program (LCP), 185
Local Initiatives Programme, 140

MacDonald, Lillian Forbes, 32–33, 35
MacGill, Helen Gregory, 27–28, 30, 33, 44; mothers' pensions and, 52, 66
MacInnis, Grace, 85, 86, 87, 93, 138
MacLean, J.D., 55, 56
MacNamara, Arthur, 76
male breadwinners. *See* men as breadwinners
marginalized women, 8, 16, 46, 95, 184, 185; *CAP* means tests, 13, 109–10, 121, 124, 144; caregiving work, 182, 185–86; monitoring of, 57–58, 59, 66, 67. as pitiable, 4–5, 20, 28, 71, 75, 93; as targets of reform, 6, 20, 26–27, 28, 39, 98, 102, 108, 183; *See also* mothers' pensions; subsidies; work-for-relief; working mothers
Marpole Day Care Centre (Vancouver), 113–18, 120
married women, 74, 76–78. *See also* marginalized women; women; working mothers

Marshall, T.H., 10
Marzari, Darlene, 162
maternal feminism, 8, 28, 197n18
maternalist concerns, 8, 44, 49, 51, 52–53, 54–55, 127. *See also* mothers' pensions
Maycock, Gladys, 115, 116–17, 124, 135
McBeath, Malcolm, 34, 35
McBride administration, 36
McCallum, D., 54
McCarthy, Grace, 138, 158, 160
McGaw, Grace, 87
McLean, Ada, 25
McNair, Mrs., 57
men as breadwinners, 8, 11, 14, 53, 73, 94, 179, 181; as discursive force, 8, 10, 13, 24, 51, 69–70, 102–3; shift in attitude concerning, 164–65
middle-class families: pre-school education, 9, 18–19, 21, 96–97; working mothers, 4, 22, 34, 43, 74, 75, 84, 95, 98–99, 106, 152, 162
Mitchell, Margaret, 138
Montreal, 28
morality concerns: about marginalized women, 6, 20, 26–27, 28, 39, 50, 98, 102, 108, 183; about middle-class women, 4, 22, 34, 43, 95, 152, 162, 164. *See also* work-for-relief
More Opportunities for Mothers (MOMs), 128–29, 137–38
motherhood mystique, 5, 49, 136, 141
mothers: burdens of care, 55–56; controversies concerning natural roles, 5, 44–47, 49, 54–56, 136, 141; duties to their children, 50; with one child, 16, 49, 56, 60, 64, 66, 67; post-World War I, 51; single mothers, 108, 143, 159–61, 169, 182, 219n41, 219n42; struggle for social rights, 70–71, 85–88; widows, 57. *See also* marginalized women; working mothers
Mothers' Allowance Act, 1938, 70, 108
mothers' pensions, 20, 45–47, 48–50, 71, 219n42; Advisory Board, 67, 205n54, 209n115; as charity, 3, 49, 52, 56, 67–68, 70; as entitlement,

14–15, 49, 52, 55–56, 59–60, 67, 70; post-World War I, 51–56; as racial barrier, 49, 52, 57. *See also* work-for-relief; *Act to Provide Pensions for Mothers*, 1920
Mulroney administration, 167, 235n89
Multilateral Framework on Early Childhood Learning and Care, 23, 172–73, 175

NAC (National Action Committee on the Status of Women), 165, 166, 167
Nanaimo Children's Day Care Centre, 157
National Action Committee on the Status of Women (NAC), 165, 166, 167
National Child Benefit, 170
National Council of Women, 29
National Day Care Conference, 1982, 154, 165
National Selective Service, 76
Needle, Miss, 25
Nelson, Lilian M., 31, 36, 39, 46, 55
Nelson Brothers Fisheries, 123
New Day Care program, 144–45, 149
New Era League (Vancouver), 44, 53, 66, 205n54
New Left student movement, 132
Newitt, Lillian, 90, 95–96
Nielsen, Dorise, 86
Novaco Day Care (North Vancouver), 141
nursery schools, 19–20, 21, 72, 95–96, 104

Oliver, John, 54
One Big Union, Ladies Auxiliary of the, 56
Ontario, 99; *Day Nurseries Act*, 1946, 94; *Dominion-Provincial Wartime Day Nursery Agreement* (WDNA), 21, 74, 75, 78–79, 94–95, 99; mothers' allowances, 16, 51, 52
orphanages. *See* boarding establishments
Ottawa, 28

paid work, 9; vs caregiving work, 183; as evidence of moral failings, 83–84; as guard against welfare dependency, 16, 49–50, 51, 60–62, 64–65, 68, 98, 159–60; as measure of moral fitness, 5, 49–51, 60–61, 65, 70, 73; as mother's choice, 7, 86, 99, 100, 121, 130, 147, 154, 169; wages, 39, 45, 61, 69, 206n68. *See also* work-for-relief
parent-teacher associations, 82, 97, 213n35
Paul, Ada, 36, 199n64
Pearson administration, 103, 108–9, 219n41; *Canada Assistance Plan (CAP)*, 102, 108, 109–10; Royal Commission on the Status of Women, 129–31
Perry, Mrs. J.O., 27
Plan for Public-Private Partnership for Day Care (PPP Plan), 112, 115
play-schools. *See* nursery schools
policy development. *See* child care policies
poor women. *See* marginalized women
Port Alberni (BC), 83–84
Port Edward (BC), 123
poverty, 219n41; feminization of, 108–9, 137–40, 219n41; rehabilitation of underprivileged children, 44, 92, 93, 102, 104, 106–7, 109, 122, 213n35; "war on poverty," 22, 102, 107–8. *See also* marginalized women
PPP Plan (Public-Private Partnership for Day Care). *See* Public-Private Partnership for Day Care (PPP Plan)
preschool education, 7, 9, 18–19, 75, 97. *See also* early childhood education; kindergartens; nursery schools
Prince Rupert (BC), 118
Provincial Child Care Council, 169
Provincial Council of Women (British Columbia): domestic labour concerns, 29
provincial government (BC), 106, 124, 168–69; amalgamation of social services, 107; Barrett

administration, 143–45, 147–48, 149–50, 156; Bennett (Bill) administration, 156; Bennett (W.A.C.) administration, 101–2, 107–25, 142–43; Campbell administration, 172; *Child Care BC Act,* 2001, 172, 175; Clark (Christy) administration, 177; Clark (Glen) administration, 170; Dosanjh administration, 171–72; Harcourt administration, 168–70, 236n97; Hart administration, 107; McBride administration, 36; rejection of role in day care, 104; Vander Zalm administration, 167–68; views on wartime child care, 74–75, 79–84; welfare reforms, 181–82
public policy. *See* child care policies
Public-Private Partnership for Day Care (PPP Plan), 112–13; Marpole Day Care Centre, 113–18, 120
publicly funded child care. *See* subsidies; tax deductions and benefits; universal child care programs; Vancouver City Crèche
Pyke, George, 57, 60–61, 62

Québec, 12, 14, 99, 170; *Dominion-Provincial Wartime Day Nursery Agreement* (WDNA), 74, 75, 78, 94

racism: BC as "white man's province," 30, 39, 54; domestic labour concerns and, 29–31, 39; mothers' pensions as racial barriers, 49, 52, 57; welfare practices and, 185
Ragamuffin, 149
Revelstoke Women's Canadian Club, 55
Rickinson, E.R., 112, 119–20, 122, 142
Rolston, Tilly, 87–88, 95, 97
Royal Commission on Equality in Employment, 166
Royal Commission on Health Insurance and Maternity Benefits, 54
Royal Commission on the Status of Women, 129–31, 165
Royce, Marion, 108–9

Saanich, 111
Sadler, J.A., 112, 122, 123
second-wave feminist movement, 17, 127–29, 161, 188n18; Wages for Housework, 8, 127, 161, 188n18. *See also* feminism; Vancouver Women's Caucus (VWC)
Service, Office and Retail Workers' Union of Canada (SORWUC), 156
SFU Co-operative Family, 127–28, 132–36
SFU Feminine Action League, 132
SFU Women's Caucus, 132, 136
Sheasgreen, Mrs., 57
Showing We Care, 1991, 168, 175
Sihota, Moe, 171
Simon Fraser University, 131–32, 157; child care co-operative, 127–28, 132–36
single mothers, 108, 143, 159–61, 169, 182, 219n41, 219n42
Skeena Terrace Welfare Rights Committee, 161
Smith, Mary Ellen, 45; mothers' pensions and, 52, 57, 66; photo of, 53; Vancouver City Crèche, 27, 30, 44
Smith, Ralph, 30
social benefits. *See* welfare policies and services
social citizenship, 7–8, 10–11, 14, 73; gender-differentiated rights and, 181; marginalized mothers and, 69–71, 102–3, 179–80; mothers' right to work and, 14, 75, 102–3, 179–80; welfare programs and, 26–27. *See also* men as breadwinners; welfare policies and services
South, Charles, 44
South Hill Day Care (Vancouver), 140, 145, 147
Spofford, Cecilia, 53, 54, 57, 58
Spring Ridge kindergarten (Victoria), 97
Status of Women Action and Co-ordinating Council, 142
Steeves, Dorothy, 71, 85, 86

stigmatization: of day care, 22, 40, 46, 72–73, 105, 116, 163–64; of institutional child care, 54–55, 72; mothers' pensions and, 56, 59; of working mothers, 22, 83–84, 87–88, 105, 111, 116, 136, 150
Strathcona Nursery School (Vancouver), 90–92, 95–96, 98–99, 118–19
strikes by child care workers, 171
subsidies, 4, 22, 153, 174; Barrett administration, 144; Bennett (Bill) administration, 157, 158; *Canada Assistance Plan (CAP)*, 22, 109–10, 114, 115, 117–20, 124, 157, 158, 168; stigmatizing requirements, 158
Sutherland, Margaret, 205n54
Sweden, 183

"Talkin' Day Care Blues," 126, 146
Task Force on Child Care, 166, 235n89
tax deductions and benefits, 153, 154, 165, 177, 234n74
temporary foreign workers, 241n29
$10-a-day plan, 23, 176–77
Thomson, Deryck, 115–16
Tolmie, Simon Fraser, 62, 66
Toronto, 28, 94
Trail (BC), 82, 83
Trudeau administration, 130, 131, 165, 166

UBC Day Care Council, 145
UCCB (Universal Child Care Benefit), 173
UCS (United Community Services). *See* United Community Services (UCS)
Underhill, Frederick T., 43
Unemployed Citizens Welfare Improvement Council, 137, 226n49
unemployment: Great Depression, 62, 67, 68–69; insurance (UI), 70; recession of 1913–16, 36–39
UNICEF: study on child care systems, 152–53
unions, 53–54, 56, 171, 236n112; views on day care, 124, 142, 156

United Community Services (UCS), 111, 149, 220n64, 222n90; Advisory Committee on Day Care, 112–21
United States, 52, 128, 182
Universal Child Care Benefit (UCCB), 173
universal child care programs, 148–49, 153, 154, 165, 179; Dosanjh administration, 171–72; federal government, 173; Québec, 12
University of British Columbia, 135, 142–43; Institute for Child Study, 97
University of Toronto, 133; Institute of Child Study, 20, 21–22, 78–79
unmarried mothers, 57
Unsworth, Desiré, 32–33, 37
Uphill, Thomas, 58

Vancouver, 37, 105, 200n81; day cares, 1910–20, 25–47; day cares, 1940s, 21, 75, 90–92; day cares, 1960s, 110–11, 112–18, 120, 222n90; day cares, 1970s, 149–50, 160; employment bureaux, 31, 38, 41, 46; feminist movement, 127–29, 131–51; preschool education, 96–97; reformers, 27–28, 52–53; social welfare concerns, 31–32, 35–42, 90–91, 137–40, 226n49
Vancouver City Crèche, 25–31, 46–47, 187n12, 198n49; attendance, 25–26, 35, 40; clientele, 26, 33, 39–42, 46; controversy concerning, 33–34, 42–46; fees, 33, 41–42, 199n52; locations, 31, 33, 35–36, 43; management of, 27–28, 32–33, 35–36, 43; photograph, 43; public funding for, 31–36; as work-for-relief project, 26–27, 31, 34, 36, 38–42, 46
Vancouver Community Chest, 111; *Report on Day Care Needs*, 1965, 105–6, 109, 112. *See also* United Community Services (UCS)
Vancouver Council of Social Agencies, 81, 84, 89–92
Vancouver Council of Women, 79, 160

Vancouver Day Nursery Association, 46, 71–72, 76, 80, 81–82, 97
Vancouver Housewives' League, 90, 92, 95
Vancouver Incentive Program. See Vancouver Opportunities Program (VOP)
Vancouver Opportunities Program (VOP), 138–40, 159, 227n58
Vancouver Resource Board, 149–50
Vancouver School Board, 96–97
Vancouver Status of Women Council, 141–42
Vancouver Trades and Labour Council (VTLC), 37, 38, 53, 56
Vancouver Women's Building, 33
Vancouver Women's Caucus (VWC), 136, 148–49
Vander Zalm, Bill, 156–58, 167–68
Vander Zalm administration, 167–68
VDNA (Vancouver Day Nursery Association), 71–72, 76, 80, 81–82, 97
Victoria, 53, 55, 80; day cares and nurseries, 28, 38, 42, 48, 92–93, 111; Family and Children's Services (FCS), 111, 140; home-based foster day care, 97–98
Victoria Crèche (Toronto), 20
VOP (Vancouver Opportunities Program), 138–40, 159
VTLC (Vancouver Trades and Labour Council), 37, 38, 53, 56

Wages for Housework movement, 8, 127, 161, 188n18
Walsey, Anne: photograph, 77
wartime. See World War I; World War II
WCTU (Women's Christian Temperance Union), 53
WDNA *(Dominion-Provincial Wartime Day Nursery Agreement),* 21, 74–81, 94–95
Welfare Institutions Licensing Act, 1938, 97, 124
Welfare Institutions Licensing Board (WILB), 97, 104, 110, 111, 112, 122, 134, 140, 216n109; Gladys Maycock, 115, 116–17, 124, 135
welfare policies and services, 50, 181; 1900–20, 26; 1930s, 69–70; 1990s, 169–70, 171; 2000–14, 173, 182–83; cutbacks, 159–61; gendered inequalities, 11, 15, 70, 137, 161–62; liberal regimes, 13–14, 26, 177–79, 182. *See also* mothers' pensions; subsidies; work-for-relief
welfare regimes, 13–14, 26, 177–79, 182
welfare states, 191n41; woman friendly, 182–83. *See also* welfare regimes
West End Crèche (Toronto), 28
Western Family Day Care Association, 166, 168
Whitton, Charlotte, 63; report, 1931, 50, 55, 62, 63–66, 67, 68, 70, 207n82, 208n90, 208n93, 208n99
WILB (Welfare Institutions Licensing Board). *See* Welfare Institutions Licensing Board (WILB)
Williams Lake (British Columbia), 140
Winn, E.S., 54, 58–59, 60, 61, 66, 205n55
Winnipeg, 28
women: left-wing activists, 37, 71, 85–86, 94, 100; maternalist reformers, 27–28, 45, 49, 52–53; post-World War II conditions, 93–94. *See also* gendered inequalities; marginalized women; mothers; working mothers
Women, Dry Those Tears, 85, 213n45
Women's Christian Temperance Union (WCTU), 53
Women's Employment League (Vancouver), 37, 38
women's rights advocacy, 154–56, 180
Wood, Betsy, 140, 145
Woodside, Frank E., 34, 42
work ethic regulation. *See* work-for-relief
work-for-relief, 4–5, 6, 20, 102–3, 179; *Canada Assistance Plan (CAP),* 22, 108; mothers' pensions, 50, 55,

60–68, 70, 207n82, 208n90, 208n93, 208n99; Vancouver City Crèche, 26–27, 31, 34, 36, 38–42, 46
worker-citizenship: barriers to women, 16, 50–51; feminist movement and, 127–29; Royal Commission on the Status of Women, 129–31
working mothers, 16, 99, 103, 105; acceptance in labour force, 99, 101, 103; ambivalence concerning, 5, 8, 18, 23, 47, 49–50, 75, 99–100, 123, 153, 178; disapproval of, 3–5, 22, 34, 43, 51–55, 95, 99, 152, 162, 164; as pitiable, 4–5, 20, 28, 71, 75, 93; as selfish, 4, 22, 34, 43, 95, 152, 162, 164; as signs of failed families, 6, 24, 46, 71–72, 83–84, 88, 179; stigmatization of, 22, 83–84, 87–88, 105, 111, 116, 136, 150; unemployment, 37, 38, 67, 68–69; wartime conditions, 3, 37–39, 74–93, 99–100; welfare reform and, 181–82. *See also* gendered inequalities; marginalized women; mothers' pensions; paid work
working women, 29; hostility towards, 34, 51, 69, 83–84, 87–88. *See also* gendered inequalities; marginalized women; working mothers
working-class women. *See* marginalized women
Workmen's Compensation Board (WCB), 54, 59, 205n54, 205n55
World War I, 37–39
World War II, 74–93, 99–100; *Dominion-Provincial Wartime Day Nursery Agreement* (WDNA), 21, 74–81, 84, 91, 92, 93, 94–95, 211n1; wartime day nurseries, 21, 75, 90–92

York, Madge, 82, 83
Yorke, Gini, 132